ACADEMIC APPROACHES TO TEACHING JEWISH STUDIES

ACADEMIC APPROACHES TO TEACHING JEWISH STUDIES

Edited by

Zev Garber

University Press of America,® Inc.
Lanham • New York • Oxford

Copyright © 2000 by
University Press of America,® Inc.
4720 Boston Way
Lanham, Maryland 20706

12 Hid's Copse Rd.
Cumnor Hill, Oxford OX2 9JJ

British Library Cataloging in Publication Information Available

Library of Congress Cataloging-in-Publication Data

Academic approaches to teaching Jewish studies / edited by Zev Garber.
p.   cm.
Includes bibliographical references and index.
1. Judaism—Study and teaching (Higher) I. Garber, Zev.
BM71.A33   1999   296'.071'1—dc21   99—048952 CIP

ISBN 0-7618-1552-X (pbk: alk. ppr.)

To the memory of my parents

Morris B. Garber
Pearl Garber

ACKNOWLEDGEMENTS

Academic Approaches to Teaching Jewish Studies is published with the partial support of the following institutions:

• The Western States Jewish History Association discovers and preserves the history of Jewish life and Jewish participation in the settling of the American West. Its goal is to preserve our history for future generations and to encourage academic research by providing publishing opportunities in its quarterly journal, *Western States Jewish History*. Gladys Sturman, is Publisher and Editor-in-Chief.

• International Judea Foundation (a.k.a. *Siamak*); Dariush Fakheri, President and Founder.

Additional assistance in the publication of this volume came from the following: Rabbi Ed Feinstein of Valley Beth Shalom, Dr. Gerald and Joyce Glanz, Gold Family Trust in memory of Esther Askenaizer and Ida Rose Gold, Rabbi Eli Herscher of Stephen S. Wise Temple, Rabbi Moshe Rothblum of Adat Ari El, Rabbi Harold Schulweis of Valley Beth Shalom, and Rabbi Isaiah Zeldin of Sephen S. Wise Temple.

The editor is grateful for their support in the scholarly dissemination of Judaica.

The editor and publisher would like to acknowledge permission for republication of the following articles:

Charles E. Vernoff, "The Contemporary Study of Religion and the Academic Teaching of Judaism," in *Methodology in the Academic Teaching of Judaism*, Zev Garber, ed. (Lanham, MD: University Press of America, 1986), pp. 15-40.

Bruce Zuckerman, "Choosing Among the Strands: Teaching Old Testament Survey to Undergraduates at a Secular University," in *Methodology in the Academic Teaching of Judaism,* Zev Garber, ed. (Lanham, MD: University Press of America, 1986), pp. 91-115.

Herbert W. Basser, "Approaching the Text: The Study of Midrash," in *Methodology in the Academic Teaching of Judaism*, Zev Garber, ed., (Lanham, MD. University Press of America, 1986), pp. 117-134.

Gilead Morahg, "Teaching Modern Hebrew Literature to American Undergraduates," in *Methodology in the Academic Teaching of Judaism,* Zev Garber ed. (Lanham, MD: University Press of America, 1986), pp. 145-164.

Eugene J. Fisher, "Theological Education and Christian-Jewish Relations," in *Methodology in the Academic Teaching of Judaism,* Zev Garber, ed. (Lanham MD: University Press of America, 1986), pp. 189-200.

Zev Garber, "Teaching Zionism: The Introductory Course," *Shofar,* vol. 13, no. 1 (Fall 1994), pp. 8-37. Reprinted from *Shofar,* volume 13, number I by permission of the University of Nebraska Press. Copyright ©1994 by the University of Nebraska Press.

Contents

Preface

At the annual convention of the Association of Jewish Studies (Boston, December 1998), Professor Hava Tirosh-Samuelson (formerly at Indiana University at Bloomington now at Arizona State University) commented on why there is a dearth of Jewish students taking Jewish Studies: the perceived dichotomy between objective scholarship and commitment to Jewish spirituality has rendered Jewish Studies irrelevant to young Jews. To correct this fault, she suggested, "We must make it very clear that the academic study of Judaism is not just about facts but also about values" (*The Chronicle of Higher Education*, February 26, 1999). As expected this ignited a heated discussion on the merits of Jewish Studies and the Jewish community at the meeting and afterwards a rambling who-is-who-isn't teaching correctly the subject on the Internet.

This debate is not new to me. In my Introduction to *Methodology in the Academic Teaching of Judaism* [MIATJ] (UPA, 1986), I raised the issue, what constitutes Jewish Studies, how to teach it, and to whom, etc. I proposed a variety of observations for learning to happen effectively: allow students to interact personally with course material; make instructors aware of what students think, feel, and understand or fail to understand; show the inseparable connection between writing and learning and thinking; and create an atmosphere where individual student concerns and rigorous academic research complement each other. My personal teaching approach in a fact-oriented curricula is thematic and student-oriented and I see myself playing the role more of knowledge-facilitator than knowledge-dispenser. Thereby the student is engaged in these learning/thinking operations: observing, recording, generalizing, summarizing, applying general to specific, integrating new ideas with old, inferring, critiquing, and questioning. This methodology speaks against the older standard chronological-structural lecture arrangement (the "facts" only school), where the student sits back and absorbs like a sponge the knowledge of a professor's lecture. In additional attempts to ensure student interest in Jewish Studies classes, I recommend the utilization of guest lecturers, audio-visual aids, and outside-of-class activities, including museum trips. Finally, contra the Scantron sheet examination, I utilize journals, reviews, personal projects, and other innovative assignments (written and oral) with the goal to encourage exploration, originality and creativity. In my opinion, the knowledge-facilitator approach provides for better and more honest student-teacher communication and contributes to a learning exchange that is comfortable, friendly and non-threatening. As R. Eliazar ben Shammua might phrase it: honor and reverence are due both learners and teachers of Torah (*m. 'Avot* 4:12). Isn't this what teaching is all about?

'This anthology responds to my rhetorical question by providing age-old responses, new challenges and directions to what constitutes Jewish Studies?, what can we learn? and how do we teach Jewish Studies and its lessons? It suggests and hopefully contributes to an academic teaching of Jewish Studies; the term "academic" makes the necessary distinction between university scholarship and proselytizing, intraconfessional, and other types of parochial instruction. The chapters reflect specific theories, methods, and issues related to a scholarly teaching of Jewish Studies. Charles E. Vernoff examines the study and teaching of Judaism in the context of "worldview" developed by scholars such as Jacob Neusner, Ninian Smart and Jonathan Z. Smith in the study of religion generally. For Vernoff, a worldview manifests itself in history, seeks like philosophy to interpret the world as a coherent system, and contributes functionally to the constitution of social reality. This is tested in four types of offerings in a basic Judaica curriculum: general and particular courses in Hebrew Bible, and general and particular courses in post-biblical Judaism. His analysis of Judaism as a "religiology" conveys distinct forms of Jewish religious reality which provide a new incentive to teach Judaism in its wholeness often lacking in contemporary Jewish education.

S. Daniel Breslauer expresses a novel way to the study of Judaism, the religion: Jewish myth. His essay begins by noting the different types of mythic material, traces them in Jewish narrative, and examines their implications for the study of Jewish religion by analyzing the stories concerning Aqiva ben Yosef's martyrdom (*b.Ber* 61a, *y.Sota* 5.20c, *b.Menah.* 29b). Each of these variants is understood as fulfilling one of the three functions of myth (political, anthropological, cosmic), while each contains several distinctively Judaic elements. His research shows how later tradition applies mysticism to Aqiva's martyrdom thereby redacting the original tales into a different composite myth. The essay concludes by offering certain general lessons about myth as a category of Jewish religious narrative.

Bruce Zuckerman considers issues and problems in teaching "Introduction to the Hebrew Bible" at an undergraduate university not associated with any religion and/or religious institution. The course targeted covers the teaching of the Bible (Tanak/ Old Testament/ First Testament) — most likely the only opportunity an undergraduate will ever have to consider the Hebrew Bible in an academic context — as part of a "liberal arts" education in a limited period of time. His essay entails an involved discussion on A) the problem of time ("educated ruthlessness" is proposed — that is, a recognition that one must sacrifice a serious consideration of much vital material in order to leave time to consider absolutely essential material); B) the issue of overall emphasis (stress is placed upon overreaching ideas, how they developed in biblical times and how they affect western civilization); C) Biblical and secondary texts (the choice of biblical text edition or editions and the problem of finding the right supporting literature are discussed); and D) issues of faith (an approach that emphasizes modern scholarly issues and basic rational problems [e.g., theodicy], but also leaves room and respect for individual faith positions).

Marvin A. Sweeney traces the emerging discussion of Tanak theology as a field of inquiry related to but distinct from Christian Old Testament theology, which is linked for the most part to some packageable Christology. His essay starts with a discussion of the rational for Jewish theological interpretation of the Bible, including both the problems and prospects for such study. It then engages with specific topics of concern in Jewish biblical theology, including the role of the Bible in Judaism and Christianity, the issue of "Universalism versus Particularism" (i.e., Israel and the Nations); the role of Israel, land and nation; the Temple as Holy Center of Israel, including its associated practices of holiness (Shabbat, Festivals, Kashrut, etc.); the concept of eschatology and history in Jewish and Christian understanding of the Bible; and the problem of evil, including the Shoah. This contextual article demonstrates awareness of the material and sources and methodologies involved in exploring a new field in Jewish Studies, Jewish Biblical Theology.

Herbert W. Basser addresses the study of midrashic texts in undergraduate and graduate classes. He begins his chapter on methods in the study of *midrash* by introducing the authors, the grand Rabbis, as *hakhamim* ("wise people"), who "solve riddles by spelling out the implications of mysterious, often apparently contradictory signs and symbols." He suggests that the instructor must stress that these techniques often involve the transformation of biblical texts by means of acoustical shifts in the Hebrew wording. Salient features of *midrash* composition are examined critically and incorporate these concerns: comparing versions, finding problems in one version which are solved by another version, locating the specific problem in a biblical text which generated the *midrash*, looking up the biblical verses in the *midrash* and showing the exegetical technique used by the midrashist, the artistic effect of the *midrash*, etc. These issues are also pointed out by Harris Lenowitz' page-by-page critique of M. Pérez Fernández, *An Introductory Grammar of Rabbinic Hebrew* (Leiden, 1997), a long awaited replacement of M.H. Segal, *A Grammar of Mishnaic Hebrew* (Oxford, 1927), for use in a course in mishnaic Hebrew. A work on rabbinic Hebrew by a Christian-Hebraist is welcomed but if the *Endzeil* is informed with Christian New Testament aims this may explain the chapter's title, "Honor It and Suspect It."

Gilead Morahg presents an integrated curricular approach to multi-level university teaching of modern Hebrew literature. He emphasizes three problem areas: insufficient competence in language skills; insufficient training in basic techniques for literary analysis and interpretation; and insufficient knowledge of the historical and cultural contexts of Hebrew literature. He offers instructional guidelines and specific techniques for overcoming these deficiencies while progressing through the various stages of a comprehensive curriculum. Basic principles for the selection and organization of literary texts, mode of presentation and learning activities are provided.

Judith R. Baskin explores some of the ways in which the implications of gender and the specific experiences of women can be incorporated into Jewish Studies teaching and research. Drawing on her previous work and works of others, she projects a variety of paths moving beyond the customary inclusion of "women worthies" to incorporate Jewish gender issues into academic courses. Some of the teaching strategies delineated are gender-specific while others incorporate the gender concerns into more general Jewish Studies courses. Each meets at least one of the following criteria : (1) to comprehend the role of gender in relationships of power; (2) to appreciate the differences among Jewish women; and (3) to challenge the traditional patriarchal disciplines which by their own *history* have neglected either overtly and/or covertly the perspectives and experiences of the Jewish People's *herstory*.

Elliot N. Dorff writes that teaching Jewish ethics and morals requires both an examination of the various views taken by Jews attempting to apply their tradition to issues in bioethics, business ethics, legal ethics, and the like, as well as describing the broad strokes which differentiate the Jewish vision from various non-Jewish views of the ideal person and society (the value of life, for example). Are Jewish law, Jewish belief, Jewish lore and Jewish ethics interwoven? If so, in what way and to what degree can Jewish sources from eras gone by reasonably be consulted to guide moral decisions related to contemporary circumstances? And in a modern setting, how beneficial or detrimental are differences in transdenominational interpretation of Halakhah vis-à-vis academia and republica? These and other questions come under scrutiny by Dorff as he relates his thinking on Jewish ethics and morals in classes designed for the undergraduate and graduate levels.

Eugene J. Fisher observes that the relationship of the Church to the Jewish People is integral to every area of the core theological curriculum, from sacred scripture to systematics and Church History. Nonetheless, there are errors in the Church's teachings about the Jews and Judaism, e.g., "teaching of contempt" theology, which need to be corrected. Fisher assesses improvements made and need to be made in ecclesiology and liturgy to correct these flaws "at the very level of the Church's own identity" (Pope John Paul II). A necessary ingredient of the theological renewal for religious relations with the Jews called for in *Nostra Aetate* (1965) and more recently in *We Remember:A Reflection on the Shoah* (1998).

James F. Moore continues his reflection on the importance of team-taught, in-class dialogue for teaching Jewish Studies generally and Judaism in particular. The strengths of team-teaching is presented as a response to the current pressing desire for courses that are global, interdisciplinary and multi-cultural. For Moore, no field of study seems better prepared to meet these new challenges than Jewish Studies since from the outset the study of Judaism on campuses has been forced to patch together courses from different disciplines as well as offer those courses that enable the student to fit the very particular study of Judaism into the wider curriculum of any student's work.

David Patterson takes the position that the Shoah can be taught as *Shoah* (not as Holocaust, a more inclusive term) only if the Event be seen from the standpoint of the Jew as victim. Drawing on diaries, memoirs, and novels of Jewish victims, written during and after the European Judeocide, he interweaves their shattered thoughts with the sacred texts of Jewish tradition (Bible, rabbinics, mysticism, Hasidic lore) thereby elucidating an intergenerational historical and metaphysical *teshuvah* (sacred response) to why the Shoah and its consequences.

My essay on "Teaching Zionism," is an invitation to study the Zionist movement as one of contemporary Jewry's most successful responses to the Jewish predicament: the Jewish People as the victim of world history. The student is exposed to the historical background beginning with episodes from the Pentateuch and continues on the road to the centennial celebration of the birth of modern Zionism (1997). The goal is to familiarize the student with what the Zionist tradition regards as its essential genius and to provide an opportunity for an appreciation of the similarities and differences between ideologies and divisions within Zionism. The subtext is that the mosaic of Zionism, a national ideology, is a movement to and not away from the teachings of Moses accepted by the Children of Israel at the dawn of their collective history.

Gill Graff surveys Jewish history as a core curriculum in secondary Jewish education. He begins by exploring the state of the field in Jewish day high schools. He suggests possibilities and methods of enhancing the Jewish history curricula of Jewish day high schools (across the span of ideological diversity) through the use of primary sources. His chapter includes applications (i.e., specific examples) of the proposed methodology. By entitling his chapter, "Back to the Future," he means the (future) prospects of strengthened Jewish day school education are for many learners (back) in the historical texts of the Jewish experience. An important point that applies as well to the teaching of Jewish Studies at the college level.

To the contributors, whose sentiments and words inform this Preface, I offer a thankful *todah rabbah*. Their diverse talents and scholarship, as expressed in their own specialties, in providing a new edition to Z. Garber, Editor, *Methodology in the Academic Teaching of Judaism* (UPA, 1986) are very much appreciated. Their contributions and preferred style of spelling (e.g. G-d and God, Jewish People and Jewish people, etc.) have been kept intact, despite the emendations necessary to ensure editorial conformity. I am deeply grateful to Steve Strande and David W. Epstein for their technical assistance in preparing this manuscript for publication. Also, I wish to thank Susan Garber for her encouragement and support and our *kelev*, Shukie, who provided solace to the many midnight hours at the computer.

The volume is dedicated to the memory of my parents, Morris Benjamin and Pearl Garber, whose journeys in Eastern European *yiddishkeit*, American democracy and Israeli Zionism are links in the unbroken continuity of the Jewish People that this volume is dedicated to teach.

Zev Garber

Erev Simhat Torah 5760
October 1999

Chapter 1

The Contemporary Study of Religion and the Academic Teaching of Judaism
Charles Elliott Vernoff

How a subject matter is taught depends, in no small measure, on what it is conceived to be; and the basic conception of a subject area is established through its academically disciplined study. For several generations, accordingly, the prevailing norms for the academic study and teaching of Judaism have been dictated by the classical tradition of *Wissenschaft des Judentums,* the "science of Judaism," flourishing on a groundwork laid by Leopold Zunz and other giants of nineteenth century historical scholarship. This tradition has been well perpetuated in America within the contemporary Association for Jewish Studies. But Judaism, whatever else it may be, is a *religion.* And during the past generation, the academic study of religion has itself been swept up in a current of rapid and indeed revolutionary change. Since the early 1960's, departments of religious studies have proliferated within the secular university. Staffed by an interdisciplinary assemblage of scholars trained in areas as diverse as theology and sociology, these departments - spurred in part by their own graduate Ph.D.'s draped with the mantle of "religious studies" - have been under ever increasing practical pressure to define their academic mandate more precisely. And that entails delineating exactly what it is they study - presumably "religion." Circumstances have thus conspired to force, as never previously in the history of scholarship, engagement with the theoretical and methodological questions of just what religion is, why it should be studied and how it should be investigated and taught.[1]

To be sure, the crystallization of religious studies as an academic domain remains a process barely underway. Long established schools of historical scholarship within particular religious traditions can continue, for the most part, in easy disregard of a development which has yet to vindicate its full legitimacy. An exception to this state of affairs, however, is the case of Judaism. No scholar of the present generation has achieved greater renown for creative and sometimes controversial innovation within the tradition of *Wissenschaft des Judentums* than Jacob Neusner. Yet this same Jacob Neusner has not only assumed simultaneous leadership within the American Academy of Religion, nurturing bed for the new religious studies, but as Jonathan Z. Smith, himself a leading scholar of religion, has observed more than once, Neusner has increasingly diverted his own programmatic concerns and scholarly agenda toward the organic integration of Judaic studies into the broader conspectus of nascent religious studies.[2] In 1983, this striking intersection of the contemporary study of Judaism with theoretical and methodological preoccupations of the newly emergent academic domain of religious studies embodied itself in a significant volume edited and partially authored by Neusner: *Take Judaism, for Example: Studies Toward the Comparison of Religions.*[3] For a scholar of Neusner's visibility to implant his work so firmly and deliberately within the vineyard of religious studies extends a peculiarly bracing challenge not only to other scholars but to all teachers of Judaica; a mandate to stretch their pedagogical horizons so as to incorporate the widest and most provocative insights and issues within the contemporary study of religion at large:

> The title of this book, then, is meant to lay down a challenge to the study of Judaism within the study of religions. *Take Judaism, for Example*—but to exemplify what? If we move *toward the comparison of religions,* what is it about religions that ... we wish to compare? Let me specify what I think we study when we study religion, and, even more specifically, what we study when we want to know about Judaism. I wish to know about Judaism. I wish further to explain why I regard the study of religion as urgent, not merely interesting—a necessity for society and a precondition for the future of humankind.[4]

The last sentence of this passage clearly, if implicitly, mediates between "study" as a scholarly activity in a research library and as a general classroom activity guided by an instructor. But tracing the potential impact of the contemporary scholarly ferment in religious studies upon the teaching of Judaism in the classroom is itself a task which can proceed only by way of example. We shall therefore examine one trajectory along which religious studies might in fact develop and consider how its theoretical insights and methodic principles may inform first the academic study and then, flowing from that, the teaching of Judaism.

An Emergent Direction in Religious Studies

During 1983, the same year *Take Judaism, for Example* appeared in print, a noted exponent of theory and method for the new religious studies, Ninian Smart, published a volume entitled *Worldviews: Cross-Cul-*

tural Explorations of Human Beliefs.[5] Smart here proposes to identify the focal subject area for this emergent academic realm:

> Thus, the modern study of religion helps to illuminate worldviews, both traditional and secular, which are ... an engine of social and moral continuity and change; and therefore it explores beliefs and feelings, and tries to understand what exists inside the heads of people. What people believe is an important aspect of reality whether or not what they believe is true ... The English language does not have a term to refer to both traditional religions and ideologies; the best expression is perhaps *worldviews.*[6]

Other theoreticians of the study of religion had been converging for some time upon the notion of "worldview" that Smart in this book elevates to special prominence. The consensus of their thinking understands worldviews as arising in fulfillment of the constitutive need of self-conscious beings for some comprehensive and integral orientation to the conditions of their existence. Raimundo Panikkar, for example, insists that each person has ultimate presuppositions, i.e., some basic view of reality, and no one stands on "neutral ground".[7] Mircea Eliade implies that human consciousness cannot even coalesce without a structure of epistemological reference and orientation which organizes and interprets one's *Lebenswelt.*[8] Michael Novak observes that *mythos* basically means "story," and the irreducible domain of religious studies is that of the integrating "stories" that all self-conscious entities, individual or collective, must tell themselves to function within the environing reality of other selves and world.[9] Peter Berger, speaking as a sociologist of knowledge, situates religion at the generative center of "world-building" and maintenance.[10] And Ninian Smart himself proposes that the heart of the study of religion is simply "worldview analysis."[11]

Within the realm of Judaic studies itself, the category of worldview was particularly highlighted in 1979 when Jonathan Z. Smith delivered the first presentation in the History of Judaism section of the American Academy of Religion upon its reconstitution at the initiative of Jacob Neusner. Smith detects important anticipations of a theoretical model for the new religious studies in the often spurned notions of the "Pan-Babylonian school" of the history of religion, which paved the way for present usage of the term "worldview" within the field:

> ... what the Pan-Babylonian school introduced was the notion of a total system, to use their favorite word, a *Weltanschauung* [worldview] ... the object of religion, for them the most total expression of "world view," is man's cultural and intellectual world, not the world of nature. It is the

inner relationships of the "elements," their system, their internal logic and coherence, that validates a "world view," not conformity to nature. Therefore, the "world view" may be articulated in a rigorously systematic manner.[12]

Smith goes on to question whether Neusner's narrow application of the concept of worldview to a literary "system," i.e., "the generative logic ... of a quite particular document," does not abandon the cardinal principle of *totality*.[13] In the epilogue to *Take Judaism, for Example,* Neusner responds to this critique:

> Our work then is to locate the logic of a given system and to relate that logic to the context of the system ... At this point I must digress to emphasize that when we speak of system, we mean only a social system ... The limits of the system are not literary but social, even though, in historical research, we tend to begin with literary evidence ... What I propose, therefore, is a way beyond the historicizing atomism which treats all things as unconnected to all others, and which therefore closes off the path to insight worth sharing, method worth repeating.[14]

Yet the "way beyond" Neusner proposes apparently can be neither that of the conventional *historian,* who seeks the particular above all, nor that of the conventional *philosopher,* who confines his interest to the universal:

> Historians treat events as singular ... But if there are patterns, they reduce the singularity, the givenness, of the singular. To historians, the search for insight is a task for philosophers, theologians, or social scientists - people who wish to bring things into relationship and to find out the universally useful truth in diverse things ... (yet) ... the theological construction of "Judaism" falls before the wrecking ball of historians, with their exceptions, their various examples, their particulars.[15]

Does the apparent crash Neusner discerns between the perspectives of history and philosophy imply, then, that the "way" toward understanding *religion as such* might lead "beyond" the horizon of the conventional academically disciplined historian, no less than that of the disciplined philosopher or theologian?

If something like "worldview" and its manifestations constitutes the object proper of the study of religion, it becomes evident that this study can indeed be neither history *nor* philosophy, yet it must have tangencies with both. First of all, from Jonathan Z. Smith's discussion of the Pan-Babylonian school may be derived, given the other theoretical concepts cited above, a working definition of "worldview": a view of "the world" as total system, by and large internally logical and coherent, which satisfies the elemental human need to *make sense of things* as the means of establishing basic sanity and maintaining a foundation for practical action. By this reckoning, any largely *self-conscious* and thus *choice-making* entity collective or individual, will need *some* orientation to reality, which entails formation of a worldview; and worldviews accordingly provide the matrices for all group and individual systems of reality manifest in societies, cultures and persons. What evidences the presence of worldviews, then, is their empirically available molding of the thought and action of concrete human beings, not only in the texts they write and rituals they perform, but in their attitudes, character and general behavior. As custodian of the human past, it is surely the historian who furnishes the model for the initial gathering and assembling of such particular data. But what allows these data to be interpreted is an understanding of worldview as vehicle of the constitutive and universal human need for *orientation,* i.e., the demand to comprehend reality implicitly as a total system characterized by internal logic and coherence. It is the philosopher who furnishes the model for the purest and most self-conscious expression of this need, which itself is the most primal expression of self-consciousness.

At one extremity, therefore, the study of religion must certainly approach the historical disciplines with their skill at practical data gathering and primary interpretation. At the other extremity, though, the study of religion requires hypothetical mapping of the general structure of a worldview as embodying the need of self-consciousness for integral orientation to reality; and this mapping must be informed by awareness of philosophic consciousness as well as by philosophic disciplines with their skill at theoretical reflection. Yet the central arena within the study of religion is the study of *religions,* for example Judaism. To understand Judaism fully might require greater coordination of theory *and* empirical practice than has yet been achieved at institutions, such as the University of Chicago, which stress the former, and Harvard or Brown, which emphasize the latter. Hypotheses broaching the general nature of worldview must be brought into close critical relation with the substantive data of Judaism in its varied manifestations at different points in time and space. Through the mutual hermeneutic interplay of the data of the manifold concrete "Judaisms" with a developing hypothesis which seeks to formulate the generic aspects of "Judaism," a grasp of the Judaic worldview in its universality and particularity, its constancy and variation, its abiding similitude and ever novel empirical differentiations, should emerge. To achieve such genuine interplay, however, necessitates devising methods of hypothesis aimed not just at temporally unfolding historical configurations nor at eternal philosophic truths but at the diachronic and synchronic reality of *worldview as such.* Here lies a developmental frontier for the study of religion, visible beyond the clash discerned by Neusner.

Should successful methods of hypothesis yield deepening understanding of the Judaic worldview, the profound manner in which this worldview structures the society, culture and psychic makeup of its host group would certainly become more evident; conversely, an acquaintance with the dynamics of society, culture and the psyche could expedite a gasp of the functioning of a worldview within its milieu and thereby lead directly to essential insight into the worldview itself. Exploration of how religion functions within its milieu as a way toward understanding religion as such has provided much of the agenda for the study of religion at schools such as Syracuse University. Is the study of religion as worldview, then, perhaps a mere adjunct to the existing *social sciences?* The term "worldview" itself, after all, has achieved its widest currency in the field of anthropology.[16] The answer to such concerns is that methods of disciplined study in the existing social sciences appropriately urge an effort at the complete suppression and functional neutralization of the scholar's own worldview since it bears personal values which may distort *objectivity.* Fully understanding *worldviews themselves,* on the other hand, requires that a scholar become precisely and vividly *aware* of his or her own worldview *as* worldview—that is, as fulfilling the universal *subjective* human need for orientation—in order to have an empathic, cognitive and critical touchstone for fathoming the worldviews of others; and this is requisite even if one's personal worldview invokes the authority of science itself. For Western humanism, of which scientism is a variant, is very much a particular worldview with developmental roots extending as far back as ancient Mesopotamia where the original precursors of the Jewish people may have sought spiritual liberation from the slave holding deities of old Sumer. Thus humanism itself may in principle have no less, but also no more, inherent claim to ultimacy than various other worldviews with differing yet coherent perspectives on the world as total system. In sum, then, it appears that "methodological self-consciousness" in the study of religion can be neither "objective" nor "subjective" in the conventional sense, but must remain faithfully transparent to the total character of the whole human person as a self-conscious entity requiring orientation to his or her environing reality.

What the academically disciplined study of religion actually necessitates methodologically may therefore best be described as a *probe of the limits* of scientific objectification, issuing in a kind of "self-transcendence" of the researcher's "objectivity" such that it cease to suppress the reality of that "subjectivity" which always accompanies it in any case. And this accommodation of subjectivity is demanded by the interests of *truth itself,* which likewise motivates the scientific ideal of objectivity as such. While not at all unscientific, then, the study of religion may stand at and delineate the *limits of* science, there admitting the rights of subjective consciousness - which is perhaps why the contemporary study of religion has evidenced notable affinity with the arts and humanities, among which it is often enumerated.

The foregoing characterization of an emergent direction in the study of religion depends, to be sure, on the assumption that the object of that study will increasingly be identified as *worldview,* in the fullest and most non-reductive sense. But granting this not implausible assumption suggests the likelihood of scholars more and more recognizing that to study religion *as* religion is to venture forth into largely uncharted methodological terrain, moving in the direction not of any other study or studies but of a novel disciplinary perspective endowed with its own theoretical grounding, methodic arsenal and systematic agenda. What we wish to consider here are the consequences for teaching of this sort of a disciplinary perspective, committed to investigating religion in accordance with its own *logos* - i.e., its intrinsic nature, empirical characteristics, and inherent principles of intelligibility. To understand the pedagogical implications of such a *religiological* approach to the subject matter necessitates closer examination of scholarly method to determine how it might inform modes of classroom instruction.

An Exemplary Methodology in the Scholarly Study of Judaism

A religiological mode of studying religion as adumbrated above may seem at once novel, insofar as it still has few operational precedents, and familiar, to the extent that it retrospectively conforms with one's intuitive sense of what place the religious dimension occupies within the compass of human existence. Yet, in truth, the necessity for a new discipline which approaches religion in accordance with its own *logos* has already gained a measure of implicit recognition at the horizon of the historical, philosophic and social scientific investigation of religious phenomena and tradition. Nowhere is this more pointedly apparent than in *Take Judaism,* for example, where Jacob Neusner, in his summary reflections, brings the enterprise of the conventional historian of religion toward its limit and there glimpses the profile of an emergent religiology:

> Why do I wish to construct a system ... and to make sense of the whole by seeking other wholes, other systems? The answer is given in the question, in use of the language, "to make sense....." It is only in discovering the choices, the contexts in which statements are made, in defining the persistent questions to which statements constitute answers, that the statements begin to make sense. Discovering similar patterns in a diversity of situations makes possible the juxtaposition for purposes of contrast and of comparison of the people who live in those circumstances and make their lives within them... These then are the decisive questions: What questions are answered and how are they answered, in the system of historical and social ecology framed and founded by a given group? How do others answer these same questions, within the same systematic structure of history and economy? And finally, what do we learn about both groups in the comparison and contrast of each with the other? These are the three exercises which respond to the questions of "Why?" and "So what?" For the answer to "so what" must be, so this is one way in which people made choices, and that is another way, and in the variables between the one and other lie rich insight even into how we are and might be.[17]

To move decisively beyond the self-limited horizon of the disciplined historian's framework, necessarily constrained to interpret "choices" solely in terms of such factors as "history and economy," no more is required than to consider afresh the *inward human substance* of those choices whose outward form the external environment of human life demonstrably conditions.

Anthropology has well understood that corporate human existence requires a coherent matrix that organizes all of life's activities into a systemic whole, and it investigates worldview chiefly as the "outer" collective form of this coherence. But human consciousness also demands an integral view of the world as the condition of *its own inner coherence.* As Peter Berger, among others, has shown, breakdown of one's "world," i.e., ones worldview, may lead directly, unless somehow mitigated, to a breakdown of self-consciousness as such into the fragmented state termed insanity.[18] Then those outward choices which determine the integral organization of one's world must conform with and reflect - constitute, as it were, the *outside of* - an inward "choice" of some *integrating focus for the organizing of conscious selfhood.* "Worldview" understood in a non-reductive way, that is, construed in its fullest and truest sense, thus not only organizes "the world" but *mediates* the coherence of the world and the coherence of the self, coordinating and thereby unifying outer and inner human reality.[19] Now, only that study which treats religion in its own terms, in its own total reality, is properly religiological. Accordingly, any religiological investigation of worldviews must take full cognizance of the inner matrix no less than the outer occasions of a given worldview; the choice of "how we are and might be" is in very truth a choice of modality for *total being,* inward as well as outward. No method for analyzing religion is yet religiological without evincing the power to probe, discriminate and compare such elemental human "choices" in their total and inclusive reality.

The choices of *modality for total being* which religiology scrutinizes perforce arise within the most encompassing context of the human situation, to whose outer *and* inner aspects alike self-consciousness must become oriented in order to negotiate the challenges of self-conscious existence. To pursue the study of Judaism religiologically therefore entails beginning with some theoretical understanding of the general "orientational needs" of human self-consciousness which give rise to *any* particular worldview. Here the relevant consideration is: What are the inescapable questions that *all* people, by virtue of their very humanness, must implicitly pose to their life situations - the primal bases of the "choices" to which Jacob Neusner refers? Or, to put it another way, what are the universal conditions of concrete human experience to which self-consciousness must coherently orient itself in order to make sense of "the world" and navigate a practical course through it on the journey from birth to death?

The outlines of an answer inhere in the query itself. To speak of "the world" conjures, in its most primary signification, the category of *space* and to speak of "birth and death" elicits the category of *time.* Within the framework of space and time, self-consciousness discovers itself *as* "self" in relation to "other selves." The experiencing of "self" and "others" unfolding within its spacio-temporal framework is universally conditioned by the presence and behavior of such spacial realities as the natural elements, whose behaviors are of course exhibited only in time, and such temporally encountered realities as pleasure or pain and birth, sexuality, sickness, death which conversely have their necessary spacial occasions. Each of these aforementioned factors, which universally condition human existence, poses the question to a newly crystallizing self-consciousness of that factor's integral *place* in the overall scheme of things — the question of its nature, structure, function, purpose and meaning within the totality of the world which, for "the world" to be recognized at all, must be presupposed by emergent self-consciousness to constitute a coherent whole. Religiological theory faces, then, the crucial early task of constructing a foundational religiological epistemology which maps the parameters of any imaginable human *Lebenswelt*. As an exemplification of such an epistemology, it is at this time still difficult to surpass the classic basic texts of Mircea Eliade, notably *The Sacred and the Profane* and *Cosmos and History.*[20] But scholars, especially of Judaica, would do well to consider also the epistemological reflections of a thinker like Martin Buber, who with Eliade belongs to the extended Neo-Kantian tradition:

> We may characterize the set and the work of entering into relation with the world as such — and, therefore, not with parts of it, and not with the sum of its parts, but with it as the world — as synthesizing apperception, by which we establish that this pregnant use of the concept involves the function of unity: by synthesizing apperception I mean the apperception of a being as a whole and as a unity. Such a view is won, and won again and again, only by looking upon the world as a world ... He who turns to the realm which he has removed from himself, and which has been completed and transformed into a world ... becomes aware of wholeness and unity in such a way that from then on he is able to grasp being as a wholeness and a unity ... the single being has received the character of wholeness and the unity which is perceived in it from the wholeness and unity perceived in the world.[21]

The religiological study of Judaism must begin, then, by confronting the particular data of Judaism with the template of universal questions proffered by a religiological epistemology such as Eliade's. *How* precisely does Judaism deal with the nature of space, time, self, others and so forth? And *why* does it do it in this and not some other possible way? No very thorough and far-reaching investigation of Judaic source materials is required to mount initial hypotheses. For example, the uniquely Judaic understanding of time as "history" ubiquitously pervades virtually all particular instantiations of Judaism, even when retreating somewhat to the background as in Rabbinic Judaism, and distinguishes the Judaic worldview in respect to time from even so proximate and indeed conjugal a neighbor as Iranian Zoroastrianism. The integral complex of tentative answers to the fundamental epistemological questions effectively constitutes an initial hypothetical formulation of the Judaic worldview, which comparison with other worldviews may draw into sharper focus. But such a formulation can be preliminary at best. How might it be further ramified and modified through engagement with the multitudinous data of Judaism? Here begins the painstaking labor of a scholarship committed to understanding Judaic religion in its own terms.

The great philosopher of religion Rudolf Otto, in his classic work *Mysticism: East and West,* clearly anticipates a fundamental tenet of any interpretive approach to the study of religion which seeks to understand religion in its own terms and not as an aspect of something else:

> It is true that somehow or other the word "mysticism" must have one *identical meaning,* otherwise there could be no conception of mysticism, and the use of the expression as a general term would be impossible. For, logically, we can only use the same term for *several objects* when they are in some determinable aspect always "the same." This is true, for example, of the term "religion." ...... But that does not exclude, it rather includes, the possibility of "religion" differing in each of these examples, and that within one and the same genus very diverse spiritual forms may be found. [italics mine][22]

Jacob Neusner illustrates this point in relation to Judaism:

> So there is no possibility of claiming there never was, nor is there now, such a thing as "Judaism" but only "Judaisms." For once we take that route, there will be no "Judaisms" either, but only this one and that one...[23]

To speak of many historically concrete "Judaisms," in other words, is logically to presuppose certain similar characteristics of "Judaism which they somehow share despite their differences. Differences and similarities, accordingly, must define *one another* and can only be grasped reciprocally in and through each other; the understanding of both can grow only conjointly. The Aristotelian method of hypothesis, which resides at the classic foundations of all empirical investigation, aims precisely to uncover generic similarity through the comparison and contrast of differential data: here is the primal root of "comparison and contrast" as a fundamental methodic element in the study of religion, as other empirical realities. On the basis of initial data samples, then, this method develops a hypothetical formulation of such generic "similarity" which is subsequently revised on the basis of additional data, even as the developing hypothesis in turn suggests what further data are required to test and refine it. All empirical thinking must, in one way or another, adapt hypothetical method. Historians, of course, utilize hypotheses in seeking the best explanation for a thoroughly particular configuration of human events. Yet philosophers, on the other hand, in their quest for the most universal understanding of the lawfulness behind all human events, likewise often devise reflective hypotheses which are submitted to tests by human reason, knowledge and experience.

A religiological approach to the understanding of "Judaism," however, really seeks to grasp neither the historical configurations of Judaism for their own sake nor the philosophic truths of Judaism but "Judaism" *as such,* i.e., the Judaic worldview and its expressions in concrete human life. Its application of the method of hypothesis must therefore begin with empirical data reflecting this worldview, assembled as much as possible into the concrete "Judaisms" of various texts, times and places, and move toward an ever more refined, complex and integral characterization of the "Judaism" they embody and express. As with any method of hypothesis, then, to depict such "Judaism" ever more precisely entails the use of *comparison and contrast*—in this case, not only internally but externally: comparison of the "Judaisms" internally to adumbrate "Judaism"; comparison of the rough emergent portrayal of "Judaism" externally with other worldviews — both more and less closely related — in order to bring its distinctive generic traits into clear relief. Working back and forth between empirical data gleaned from the history and texts of Judaism and an initially sketchy hypothetical formulation of the Judaic worldview, the religiologist thus traces patterns of coherence which with increasing degrees of exactitude specify that generic "Judaism" such that all particular "Judaisms" disclose themselves as varied instantiations of it.

Each of these particular Judaisms, it must be stressed, proffers a hermeneutic challenge to the generic portrait of "Judaism" insofar as it incorporates peculiarities demanding explanation or—more to the point— justification as a modality of "Judaism" not inconsistent, after all, with the generic portrait. The latter depiction will inevitably expand and deepen, not to say radically change, in the process of accommodating the peculiar "Judaisms" of the concrete historical tradition. On the other hand, features of these "Judaisms," perhaps otherwise unintelligible, will be illumined by the ideal-type model of "Judaism" itself. Some distinguishing characteristics of "Judaism" which this hermeneutic circle could elucidate might include: Judaic stress on the unique and irreducible value of the individual element, whether a component of natural creation, a human being, or a temporal event, unity, wholeness and integrity as central values with peculiar Judaic valences needing analysis; Judaism's affirmative attitude toward nature as divine creation, in contrast with a variety of "world-negating" religious traditions; creation, revelation and redemption as cardinal moments of Judaic temporality; justice and mercy, bearing their peculiarly Judaic valences, as essential attributes of authentic personhood. To fathom the signification of any such possible characteristic of "Judaism" necessitates tracing its manifold significations for the "Judaisms," striving to grasp the essential form systemically common to all of them in whatever permuted fashions. The viability of a crystallizing hypothetical formulation of "Judaism" is shown forth most persuasively in its capacity to distill some coherence even from apparently "exceptional" data, while such data in turn compel the hypothesis toward ever greater adequacy in explaining atypical or marginal Judaic phenomena.

What must continue above all, though, to monitor any such religiological investigation is a basic theoretical understanding of the nature of worldview in general, e.g., recognition that it is precisely through the development of worldviews that self-consciousness endeavors to construct its *Lebenswelt* into a coherent whole. The need of self-consciousness for coherence, which the religiologist comes to intuit in part by locating it at the dynamic motivational core of his or her own worldview, supplies a fundamental touchstone for searching out the coherence within each historical "Judaism" as well as the larger integrity of "Judaism" as such which each variant must in its own way reflect. But the profoundest comprehension of this larger coherence will come, only through the uncovering of its relationship not only to *exterior* circumstance but to the *interior* coherence and structural characteristics of human personhood itself only when the outer yields up direct insight into its veiled and innermost core. In principle, religiology's quest for the most illumining perception of any given worldview can cease only when its ground in some universal aspect of human being, providing an integral focus for orientation *from the inside,* discloses itself at last to the researcher's patiently alert, painstaking and meticulous attention—as it attends, way beyond all outward data, upon an *objectivated subjectivity* whose obscurer recesses the vision that sees within as that without alone might pierce.[24]

An Exemplary Methodology for the Academic Teaching of Judaism

From this cursory description of a religiological approach to the study of Judaism, it may become evident that a peculiarly strong continuity must exist between the activity of the disciplined research scholar and the classroom instructor bringing religiological perspectives to their respective tasks. This is the case for two reasons. First, the religiologist ultimately works with higher level data configurations, seeking the larger global patterns of coherence which reveal lineaments of worldview. For the practicing scholar involved with immediate gathering of data, a religiological perspective will assist in directing research toward corroborating suspected patterns of coherence within the materials of some particular textual-historical *Sitz-im-Leben.* The teacher, in contrast, will rely more upon data substantially gathered by others. Yet the quest for coherence within the data will be similar, whether conducted by a research scholar directly or implemented by a teacher reflecting upon primary and secondary texts. Since a conventional historian of Judaism need not employ a religiological hermeneutic at all, for example, it may well fail to the classroom instructor to discover how the writings of such a scholar advances understanding of the Judaic worldview.

A second reason for intimate connection between scholarship and teaching in religion is that the ultimate intellectual operations which produce religiological understanding resemble humanistic interpretation more than they do technical scientific analysis. The rubrics which guide these operations exist as fully in the classroom as in the research library or laboratory; e.g., the awareness of self-consciousness of its own innate need for coherence. The whole strategy of teaching religion from a religiological perspective must indeed be to catalyze the student's capacity for *experiencing the coherence of reality in a way different from that native to him or her.* To be sure, the teaching process must begin with the technically constructed empirical data carrying another worldview, but it achieves its ideal end only when the student is able to synthesize and internalize these data so that his or her own self-consciousness, through tutored empathy, can vicariously and temporarily - yet vividly - "inhabit" their configuration as a plausible view of the world in its wholeness. Though more radical, religiological understanding thus has manifest affinities with such classroom occupations as in-depth literary appreciation through which a student "enters into" the vision of an author or a specific text; it is surely worth pondering that humanistic interpretation in general has a primary aim of analyzing and apprehending the internal coherence of what contemporary hermeneutics would call its "text," whether that text be literary, graphic or musical. The ultimate common ground shared by teacher and student exploring religion is indeed the ability of self-consciousness to intuit its own nature and especially its profound need for coherence, proceeding from a more conscious apprehension of its own overall worldview toward an educed skill at "entering into" the worldview of another.

In a significant sense, then, no firm boundary demarcates the practice of religiology in the research library from that in the instructional classroom. Scholar and teacher alike must gradually construct ever more adequate hypothetical formulations of a worldview on the basis of its pecu-

liar characteristics and particular exemplifications. Each new exemplification tests and may modify the preexisting hypothesis. The hypothetical formulation of a worldview must be honed and sharpened through
comparison and contrast with worldviews - their inward matrices no
less than their outward occasions originating in other religious traditions. A widening grasp of the peculiarities of a given worldview spurs,
for scholar and teacher alike, the attempt to formulate a hypothesis which
adequately explains and integrates them. And the common coinage which
allows for transmission of understanding of a worldview, whether from
source materials to a scholar's mind or from a teacher's informed awareness to a student's mind, is the universal characteristics and orientational needs of human self-consciousness. Elsewhere, in a provisional
fashion, I have sought to exemplify both a genuinely religiological approach to adumbrating the Judaic worldview through comparative analysis of the Semitic monotheist traditions, and a more elaborated model of
generic "Judaism."[25] How might a similar religiological perspective specifically inform the academic teaching of Judaism? Let us consider possible strategies for devising the four typical sorts of offerings in a basic
Judaica curriculum: general and particular courses in Hebrew Bible, and
general and particular courses in post-biblical Judaism.

1. General Course in Hebrew Bible

How would a religiological approach to surveying the Hebrew Bible
differ in principle from other teaching strategies and how might such an
approach be implemented in practice, utilizing currently available resources
that for the most part reflect other methodological standpoints? These
issues could themselves be addressed inductively by explicitly eliciting
from students the range of conventional interests in this text, which might
include:

A. *Historical* - The Hebrew Bible is a *source* for history, that of the ancient Near East, and as such belongs to archaeology, paleontology, and
the history of antiquity.

B. *Cultural* - The Hebrew Bible is the *basis* of a history, that of a corporate people, and as such falls within the specific purview of social and
cultural anthropology, folklore and "Jewish studies" generally.

C. *Textual* - The Hebrew Bible *has* a history, that of its textual evolution,
and as such is of interest to form criticism, redaction criticism and
similar modes of purely textual scholarship.

D. *Literary* - The Hebrew Bible portrays a history, that of the Jews from
their ancestral beginnings, and as such incorporates dramatic narra-

tives worthy of purely literary analysis and appreciation, not to mention superb poetry and other prose.

E. *Theological* - The Hebrew Bible explains "history" as a divinely meaningful progression, and as such constitutes the religious foundation for the history-oriented faiths of Judaism, Christianity, Islam and humanism.

F. *Philosophical* - The Hebrew Bible is based upon "history as a way of experiencing time and the human condition, and thus presents a modality of humanness of central import for the philosophy of religion, culture, time, and so forth, as well as for any general philosophical anthropology.

These characterizations highlight in assorted ways, of course, the centrality of *history* as a formative principle of Western humanity, consciousness, thought and academic enterprise. The religiological interest, then, resides in grasping the *worldview* of the Hebrew Bible as itself the fountainhead of this - and not only this - formative principle of the Western civilization reality, apprehending that worldview entails considering the Hebrew Bible from all the above perspectives in order to fathom its worldview's influence in its entirety.

Through historical and cultural perspectives from the *social sciences* the formation and influence of the Hebrew Bible's worldview can be traced in an "objective" and external manner. The textual and literary concerns of the *humanities* permit entering into the substance of the worldview itself in a mediate aesthetic way which still admits of critical distance and phenomenological bracketing. In bringing to bear the theological and philosophical interests of *religious thought* proper, however, the Western student of the Hebrew Bible is apt to discover the extent to which his or her own very "subjective" identity and *Lebenswelt* have been hewn by the formative power of that text. With this awareness, the student has arrived at the threshold of a religiological understanding which transcends the dichotomy of "objective" and "subjective" to appropriate the Hebrew Bible in its operational relationship to immediately experienced *"world"* and worldview, To conduce toward such an understanding, a course structure must simultaneously apply social, scientific, humanistic and religious perspectives to its encounter with the reality of the Hebrew Bible. Through the non-linear interaction of all three sorts of perception, a religiological grasp of the text will gradually crystallize.

For example, literary analysis of the biblical narrative might be framed by the historical scholarship of Yehezkel Kaufmann, on the one side, and the biblical theology of Martin Buber, on the other.[26] While both authors regularly advert to concepts such as freedom, unity and transcendence, Kaufmann's discussion is anchored in the realm of "objective" empirical research whereas Buber's penetrates the sphere of ultimate "subjective" meaningfulness. Situating the student between, obliged to wrestle with their relationship, will invite the efflorescence of an ever deeper consciousness of the Hebrew Bible as a living power organizing the students "world" without and self within; the student may then come to recognize himself or herself as a virtual subject of the literary narrative he confronts at the mediate intersection between outer and inner, insofar as his very existence as concrete person has absorbed and been shaped by human modalities which first dynamically appear in biblical ethos, personalities and socio-cultural milieu. Non-Western students will resonate to some extent with these modalities insofar as they have infused and molded global industrial society, which emanates from the West. Conversely, the inward sensibility of such students can provide a comparative foil to elicit general perception of the peculiar characteristics of Western sensibility which hearken back to biblical precedents.

2. Particular Course in Hebrew Bible

No axiom is more foundational to the religiological perspective developed herein than the inherent need of self-consciousness for coherence. This axiom governs, among other aspects of general religiological method, the analysis of particular elements within a whole: as hypothetical understanding of a coherent and systemic whole clarifies, it becomes possible to identify with increasing precision the logical function of each element within it. Applied to interpreting texts in the Hebrew Bible, this rubric likewise presumes that the quest for coherence shapes each element internally as well as determining their integral relation. Thus a religiological hermeneutic of the Hebrew Bible, although indebted to historical and linguistic scholarship for its critical preparation and corroboration, reposes its essential confidence in the need for coherence innate in the redactor's own self-consciousness and manifest in his conscious judgments. Its methodology recalls Franz Rosenzweig's famous avowal that he reads the "R" for redactor as "Rabbenu," implying that one must trust the wisdom of the canonizers as persons of inspired aesthetic and spiritual genius whose final product must be approached with the reverent attention accorded to any great and presumably unified work of art and spirit if one would probe its deeper strata.[27]

The interpretive power of such a hermeneutic might best be illustrated through application to a subsection of the Hebrew canon, itself

arranged as a whole composed of parts. Teaching of the third section of
the Bible, the Ketuvim *(Writings)*, has not been salient as an especially
rich area of pedagogy. With its axiomatic confidence in the redactor,
though, a religiological hermeneutic would examine these texts in an
attempt to identify their function within the Hebrew Bible in its totality,
afterwards seeking to understand the view of reality each expresses individually and together as a possible subsystemic whole. An exemplary
hypothetical formulation of the general function of the Ketuvim within
the Bible overall might run as follows: *Torah* proper, the first section of
the Bible, details the binding of God and the people of Israel *together* in
a normative Covenant. Granting this much, the Bible's second section,
Nevi'im (Prophets), evidently offers historically specific corrective guidance from *God* regarding violation of express provisions of the Covenant. But not every human situation is amenable to the intrusive witness of explicit covenantal norms. Most of the time, indeed, people
must assuredly take counsel with *themselves* in order to determine their
stance toward the situations with which life presents them - including
those "metacovenantal" situations in which human relationship with
God is itself vexed or otherwise at issue and in need of basic
reconfiguration. Self-consciousness is, after all, prior even to consciousness of God. Does this mean that humanity shall be left to its own devices in confronting the manifold ambiguities and subtly shifting modalities of creaturely existence? From a biblical standpoint, the totality
of God's concern would seem to preclude the likelihood of this. What is
required alternatively is some sort of prudential wisdom capable of
molding human awareness from within, insinuating itself so that guidance when needed might be forthcoming from persons, as it were, to
themselves. Such guidance, then, would come from God not directly
but indirectly, issued not by prophetic fiat at specific historical moments but rather taking the form of inspired tales, poems, object lessons
and general nostrums always instantly ready to hand and also there to
be gradually and freely absorbed into one's character as a transforming
leaven. Whereas sporadic prophetic guidance descends, so to speak,
transcendentally "from above," that is, from *without,* this abiding guidance by prudential wisdom could then arise mundanely 'from below,"
that is, from within, in the consciousness of a person consulting a
selfhood shaped by spiritually nurturing instruction. It is just this sort
of companionable wisdom which the *Ketuvim* appear to embody—a
wisdom for every typical human condition.

But the *Ketuvim* include not only such "wisdom texts"; they incorporate as well four texts of sequential narrative history, i.e., the two books of Chronicles, Ezra and Nehemiah. The presence of these generically distinct texts in the third part of the Hebrew Bible poses a special interpretive problem. By virtue of what organizational principles do they constitute an integral and coherent element of the *Ketuvim?* The basis for any answer may reside in two mutually supportive facts of the canon's organization: first, the books of Chronicles closely parallel the books of Kings, included in *Nevi'im;* second, the actual chronological span covered by other texts within *Nevi'im* and *Ketuvim* is similar, ranging from the time of the Judges to the Persian period. A final clue is that, despite the close parallel, the tone of Chronicles differs from that of Kings by virtue of an editorial tendency to extract moralizing wisdom from historical events, e.g., II Chron 15-16. All this suggests that prophetic guidance "from above" and prudential wisdom "from below" are to be regarded as devolving in tandem after Torah was received and Israel had entered the Land. Moreover, each type of sacred knowledge implies a viewpoint of its own within which to perceive historical events, and the more mundanely oriented historical consciousness of the "wisdom" perspective shades directly into a scribal transition to the even more mundane consciousness of the Rabbinic period. Then the problem of historical narrative within the *Ketuvim* proper appears resolvable. But what of the integral design of the nine remaining texts which bear, in varying ways, the stamp of "wisdom" as such?

Scrutinized in the light of the foregoing hypotheses, the "wisdom books" of *Ketuvim* do indeed disclose themselves as subsisting within a coherent organizing matrix which may be diagrammed and explicated as follows:

Closeness:
Song of Songs *[THEORY]*
Psalms *[PRACTICE]*

	G	
Stability:	W O R L D	**Change:**
Ecclesiastes *[T]*	D	Daniel*[T]*
Proverbs *[P]*		Esther/Ruth*[P]*

Distance:
Job *[T]*
Lamentations *[P]*

Human life transpires in a reality structured both by direct "vertical" relationship with God as well as by "horizontal' relationship with the world as such and its ongoing continuum of events. Within this ontological field, human beings require the help of prudential wisdom in four distinct modes to deal with the basic situational realities of (a) *closeness* to God; b) *distance* from God; (e) *stability* in the world; (d) *change* in the world. The wisdom operative in each mode must furthermore be of two kinds: an orienting theoretical wisdom which describes the situational reality in its ultimate ideal dimensions and an instructive practical wisdom to guide action in the midst of that reality as it actually impinges. This system delineates a coherent hermeneutic framework which specifies eight functional niches that assign a meaningful order to all the texts of the *Ketuvim;* two texts occupy one niche, that of the "practical wisdom of change," insofar as the helping Providence which faith must affirm operates behind the scenes of challenging worldly circumstance may either show itself openly in the short range as with Esther, or remain hidden for the long range, as was the case with Ruth.

While space restrictions forbid additional analysis of individual texts in accordance with the hypothetically described hermeneutic framework, and only such analysis can buttress conviction that the framework completely "makes sense," it may at least be observed that this method has already modeled an internally logical and coherent system of prudential wisdom that may potentially clarify an area of biblical worldview - an area, moreover, which comparative analysis of the Hebrew Bible in its entirety could confirm is indeed a functionally requisite and textually instantiated component of that worldview. At any event, the present hermeneutic - as in every case where religiological analysis discerns a hypothetical configuration imbued with some inner logic—serves, even if merely plausible, the immediate pedagogical end of providing a natural heuristic through which a teacher may utilize socratic methods to engage students with the texts at hand.[28]

3. General Course in Judaism

Courses in Hebrew Bible exhibit a fundamental groundedness and finitude by virtue of their limited commitment to expound particular texts, however central. An introductory course in Judaism offers, in contrast, an arena of unlimited horizon within which the teacher may experiment both with presentation of the generic Judaic worldview—or more properly a current hypothetical formulation of it—and with the attempt to justify that formulation through appeal to the "Judaisms." Exigencies of practicability in an undergraduate survey course dictate that material be expounded deductively, working from "Judaism" to the "Judaisms," i.e., from abstract ideality toward concrete reality. Given this trajectory of exposition, three progressive levels of delineating the subject matter suggest themselves, corresponding to course subdivisions. First, the metaexperiential "core elements" of the generic Judaic worldview may be ideally laid out and these major structural components characterized individually and in relation. Secondly, this core in all its particularity may be situated within the universal framework of human experience by raising the question of how the Judaic worldview in principle structures existence in space and time. Thirdly, Judaism can be brought down to full concrete reality through investigating the specific actualities of Judaic experience within the context of a particular "spacio-temporal" community, whose modes of Judaic life and thought might—time permitting—be compared with those of other similarly concrete "Judaisms."

The core of Judaism, more precisely, is the freely committed or *covenantal* relation between the two "selves" or "persons" God and Israel, a relation defined by and subsisting in Torah. This relation becomes grounded within the framework of space and time through identification of components of space and time with the Covenant itself. The Land of Israel is that area of *space* especially designated for the full living out of the covenantal relation, and Israel may consequently occupy it only when enacting basic commitment to this relation; the Sabbath is that realm of *time* especially set aside to exemplify the quality of fully lived out covenantal relation and honoring it thus itself becomes the paradigmatic enactment of Israel's basic commitment to the Covenant. Because Israel's commitment to the Covenant is not in fact initially complete and must be deepened through learning experience, the wholeness of the covenantal relation can be actualized only gradually within the spacio-temporal framework of human life. Such defective progression toward eventual wholeness of relation imbues this framework with the character of "history," i.e., the developmental movement of events from a time in which Israel's hold on its designated space remains tenuous, continually threatened by the divinely ordained instrumentality of peoples hostile to Israel, toward a time at which Israel's residency in its appointed space has been fully consolidated and, as prerequisite, its relations with hostile peoples mended by virtue of Israel's completely actualized living out of its covenantal commitment. The Judaic worldview thus endows the common spacio-temporal framework of human life with a coordinated empirical *directionality* toward the Land of Israel in space and the period of consummated covenant relation in time; and it is this characteristic directionality, with the unique narrative significance it bestows upon the particular empirical realities of spacial locus, temporal occurrence and human person - individual and collective - that the Judaic sense of "history" properly entails. Awareness of this directionality, which constitutes the very career of the Covenant on earth, remains vivified through representation of its basic structure—creational beginning, revelatory middle, redemptive end —by the Judaic year's three seasonal pilgrimage festivals, whose pattern the three periods of the weekly Sabbath day —evening, morning, afternoon—itself replicate.

Specific observances which enact Sabbath and festivals are best reserved for the third unit of a course in Judaism, which may take up the details of Judaism in practice. An excellent vehicle for presenting such material, treating Judaic practices within living historical context, are anthropological studies like the classic *Life Is With People,*[29] a masterful tribute to the now extinct Eastern European Jewish *shtetl.* Its chapters at one point or another cover most of the significant Judaic teachings in regard to personal and communal behavior, both the dynamic moral substance and the ritual disciplines to promote acquisition of that substance. This presentation of "living Judaism" invites supplementation by source texts expounding religious doctrinal and ritual concepts and background reading in the history of Judaism. Elements of the Judaic worldview schematically explicated in the course's earlier units may be verified, exemplified and concretized by the witness of a concrete manifestation of Judaism. And the view of Judaism which emerges may be further tested and corroborated through selective examination of other representative historically embodied "Judaisms."

4. Particular Course in Judaism

A teacher or scholar approaching Judaism religiologically seeks to construct, over the long term, an ever more adequate model of generic Judaism. In its most compact and schematic form, the current state of such a model might be sketched out as prolegomenon to an introductory course in Judaism and ought to serve, on the other hand, as implicit context and foil for the presentation of more bounded topic areas within Judaism. A generic model of Judaism might, for example, discern a characteristic Judaic intention to relate transcendental unity, however conceived, to the unique particulars which become immanently unified into an integral whole by virtue of that transcendental unity. In the Hebrew Bible, this "logic of Judaic unity" governs both creation in space, resulting in the formation of an integral cosmos, and occurrences in time, guiding the unfolding of an integral history. The identical concern emerges in the methodic principle of the Rabbinic period that each element of Torah constitutes a unique and indispensable part of a unified whole. For Maimonides, contemplation of the integral role each element of the natural creation plays in the functioning of the whole discloses the unity of design within that whole, leading to awareness of the Unity of its Creator. In the Zohar, each *Sephirah* performs a unique function as an indispensable part of an integral whole unified immanently and transcendentally by the *Ein Sof.*

The most effective hermeneutic for a particular course in any such text and period of Judaism, it appears, may be furnished by the teacher's own currently revised model of generic Judaism. As the above example indicates, such a model should implicitly suggest deep structural relations between the designated topic area and many others throughout the sweep of the historical Judaic tradition, equipping the teacher to venture with broadly based as well as narrow comparisons which draw upon various manifestations of Judaism. At the same time, any new course preparation becomes an opportunity to test, revise and embellish the model itself. The model functions throughout as a heuristic directing attention of teacher and student alike at underlying structural features of the Judaic worldview, perpetually raising questions not only as to why each feature is what it is and what constitute the parameters for its variant forms in different historical manifestations of Judaism, but also questions of elemental "choice"— e.g., what aspects of universal human existence or personhood the model most aligns with and how the model constellates within larger comparative frameworks. Thus, to pursue the above example a bit further, the religiological investigation of Judaism fairly swiftly confronts the scholar and teacher with the demand to specify exactly what "unity" means generically for Judaism in contrast with its root meaning for other religious traditions, as well as to account for variant significations of "unity" as understood within the manifold of the "Judaisms."[30]

One conspicuous way in which scholars of religion have been treating what many increasingly apprehend to be the distinctiveness of the domain they study, we have noted, is through the rubric of "worldview," a concept now being crafted into an ever more subtle and refined vehicle for insight into the nature and structure of religion. This concept has served as present basis for illustrating the impact recent developments in the scholarly study of religion might have upon the academic teaching of Judaism. Nonetheless, more primary than any such specific example stands the advancing understanding that the subject matter of religious studies may constitute an area of human reality no less distinctive nor any more reducible to some tangential realm than are other subject matters currently investigated within their own respective disciplines. The more that the most telling insights into this area prove to yield themselves only to *sui generis* methods conformed uniquely to the nature and structure of religion, the more the study of religion may acquire its own acknowledged status as a religiology. But "religiology" begins whenever a scholar or teacher is grasped by the awareness that religion has a *logos* of its own, an intrinsic mode of being that can be penetrated only when honored in its uniqueness, even though the methods of existing disciplines may enable partial access to it.

Most scholars and teachers of Judaism have been trained in the methods of extant disciplines within the humanities and social sciences, yet many have glimpsed the integrity peculiar to Judaism as a form of *religious* reality whose fullest disclosure may demand transcending standard disciplinary bounds. To this extent, many teachers of Judaism have already found their way to the threshold of incorporating a religiological perspective into the presentation of their subject matter, if only as ancillary to more conventional stratagems for classroom instruction. To these, a view from the horizon of the contemporary study of religion encourages persistence in the endeavor to see Judaism whole and clear, in its own innate character, even when its reality can be captured only through a wholesale breaching of traditional intellectual frontiers which resorts to innovative procedures, exotic approaches, novel angles of vision. To others, content with established methods of teaching, the emergence of ever more articulated religiological perspectives for the study of Judaism may jostle complacency, stir fresh ideas, and issue a salutary challenge for more creative employment of proven instructional techniques. In the last analysis, though, the worth of any new perspective for examining Judaism will be judged by how compellingly, comprehensively and profoundly it reveals the lineaments of its object. From this standpoint, the contemporary study of religion may commend to all academic teachers of Judaism the possibility of unprecedentedly bold and stimulating experiments in determining and conveying that truth toward which all those pledged to the life of the mind aspire.

Indeed, the most bracing promise of such experimentation toward truth might be nothing less than a wider revitalizing of the life of the mind as such. Jacques Barzun, in an essay entitled "Scholarship Versus Culture," has eloquently decried the usurpation by a deadeningly analytic modern scholarship—its repercussions permeating even lay society —of a whole territory which human sensibility formerly allocated largely to that true cultivation of mind and spirit previously denoted by the term "culture":

> ... by the same human mind that has created science but the analytical method can work in an entirely different way ... The other use, direction, or bent, Pascal called the *esprit de finesse,* we would say "intuitive understanding." It goes about its business just the other way. It does not analyze, does not break things down into parts, but seizes upon the character of the whole altogether, by inspection short or long ... The objects that go to make up culture are designed to be understood and remembered and enjoyed by the operation of finesse; they are for inspection as wholes, not for analysis.[31]

Barzun fiercely indicts the negative impact of the modern academy and its procedures upon true cultural vitality:

> In the use of "method," whatever it be, the role of self-consciousness is evident. Here is a work of art: not *Let us read it* but *How do we deal with it?* Our jargon word *approach* is revealing: we creep up; we are on safari; we bring down the big game. The procedure naturally varies not only with the doctrine but also with the mental qualities of the practitioner ... But coping with a problem by analytic methods is the unquestioned aim.[32]

Yet religiological insight finds, at the primal core of that very self-consciousness to whose overextension Barzun unarguably ascribes much endemic alienation, precisely a drive toward *coherence* which knows no peace until it "seizes upon the character of the whole altogether .." To follow the tracery of this impulse is to voyage toward overcoming the fragmentation of the human spirit at its crux to recover the wholeness of object and subject, of "outside" and "inside," itself. But if the quintessential rubric of religiological *method* is itself the elemental pursuit of *wholeness* or coherence, can it be that within its purview even the split between overspecialized scholarship and disenfranchised culture might find mediation and eventual healing? At the very least, an emerging ethos within the contemporary study of religion, far from being averse to the cultivation and hence true *education* of the whole human person, can perceive much of its own innermost soul in words that Barzun reserves to contrast culture with scholarship—and in this hopeful similitude the thoughtful teacher of religion might perhaps recognize the highest of pedagogical callings:

> Culture in whatever form—art, thought, history, religion—is for meditation and conversation ... As for a true meditation, it radiates in all directions, excludes nothing; its virtue is to comprehend—in both senses: to understand and to take in the fullest view. Both are actions of the mind *and spirit,* and therefore charged with the strongest relevant feelings. Indeed, both the interior monologue and the spoken dialogue aim at discerning which feelings and what degree of each belong to which idea or image. That is how culture reshapes the personality; it develops it by offering the vicarious experience of art and thought; it puts all experience in order gradually, through reflection, meditation, and conversation.[33]

Drawn into conversation with Martin Buber and Jacques Barzun, then, the words of Jacob Neusner may finally speak with even deeper resonance and issue a profounder summons to the exploration of religion than they could originally have intended, but which those learning to see religion fully will nonetheless be able truly to hear:

> Seeing the whole whole, finding out what makes it whole, establishing definitive context, discovering the questions to which systems constitute answers—this is the sort of description which makes possible the labor...[34]
> ✿

Endnotes

1. Further analysis of the current state of religious studies may be found in the authors articles "Naming the Game: A Question of the Field," *Bulletin of the Counsel on the Study of Religion,* 14/4 (October, 1983), pp. 109-113; and "Response" to "Insiders and Outsiders in the Study of Religious Traditions," *Journal of the American Academy of Religion,* LI/3 (September, 1983), pp. 480-484. The latter more thoroughly treats the relationships of "objective"/"subjective" and "outside"/"inside" which figure crucially in this chapter, for which a companion article - emphasizing theory rather than pedagogical *praxis*—is now in preparation under the title "The Contemporary Emergence of Religiology from the History of Religion: An Example and Prolegomenon."

   In regard to the current state of Jewish Studies a number of helpful bibliographical essays and surveys have been published within the past two decades. Notable among these are the following: Arnold J. Band, "Jewish Studies in American Liberal Arts Colleges and Universities," *American Jewish Yearbook,* 1966 (Volume 67), edited by Morris Fine and Milton Himmelfarb (New York and Philadelphia: Jewish Publication Society of America, 1966), 3-30; Zev Garber, "Jewish Studies at a Two-Year Public College," ERIC, 1974 (ED 086 269); idem, "Alternative Teaching Methods in Teaching Introduction to Judaism," ERIC, 1976 (ED 114 *151*); idem, "Teaching the Holocaust at a Two-Year Public College," ERIC, 1983 (JC 830 218); Abraham I. Katsh, *The Biblical Heritage in American Democracy* (New York: Ktav, 1977); Jacob Neusner, *The Academic Study of Judaism: Essays and Reflections* (New York: Ktav, 1975, second edition, Chico: Scholars Press for Brown Judaic Studies, 1982; Second Series, New York: Ktav, 1977; Third Series, New York: Ktav, 1980); idem, *Judaism in the American Humanities* (Chico: Scholars Press for Brown Judaic Series, 1981; Second Series, Chico: Scholars Press for Brown Judaic Series, 1983); idem, ed., *New Humanities and Academic Discipline: The Case of Jewish Studies* (Madison: University of Wisconsin Press, 1984); idem, *Judaic Studies in Universities: Toward the Second Quarter-Century* (Durham: Duke University, 1984), idem, *Major Trends in Formative Judaism,* Second Series (Chico: Scholars Press for Brown Judaic Series, 1984), pp. 123-149.

2. Jonathan Z. Smith, *Imagining Religion* (Chicago: The University of Chicago Press, 1982), pp. 19-20; and "No Need to Travel to the Indies: Judaism and the Study of Religion," *Take Judaism, for Example: Studies Toward the Comparison of Religions,* ed. Jacob Neusner (Chicago: The University of Chicago Press, 1983), P. 215.

3. *Ibid.*

4. *Ibid.,* p. xi.

5. Ninian Smart, *Worldviews: Cross-cultural Exploration of Human Beliefs* (New York: Charles Scribner's Sons, 1983).

6. *Ibid.,* pp. 1-2.

7. Raimundo Panikkar, *"Aporias* in the Comparative Philosophy of Religion," *Man and World,* 13 (1980), pp. 357-383. *Man and World* is published in the Hague by Mutinus Nijhoff.

8. Mircea Eliade, *The Sacred and the Profane* ("Harvest Books"; New York: Harcourt, Brace & World, 1959), esp. Ch. I.

9. Michael Novak, *Ascent of the Mountain, Flight of the Dove: An Invitation to Religious Studies* (New York: Harper & Row, 1971).

10. Peter Berger, *The Sacred Canopy: Elements of a Sociological Theory of Religion* (New York: Doubleday & Co., 1967), Ch. 1 and Ch. 2.

11. Smart. p. 5.

12. Smith, *Imagining Religion,* P. 26.

13. *Ibid.,* p. 34.

14. Jacob Neusner, "Alike and Not Alike: A Grid for Comparison and Differentiation," *Take Judaism, for Example,* ed. J. Neusner, pp. 233, 235.

15. *Ibid.,* p. 235.

16. The most compendious anthropological theory of worldview to date was published just a year after Ninian Smart's volume of similar title;

i.e., Michael Kearney, *World View* (Novato: Chandler & Sharp, 1984). Among the most powerful influences upon theory of religion at the present time is the work of the anthropologists Clifford Geertz, Victor Turner and Mary Douglas.

17. Neusner, pp. 234-5.
18. Berger, pp. 16-17, 22-24, 44ff.
19. That worldview mediates between external cultural "world" and internal integrity of the self suggests that the disciplinary niche for religiology may lie between anthropology and psychology (cf. Vernoff, "Naming the Game," p. 112). On the relation between external and internal human reality, "outside" and "inside," cf. Vernoff, "Response," pp. 482-83, and notes 24 and 29 below.
20. Mircea Eliad, *Cosmos and History* ("Harper Torchbooks"; New York: Harper & Row, 1959).
21. Martin Buber, *The Knowledge of Man,* ed. by Maurice Friedman (New York: Harper & Row, 1965), pp. 62-63.
22. Rudolf Otto, *Mysticism: East and West* (New York: Macmillan, 1970), pp. 157-58.
23. Neusner, p. 235.
24. For a specific example of experimental comparative method in what might be called "depth religiology," cf. the author's article "After the Holocaust: History and Being as Sources of Method within the Emerging Interreligious Hermeneutic," *Journal of Ecumenical Studies,* 21/4 (Fall, 1984), pp. 639-663. Utilizing this method allows tracing the interior, intrapsychic and intrasubjective grounding of the Judaic and Christian worldviews respectively within universal ontological structures of *personal identity* and *personal consciousness.* The resulting model of generic Judaism is further elaborated in the author's article "Unity," *Contemporary Jewish Religious Thought,* ed. Arthur A. Cohen and Paul Mendes-Flohr (New York: Charles Scribner's Sons, 1986). It should be noted that the present chapter intends to adumbrate religiological method only in the most general way; the horizon of this new disciplinary realm stands open for the development of many sophisticated methodic approaches toward penetrating the nature and structure of and systematic relations among modalities of religion.
25. See note 24 above.
26. Yehezkel Kaufmann, *The Religion of Israel,* trans. by Moshe Greenberg (New York: Schocken, 1972). An excellent source of Martin Buber's biblical theology for teaching purposes is the essays in *Israel and the World: Essays in a Time of Crisis* (New York: Schocken, 1963).
27. Cf. Nancy Fuchs-Kreimer, "Christian Old Testament Theology: A Time for New Beginnings," *Journal of Ecumenical Studies,* 18/1 (Winter, 1981), P. 86: "I would argue that the redaction which scholars cut through to find the 'acts of God' is, in itself, the evidence of God."

28. I am indebted to discussion with Rabbi Ephraim Rottenberg and Mr. Natan David Seidel for insight into the historical consciousness of the *Ketuvim*. Further publications dealing with this hermeneutic of the *Ketuvim* and its application are in progress.

29. Mark Zborowski and Elizabeth Herzog, *Life Is With People* (New York: Schocken, 1962). Part V, "As the Shtetl Sees the World," splendidly exemplifies the anthropological rendering of Judaic worldview. It is particularly instructive to compare this with the exemplary rendering of Judaic worldview in a religiological mode found in the author's article "Unity." Although the two approaches are mutually complementary, the former understands worldview more limitedly, chiefly as the integrating matrix for a given culture; it stresses "view," as it were, rather than "world." In religiological perspective, on the other hand, worldview becomes situated in the context of *reality as a whole* in a way that bridges, transcends and finally abolishes the dichotomy of "object" and "subject." From this perspective worldview finds its place within the nested and interactive contexts of the ontoepistemological structure of *human personhood;* the perceptual *mediation* between human personhood "inside" and the reality "outside" which generates any "view" of the "world;" and the ontocosmological structure of that wider *reality itself* in its conditioning of all human existence and experience.

30. Cf. Vernoff, "Unity," for an exemplary model of generic Judaism.

31. Jacques Berzon, "Scholarship Versus Culture," *The Atlantic,* pp. 254/ 5 (November, 1984), p. 99.

32. *Ibid.,* 100.

33. *Ibid.,* 104.

34. Neusner, p, 235.

Chapter 2

Reading Myth:
A Strategy for a Methodological Introduction to the Study of Jewish Religions
S. Daniel Breslauer

The Study of Jewish Myth as a Postmodern Approach to Jewish Religion

The well-known story of the blind men and the elephant often occurs in unexpected places. The Sufi mystics, for example, use the story as an allegory for human knowledge of the divine. Like men stumbling upon an elephant in the dark, they grasp onto whatever they confront and claim that they have comprehended all that there is to know.[1] The same condition applies to academic scholarship. A model or a paradigm, true enough as a partial glimpse of reality, becomes in the hands of some investigators the single key to unlock every door. Joseph Dan, for example, reports that he once met a Jungian scholar who was quick to point out to him that the cosmic vision portrayed in the kabbalistic book, *Sefer Yetzira*, in fact resembled a Jungian mandela.[2] There is much in that book to confirm such an impression. The book takes as its point of departure the magical properties of the alphabet, of the human body, and of other aspects of the human and natural world. It would be strange if these elements, common to all human experience, could not fit into a Jungian pattern. Nevertheless, the specific problems -of dating *Sefer Yetzira*, of determining its provenance, its place in the history of Jewish mystical speculation, and its relationship to non-Jewish mystical works, remain unresolved by applying such a Jungian panacea. A more profitable approach would be to use the Jungian model as one of several equally illuminating ways of discovering the varied dimensions of that mystical text.

The task of the teacher of Jewish studies in the modern period is precisely that of resisting the impulse exhibited by the Jungian disciple whom Dan encountered. Jewish studies faces a new challenge and a new opportunity. Freed from doctrinal or institutional limitations, this scholarship can uncover the diversity that marks human creativity generally and Jewish creativity in particular. Raphael Jospe comments that the current generation of Jewish scholars stands at a crossroads. He explains this by the historical development of Judaic studies beginning with the "the giants of European *Wissenschaft des Judentums*" and being carried on now by the profusion of studies in Israel and the United States.[3] Certainly contemporary studies of Jewish religion stand between two worlds, but these may better be understood as the modern and postmodern rather than as the European and the Israeli-American. The modern approach sought to uncover the essence of Judaism, its historical, intellectual, and religious uniqueness. Moderns used the techniques of Western science to reveal the hidden heart of Jewish religiousness. Postmoderns are skeptical of the possibility of finding any such essence. They rejoice in the proliferation of possible Jewish religions, in the variety of expressions that can go by the name Judaism. The challenge for the academic study of Judaism today lies in being able to utilize the tools inherited from past generations of scholars in the new pursuit of diversity and pluralism.

A study of Jewish myth can generate such a vision of a diverse Judaism because myth itself often grows out of the soil of difference and plurality. Will Herberg, for example, prepared notes on the variant meanings of the word "myth." After reviewing several possible nuances to the word he raised the question of whether the term "in any of its nuances can be conscripted to serve in the understanding of the scriptures of the Bible, both Old Testament and New Testament, which are at once so thoroughly historical and so thoroughly dramatic."[4] The defining of the term must come first and then its application to texts which resist easy classification.

Herberg's effort, published posthumously represents a valiant foray into an arena fraught with complexity. The study of myth has itself mirrored the division between the moderns and the postmoderns. Joseph Dan notes two approaches to myth: one looks for eternal, universal patterns and the other focuses on the specific, the particularistic expression of myth in one cultural group.[5] Students of Jewish myth also sought both the specific and the universal in Judaism. Gershom Scholem, for example, whom Dan credits with reopening the question of myth in Judaism as a viable possibility, illuminated the detailed and specific myths of Jewish mystics. Against claims of scholars such as Yehezkel Kaufmann and Umberto Cassutto, Scholem portrayed a continual mythic substratum which resurfaces in Jewish life again and again.[6] Jewish myth gives testimony to an ambivalence within Jewish religiousness. While many proponents of Jewish religion held to an anti-mythological and strictly legal perspective—others cultivated myth as an alternative route to piety. Sometimes Jewish myth and Jewish law join forces in a single expression. At other times they play off against each other in a round of challenges and responses. Discovering myth may mean discovering the key to hidden difference, to a pluralism that kept itself undercover and avoided obvious detection.

Attention to myths does not mean a rejection of scholarship or an unwillingness to set boundaries of some sort to the study of Jewish thought and practice. Umberto Eco has pointed out that myth traditionally sets limits on the human imagination. Traditions generate myths to contain the imaginative overflow that spills out from speculation and thought. Eco complains that modern views of myth no longer recognize this function. The modern view of myths, he thinks, "no longer recognizes the discipline that myths impose on the symbols they involve."[7] Studying myths means understanding the restrictions they place on how people imagine the world no less than understanding the variety of possibilities that they open up. A study of Jewish myth requires the recognition of the purpose behind such myth -- to establish a definitive view of Judaism, to evoke a compelling and comprehensive portrait of what constitutes reality. The meaning of mythology generally then offers the indispensable tools by which to understand what Jewish myth seeks to express.

The Study of Mythology

An approach to Judaism through myth begins by asking the function and meaning of myth in general. The first task is that of defining "myth," a word that seems as various in its interpretations as the illustrations used to exemplify it. Loyal D. Rue considers myth as a story that provides "a shared matrix of meanings." He sees it as a mixture or a "confusion" of artistic presentation, cosmology, and moral tenets.[8] This suggests that myth represents a conscious construction, a poetic evocation of ideas and ethical values. Studying Jewish myths will entail examining several narratives, each of which brings together, or confuses, a view of reality, a sense of moral duty, and evocative artistry. Introducing the idea of myth itself then, already advances the cause of diversity; students learn that myth is not all of one type, that Jewish myths may fall into several of the different categories, and that not all Jewish scholarship accepts the premise that Jewish mythology, as such, can even exist. Against Rue's complaints that modern scholarship suffers from "amythia" or an antagonism to myth, students should take seriously the criticism of myth offered by serious Jewish thinkers. Emmanuel Levinas, for example, continues a polemic of Franz Rosenzweig against myth. He sees Jewish approaches to texts as a strategy of continual demythologization. Myth evokes eternal patterns, unchanging rhythms. Jewish interpretations always re-read texts, always find something new in an inherited text. He calls this process "a quest for meaning to be renewed."[9] The interesting feature of this approach is that it criticizes myth for being not creative enough, not diverse enough, not flexible enough. Students can learn to question whether myth makes something fixed and unchanging or whether it opens the way to greater creativity and innovation.

The diversity of myth becomes clear when reviewing the typology used to categorize different stories. Some types of narratives cluster into a single category. G. S. Kirk, for example, studies several examples of myths from Mesopotamia and Greece in an effort to discover the usefulness and limitations of various ways of examining myths. He concludes his study with "A suggested typology of functions" of myths.[10] His second class of myths—ones that he calls "operative, iterative and validatory"—correspond to the narratives studied here. The three purposes of myth in this category reflect the range of functions that Jewish myths tend to perform. The first type is basically cosmological in its orientation. It rehearses the natural cycle, the rhythms of life, the regularity of the seasons. Some myths tend to celebrate this regularity, others seem to help maintain it. Invariably these myths present the hidden skeleton of existence for all to see. Science and philosophy explain the world to people. They offer rational descriptions of how things began and how they function. Myth, on the other hand, offers a way of interacting with the pattern behind all things, of treating the structure of being as an entity in itself. As John L. McKenzie notes concerning biblical myth, myth transforms the facts of science into a "thou," or an "other" with whom people can have a relationship.[11] This type of myth can be called a "cosmological" myth, meaning a myth that focuses on creation, nature, and the reality with which human beings struggle daily.

The type that Kirk calls "validatory" act, in his words, as a "charter" or model for social and institutional practices. He shows how such an intention animates the Mesopotamian Gilgamesh epic. That epic, however, reveals another aspect of these myths—they validate institutions by analyzing human nature. Social life is justified by the way human beings inevitably behave. Part of the purpose of the Gilgamesh epic is to expose the human dynamics motivating kings and heroes and to suggest civility as the cure for the common psychological ills affecting all people. These myths, then are really "anthropological" or "psychological," because they expose the hidden urges and necessities that form the basis of all social life. These myths do, indeed, legitimize social life, but they do so on the basis of how human beings exist, on the way life is inevitably carried out. Erich Fromm speaks of myths that enable people to remain in touch with their psychological realities. Through symbols and myths, he thinks, human beings project their inner world outward so they understand themselves and grapple with their lives. He interprets such myth as a special type of language, a forgotten language, which requires a special logic to decode its mysteries. That logic is the logic of the psychic realities within consciousness. Several myths provide this way of understanding the inner meaning of human nature. Fromm looks at mythic rituals such as the Jewish Sabbath and its traditional explanations and at folk tales such as Little Red Riding Hood to discover how they communicate a message about what it means to be human. He sees each symbolic pattern evoking a portrait of the human soul.[12]

Kirk concludes his typological suggestion by remarking that "one category that is not particularly well served by this suggested typology is that of eschatological myths."[13] He does himself a disservice. That final type of myth, one that describes the end of history and the world beyond this existence, is more generally a myth seeking to understand and justify human historical experience. Such myth is predominantly political. It uses symbols and artistry to evoke a political program, to affirm and confirm the view a group holds about itself and its place among human communities. This type of myth fits the category of the "iterable"—the articulation of social reality. As Gilbert Morris Culbertson remarks, ever since Nietzsche, students have recognized the political functions that myth plays in creating a consensus about political values and taboos.[14] Myth serves the political body by explaining suffering, justifying triumph, and legitimating the social situation in which people live. Myth makers create stories that span present, past, and future to weave a seamless tale of continuity. They construct the past and the future so that the present takes on value and significance for their audience. Political myth is an address to a present audience that seeks to persuade them about the past and the future. The validity of such narratives depends on their reception by those who hear them. Political myth requires a living present to authenticate its claims about both the past and the future[15] For this study "political" is too loose and broad a term. Cosmological and certainly anthropological myths have political consequences. While the myths that speak of eschatology are "political" in so far as they bridge past and future for a community, they are above all historical. The third type of myth examined here, then, is historical myth.

Cosmological, Anthropological, and Historical Myths in Judaism

Contemporary Jewish scholarship suggests that each of these types of myth occurs within the Jewish tradition. There are some, like Yehezkel Kaufmann, who reject the claim that Judaism can contain cosmological myth. This view identifies Jewish monotheism as inherently antagonistic to myth. The idea of a single and unified world creator is, according to this approach, incompatible with the mythic evocation of a personally accessible reality. Myth makes the world present to the believer. Monotheism it is claimed requires a greater sense of distance and awe. While Jewish tradition may borrow elements from the myths of other cultures, this view concedes, it uses them selectively and non-mythically.[16]

Despite this view, however, Jewish scholars have found in both biblical and post-biblical writings evidence of that personalization of creation and sense of relationship to nature that defines cosmological myth. Perhaps none have done this so eloquently as Martin Buber. Buber explains myth as a narrative by which a human being reports an event of relationship. For Buber myth, whether in the Bible, in later Jewish literature, or in more recent Jewish writings, represents a trace of an I-You relationship. Buber defends myth within Judaism as a means for keeping alive the continuing possibility for I-You meeting. He characterizes myth as a form of creative speech whereby a special dimension of being ordinarily dormant comes into vibrant life. This evocative character of myth marks it as a cosmological communication about the nature of reality.[17]

Judaism has been declared independent of myth understood as anthropological or psychological charter narratives no less than of myth seen as cosmological. Rene Girard analyzes the psychological meaning of myth and its connection with human violence. Through mythology, he argues, a society projects its violence outward onto a scapegoat. Myths of the Greek God Zeus and of the Scandinavian Baldr exonerate their heroes from charges of mass murder. Such myths, Girard argues, teaches a people to accept its own violence as both necessary and even virtuous. He claims that only when people face up to their violence, as for example in the Hebrew Bible or the New Testament, do they move beyond their "natural" inclinations and advance morally. He looks to an abandonment of myth as a sign of human maturation.[18] Girard notes that "the representations of historical persecutions resemble mythology" but he makes this crucial distinction, "The face of the victim shows through the mask in the texts of historical persecutions. There are chinks and cracks. In mythology the mask is still intact; it covers the whole face so well that we have no idea it is a mask." Because of this, myth dilutes the moral outrage that should accompany violence. The historical narrative has a more forceful affect, makes a more powerful impact, and is more morally effective than myth.[19]

Advanced societies, therefore, should dismember myth and concentrate on history. Yet masks mark the reality of every society. The expectation that violence can be contained rather than merely recognized and accepted seems naive and overly simple. A study of Jewish myth may, indeed, reveal only the masks of the victim. Recognizing those masks helps identify the myths and masks of the present. Claiming that myth has been replaced by history raises dangers of its own. Galit Hasan-Rokem surveys the controversy over myth in Judaism and concludes that whatever the truth has been in the past, present Jewish thought often represents mythic ways of thinking. She claims that secular ideologies, paradoxically but not really surprisingly, "revalorize traditional mythical ideas and idioms." That is, the way Zionists, socialists, and various modern Jewish religionists invoke a typology of human nature that reinforces their political agenda.[20] Learning to see modern views in their mythological function helps students recognize that whether or not myth is an advance or a decline, its presence, potential for violence, and ability to mask institutional power as an inevitable aspect of human existence make it an important phenomenon to study.

This historical dimension of myth contrasts with the critique of mythology that Hermann Cohen launches in the name of Jewish ethical monotheism. Cohen takes the Jewish idea of a messianic redemption at the end of time, an idea that Kirk would understand as an eschatological myth as an example of an extreme rejection of mythology. Myth, Cohen avers, posits an eternal return to origins. Instead of history, Cohen suggests, myth focuses on continual return, on regeneration. The world recreates itself again and again in myth; humanity need add nothing to the processes that eternally ensure the enduring patterns of nature. The idea of the Messiah, he argues, rejects such complaisant thinking. The Messiah represents human suffering and human activism. The messianic time will occur through continual progress, growth, and change, not through a process of eternal rebirth. Under myth, Cohen concludes, human actions have no real consequence; there is no judge or judgment for how people live. In ethical monotheism, on the other hand, judgment and divine justice are of the highest concern. True being does not come on its own, it must be earned by human struggle and striving. Judaism, Cohen thinks, rejects myth because myth undermines the moral seriousness of human action. [21]

A myth, however, may appear to be describing eternal patterns but actually revealing the philosophy of history governing its author. Jonathan Z. Smith, for example, looks to the function of myth rather than its content to uncover its view of history. He discovers in the myths of a group evidence of its past and its theory of history. He rejects the idea that myth tells a story of continual repetitions and history a tale of unique events. Instead, he declares, that he likes "to reflect on the historicity of myth ... the historical context of myth and the question of the utility of concern" for the historical. His question is not whether authors think they are writing history or not. Historians do not often realize the mythic aspects of what they write, and myth makers do not often recognize the history within their myths. In both cases the "function" of historical or mythic writing is more a matter of the reader's perception than of the author's intent.[22] A study of Jewish myths about history, whether focused on eschatology or on the meaning of present experience illustrates the goals and values of the authors of those myths. While Cohen may be right in his contrast between "myth" as eternal return and "Jewish monotheism," examination of stories that seem to address this issue will illuminate the variety of "histories" that Jews have imagined. Historical myth, although a self-contradiction for Cohen, represents an authentic type of Jewish expression validating experiences in the present in the light of past and future.

With these tools in hand, students can begin looking for the variety of Judaisms, the diverse ways in which Jews imagine the cosmos, human nature, and history. Students are prepared to find one group of Jews opposing another in the views of the world. They are ready to understand how history and context shape the stories that people tell. The next section looks at one set of stories, those about the martyrdom of Rabbi Aqiva ben Yosef, as a test case. This case of interrelated tales shows how cosmological, anthropological, and historical myths can utilize the same basic narrative to create different versions of Jewish religion.

The Myth of Rabbi Aqiva

In the introduction to his 1936 study of Rabbi Aqiva, Louis Finkelstein claims that this rabbi shares with Moses the prophet and Moses Maimonides the philosopher a dominant place in eighteen centuries of Jewish life.[23] Far from denying myth, the story of Aqiva shows, the rabbis themselves established the myth of a hero who could replace Moses. The rabbis delighted in similarities between Moses and Aqiva and pointed to the same chronology—both lived as outsiders for forty years, both trained to be leaders for forty years, and both served in positions of authority for forty years. The story begins with Aqiva as an outsider, as alienated from his people as Moses was from his. Finkelstein remarks that "Aqiva hated those to whom he should rightly have belonged..."[24] He stood outside of traditional scholarship, an "*am haaretz*," of proverbial ignorance and boorishness. He rose from this position to become a leader of his people who demonstrated a novel way of serving God. His alienation from the scholar class turned into imitation through the catalyst of love, through a romantic attachment. Strangely enough, however, the theme of alienation continues even through this emphasis on love. Aqiva, in order to become a scholar, must be estranged from his wife, first for seven years and then for another set of seven years. As with Moses, one alienation leads to another. Only when Aqiva returns to his wife as a great scholar does he overcome this gap of alienation and draw her to him, informing his disciples that all he has become and all that they have derived from him comes ultimately from her.

The tradition does not focus on this theme of alienation and return but it does compare Aqiva to Moses as creative thinkers who reshape Jewish religion. Each hero offers the sharp critique of external evaluation, of distance, together with a sense of belonging, of self-association. For Jews to whom leadership means scholarship, however, the image of Aqiva, turning from a life of ignorance to one of knowledge, holds greater power and significance than that of Moses. The myth of alienation as the basis for return to tradition takes on power for a nation of students when that alienation applies to the one sphere in which they feel most at home. The image of Aqiva replaced that of Moses precisely because the alienated Jews of the rabbinic period found in him a more accurate revelation of how the divine interacted in their own situations.

Aqiva's contribution as a Jewish teacher, as a hero of scholarship, came from his innovative approach to understanding the Torah. While his decision to become a scholar represents a turning point in his life, his conversion may be identified with his choice of Nahum Ish Gamzu rather than Eliezer ben Hyrcanus as his mentor. The difference between these teachers lies in their flexibility and responsiveness to human needs. Eliezer, a staunch traditionalist, insisted on the rigorous acceptance of past authority. Nahum, whose influence on Aqiva, according to Finkelstein, extended basically to the teaching of a method by which to interpret the Torah, represented the "poverty and ... cheerful resignation in the face of the most dreadful personal disasters." [25] Learning this new method, however, changed Aqiva. He became "completely transformed

... his interests now transcended his provincial origin."[26] At the same time, however, he heard the echo of his older affiliation, his roots with the common Jew. Heeding that echo, he created a responsive view of Torah that "could have no other aim than the increased prosperity of Jerusalem, and especially of its workers and artisans."[27] In this way he remained true to his origins. Unlike the elite, such as Eliezer ben Hyrcanus, Aqiva recalled the common person, the ignorant and the abandoned. His concern for these forgotten ones led him to develop a means of exegesis that challenged even Mosaic creativity.

The most audacious comparison of Aqiva to Moses comes when the rabbis claim that even Moses could not comprehend everything that Aqiva would teach. According to the story, Moses complained to God concerning the small "crowns" (the "tittles") adorning the Hebrew letters of the Bible. God replied that a later scholar, Aqiva, would interpret them and derive mountains of law from them. Moses asked to visit this sage, and God obliged. Moses, however, could understand nothing of Aqiva's discourse, being comforted only when a disciple assured him that this was "the Law of Moses." This variation on the theme of "his father's voice" deserves comment. Aqiva contributes to his people because in the midst of his distance from his roots he still hears the echoes of those who do not understand the mysteries of Torah. Finkelstein notes that "Aqiva drew on every source of experience. Sometimes he would even fall back upon his knowledge of animal anatomy..." His compassion for the poor, for women, for the beleaguered middle classes, suggests that his leadership stemmed from an ability to listen to voices from the past, to background echoes.[28]

Whereas Moses became a leader when he discovered the voices of his past in his place of exile, Aqiva's leadership lay in his ability to hear the voices of the forsaken exile even when he becomes part of the Jewish elite. Once again the difference in setting plays an important role in the choice of mythic heroes. A people devoted to Torah may become lost, not through the temptation of external persuasions, but through an insensitivity to those within their own midst. Moses left his relatives behind because he had assimilated into an alien culture. Aqiva's temptation lay in the possibility of forgetting his humble origins. For rabbis prone to self-indulgent piety, the father's voice heard in a distant land has less relevance as a mythic symbol than the ancestral voices of the average Jew echoing through esoteric scholarly debates. Such a lesson, that God's hand directs scholars to remember their roots, provided balance in rabbinic leadership.

Moses' covenantal ceremony suggests the public witness with which Jews integrate private and communal loyalties. For Jews, of the rabbinic and medieval period, however, the constraints of living in a world constructed by foreign religions—Islam and Christianity—made such public ceremony natural and unexceptional. The final integration of selfhood often entails a mixture of pain and joy. That realization of the need for suffering, created the impetus to expand the myth of Jewish heroes. The mythic story of the Sinai experience remains the central narrative in Judaism, but the mythic significance of that story was often conveyed by tales of suffering and martyrdom.

A legend concerning Aqiva's death suggests that such covenantal suffering represents a transition from this world into the world to come. Aqiva's transformation from origins as an outsider into an ambivalent insider reaches its conclusion as an angel welcomes him into the life of the world to come.[29] The story tells that during or after the Bar Kochba rebellion, government officials—the Romans—forbid the study of Torah. Aqiva ignores the prohibition and, against the advice of friends, continues his teaching. A Jew, Pappus, a Roman sympathizer, argues unsuccessfully against this strategy. Predictably, Aqiva is seized and imprisoned; while in jail he meets Pappus whose crime was some trivial offense. "Happy are you, Aqiva," he exclaims, "that you were arrested for studying Torah. Woe is me, for I was arrested for foolishness." This testimony from an erstwhile opponent demonstrates that Aqiva has become a model not only for dedicated scholars but even for those who have chosen to ignore that world and its rewards. He has integrated the elite tradition of Torah learning with a sensitivity to human needs, and by so doing, he has become a hero who presents a type of religiousness that even non-scholars can appreciate and respect.

Aqiva's mythic image attains its final shape in his courageous self-sacrifice. The drama of Aqiva's last days begun in his dramatic defiance of the Romans continues through his imprisonment, the torture he endured, and his manner of death. When finally brought out to die, the hour is that set aside for the "reciting of the *shema*"—the prayer proclaiming God's unity and the Jew's duties toward God that extend even to the giving up of one's life. His disciples are amazed that Aqiva seems happy at his fate. They question his calm serenity. In reply he announces his joy at being finally able to fulfill this commandment which he had recited every day. He dies reciting that prayer declaring that God is One. A *Bat Kol*, or heavenly voice, sounds forth commenting, "Happy are you Aqiva that your soul departed on the word One." Aqiva has been

initiated into the life of the world to come, he has recognized the purpose for which he had been created and the supernal beings recognize
him as a human being whose task has been accomplished.

In this story Aqiva appears as a model for all Jews during a time of
trouble. His affirmation of Jewish rituals and of the study of Torah reminds them that Judaism stands for more than convenience, it points the
way to self-transcendence. Throughout the middle ages the example of
Aqiva, recounted during such solemn days as the Day of Atonement,
suggested to Jews the ideal goal of religious life. Alienation had led to
creativity that in turn resulted in a new model of Jewish religious loyalty, that of the individual whose readiness to forfeit this life wins entrance into purity and the life to come. Three distinctive myths combine
in the Aqiva narrative: a cosmic myth which justifies the divine ways of
interacting with the world, an anthropological myth concerning insiders
and outsiders, and a political myth that legitimates rabbinic leadership
in the world. While apparently reconciled into a single narrative, these
themes actually work at cross currents to each other. No where is that
more evident than in the stories of Aqiva's death. Enabling students to
see how the Aqiva myth of a new Moses generates a variety of mythic
responses to the world helps them realize the variety of the Judaisms
they study.

The Variant Traditions Concerning Aqiva's Death
Students of the rabbinic literature have long realized that the stories
about the death of Rabbi Aqiva give evidence of a long evolution. Ephraim
Urbach examines those stories in the context of suffering and death in the
rabbinic tradition. He concludes that originally the tale did not include a
theodicy which questioned divine judgment and then resolved that question. Herbert Basser goes beyond this to suggest that the Aqivan story
raised the problems of theodicy that later tales like that of the martyrdom
of Hanina ben Tradyon, introduce the idea of theodicy, of suffering as
earning a reward in the world to come, and showing "how the Rabbis
used history, Scriptures, and stories in the service of theology and faith
in the most difficult times." [30] Other scholars have compared different
versions of the death of Aqiva to show the dynamics at work in rabbinic
writings. Daniel Boyarin, for example, traces the mythic linkage of Eros
and Thanatos in the Aqivan tales. He suggests that the narratives of
martyrdom in rabbinic literature combine to offer an alternative to the
glorification of death found in the Hasmonean stories of the Maccabees.

There, he suggests, martyrdom is proof of loyalty to national values. With the Aqiva tales it becomes "the only possible fulfillment of a spiritual need."[31]

Michael Fishbane takes a different approach. He suggests that the variant traditions arise because a new mythology was taking shape. At the time of Aqiva, he claims, the idea of martyrdom was undergoing a dramatic change. It shifted "away from the more general idea of given honor to God and Judaism (its norms and *mitzvot*) and toward the exclusive commitment of martyrdom." The Akivan material illustrates this shift. Looking at the variants, Fishbane considers the talmudic version in *Ber.* 61b less plausible than other versions, and thus probably later than them. He characterizes this talmudic variant as "a stylized martyrology to inspire inspiration." As he reads the stories, then, they move from seeing martyrdom as a symbol of loyalty to Jewish tradition to martyrdom as a spiritual act to martyrdom as the spiritual act of affirmation of the rabbinic values of scholarship and piety. [32]

Aqiva's Death in the Babylonian Talmud

An approach to the texts seeking their mythic meaning rather than a historically prior original version reads them slightly differently. The context of the story in *Berachot* stretches over several narratives. These include tales of how Rabbi Aqiva would contend that a person should always affirm that "Whatever the Holy One Blessed be He does is done for the best," of the struggle within every soul between the good and evil inclination, of the ambivalence of humanity made in the image of God. The story of Aqiva's martyrdom begins by narrating how the government proscribed Torah study and how Aqiva refused to abide by that injunction. It includes Aqiva's confrontation with Pappus who first advises Aqiva to stop studying Torah and then, when arrested himself on a trivial charge, admits that Aqiva was wiser to be imprisoned on an important charge rather than on an insubstantial one.

That tale leads directly into the story of Aqiva's death. It tells how when Aqiva was to be executed it was the hour for the recital of the *shema* and that he was "accepting upon himself the kingship of heaven" just as the torturers combed his flesh with iron combs. At that point his disciples asked him "Even unto this point?" and he explained that all his life he had wanted to fulfill the injunction of the *shema* to love God with all his heart, life, and substance. He had achieved the first and third, now he was able to fulfill the second. At that point he died and a heavenly voice proclaimed his reward: Happy are you Aqiva since your soul has departed on the declaration of unity. Yet, despite this happiness, the angels, in the story, raise the question of theodicy. Citing several verses from the Bible they ask whether such Torah as Aqiva possessed should be rewarded by such a death. God replies that the reward is immortal life, and the heavenly voice reiterates its praise of Aqiva, this time for having inherited immortal life.

Three elements are clear in this story, each of them connected with the importance of the study of Torah. The first focuses on the importance of ritual observance. Aqiva's students wonder whether the requirement of fulfilling the law extends to those facing imminent death. They query him as to the limits of the legal injunctions to say the *shema*. This inquiry reflects a debate attributed to the houses of Hillel and Shammai. The school of Hillel argued that the recitation of that prayer requires no extra effort—such as rising to say it in the morning or reclining to recite it at night. The opposing view demanded that the prayer be accompanied by appropriate actions. The discussion following that argument includes a notation of times when one is not required to recite the prayer (*Ber.* 10b-11a). This consideration is expanded by other scholars (*Ber.* 16a-b). The disciples here wonder whether martyrdom constitutes one of those occasions on which it is permissible to omit the saying of the *shema*. Aqiva responds that the prayer itself suggests the limits of loyalty required all one's possessions, all one's mind and all one's life. This part of the story acts as a political myth, justifying the authority of rabbinic instructions, even if those instructions lead to dangerous situations. Aqiva's answer to his disciples is that the religious act of self-sacrifice is already included as a part of the *shema* and therefore does not obviate the need to recite it. The prayer is the rabbinic justification of giving up oneself for the sake of loyalty to the tradition.

This theme continues into the justification of martyrdom as a means of attaining eternal life. The angels declare that Aqiva is "happy" (fortunate) because he has died with the word "One" on his lips. This suggests that the purpose of human life consists in opportunities to fulfill the commandments of the Torah. The earlier sections in the talmudic discussion of Aqiva reinforce this impression. Aqiva is lucky to have suffered for the sake of Torah rather than for the sake of some trivial matter. Suffering, then, is inevitable, but the reason for the suffering makes the difference between a lucky or unlucky human life. This legitimation of a life of Torah, however, seems to have been understood as somewhat unpersuasive. The text could have ended with the declaration of the angels concerning Aqiva's good fortune. The fact that the story goes on with the angelic complaint to God followed by a second declaration of Aqiva's happiness suggests that the original ending was perceived as insufficient. In the second ending the reward of martyrdom is eternal life. Loyalty not only fulfills the purpose of being human, but it leads to the final perfection of the human being in the world to come. Torah may not lead to happiness in this material world, but, the story suggests, such happiness is not the true goal of human existence. To be human, rather, means to aim for something that transcends this life, and that aim finds its realization in a life of Torah.

The conversation between God and the angels is the one place in which the question of theodicy occurs. The angels raise the issue of reward and punishment, of divine justice. They ask whether the Torah that Aqiva knows deserves such a painful consequence. The obvious answer is that Aqiva's death is really a blessing in disguise, it is his ticket into eternal life. Yet this answer itself leads to another question. Why should God make this final blessing contingent on such painful suffering? The story never raises this question. Instead, it assumes a basic calculus in the universe—great rewards must be attained through great suffering. The cosmic vision is of a universe in which the good find their recompense in a better world than this sublunar world of pain and suffering. Why this should be so is not made clear, but is insisted upon as the basis of social and moral life. At the heart of this myth, then, is the study of Torah as the basis of human perfection and an affirmation of a utilitarian cosmology. The myth of Aqiva, as developed in *Berachot* is a myth of Torah as politics, anthropology and cosmology. This way of reading the story, however, is not the only interpretation of cosmos, anthropology, or politics that can emerge from it. Looking at the alternative readings shows the variety of myths found in rabbinic tradition.

Aqiva's Death in the Jerusalem Talmud

The death of Aqiva can serve a very different set of mythic concerns as is evident from the rendition given in the Jerusalem Talmud. That version suggests the variety of Jewish myths possible from a single story. Michael Fishbane recognizes the mythic elements in the report of Aqiva's death in the Babylonian Talmud and considers the report given in the Jerusalem Talmud (*Ber.* 9:14b) to be a more "plausible sequence of events and motivations.[33] Other scholars also turn to the alternative account because of its special elements.[34] Even traditional accounts of the events in later Jewish literature, like the *Midrash Proverbs* incorporate parts of this tale because they are so striking. According to this rendition, Aqiva was brought before the wicked Tinnius Rufus and scourged in public. When the time came for the recitation of the *shema,* Aqiva began reciting and laughed. At that point Rufus inquires whether he is a magician or impervious to pain. Aqiva then points to himself and says "this person is granted a special pleasure," and explains that whenever he had previously read the verse requiring self-sacrifice for the sake of God, he had been saddened at the thought that he could not fulfil it. Now that the time for self-sacrifice and the time for reciting that verse coincided, he no longer felt the disturbance he had before. No sooner had he finished making this statement, the text declares, than Aqiva gave up his soul in death.

The mythic elements here are more subtle than in the Babylonian Talmud. The cosmology here does not require the theodicy elaborated in the previous text. For this story, the world is made for the maximization of pleasure and minimization of pain. The theory of reality behind the tale is a this-worldly rather than other-worldly utilitarianism. Neither Rufus nor Aqiva disagree with the principle that it is good to experience pleasure and bad to experience pain. They differ, however, in their evaluation of what constitutes the greatest pain. For Rufus, physical pain is the most severe. He thinks only someone superhuman can withstand it. Agave, however, explains that psychological pain is far more devastating. The joy of no longer undergoing that psychological disruption which he had previously felt over the recitation of the *shema* outweighs the physical suffering he undergoes. From this perspective, the purpose and meaning of life lies in avoiding the worst possible pain which is psychological rather than merely bodily.

That view of the world colors the view of humanity entailed here as well. Rufus and the Romans understand what it means to be human no less than does Aqiva. Unlike the Babylonian Talmud, this anthropology does not distinguish between insiders and outsiders. The Romans and the Jews share a common human condition. They both live life in similar ways. Torah practices do not alter human nature in this story the way they seem to in the Babylonian Talmud. The Romans can appreciate the psychological message that Aqiva gives to them. The mythic message here testifies to a natural affinity that binds all people to one another.

That anthropological statement resonates with a political myth as well. Aqiva treats his tormentors as students; he gives them a courteous and honest response. He neither upbraids them for their actions against him nor condemns them for persecuting the people of God. Aqiva appears in this story not as a revolutionary activist who has provoked the Romans into killing him but as a civil member of society who regards the rulers of the community with respect. This portrait of Aqiva fits with stories found about him in the Babylonian Talmud as well. The Babylonian Talmud in *Baba Batra* 10a describes an intellectual debate between Aqiva and Rufus. Rufus asks Akiva why God allows poverty to exist if God loves the poor. Aqiva answers that the poor provide the more well to do with an opportunity to please God by helping them. Rufus suggests that God should be angry if human beings help those whom God has seen fit to punish with poverty. Aqiva gives a clever response to this by suggesting that as a king will look the other way if someone cares for the king's son who has, presumably justly, been put in prison. So too God will honor those who help the poor, even if that poverty is divinely ordained. The content of this story, like that of the confrontation in the Jerusalem Talmud, assumes that both Aqiva and Rufus use the same logic, respond to life from the same human perspective. Beyond that, this story like the one of Aqiva's martyrdom shows the sage treating the ruling power with respect and honor. That message of obedience to government expresses a myth of political power as a divinely given ordinance, as a fact of life that must be respected rather than resisted.

The Jerusalem Talmud thus offers a more universalistic, humanistic, and quietistic view of Aqiva's death than does the Babylonian Talmud. It evokes a world of cooperation and human compassion, even while relating a tale of torture and suffering. Both Talmuds, however, have a general sense of logic and reason in their telling of their tales. While the cosmology of the Babylonian Talmud is that of divine fiat, the context in which that arises is placed within an angelic sphere, a supernatural realm where such answers might be expected.

Aqiva and Moses: Aqiva's Death in *Menachot* 29b

A third version of the death of Aqiva emphasizes the unusual and supernatural to an even greater extent than the tale of the Babylonian Talmud. In that version the cosmology, anthropology, and political meaning of the myth of Aqiva's death takes on extraordinary significance as an almost magical event. The context of this final description of Aqiva's death consists of what has been termed a "Charter myth" of rabbinic teaching. According to Rabbi Yehudah, Rav taught that when Moses ascended to heaven to receive the Torah he found God sitting and decorating the letters with crowns. Moses asks why God takes the time for such delaying flourishes, and God responds by sayings that a future scholar will be able to derive heaps of laws from these decorations. Moses asks to be shown this wondrous scholar and is transported to Aqiva's lectures where he cannot understand a word of what is being said. This disturbs Moses until a student asks Aqiva to give the source of the laws he's teaching. Aqiva responds "These come from the legal tradition given Moses at Sinai." That response calms Moses' spirit.

The political implication of this myth is fairly clear. The story reflects rabbinic recognition that much of their teaching seems unrelated to the biblical texts they claim to interpret. They contend through this story that even Moses at Sinai recognized this apparent problem. Their seemingly tangential derivations of law, however, are authorized by a power higher than Moses, that of the divinity. More than that, Moses acquiesces in affirming the appropriateness of tracing the legitimacy of those teachings back to Sinai. The myth answers the question of how the tradition of Torah interpretation used by the rabbis began through divine intention. It begins, as does all Torah, with Moses, even though Moses would not comprehend much of that interpretation. Self-identification with Mosaic authority, rather than actual correspondence to Mosaic intention, provides legitimacy for rabbinic exegesis.

While this political dimension of the myth is clear, the cosmological dimension, equally prominent in the talmudic passage, has often been overlooked. When analyzing the martyrdom of Aqiva, Michael Fishbane notes that while the passage in *Ber.* 61b has the angels raise the question of theodicy, in the *Menahot* passage, Moses does.[35] Yet that is not the first place in this passage where Moses questions divine wisdom. After returning from the study session with Aqiva, Moses asks in wonder, "Master of the world, you have a man such as this and you would send the Torah by means of me?" God replies here, as he does not to the angels in *Ber.* 61b, "Shut up! That's what I think is best." Here the arbitrariness of the divine finds explicit expression. God does not look at the talents and capabilities of human beings and judge them accordingly. The teaching of Torah is not either as a means of potentiating human abilities or an example of a generally human experience. The anthropology of *Ber.* 61b, which sees Torah as a gift that improves human nature or the anthropology of the Jerusalem Talmud which understands the effects of Torah on Jews as parallel to effects of other stimuli on other human beings give way before a different view entirely. In this version of the Aqiva story human life and destiny follows an entirely arbitrary pattern. Neither human nature nor acquired learning account for a person's experience. Instead, that experience reflects an incomprehensible divine whim which human beings cannot understand. Luck rather than human nature or divinely given instruction lies at the heart of a person's life story.

The same sense of arbitrary and incomprehensible divine power dominates the cosmology of this text as well. After Moses has been told to shut up about why God selected Aqiva in the first place, he then asks to see the reward that Aqiva receives. At that point, God displays the torturous martyrdom that Aqiva endures. Moses, not the angels as Fishbane points out, then responds by questioning divine wisdom and justice, asking "Is this the Torah and this its reward?" Again he receives the same answer "Shut up! This is what I think is best." That reply appears like an ironic comment on the earlier story in *Berachot* in which Aqiva claims that whatever God does is done for the best. Yes, of course, it is done for what God thinks is the best. What looks like the "best" to God, however, may be rather painful and unfortunate for the human being involved. Here is a rather skeptical cosmology. The meaning of the world cannot be reduced to a utilitarian calculus of reward and punishment. Just as the biblical book of Proverbs which advocates hard work as the means to achieving a successful life finds its antidote in the skepticism of the biblical book of Ecclesiastes, so the utilitarianism of *Berachot* finds a retort in the arbitrariness of God's view of what is "the best" in *Menahot* 29b. Human beings should not question the divine decisions about a world which they cannot understand. *Menahot* 29b, then, represents a third alternative to the politics, anthropology and cosmology of rabbinic Judaism. It offers a politics of interpretation rather than that of study or self-sacrifice, an anthropology of luck rather than of Torah as a special cure for human nature or as an example of a common human experience, and a cosmology of incomprehensibility rather than of either a supernaturalist or realistic utilitarianism.

The Omitted Alternative: Aqiva's Mysticism

One characteristic of the rabbinic and post-rabbinic view of Aqiva finds no echo in the rabbinic stories of his martyrdom, that of his mysticism. A famous tale tells of Aqiva's ascent into the heavenly spheres, into PaRDeS (Tosefta *Hagiga*, Chapter 1; Jerusalem Talmud *Hagiga* 2:77b, Babylonian Talmud *Hagiga* 14b-15b).[36] Of several rabbis associated with an attempted ascent, only Aqiva is said to have entered whole and left whole, that is he was the only one who achieved mystical experience without being left impaired. Later Jewish tradition emphasizes this aspect of Aqiva's personality so that he becomes the ideal Jewish mystic. Isaac Luria, for example, understands Aqiva's martyrdom in terms of mystical experience.[37] One of the most interesting mystical uses of the Aqiva tale is that of Luria's contemporary and rival Moses Cordovero.[38]

Cordovero, himself someone lacking in ancestral status, emphasizes that Aqiva is described as originally ignorant and from a family without prestige. He imagines the scene between God and Moses differently. When God says to Moses "This is what I think is best," Cordovero notes that it literally means "This is what arose before me in thought." He understands that mystically - this is how a soul can arise through meditation. The death of Aqiva is an example of the mystical reparation of souls, the elevation of an originally lowly and insignificant individual to heights of spiritual achievement. Cordovero makes two points about Aqiva. The first is that he suffers greatly because he has achieved greatness. Someone who has the scholarly status of Aqiva, Cordovero insists, must pay dearly for even the slightest of his sins. In a type of mystical noblesse oblige, Cordovero insists that because of the special rank of the mystic, no infraction, however insignificant, occasions inordinate suffering. Secondly, Cordovero claims that because Aqiva lacks ancestral merit he must earn his own place before God. His martyrdom provides him with the ticket that for others earlier, more illustrious forebearers supply. Aqiva creates his own heritage, just as Cordovero claims he has done for himself. These two contentions reveal the mythic pattern that a mystic might see in the story of Aqiva. First, the politics legitimate seeing hidden meaning within a text. Cordovero goes beyond any of the three explicit stories of Aqiva's death. He implicitly claims that only those exegetes who probe below the superficial story understand its message. This emphasis legitimates the mystical leader who, while not rejecting the legalist tradition, considers normative rabbinic teachings too obvious and mundane to have ultimate relevance. Secondly, Cordovero derives still another anthropology from the tale. Human beings make their own destiny and their own history through either their own actions or their inherited merit. This anthropology negates the view of Torah as the tool by which all people meet the everyday challenges of life. Torah is rather a means to extraordinary living, to a transcendent status beyond that of ordinary people. Cordovero's anthropology also goes beyond the universalism of the Jerusalem Talmud. Only elevated souls, those tutored by the Torah, can attain the condition that Akiva, and by extension Cordovero, have reached. Torah is meant for the elite among the Jews, a status that can be earned for oneself or inherited from the past. Finally,

Cordovero defends divine justice in a strange way. He does not deny that the "reward" Aqiva receives is rather extreme. He claims, however, that divine justice demands that those who are greater pay a greater price for their errors. Cordovero suggests that people can indeed know what the divine intends, what makes up divine justice. That justice, however, is not merely earning a place in the world to come or achieving psychological satisfaction. It is rather a justice that is tailored to each person's status. This sliding scale of justice goes beyond either naturalistic or supernaturalist utilitarianism and also rejects the ploy of saying that divine actions lie outside of human comprehension.

Conclusions

The story of Aqiva's martyrdom takes various shapes in Jewish writings. Students looking at the sources in rabbinic literature will note the three alternatives offered. This suggests that there is no single Jewish myth with a univocal political, anthropological, or cosmic message. More than that, students will discover the necessity to look for the myth that is absent, the myth that is implied but not utilized. The example ofCordovero's mystical myth of Aqiva highlights the possibilities untapped by rabbinic writings. Such a detailed study of different versions of a single event shows how attention to Jewish myth brings into focus the variety of Jewish theories about the world, humanity, and Jewish leadership. The more one looks at specific Jewish myths, the more the diversity of Judaisms, of Jewish religious expressions, becomes inescapable. ✡

Endnotes

1. See Arthur J. Arberry, *Tales From the Masnawi* (Richmond: Curzon Press, 1993), 208.
2. Joseph Dan, *On Sanctity: Religion, Ethics and Mysticism in Judaism and Other Religions* [Hebrew] (Jerusalem: Magnes Press 1997), 162-63.
3. Raphael Jospe, " Introduction," *Jewish Philosophy and the Academy*, Emil L. Fackenheim and Raphael Jospe, eds. (Madison, New Jersey: Fairleigh Dickinson University Press, 1996), 9.
4. Will Herberg, "Some Variant Meanings of the Word "Myth," in his *Faith Enacted As History: Essays in Biblical Theology*. Bernhard W. Anderson, ed. (Philadelphia: Westminster, 1976), 147.
5. Dan, *On Sanctity*, 'Myth and Research on Myth," 155-78.
6. *Ibid.*, 175.
7. Umberto Eco, *The Limits of Interpretation* (Bloomington: Indiana University Press, 1990), 2 1.

8.   Loyal D. Rue, *Amythia: Crisis in the Natural History of Western Culture.* With a Foreword by William G. Doty. (Tuscaloosa: University of Alabama Press, 1989), see especially 49-54.

9.   Emmanuel Levinas, *In the Time of the Nations,* trans. by Michael B. Smith (Bloomington, IN: University of Indiana Press, 1994), 168. See the entire discussion beginning on 157.

10. G. S. Kirk, M*yth: Its Meaning and Functions in Ancient and Other Cultures* (Berkeley: University of California Press, 1970), 252-61.

11. John L. McKenzie, "Myth and the Old Testament," in his *Myths and Realities: Studies in Biblical Theology* (London: Geoffrey Chapman, 1963). 182-200.

12. See Erich Fromm, *The Forgotten Language: An Introduction to the Understanding of Dreams., Fairy Tales and Myths* (New York: Grove, 1951.

13. *Ibid.,* 2,60.

14. Gilbert Morris Culbertson, *Political Myth and Epic* (East Lansing, MI: Michigan State University Press, 1975), 2-3.

15. See Christopher G. Flood, *Political Myth: A Theoretical Introduction* (New York: Garland, 1996).

16. See Yehezkel Kaufmann, *The Religion of Israel: From Its Beginnings to the Babylonian Exile,* Moshe Greenberg. tr. (Chicago: University of Chicago Press, 1960), 77, 244, 316 and the Hebrew original *Toldot HaEmuna HaYisraelit Mimei Kedem Ad Sof Bayit Sheini* (Bialik Institute/Devir: Tel Aviv, 1937), Volume 1.

17. See S. Daniel Breslauer, *Martin Buber on Myth: An Introduction* (New York: Garland Press, 1990).

18.   See Rene Girard, *Things Hidden Since the Foundation of the World* (Stanford: Stanford University Press, 1987) and his *The Scapegoat,* trans. by Yvonne Frecerro. (Baltimore: The Johns Hopkins University Press, 1986) as well as Richard J. Golsan, *Rene Girard and Myth: An Introduction* (New York: Garland, 1993).

19. Girard, *The Scapegoat,* 33, 37, 41.

20. See Galit Hasan-Rokem, "Myth," in *Contemporary Jewish Religious Thought: Original Essays on Critical Concepts, Movements, and Belief,* Arthur Allen Cohen and Paul Mendes Flohr, eds. (New York: Scribner, 1987), 661, and the entire essay 657-61.

21. See the discussion in Hermann Cohen, *The Religion of Reason: Out of the Sources of Judaism.* trans. by Simon Kaplan, (New York: Frederick Unger, 1971), 244-91.

22. See Jonathan Z. Smith, "The Unknown God: Myth in History," in his *Imagining Religion: From Babylon to Jonestown.* Chicago Studies in the History of Judaism, Jacob Neusner, William Scott Green, and Calvin Goldscheider, eds. (Chicago: University of Chicago Press, 1982). 66-89.

23. Louis Finkelstein in his *Akiba: Scholar, Saint and Martyr* (New York:

Athenaeum, 1978), 1; note the comparisons between Moses and Aqiva throughout the book as well as the sympathetic treatment of the myth of Aqiva.

24. *Ibid.,* 22.
25. *Ibid.,* 76,88-89.
26. *Ibid.,* 94.
27. *Ibid.*
28. *Ibid.,* 155-59.
29. *Ibid.,* 235-77.
30. See Ephraim E. Urbach, "Acesis and Suffering in The System of the Sages," [Hebrew] in Salo Baron, ed., *Yitzhak F. Baer Jubilee Volume on the Occasion of His Seventieth Birthday* (Jerusalem: The Israeli Historical Society, 1960), 48-68 and Herbert Basser, *In the Margins of the Midrash: Sifre Ha'azinu: Texts, Commentaries and Reflections,* (Atlanta: Scholars Press, 1990),52.
31. Daniel Boyarin, *Intertextuality and the Reading of Midrash* (Bloomington: Indiana University Press, 1990), 126; see the entire discussion "Between Intertextuality and History: The Martyrdom of Rabbi Akiva," 117-129.
32. Michael Fishbane, *The Kiss of God: Spiritual and Mystical Death in Judaism.* The Samuel and Althea Stroum Lectures in Jewish Studies. (Seattle: University of Washington Press, 1994), 70-71.
33. *Ibid.,* 68.
34. See Boyarin, *Intertextuality,* 126.
35. Fishbane, *Kiss of God,* 82.
36. *Ibid.,* 34-36.
37. *Ibid.,* 114-16.
38. See Bracha Sack, *The Kabbalah of Rabbi Moshe Cordevero* [Hebrew] (Ben Gurion University of the Negev Press, 1995), 238-39.

Chapter 3

Choosing Among the Strands:
Teaching Hebrew Bible Survey to
Undergraduates at a Secular University
Bruce Zuckerman

Each time I start my one semester survey course on the Hebrew Bible—
or, as it is frequently entitled, "Old Testament"[1] I focus the class' attention on the word "Bible"[2] and its derivation from the Greek. After all,
this is an obvious point of departure. If one is going to study "the Bible,"
or at least a major part of it, one should know whence the term comes:
namely from *ta biblia,* neuter plural of *to biblion,* "book": Hence, "the
books" or, more properly, "the Books" *par excellence.*[3] Indeed, the other
common designation of the Bible as "the Holy Scriptures" is most appropriate, since "Scriptures" (note the plural) is a good rendering of the
sense of *biblia* while "Holy" captures the nuance of specialness which
makes these writings venerated above all others in the Western world.

But I also begin my survey course with the derivation of "Bible" for
another reason: because the term *biblia* can serve as an effective metaphor that catches the sense of biblical study as I think it should be conveyed to an undergraduate class. For *biblion* also means a strip or strand
of *biblos*—the inner bark of the papyrus plant from which the first paper
was made.[4] Thus, the plural biblia can also be taken as the aggregate of
many such strips laid (as was the practice) warp and woof to form an
ancient papyrus scroll. Seen in this light, *ta biblia* is revealed to be a
very complex grouping of strands no two of which are precisely the same
in a labyrinthian web as individual and multifarious as the whorls of a
human fingerprint.

Utilization of this metaphor allows one to draw an appropriate analogy: for the Bible is very much like the papyrus scroll on which it often
must have been written in ancient times. It too is a maze of strands of
many types and kinds; so many that we can hardly hope to identify, let
alone keep track of all of them. The central problem that faces any teacher
of Hebrew Bible, especially one who must teach a course that purports to
"cover" the Tanak in a one semester time span (approximately 15 weeks
or so of lecture and discussion) is how to handle such a welter of material
in a responsible fashion, how to choose among the strands of ancient ma-

terials and modern interpretations in order to convey to one's students a
sense of the fabric that makes up this complicated weave.

There is, of course, no definitive answer or set of answers to this
question. Teaching, much like acting, is an individual art; each teacher
will and should approach so commanding a subject as the Bible in his or
her own particular way. I certainly have no intention of issuing to my
fellow "Bible" teachers anything resembling detailed pedagogical pro-
nouncements. Instead, I will only offer my particular midrash on the
subject with the proviso that there is always "another interpretation"
equally valid, perhaps more so. In light of this, the following discussion
of teaching Tanak will be limited to a consideration of selected broader
issues of method and approach, and how I perceive them.

At the outset of this discussion, we should perhaps define our terms:
among the essential considerations for teaching any course are an awareness of what one's target audience needs to learn, the environment in which
the learning experience is taking place and, not least of all, the precise
nature of that audience. Our working assumptions will be first, that the
target group needs to learn what is concomitant with the goals of a liberal
arts education; second, that the educational environment is secular; and
finally, that the audience is undergraduate. In teaching Hebrew Bible, one
must be self-consciously sensitive to the implications that go with each of
these classifications; for they inevitably shape the manner in which one
constructs the course of study.

As regards the "liberal arts" classification, a teacher must recognize
that there are certain responsibilities that go with teaching the Tanak as
part of a liberal arts education. Of course, there was a time when a liberal arts education and knowledge of the Bible were considered essentially synonymous. That is, it was assumed that knowledge of the Bible
was, along with knowledge of the classics, the essential foundation of
the humanities. While this is hardly true today, a teacher of Hebrew
Bible must nonetheless recognize that his or her role has not really
changed that much. Granted, the teacher of Tanak can no longer claim
that one must learn the Scriptures because they are the source of all
essential truth in the universe (a claim that might have been made from
a university podium in earlier times and which remains viable in non-
secular contexts). Still, he or she can maintain that knowledge of the
Bible is basic; for, whether one believes its worldview or not, that
worldview has largely molded the context of modern Western civilization. Moreover, students enroll in a course in Hebrew Bible courses today for essentially the same reason they did so in the past. As a rule,

there are few undergraduates who seek out an a Bible survey course because they are majoring in Religion or even because they are interested in the Bible per se. Rather, the vast majority of one's students (whether they have thought this out or not) have elected to take Hebrew Bible survey because they wish to grasp some sense of why Western civilization has developed in the manner that it has. Consciously or unconsciously, they have recognized that it is impossible to do this without taking into account the informing influence of the Bible. Thus, the appeal of a course on the Tanak to undergraduates is very much in line with the old liberal arts assumption: that one simply cannot be considered properly educated without a decent comprehension of the Bible.

Because the study of the Bible therefore remains one of the traditional bastions of a liberal arts education (at least for those who have sought out a course thereon), the teacher of the Hebrew Bible has the responsibility to cover all the essentials of the material. That is, he or she should begin in Genesis (or wherever else one wishes to begin) at the outset of the course, end in Daniel (or wherever else one wishes to end) some 15 weeks later and move through the main body of the biblical writings during the intervening weeks.

The need to move comprehensively through the material in any survey course may seem so self-evident as to not require mention. Certainly, a vast majority of Hebrew Bible teachers would ascribe to this viewpoint in principle. However, as is also often the case in survey courses, the practice does not necessarily hold to this ideal. There is a strong temptation for a university teacher to follow his or her scholarly instinct to dwell extensively upon the details of the subject matter. But this instinct, however motivated by one's honest desire to give a full presentation of the issues at hand, ultimately can result in too little material being covered too well. In the particular case of biblical study, the result can be a full-blown picture of Genesis and/or Exodus at the beginning of a course, while the Wisdom literature or the post-exilic writings get short shrift (or perhaps no meaningful discussion at all) at its end.

In other survey courses in the humanities, the truncation of the coverage, while not to be condoned, can perhaps at least be tolerated. However, this is not so in a Hebrew Bible survey course. Because the material in all its major forms and types is such a formative influence on Western civilization, it should be broadly covered and not under-represented in any of its major aspects. To give less than a full presentation of the Tanak can only serve to undermine its importance as a basic point of reference in a liberal arts education.

On the other hand, one cannot hope to cover the Hebrew Bible in any significant depth during a fifteen week period. A rigorous selectivity is absolutely essential. Indeed, I strongly feel that a teacher of biblical studies must be more-or-less ruthless in cutting down the breadth of the material in recognition of the serious time constraints imposed by a survey course. I do not even try to touch upon every biblical book during the course of study. Rather, I try to rely on a textbook to expose one's students to supplemental texts which have not been specifically focused upon in class. Overall, one must be willing to sacrifice material that is highly important in order to give full coverage to the absolutely essential.

One might well claim that the cases I have just made above, first in favor of comprehensiveness and subsequently in favor of rigorous selectivity, are contradictory. However, while the demands of these competing interests manifest an inevitable tension, they should not be seen as necessarily at odds. An educator must try to strike an appropriate balance between them: He or she should aim to give students a full sense of the variety of biblical material while at the same time allowing them the opportunity for selective concentration, even on occasion, detailed text analysis of the salient features of Tanak.

There is yet another important aspect of teaching Hebrew Bible survey as part of a liberal arts education that a teacher should carefully consider: exactly *what* should be the dominant emphasis in the course? To put this another way, ten years after a student has taken one's survey of the Tanak, what (if nothing else) should the teacher want his or her students to remember?

To judge from the titles and course descriptions for survey courses on the Hebrew Bible commonly found in college bulletins, this question has often been answered in a manner that I, at least, feel is incorrect. Thus, for example, when I first began teaching the course on the Tanak in a university context, I inherited a course entitled "Old Testament Literature and History." Such a title is typical and, in this respect, highlights what I think is the problem. For I strongly believe that, although a teacher should neither ignore the literate nor the historical aspects of the Bible, he or she should also not allow either one to be the dominant emphasis in a Hebrew Bible survey course.

These days, the "Bible as literature" type course has had a particular prominence on the college campus, stimulated no doubt by the recent influx of literary critical studies of biblical texts in the scholarly literature. Yet even the designation, "Bible as literature," has about it a sense of "special pleading" that should alert one to consider the implications of teaching the Tanak from this standpoint. One never hears of other courses taught in an analogous manner. For example, one can look in vain for college course offerings on "physics as mathematics" or "social science as statistics." Obviously, this does not mean that mathematics is less than essential for the study of physics or that statistics are unimportant for explaining social phenomena. Nor would I wish to argue that the Bible is not "literate" and that literary analysis of the Hebrew Bible is a fruit-less endeavor. Far from it. But to isolate this particular "literary" side of biblical study largely to the exclusion of other aspects is both misguided and wrongheaded. To put it more bluntly, to see the biblical texts solely as literary documents to be interpreted as one would a novel or a sonnet, completely misrepresents the Bible in a survey class.

At best, an approach of this sort is simplistic. The Bible is not "litera-ture" or, at least, not literature in the sense we usually understand that term. Generally speaking, modern literary criticism looks at a given piece of writing as "the work of an individual who determines its final form and publishes it under copyright at a particular date."[5] More to the point, the "literary" approach to the Bible assumes one can take a given bibli-cal text in a manner consistent with this view of literature. Thus, a bib-lical text is seen as a unified work presented from a consistent perspec-tive-as though written by the hand of a single author. As Simon Parker has noted:

> The new literary criticism of the Bible treats the texts as ahistorical, as
> removed from all aspects of historical existence except as the object of
> the present critic's reading. They are simply literary objects in our world,
> not avenues to or messages from an ancient world.[6]

I would argue that such a literary-critical approach to the Bible is seriously in error under any circumstances. However, whether or not this modern literary approach to the Bible can be defended as a valid scholarly endeavor, I believe it is quite impossible to countenance as the dominant viewpoint in a Hebrew Bible survey class. Certainly, one may be tempted to approach the biblical writings as though they were ahistorical. One can then "short-circuit" all of the technical problems involved with analyzing an ancient collection of texts with long text traditions (both at the oral and written stages of composition) which emerged from a culture quite distinct and remote from our own. But that is just the point. Simply by pretending that these problems are irrelevant to a "literary" understanding of the Tanak does not make them go away. The biblical texts are historical documents-very complex historical docu-ments, indeed. Their concomitant historical-critical problems are always present and do affect interpretation in decisive ways on virtually every page. More often than not, these issues rise as awesome barriers that impair interpretation, making all approaches to Hebrew Bible to some extent uncertain.

A teacher of Tanak must be sure that his or her students are not directed to find the sort of "easy" interpretations that might be sanctioned by the literary-critical approach. The problems inherent in gaining confident insight into the Bible should be continually highlighted: especially the most basic issues of text and language. In my own Hebrew Bible course I spend the first two sessions solely on these issues. At the outset, I want to make sure that my students understand that what constitutes the biblical canon is and has always been under dispute, that the texts of the Bible (rather than "The Text") are impossible to establish firmly based upon the evidence of the ancient manuscripts, and that the biblical languages are inherently ambiguous due to their consonantal orthography as well as a grammar and vocabulary that are far from well understood. Only after these difficult historical problems have been brought to the forefront do I feel that my students are sufficiently sensitized to the limits of biblical interpretation and thus can proceed with appropriate caution.

The literary-critical approach, because it does not recognize the limits of what one can actually *know* about a biblical text and because it essentially throws caution to the winds, delivers the wrong message to one's class. In fact, there is a cultural chauvinism, if not arrogance, underlying the "Bible as literature" perspective—as if to say that this (and presumably all "literate" works) can be seen as though they were products of Western civilization and a Western mind-set. Fostering this approach in class can therefore only aid in skewing students' views of the roles of the Bible in Western civilization. It ignores what I think is a fundamental principle in teaching Tanak: that before one can properly speak of the formative influence of this book on the Western world, one must see it first in the context of the Ancient Near Eastern world and its culture.

Despite the obvious weaknesses in a teaching approach which confines study to the "literary" approach to the Bible, this type of course has remained (and probably will remain) popular in many college curricula. I think there are subtle but largely unstated reasons why this is so, and they bear looking at critically. In fact, there is quite often a hidden agenda involved in teaching the "Bible as literature." Not only is this type of course easier to teach because of its ability to sidestep the technical problems inherent in biblical interpretation, it is also the avenue of least resistance for a teacher who wishes to avoid confronting the religious sensibilities of his or her class. In particular, the "Bible as literature" course is very serviceable as a means of avoiding dealing seriously with students of a traditional or conservative background who take for granted a "fundamentalist" interpretation of Scripture.

This is true for essentially two reasons. First, the "literary" approach largely can be seen to fall closely in line with the basic fundamentalist assumption that biblical books are unified literary works, composed or rather inspired by a single author, namely, God. The literary-critical assumptions, as applied to the Bible, actually constitute a secularized fundamentalism which "true" fundamentalists can happily embrace. Thus they remain content; and, as a consequence, the teacher need not deal with the delicate and difficult issues that necessarily arise when the Bible and its historical/cultural background are both focused upon. Second, the "Bible as literature" course not only ignores the historical context of the Bible, but also completely avoids any consideration of the Bible as a religious document written for explicitly religious purposes. A typical stance of a teacher who presents the "Bible as literature" is that his or her "literary" analysis has "nothing to do" with religion, that issues inherent in a discussion of the Bible as religious record "are not relevant" to the course. With this credo stated at the outset, the teacher can remain insulated from the controversies that naturally occur when the Bible's religious perspective is fully explored. Once again, this would seem a secularized manner of teaching the Bible; but, on a more subtle level, it again offers an easy way to keep fundamentalists content (or at least at bay). For this approach really never considers the validity of the fundamentalist interpretive assumptions, or, for that matter, any others outside the literary-critical purview. Thus a "truce" can be effected between teacher and conservatively religious student. The teacher agrees to avoid seriously considering the fundamentalist interpretation because it is "not relevant," and the student agrees to pursue his viewpoint—but outside of the classroom. Since, as previously discussed, the mechanics of the literary approach are very much akin to the fundamentalist assumptions in any case, the educator can proceed to teach the Bible as a completely noncontroversial subject. He or she can pretend that the mode of presentation is completely academic and has nothing to do with religion—even though a desire to avoid religious controversy has played a major role in shaping the way the course is presented.

Such a hidden agenda comes very close to being a type of masquerade; for it purports to be one thing while in fact it is quite another. The "Bible as literature" course pretends to have nothing to do with religion while it is precisely the fear of religious controversy that makes this the avenue of choice in so many instances. In fact, there is very little that separates this teaching strategy from other approaches that stand in the shadow of religious sensibilities. One is reminded, for example, of the so-called "creationist" approach to teaching biology. The creationist teacher pretends to present a strictly scientific theory based solely on empirical evidence regarding the origin of life. But, as above, there is a hidden agenda to this pseudo-scientific theory of evolution. Creationism exists solely for the purpose of coordinating "science" with Genesis even though Genesis itself is not usually mentioned explicitly in creationist theory. While the literary approach to the Bible is not as blatant as creationism in the manner it accommodates to religious sensibilities, it nonetheless shares with it a kind of tunnel vision that borders on self-censorship. In this regard the "Bible as literature" approach runs entirely counter to a fundamental tenet of a liberal arts education: that the university is an open market place in which all aspects of a subject are to be pursued, tested and judged against the full range of evidence.

Another factor also plays a role in the fostering of the "Bible as literature" course on the college campus. Because the literary-critical assumptions give one license to shunt aside the technical aspects of biblical study, teachers without training in biblical languages or serious knowledge of Ancient Near Eastern culture feel free to teach "Old Testament," usually offering the course as part of the curriculum of an English or Literature department. The Bible, after all, is integrally tied up with literature in the Western world. It is therefore only natural for literature teachers to turn to this seminal influence—much as they would turn to Beowulf or other early antecedents of writing in the West.

I do not want to suggest that only someone with a Ph.D. in biblical studies and/or Ancient Near Eastern languages and cultures is qualified to teach Tanak. In fact, there can be no doubt that scholars with a critical background in the study of literature can offer insightful perspectives on the Hebrew Bible. But rarely do teachers, who received their professional training outside the field of Ancient Near Eastern studies, make the effort (or even feel the need) to master the technicalities of biblical studies or, lacking that, seek assistance from scholars in the field who can give them advice and guidance. Instead, they present the "Old Testament" as another book alongside other works on the Western literature bookshelf. We have already noted the inherent chauvinism that sanctions such an approach; but beyond this, there are, in my view, serious academic questions involved in the fostering of courses in a university environment taught by personnel who really are not expert in a given field. Of course, it would also be an error to draw the lines between fields too strictly—an overly rigorous academic territorialism can only inhibit academic freedom and stifle cross-pollination among scholarly disciplines. Nonetheless, in the specific case of the "Bible as literature" concept, there is not generally a serious recognition that a line *does* exist—that a teacher who presents such a course has a responsibility to set the Bible within its own environment. Once again, one can only question the appropriateness of such a course as part of a liberal arts education.

Finally, there is one other aspect of the "Bible as literature" course that helps to keep it popular and which merits consideration. The fact is, the inclusion of the "literature" designation in the course description helps significantly to "sell" the course in the undergraduate marketplace. For a number of reasons, students are attracted to a course that purports to present the literary aspects of biblical study. The more conservatively religious student, as already noted, will see in this designation a signal that his or her own belief system will not come under scrutiny or challenge. A non-religious student, on the other hand, will see in the "literature" label an indication that the class will be concentrating on "Bible stories" rather than more intimidating technical biblical material (like laws or genealogies) or the drier tenets of theology. A biblical literature course of this sort is thus generally seen as being both fun and safe; it usually also has a reputation of being easy—in any case, easier than a "regular" Bible course.

Teachers of the Hebrew Bible are fully aware of the salability of the "literature" label; they also are often under subtle pressure from their colleagues or university administrators to fill as many seats in their class as possible. Religion departments, after all, generally do not live by their majors; they are service departments that are expected to attract a broad clientele of elective students. There is thus a temptation to work the word "literature" into the title of a Hebrew Bible course because it will deliver a better body count. There is even the possibility that teachers will simply use the "literature" label without any serious intention of discussing the "Bible as literature" at all. The designation simply functions as attractive advertising, and much like advertising, tends to mislead.

One might argue that there is nothing wrong in offering students a course they can more easily relate to which will attract them to biblical study when a course perceived to be more intimidating will not. However, the "sugar-coating" of a course of study (or advertising to this effect) is not an appropriate goal for Hebrew Bible survey offering—nor should it be tacitly encouraged or condoned in a university setting. Granted, it is a teacher's job to impart knowledge in a manner that is sufficiently entertaining to be effective; still, the primary stress must be kept on education, not on entertainment or, for that matter, marketability.

This excursus on the problems of the "Bible as literature" approach to Hebrew Bible survey might seem to lead to an obvious conclusion: that the only appropriate way to teach the Tanak is as a record of history. This is, in fact, a common approach utilized by scholars who concentrate in Ancient Near Eastern and/or biblical studies. Yet the "Bible as history" approach also needs to be examined critically in terms of its appropriateness as an integral part of a liberal arts education.

The historical-critical approach to the Hebrew Bible basically seeks specific, factual information about the times and cultures in which the biblical texts evolved, the individuals and groups that were instrumental in their composition, and the parties and forces that shaped the manner in which the texts were edited and preserved. To put this more succinctly (although somewhat tautologically), the historian seeks truth in Hebrew Bible in what it reveals about the objective reality of Ancient Near Eastern history. Since the historian inevitably must look at biblical writings as far from objective in presentation, he or she therefore focuses upon extricating the history embedded within the Tanak. Naturally, at the same time, the historian also endeavors to classify what is historically unreliable and formulates criteria by which to distinguish fact from tradition.

Because the hard evidence required for historical analysis of Hebrew Bible is so limited, the historical-critical approach to the Tanak has developed a number of means by which to reclaim or, if need be, reconstruct the factual record. On the practical side, the historian has taken full advantage of the accumulating evidence about the Ancient Near East that archaeologists have uncovered. Also, the discovery and collation of ancient biblical manuscripts and related written works from libraries and other repositories worldwide have offered the historian significant insights into the biblical tradition and how it was formulated and passed on. On the theoretical side, the historical-critical approach has developed powerful analytical tools by which to gain insight into the Hebrew Bible based on internal evidence alone, among them, source and form criticism being, of course, the most prominent and broadly accepted.

Overall, there can be no question that the various disciplines within the historical-critical purview have proven successful in delineating the record of history in the Hebrew Bible. In fact, the historical-critical approach has accomplished so much and the prospects for continued advances look so bright that it is only natural that the historian of the Tanak and/or the Ancient Near East should wish to showcase the success of the methodologies in the classroom. The "Bible as history" type course is a frequent result.

Obviously, I do not wish to suggest that biblical history should be ignored; my remarks above in connection with the literary-critical approach to the Hebrew Bible have already made this quite clear. What concerns me is a course of study in which the history in the Bible becomes an end unto itself rather than a means towards analysis of the Tanak. The problem here is that the historical-critical approach actually tends to look past the Bible towards its antecedents and to make those antecedents the object of minute study. If, as I suggested at the outset of this discussion, the Hebrew Bible is a complicated weave of many strands, then the general intent of the "Bible as history" teacher is to disentangle (to the extent that this is possible) each and every strand and appraise each respectively in its own right. The historical-critical approach to the Tanak thus tends to be a process of fragmentation more concerned with the component parts of the Bible than with what resulted when the parts came together.

Granted, this is not entirely the case, especially in light of the recent interest in canon criticism or criticism of the Bible as Scriptures. Still, the focus predominantly remains on the delineation of subtle clues within the biblical text which show the historical process acting upon the Tanak. Such a focus is quite appropriate in graduate level course work or even in the context of an advanced Hebrew Bible offering for undergraduates. But this is the wrong emphasis in a survey course. For if the course of study becomes too deeply embroiled in the nuances of historical-critical study—for example, too caught up in distinguishing the subtle differences between one editorially distinct fragment and another or too embroiled in considering the pros and cons of competing historical chronologies or too preoccupied with the complicated picture of settlement and resettlement that the archaeological record indicates—then the larger picture will become submerged in detail and thus less well depicted. Certainly, there is something laudable in a course of study that uses the Bible as a means to open a window on an ancient world; every Hebrew Bible survey class should do this to some extent. But if a survey of the Tanak *only* ends up directing students' attention backwards, then I think the course has failed in large part to fulfill its function as part of a liberal arts education. Rather, the ultimate goal should be to look forward from the biblical times to our own. The historical perspective on the Bible must be kept subservient to this aim in a Hebrew Bible survey course.

One has to query whether there is not as much of a hidden agenda involved in teaching the "Bible as history" as there is in the "Bible as literature" approach. There is a strong desire among scholars involved in Ancient Near Eastern studies to disengage, one might even say emancipate, the study of that time and culture from the Bible and especially to bring the discipline out from under the overarching shadow of biblical religion. This may best be seen as an effort to secularize the field of study, indeed to defend it as legitimate academic endeavor, alongside similar secular approaches to the study of history. The field of Ancient Near Eastern history is thus affirmed to be intrinsically important, not merely important because of the light it throws upon the Bible and its theology.

The discussion that has arisen recently regarding the appropriateness of the designation "Biblical Archaeology" is illustrative of this tendency. Some archaeologists and historians feel compelled to eschew this label since it clearly implies that the excavations and concomitant analyses of Ancient Near Eastern sites are only important because they teach us more about the "Holy Land." Likewise, in my own educational experience, I can recall a teacher of Mesopotamian History and Akkadian Languages who would severely reprimand any student who dared to draw a biblical parallel to the culture and literature of the Eastern Semitic world during his class. In cases like these, scholars are by no means denying the relevance of their work to an understanding of the Bible; rather, they are simply "defending their turf" lest it be taken over and perhaps even drastically distorted by interpreters whose sole interest is to exploit the biblical perspective on the Ancient Near Eastern world.

One can only be sympathetic to this desire to defend the integrity of Ancient Near Eastern history as a field academically important in its own right. Certainly, it is appropriate to question a designation like "Biblical Archaeology" within a specifically academic context[7] after all, one is not excavating the Bible but rather the civilizations of the Ancient Near Eastern world. However, in one's zeal to preserve the academic integrity of the field, one should take care not to distort the way the Bible itself should be taught in a liberal arts survey course.

In fact, consciously or unconsciously, an historian may tend to feel that *any* Hebrew Bible survey course inherently depicts a slanted view of the Ancient Near East. After all, from a contemporary standpoint, the Israelite and Jewish civilizations were only of minor importance. An historian may thus feel that to portray this world from a biblical stand-point is essentially to portray it "inside-out"—rather like looking through the wrong end of a telescope. This feeling can be significantly exacer-bated when, as is sometimes the case, an historian is compelled to teach the Hebrew Bible more-or-less against his or her will. Obviously, there are far fewer academic positions in Ancient Near Eastern History and/or Archaeology than there are in biblical studies; and, in today's constricted academic job market, a scholar takes what he or she can get. The result can therefore be a situation where an historian is teaching the Bible instead of what he or she would prefer to teach: Ancient Near Eastern History. Given such a set of circumstances, an historian's sense of the unfairness of the biblical perspective may shade into a genuine resent-ment of the biblical worldview. Couple this with the chauvinism for the field of Ancient Near Eastern studies already mentioned above, and the result can be a "Bible as history" course that tends to depict the Tanak as but one faint voice amidst a cacophony of voices—many of which well anticipated salient biblical ideas and concepts.

Of course, this is a legitimate way to view the Hebrew Bible. Indeed, if one were teaching a survey course in Ancient Near Eastern History, it would be quite correct to portray the civilization that produced the Bible as essentially a socio-political backwater. It would also be appropriate to consider Tanak mainly in terms of the contribution it makes to Ancient Near Eastern history and further to examine in detail the complex of criti-cal theories and comparative evidence by which one may determine the dimensions of this contribution. But in a Hebrew Bible survey course, this approach is as wrongheaded as was the "Bible as literature" approach discussed above. Once again, the guiding principle should be the role of Hebrew Bible survey as part of a liberal arts education. Regardless of how unimportant the Bible was in its contemporary surroundings, it is vitally important in terms of its influence on Western civilization. It is this influence that must be underlined if a Hebrew Bible survey course is to fulfill its proper function within a liberal arts curriculum. To the ex-tent that the hidden agenda in teaching "Bible as history" turns students away from a full-scale encounter with the Bible as a primary shaper of Western consciousness, it is a wrong approach.

But if neither the "Bible as literature" nor the "Bible as history" ap-proach properly portrays the Tanak in a survey course, then precisely how should it be portrayed? One answers this question by posing another one: Precisely in what manner does the Bible in general and the Hebrew Bible in particular penetrate and mold Western civilization? The answer, of course, is obvious: it does so as a *religious* influence. Thus, the emphasis in a Hebrew Bible survey course should be first and foremost on the Tanak as a religious document. Obviously, the historical and literary aspects of the Bible must play an important role in Hebrew Bible survey course; but they must be kept in their place: they must primarily be used to lay a foundation for the presentation of the major ideas and concepts that are at the core of biblical religion.

Let us consider several examples to illustrate the point: One should not bring in comparative evidence of the Ancient Near Eastern flood stories of Gilgamesh of Atra-hasis simply to set the Bible's Noah story in a broader cultural setting. It is far more important to use this comparative material to show how the biblical writers/editors both assimilated an ancient narrative tradition from the wider culture and simultaneously reacted against it. Thus, if in Mesopotamia the flood hero is portrayed as stoic, responsible and completely moral, while the gods, in contrast, are shown to be childish and frivolous, without any sense of morals at all, then in the Bible just the opposite will be so: God in the biblical flood story will be shown to be completely responsible and moral in action—it is mankind, whose make-up is wicked from youth, who acts immorally and thus rightly brings upon his race a drastic punishment. Indeed, it is only God's mercy and love that saves him from being utterly destroyed. In teaching about the Flood, one must clearly mark the contrasts between the Mesopotamian and biblical perspectives, not because they are intrinsically interesting, but rather because this allows significant insight into the biblical view of God and mankind and their relation to one another. Thus, the excursus on the Flood serves its correct purpose in Hebrew Bible survey: to clarify concepts at the foundation of biblical religion.

To take another case, one does not present the theory of the Deuteronomic Redaction of the Former Prophets merely to place the editing of this material within a proper historical-critical framework. Instead, one analyzes the nature of Deuteronomy because this is the decisive theological viewpoint in the Tanak. Its presentation of God's action in history, its justification of God's punishment of His chosen people as a direct consequence of covenental violations demonstrate why one properly calls the account from Joshua through Kings prophecy rather than history.

Another example: One does not present the so-called "Court History," the story of David as king until his death and the succession of Solomon, solely as a great literary masterpiece, indeed, the consummate prose work in the Hebrew Bible. The portrait of David presented by the Court Historian can stand alongside the greatest tragic depictions in Shakespeare (indeed, it probably played a role in shaping Shakespeare's flawed heroes); and certainly one should spend time showing a class how the greatest of biblical prose writers used his spare but elegant narrative art to depict the great king, his children, his court, his friends and his enemies. However, ultimately one must draw back from mere literary analysis to consider how important this portrait of David is to the concept of kingship in the Former Prophets. For David is one of the Bible's greatest paradoxes; the most promising hope as a king, the most terrible disappointment as human being. Indeed, he functions as the very embodiment of what makes kingship in the Bible an institution with so tragic a dimension. For the establishment of kingship is seen in the Former Prophets as both a great evil and a great good: a great evil because it is a pagan office in which a man takes on the role of God; a great good because it intensifies the relationship of God to his people by focusing it through the intermediary of a single man and office, and no less because it points towards God's promise of rescue from despair through the agency of a king-to-come. All these conflicting ideas are wrapped up in the figure of David as he is shown to us in the Court History. He is not simply a literary figure but a religious focal point in a climactic position in the Former Prophets, and so he must be presented in a Hebrew Bible survey class.

Finally, let us consider the Book of Job. Job has many editorial layers—the Prologue/Epilogue, the Poem, the Hymn to Wisdom (chapter 28) and the Elihu speeches, to name the most widely *accepted*.[8] Also, the end of the dialogue between Job and his three friends has been textually disturbed (or censored) and thus has become somewhat mixed-up and garbled. Moreover, the language of the Poem itself bristles with grammatical problems that inhibit interpretation of many individual passages. One cannot, I think, ignore these problems and complexities in Job and then pretend that it is a unified literary work to be interpreted and taught accordingly. Job is a document with a complicated history, and one's class must be made aware of this history, if they are to understand Job properly.

Job is also a masterful work of literature. The Prologue/Epilogue is a finely crafted but simply developed retelling of an old story, a superb example of the folktale genre. The Poem, in contrast, is a highly sophisticated and complicated work that draws upon literary forms (e.g., the dialogue form one finds attested in Mesopotamian Wisdom contexts) and literary antecedents (e.g., the rich Canaanite mythology which we now know from Ugarit) to produce the most clearly "literary" work in the Bible. This aspect of the work must also be conveyed to a class that would properly understand the Book of Job.

But neither the historical-critical nor the literary aspects of Job should be allowed to take over when one presents Job (in the one or two lectures available) in a Hebrew Bible survey course. Rather, it is its function as a specifically religious inquiry into the nature of God that must be the focus of concentration. The Book of Job, in all its layers, centers on this basic issue; and depending on how one sees Job resolving it (if the issue is in fact resolved), so one understands its writers' grasp of the human condition. One must recall that Job is not in the Bible because it is a great literary masterpiece, nor is it there because it is an important historical artifact. Job became a part of the biblical canon because it has something important to say about God and humankind; the questions it raises are religious questions and thus it is as a religious document that it should be explored in a biblical survey course.

Obviously, each teacher of the Hebrew Bible will take his or her own particular line on how to present the Noah story, Deuteronomy, the Court History and Job; and I certainly do not wish to imply that the way I discuss these sections of the Tanak (or other sections) is the only serious way in which to do so before an undergraduate audience. But I do believe that the priorities reflected in my examples are correct. However far afield one goes into the comparative evidence, the critical theories, the grammatical problems, the archaeological record or the art of literature in order to interpret the Bible, one must begin with religious ideas and end with them: they must always be the point of reference if one's survey course is to achieve its ends as part of a liberal arts education.

But if it is the religious perspective that a teacher must emphasize, another question then must be raised: How does one properly present the Bible as a religious document in a Hebrew Bible survey course? Regarding this issue, I once had the parent of one of my students query me: Why should not Jews teach the Old Testament from a Jewish perspective, Christians teach New Testament from a Christian perspective, and for that matter, Buddhists teach Buddhism from a Buddhist perspective, etc.? I could only reply that a university's stance is and must remain *academic* and that, at least ideally, the academic perspective is dispassionate. To the extent that a teacher would allow his or her podium to become a position of advocacy, religious or otherwise, to that extent the teacher has exceeded his or her mandate. For a university is not a church, a synagogue or even a divinity school but rather a secular institution whose educational aims must also be secular. Thus, although a teacher should focus the class' attention on biblical religion, he or she should not do so *from* a religious standpoint. The only responsible position for a teacher to take, in presenting Hebrew Bible survey, is an uncompromisingly *secular* position.

However, it is not easy to present a secular view of biblical religion to a class of undergraduates. In particular, it is difficult to guide one's students to perceive that there are definitive, if subtle, distinctions between the religious concepts in the Tanak, the teacher's secular presentation of same, the teacher's personal religious commitment (or lack thereof) *vis á vis* the Bible and especially the individual student's own religious stance regarding the truth of the biblical message. For most students these distinctions tend to blur together; and, however dispassionate the teacher's stance in teaching about religion in the Bible, the typical student will nonetheless react passionately, not academically, to what he or she encounters in the course of study. In particular, two common reactions are to be expected. First, when the student sees the teacher presenting biblical religion from a secular instead of a religious position (as would one's minister or rabbi), he or she assumes that the teacher must not be personally religious. Second, the student will interpret the teacher's secular presentation, not as religiously neutral, but in terms of the student's own religious commitment. If the student is not particularly religious, he or she will assume that the teacher is "just like me," someone who does not take "this religious mumbo jumbo" seriously. On the other hand, if the student has a strong religious commitment, he or she will assume that the teacher wishes to challenge if not attack that commitment and therefore is someone not to be trusted.

A teacher of the Hebrew Bible survey should go to considerable lengths to combat problems of this sort that are the product of teaching the Bible and biblical religion from a secular viewpoint. In my own experience, I have found several strategies to be effective. First of all, I believe that teacher should not reveal the nature of his or her religious commitment to an undergraduate class; at least, I have found that my position as a dispassionate educator is easier to maintain when my students have no certain grounds by which to judge my own religious convictions. Such personal information is simply too prejudicial. For no matter what you say about your religious belief, your students will incline towards the conclusion that what you are teaching must fall in line with that belief system. That is, they will conclude that you are only highlighting a given line of interpretation of biblical religion because you are a Jew or a Catholic or an atheist, etc. Such a circumstance can only hinder one's ability to present the Bible in a proper fashion.

Of course, eventually (usually sooner than later), someone will ask the teacher in class "what do you believe, anyway?" When this happens, the teacher should make an emphatic point of refusing to answer and then proceed to give a full-scale justification for that refusal. I have often used what I call the "Dan Rather" defense at such a juncture. That is, I will query the class as to why the newscaster does not make clear to the public his political persuasion. The answer, of course, is that, if he did so, everyone would then inevitably tend to look at his presentation of the news as either Democratic, Republican or whatever. More to the point, the newscaster refrains from revealing his own politics because he wishes to underscore his intention to give a depiction of the day's events that is independent of politics—neither Republican nor Democratic, only fair-minded. Thus, in making no statement about his position on the political spectrum, Dan Rather is making a strong statement about his commitment to the aims of journalism—to bring before the public a non-prejudiced and honest interpretation of the news. One then proceeds to note that an exactly analogous situation applies to the position of a teacher of the Hebrew Bible to his or her class and are thus appropriate grounds for keeping the teacher's religion out of the classroom. Laying out a position of this nature can be most beneficial. Not only does it preserve one's neutrality as a teacher of religious ideas in the Bible, but it also makes a prominent issue of that neutrality. One's students come to recognize that the teacher is trying to avoid any hint of religious advocacy and instead desires to keep the discussion on a strictly academic and secular level.

But a teacher cannot simply stake out a position of academic neutrality and assume that his or her students are sophisticated enough to grasp the full implications of such a stance. Beyond this, one should also take pains to articulate carefully what the secular role of a teacher should be, especially in contradistinction to the theological advocacy role of a person holding a religious office. To put this in more philosophical terms, a teacher of Hebrew Bible survey must try to make sure that his or her students understand the difference between knowledge and faith as applied to biblical interpretation.

I often develop this issue with my Hebrew Bible class by noting the different manner in which Tanak should be taught in the context of a university and a divinity school. A university and a divinity school teacher begin on common ground by discussing and analyzing the evidence and theories that characterize the current state of academic knowledge *vis á vis* the Bible. But a divinity school teacher can and should go further. He or she is speaking within the framework of a religious community to a student body who, by their very presence at the school, have signaled their willingness to accept a given theological viewpoint. Thus, the teacher can rightly proceed to note that beyond what one can know or speculate about a given aspect of the Bible, academically speaking, his or her religious community further believes in a particular doctrinal position based upon faith.

A teacher of the Hebrew Bible in a university setting does not operate under the same theological umbrella. Certainly, the teacher has the responsibility to present the full academic context of biblical study and, in doing so, to consider the specific tenets upon which religious doctrines, biblical or otherwise, are built. However, he or she has no right to take the further step that the divinity teacher must take. Indeed, I believe it would be unethical for a teacher in a secular context to endorse a doctrinal position of any sort or to make any value judgment regarding a given student's faith commitment, even in terms of how it relates to the Bible.

Using this or a similar line of classroom discussion as a springboard, a teacher of the Hebrew Bible should further emphasize that, while academic knowledge and religious faith are not necessarily at odds with one another, they are quite different in the scope of biblical interpretation that they respectively allow. The academic viewpoint is circumscribed, tied to the empirical evidence available. To the extent it theorizes, going beyond what the evidence clearly shows, it does so in relationship to and with allegiance toward the empirical evidence. Hence, if one's theories are demonstrated to contravene the evidence (or new evidence appears which compromises one's theories), then they are restructured or abandoned accordingly.

The religious viewpoint is far more wide-ranging. It is not confined by the evidence available but rather transcends it. To the extent that what one knows confirms what one believes, well and good; but faith, virtually by definition, leads to interpretations that cannot be empirically established. Indeed, faith can lead one to take religious positions which appear—on strictly empirical grounds—dubious in light of the preponderance of the evidence.

In light of these distinctions, a teacher should therefore note that the kinds of answers pursued in a secular Hebrew Bible survey course must be different from the answers to which one is guided through one's religious faith. In fact, in the final analysis, an academic pursuit of religious concepts in the Tanak, when taken to its logical limit, leads inevitably to questions rather than answers. Indeed, if there is one overriding concept that I try to establish in my own biblical survey course, it is this: that the Bible is not an "Answer Book." That is, one will never be able to look into the Bible, rationally to analyze depictions of God and His actions towards mankind and *make complete sense* of them. Secular, academic inquiry is simply not up to that task. Only through a given faith commitment can one find the inspiration to answer the sort of rationally unanswerable questions that the Bible poses. But it is not the job of a university teacher to articulate this faith or to supply this inspiration. As I often have told my students: Everyone of you has the choice to make a "a leap of faith" (or not). My role is not to tell you when or how to do so; rather, my role is to show you where you are standing before you come to a decision to jump. Only when the role of a teacher of Hebrew Bible survey is thus defined in this or similar ways to one's class, can an educator hope that his or her academically secular presentation will be properly understood.

The discussion above of the secular context of a Hebrew Bible survey course highlights what every teacher of Tanak knows, in any case: that this is a very sensitive subject matter—a subject matter that tends to affect people's lives in a more direct and personal manner than most courses in the college curriculum do. Thus we must turn, finally, to a consideration of this issue: How does a secular presentation of biblical religion impact upon undergraduates, especially undergraduates who come into class with a strong religious commitment? In my opinion, this is the aspect of teaching Hebrew Bible to which a teacher should show greatest concern. For one cannot simply assume that this impact will be ultimately beneficial instead of detrimental.

When faced with the issue of how an OT course personally affects students, a teacher may have a tendency to take an academically aloof position. It might even be argued that such an aloof position is the only one possible for a teacher to espouse, if he or she wishes to maintain the academically dispassionate stance discussed above. Such a line of reasoning might lead a teacher to conclude that one must "let the chips fall where they may" during the presentation of a course on the Tanak, that one must go where the empirical evidence leads and never duck the hard religious issues and implications that will therefore arise—even if students become upset as a result.

To a large extent, this is a correct way to approach a Hebrew Bible survey course. One must never shortchange the academic ideals of a liberal arts education by compromising the pursuit and exposition of knowledge that is at its heart. But in practice this idealistic stance must be tempered by the recognition that one is teaching undergraduates—students who are not necessarily as well armed for the academic fray as the teacher is and whose developing intellects are both impressionable and fragile. One should be acutely aware that undergraduates, by and large, have not developed the maturity and intellectual self-confidence required for independent judgment. This potentially leaves them psychologically vulnerable, and a teacher of the Tanak should be sensitive to and sympathetic towards this vulnerability.

No type of student is more vulnerable in this respect than the one with a strong, traditional religious background and training. Such a student, generally speaking, has an extensive knowledge of the Bible, but that knowledge has been nurtured within a religious environment which reinforces a particular viewpoint of the Scriptures which is more or less taken as a "given." Faced suddenly with an entirely different approach, one which examines all biblical issues critically and accepts none as self-evident, the traditionally religious student may feel that he or she has gone "through the looking glass": The territory may look familiar but it all seems twisted around wrong.

Moreover, this "Looking Glass" world will almost certainly be viewed by such a student as a hostile environment, and this in turn often triggers a hostile reaction towards the teacher. Thus, it is to be expected that a teacher of the Hebrew Bible will be faced with encounters, often of a vociferous nature, with students who are bent upon advocating their conservative religious understanding of the Bible, an understanding which they perceive to be under attack.

It is just at such a juncture that the teacher of the Tanak must take special care. The temptation to react combatively to the traditional student's challenge, though often hard to resist, should nonetheless be resisted at all costs. Of course, there are good reasons why a teacher of the Hebrew Bible may tend to lose patience with students who insist upon injecting their conservative biblical interpretations into the middle of his or her survey course. The traditional student's comments can often come close to being derogatory, implicitly challenging not only the teacher's authority but even his or her competence. Moreover, the remarks can also be ill-timed and distracting, coming in the middle of lecture, for example, and thus upsetting one's momentum and throwing off a carefully plotted and timed presentation. Also, the issues raised by a conservative student are often couched in a naive, even an unthinking manner. Thus, the teacher may be irritated that he or she has had to stop everything in order to answer "another silly question."

All of these factors can join together to lead a teacher to respond in kind to a student's belligerent advocacy of a traditional religious viewpoint. Moreover, in general, it is easy to do so with considerable success. After all, the teacher has an arsenal of knowledge—especially technical knowledge of languages and cultures—with which the student can rarely complete. The teacher also has both the weight of professorial authority as well as parliamentary control of the class. Thus, a skillful teacher can use his or her considerable advantages to outmaneuver and out-debate a traditionally religious student, deftly undercutting the less sophisticated arguments—indeed, "skewering" the student before a class that, in such circumstances, inclines to side with the teacher, in any case.

One can hardly expect a traditional student, counterattacked in this manner, to react positively. More likely, he or she will respond in one of two manners: retreat or surrender. If the student retreats, he or she withdraws from further serious academic discussion and turns a deaf ear to what the teacher is saying about the Hebrew Bible. In such an instance, the educational process essentially ceases to operate; in the most extreme cases, the student simply drops out of the class. This is bad enough, but the alternate response is far more serious. When the student is suddenly exposed to heretofore unconsidered critical interpretations of the Bible, especially under "battle conditions," he or she can be deeply affected, perhaps even traumatized. After all, it is often the case that a student's traditional faith, while strong, is also both inflexibly brittle or untried. If the traditional interpretations that have served as the armor for this faith are perceived by the student to be in any way penetrated, then his or her faith commitment itself can also be shattered. The student is then left like Humpty Dumpty—and none may be able to put his fragmented psyche back together again.

A teacher of Hebrew Bible survey must therefore recognize that he or she has tremendous power—and that the power is double-edged: one may educate but one may also do damage. To be sure, the teacher of any course has a similar power to affect his or her students' lives. But I believe the capability to do damage is particularly acute in a survey course on the Bible. Students, like most people, have a tendency to compartmentalize what they know. If a conservatively religious student takes a course in physics or even biology, he or she can usually isolate that type of knowledge from religious knowledge, guided by faith. Science and religion can be perceived as simply not being relevant to one another. If the fallacy of such a position is suggested, the traditional student can always take the viewpoint that physics and biology are wrong—that their teachers, after all, do not really know and understand the truth of the biblical message.

Even other courses in religion or philosophy that challenge a traditional student's faith can be effectively parried in a similar manner. Religious and philosophical ideas are usually presented as abstract concepts open to interpretation and challenge. Thus the traditionally religious student can conclude that what Plato, Buddha, Zoroaster or even Kierkegaard has to say, though interesting, is also misguided. The theologians and philosophers can be dismissed because they either did not know or they misunderstood the text of the Bible. And it is the text of the Bible itself upon which all faith hinges in most conservative circles.

However, it is precisely the text that is a central focus in any Hebrew Bible survey course. Thus, when a teacher raises issues about basic interpretation of the Bible—chapter and verse—he or she is shaking the rock upon which much conservative religious belief has been built. The shocks to a traditional student's religious faith are not so easily cushioned in such a circumstance, and the results can sometimes be no less than devastating. Indeed, I know of cases where students have spent years recovering from the trauma of being exposed to a critical inquiry into the Bible, and most teachers of the Bible, who know their students well, can recall similar situations.

The students who worry me most are not the ones who make their traditional viewpoints known in one's course but rather the silent conservatives, who, either out of shyness or fear of ridicule and/or retaliation, keep their religious faith under wraps. They too can be traumatized by a Hebrew Bible survey course; but their trauma can be far more intense because it stays beneath the surface, unarticulated by the student, unknown to the teacher. Nonetheless, one must always be aware that the silent ones also are out there in the classroom. An educator must recognize that in teaching about the Bible he or she is doing more than teach: lives are being affected, sometimes seriously, and even if the teacher does not always know whose or how, he or she should care enough to be self-consciously concerned.

So, in light of these concerns, how should one handle undergraduates in a Hebrew Bible survey course? For one thing, a teacher should not seek out confrontation. Recently, a student told me about a teacher of Bible whose lecture strategy each week was always the same: According to this student, the teacher would focus upon the lecture topic of the day (labeled by the teacher as a "cherished belief") and then challenge the class in these terms: "You believe such and such? Well, you're wrong!" Such an approach has the obvious advantage of being dramatic and thus riveting to a student's attention. However, in my opinion, the price is too high. One should recall that exposure to critical knowledge of the Bible is a potent and dramatic enough experience for many in one's class. One should not indulge in confrontation-overkill; for, in doing so, one may end up running roughshod over students' sensibilities.

Secondly, one should be patient with even the most vociferous of traditional students. The teacher must not look upon such students' comments as challenges to his or her authority or as silly distractions from the issues at hand. Students are raising questions because they are seriously concerned about the answers. While the ramifications of these questions should be fully explored with nothing held back, this should be done in a sensitive manner. Students should not be made to feel foolish; if their questions are obviously naive, then an issue should not be made of this naiveté. Rather the teacher should always try to frame a response to a particular question so that the question itself appears intelligent. Beyond this, the student must never be dismissed as an inferior opponent. Instead of isolating the student in this manner, the teacher should rather take pains to reinforce the collegial teacher-to-student relationship that encourages the broadening of intellectual perspectives rather than their diminishment. Such a non-hostile and open attitude may even have the effect of drawing a response from the silent conservatives, alluded to above. Once such students feel that they will not be made to look foolish or that they will not be penalized (in terms of their grade) for taking a traditionally religious stance, they too may become engaged actively in the issues raised by Hebrew Bible survey rather than staying on the sidelines, perhaps suffering silently.

Finally and most importantly, the teacher should respect students' religious beliefs and leave them room for their faith. Students should not be made to feel that they are intellectually inferior or ignorant simply because they hold to their own religious convictions during the course of a Hebrew Bible survey class. Indeed, any teacher should recognize and make clear to his or her class that the academic, secular worldview has its own credo, its own dogmatic positions and its own axioms which ultimately depend as much upon faith (invoked in the guise of "common sense") as anything else. While it is certainly appropriate for an educator to act as defender of the academic faith in the classroom, he or she should not further proselytize students into believing that this is the only possible way for "right-thinking" people to look at things. It may be true that the secular worldview has the high ground within the confines of a university, but one must admit at least the possibility that there are more things on heaven and earth than are dreamed of in its philosophy. One's students certainly have the right to believe so, and a teacher should not only respect that right but also not discourage its exercise.

Of course, in teaching a Hebrew Bible course, one must consider not only its effect upon students with a strong religious commitment but also its influence upon the wide range of other students who find their way into such a course. A most challenging aspect of teaching the Bible is that it tends to attract all kinds—not only undergraduates who read the Bible everyday, but also those who have never opened it even once; not only students at home in the humanities but also those who have chosen this course as the one diversion from their study in the hard sciences. Overall, the vast majority of one's students will be those who have never looked at biblical religion seriously, and one must be just as sensitive to their concerns as to the concerns of the religiously committed student.

The fact is that the field of Bible study can appear most intimidating to those unfamiliar with the Tanak. There is so much material to assimilate, so many different types of writing for the student to encounter, such a lot of technical issues with the inevitable technical jargon to take in, that it is normal for students to feel overwhelmed. A common reaction that many students have is that the teacher expects them to be familiar with the Bible even before they have entered the classroom. Moreover, as the teacher begins to engage in dialogue with the religious students who know their way around the biblical text, the sense that many students develop of being uninitiated outsiders can be further intensified.

In my own classes I have found that the best way to redress this sort of alienation is through the establishment of an easy and open procedure by which students may ask questions at any time. Questions tend to open up a Hebrew Bible class; individuals discover that they are not the only ones who are feeling both isolated and confused. Moreover, if the teacher makes it unmistakably clear that questions are not only expected but a *necessary* aspect of the class, then the question periods and the dialogues that develop as their result can turn out to be the most educationally beneficial parts of the entire course.

Obviously, questions are always an integral part of most courses of all types; however, I believe that the students' need to pose questios to the teacher is especially pronounced and therefore of crucial importance in a course on the Tanak. In my own class I have noticed that there is a revealing pattern to the way questions come. Over the initial period of four to five lectures the class will have little to ask; and then in a subsequent lecture period, an outpouring of questions will occur, so many that not infrequently I find myself spending most of the class hour answering them. Moreover, in such a question period there is an "edge" to the way the questions are posed, as if the class is using questions as a therapeutic means by which to come to terms collectively with the larger issues inherent in the study of biblical religion. For in such a question period, however picayune the questions begin, they almost inevitably turn towards issues of a much broader nature.

.In the best of such question periods, everyone becomes engaged: teacher, religiously committed student, the student without religious background and all the shades in between. Together, like Jacob wrestling with the angel, they struggle with the basic questions which the Bible poses; and, if like Jacob, they no more succeed in gaining the answers sought, perhaps they too are changed by the process. I personally feel that no class of mine has been worthwhile if it does not have moments of this sort. They represent the best of what a Hebrew Bible survey can offer to undergraduates.

In the final analysis, one has to consider what is the most important thing that a teacher of the Tanak has to offer his or her undergraduates. As I mentioned before, a characteristic of the undergraduate intellect is that it has generally yet to gain the capacity for confident, independent judgment. The most important aim that a teacher of the Bible should try to achieve is to give students the tools through which they can further formulate this capacity for independent judgment, the ability to look at the Bible intelligently and knowledgeably, but also in their own terms, independent of the teacher's viewpoints. A teacher's efforts and methods should ultimately tend towards this final end. After all, there are far too many strands in the biblical weave, and one can only pass the fabric quickly before one's students' eyes during a Hebrew Bible survey course. At the beginning of a course on the Tanak, the teacher must do all the choosing among the strands, but by its end it is the students' ability to choose for themselves that is of decisive importance.

Each time I conclude my one semester Hebrew Bible survey course, I do so with a strong feeling of discouragement and failure. By its very nature, a survey course dramatically abridges and therefore distorts its given subject matter. Such a course ultimately never can succeed in conveying to one's students anything approaching a genuine grasp of the subtleties of a particular field. Survey courses are the blunt instruments in a college curriculum—they achieve their ends in the broadest sense, but with little fine detail and less finesse.

Teaching the Tanak within the framework of a survey course can be a difficult enterprise, full of frustrations and small defeats. The process of communication between teacher and class is always tenuous and, by the time my Hebrew Bible course has reached its end, I am always acutely aware that far too many of my students have failed to grasp even the most basic of concepts that I wished to convey.

Yet teaching Hebrew Bible survey can also prove to be more than simply a necessary evil. For even as Hebrew Bible survey fulfills its role for students as part of their liberal arts education, it can serve as a valuable experience for the teacher as well. Such a course compels the teacher to step back from his or her more myopic scholarly endeavors and reconsider the larger picture of biblical studies, reviewing the broader issues and asking again the essential questions. This experience of rethinking the Tanak is, at least for me, not a repetitive exercise but rather an evolving process. As I choose among the strands of biblical ideas that I wish to present to my class, I find that each semester they are somewhat different strands that entail different approaches and fresh conclusions. By watching how students react to their encounter with biblical ideas, I find myself getting back in touch with those intangible attractions that brought me into the field of biblical studies in the first place. And, of course, there will always be more strands in the biblical weave to encounter and new ways to look at them. Because this is so, teaching the Hebrew Bible to undergraduates at a secular university will remain for me the difficult pleasure that it has always proven to be. ✡

Endnotes

1. There is, of course, the question of whether one should ever use the term "Old Testament," since it is potentially offensive to Jewish sensibilities. Certainly, if one is lecturing or teaching to an audience under specifically Jewish auspices (for example, in an adult education class at a synagogue), one should make particular point of using the more neutral "Hebrew Bible" (a slight misnomer since a small percentage of the "Hebrew" Bible is written in Aramaic) or the traditional "Tanak" (the acronym for Torah-Nevi'im-Ketuvim=Law/Teaching, Prophets and Writings), designating the threefold division of Scripture. However, in a secular environment one cannot ignore the use of "Old Testament," since it is the most widely understood designation for the biblical writings outside of the Christian canon or New Testament. Indeed, "Old Testament" is the dominant designation used for subject indexing in virtually all libraries. The reason why was once explained to me by a librarian at a Jewish seminary: "You can't fight the Library of

Congress." So "Old Testament" as a designation for the Tanak is not going to go away. In light of this, the best approach in the classroom is first to explain the term and why the label by its very nature assumes a Christian perspective. Then one simply tolerates the term as the common, if not ideal, secular label that will be deemed acceptable, if not inevitable nomenclature.

2. Although this study specifically focuses upon teaching Tanak, many of the issues discussed are inevitably more broad and thus relevant to teaching "the Bible" in general or, better, texts of a biblical nature (including not only New Testament books but also those in the Apocrypha and Pseudepigrapha). It is in fact quite impossible entirely to isolate issues unique to teaching Hebrew Bible from those relevant to teaching the range of biblical texts. In any case, this will be the working assumption in the discussion that follows, and the terms "Tanak," "Hebrew Bible" and "Bible" will be used interchangeably throughout.

3. Cf. *A Greek-English Lexicon,* ed., H. G. Liddel, R. Scott (Oxford, Clarendon: 1968) s.v. biblion, p. 315; also *The Oxford English Dictionary,* vol. 1, ed., J. A. Murray et al. (Oxford, Clarendon: 1933; rpt., 1970) s. v. "Bible," p. 846; 2nd ed., vol. 2., ed., J. A. Simpson, F. S. C. Weiner (Oxford: Clarendon, 1989) s. v. "Bible" p. 168

4. Cf. Liddel and Scott, *ibid.,* s.v. *biblion,* p. 315 and *bublos,* p. 333.

5. The quotation comes from an unpublished paper, "What has Literary Criticism to do with History?" read by Simon B. Parker at the annual covention of the Society of Biblical Literature, December, 1984. I am very grateful to Dr. Parker for furnishing me with a draft copy of that paper. Much of the following comment on the difficulties of reading and interpreting the Bible simply as "literature" rely heavily on the insights of Parker's paper, and my debt to him is acknowledged forthwith.

6. *Ibid.*

7. One must recognize, however, that Ancient Near Eastern history and especially archaeology in the Near East do not function solely within an academic environment. Cognizance must be taken of the public's interest in and support of research in these fields, and by and large the public is interested in what history and archaeology have to say about the Bible and "biblical times." Thus if historians and archaeologists (not to mention linguists and philologists) wish to keep the public's interest and thereby attract the funding that will keep their research and excavation efforts viable, they will have to continue to focus some of their attention towards the relevance of their fields to the Bible. Thus, labels like "Biblical Archaeology" will and should remain in a scholar's arsenal of public lecture titles.

8. Many would also divide the poem into further discrete editorial layers, e.g., viewing the Theophany as an addition to the rest of the Poem or seeing the Behemoth/Leviathan speech as an interpolation at the end of the Theophany.

Chapter 4

The Emerging Field of
Jewish Biblical Theology

Marvin A. Sweeney

I

The past three decades have seen tremendous growth in the numbers of Jews who are trained as critical biblical scholars and who now hold academic teaching and research positions in universities, colleges, and even in Christian theological seminaries. This stands in striking contrast to past generations in which Jews were largely absent in the field. Various reasons explain this absence. On the one hand, Jews were systematically excluded by schools and departments of theology or religion who saw the teaching of the "Old Testament" as a strictly Christian theological endeavor related to the fields of New Testament, Church History, Practical Theology, and Systematic Theology. On the other hand, Jews themselves saw biblical studies as part of a much broader spectrum of Jewish studies, Hebrew language and literature, or Ancient Near Eastern studies in general, and had little interest in a field that was derived from the concerns of Christian systematic theology. As a result, very few Jews have been engaged in the field of biblical theology until relatively recent times.

With the emergence of Jewish Studies programs and departments among secular universities and colleges and the wider participation of Jews in the general fields of biblical studies in particular and religious studies in general,[1] the past few decades have seen a growing interest in Jewish theological interpretation of the Bible.[2] Various scholars have published a growing number of books and articles that either directly or indirectly address the field of biblical theology from a Jewish perspective.[3] In light of this interest, it is appropriate to provide an overview and assessment of this emerging field. This essay will treat several foundational topics in the field, including the rationale for Jewish biblical theology, the recognition of a distinctive Jewish Bible, the role of the nation Israel, the Temple as holy center, the problem of evil, and the role of post-biblical Jewish tradition.

II

The first question that must be addressed in any consideration of Jewish biblical theology is why do it at all? The impetus for Jewish biblical theology comes from the corresponding field of Christian Old Testament theology, which in turn is derived ultimately from the concerns of Christian systematic theology. Although the roots of the field lie in the concerns of the Protestant Reformation, the origins of Christian Old Testament theology may be traced to Johann P. Gabler's 1787 inaugural lecture at the University of Altdorf in which he argued for a distinction between the fields of biblical and dogmatic theology.[4] His fundamental goal in making this distinction was to provide a basis by which the Bible, historically interpreted according to its original meaning, would inform the development of Christian dogmatic theology rather than the reverse. He, of course, understood biblical to refer to both the Christian Old and New Testaments. Such a program was in keeping with Protestant Christianity's emphasis on the Bible as the only true source for the understanding of G-d, humanity, and the world, including its perspective that Jesus must be understood as the true fulfillment of the destiny of Israel in the world.

Obviously, the subsequent development of the field of Christian biblical theology demonstrates its distinctively Christian character and concerns. Gerhard von Rad, for example, emphasizes the concept of salvation history in the Old Testament that points ultimately to Jesus Christ,[5] and Brevard Childs emphasizes the canonical interpretation of the Bible in which the writings of the Old Testament must be read in relation to the entire Christian canon, including both the Old Testament and the New Testament.[6] Indeed, Jon Levenson emphasizes the specifically Christian character of the field of biblical theology in raising the question as to why Jews should be interested in biblical theology at all.[7] In addition, he points to the clearly anti-Jewish character of the field that derives from the long *adversus Iudeos* tradition in Christian history and thought.[8] Christian Old Testament theologians frequently take the opportunity to denigrate Jewish practices, beliefs, and institutions in relation to the "ultimate triumph" of Christianity. Julius Wellhausen, for example, speaks of Judaism as "a mere empty chasm over which one springs from the Old Testament to the New,"[9] and Walter Eichrodt speaks of the "torso-like appearance" of Judaism in relation to Christianity.[10] If biblical theology is fundamentally Christian and anti-Jewish, it has little to say to Jews. Why then should Jews be interested in biblical theology?

There are two basic reasons for Jewish interest and participation in the field.[11] The first reason is to serve the interests of Jewish self-identity. By asserting a distinctively Jewish presence in the general field of biblical interpretation, Jewish biblical theology provides a means to demonstrate that the Hebrew Bible is fundamentally Jewish literature that must be read in relation to Jewish concerns and later Jewish tradition. Christian biblical theology has generally addressed its own concerns that are derived from the larger field of Christian systematic theology, i.e., the nature of G-d who brings judgment against the people of Israel for sin and then sends the divine son Jesus to redeem the entire world; the role of the human being, with particular emphasis on the sinful character of humanity; and the process of salvation by which all of humanity will be redeemed by G-d's son the messiah. Jewish tradition has a very different set of concerns that are rarely or inadequately addressed in Christian biblical theology. Judaism shows far less concern than Christianity in exploring the nature and character of G-d; the definition or portrayal of G-d is discouraged in Judaism as it tends to compromise the sanctity of G-d and promote idolatry.[12] Indeed, Judaism is intimately concerned with G-d, but it focuses much more on the areas for which human beings are responsible, i.e., human action, including the care of creation and the role of the Jewish people in meeting that responsibility. Thus, Judaism is concerned with the character and role of the nation Israel, not simply as an ancient entity that suffered destruction, but as a continuing reality that embodies the Jewish people; the development of halakhah or Jewish practice that defines the life of the Jewish people through the present day; and the problem of evil, in which the continued existence of the Jewish people is challenged by the destruction of the Temples, the Shoah, or other disasters in Jewish history. In essence, Judaism posits that human beings were created to serve as partners with G-d in completing and sanctifying creation, and the revelation of Torah to the people of Israel provides the foundation by which humanity will accomplish this task.[13] Although Judaism posits the transcendental nature of G-d,[14] it tends to be oriented to an immanent understanding of G-d, in which the divine presence or sanctity is manifested or expressed through the mundane reality of this world.[15]

The second reason for Jewish concern with biblical theology is to influence the field of Christian biblical theology. Jewish biblical theology provides a means to assert that Judaism is not simply a prelude to the advent of Christianity that will ultimately be absorbed as Jews come to recognize Jesus as G-d's messiah, but that Judaism constitutes a distinctive, continuing, and legitimate theological reality that must be accepted and engaged as such in Christian theology.[16] Judaism and Christianity are related, but they are not one and the same. Whereas Judaism maintained the concept of the continuity of the Jewish people and their relationship with G-d throughout its history,[17] Christianity abandoned its originally Jewish character in the aftermath of the destruction of the Temple and Judean homeland by the Romans in the revolts of 66-74 C.E. and 132-135 C.E. Instead, it looked to the pagan Gentile world as the basis for its continued growth and theological development as it absorbed the peoples and religious systems of the Greco-Roman world and beyond. The result was a very different understanding of the nature of G-d and the human being that was expressed in the New Testament and later Church writings in which human beings were ultimately incapable of overcoming their sinful condition and required divine intervention in order to achieve salvation. The recognition of the distinctive characters of Judaism and Christianity must begin with the recognition of their distinctive constructions of their communal scriptural base and their respective self-understandings that are derived from that base.

III

The recognition of Judaism's distinctive character and its implications for the development of Jewish biblical theology must begin with consideration of the Bible itself or the Tanak as it is known in Judaism. Such consideration is necessary not only because the Tanak constitutes the necessary basis for Jewish biblical theology but because it is claimed by Christianity as a major component of its own scriptural canon, the Old or First Testament, as well. Although there are very clear differences in the manner in which Judaism and Christianity respectively interpret the Tanak or Old/First Testament and apply its teachings,[18] there is a tacit assumption among many modern critical interpreters, whether Jewish or Christian, that the Tanak and Old/First Testament are one and the same document that stands as the common basis for both Judaism and Christianity.[19] Fundamental to this assumption is the view that the authors of the biblical books employed their own purposes and world views in writing the books and that it is the task of the biblical scholar to interpret the book in relation to those purposes and world views. There might be differences in the interpretation of the Tanak and Old/First Testament in Judaism and Christianity as Jewish scholars will tend to study topics of specifically Jewish concern, e.g., Torah, the land of Israel, etc., whereas Christian scholars will choose topics of Christian concern, e.g., the concept of sin, messianism, etc., but such concerns are essentially topical and do not materially challenge the perceived singular character of the Hebrew Bible as a whole. In order to emphasize the uniquely Jewish character of Jewish biblical theology in relation to the study of the Hebrew Bible that is shared by both Judaism and Christianity, Moshe Goshen-Gottstein advocates labeling the field Tanak theology and calls for the pursuit of biblical themes that are of importance for Judaisim e.g., G-d, people, and land.[20]

Nevertheless, there are major differences between the Tanak of Judaism and the Old Testament of Christianity which must be examined and understood in relation to the call for the establishment of a field of Jewish biblical theology.[21] Such differences involve the overall conceptualization of the Hebrew Bible as either Tanak or Old/First Testament as well as the respective structures of each, including their respective selections and arrangements of the books that comprise the Hebrew Bible. Although there is considerable overlap, especially in the selection of the constitutive books, the Tanak and the Old/First Testament must be recognized as distinctive literary works that are presented according to distinctive hermeneutical and theological agendas. The conceptualization, structure, and arrangement of the Tanak is distinctively Jewish whereas the conceptualization, structure, and arrangement of the Old/First Testament is distinctively Christian.

The theological implications of the term Old/First Testament have long been recognized.[22] The term "testament" denotes "covenant" or "agreement," and refers to the "covenant(s)" between G-d and human beings that appear in the Bible. Christianity posits that a covenant was made between G-d and Israel at Mount Sinai in which the Mosaic "law" or "Torah" would serve as the governing principles for the establishment of Israel as G-d's people who then serve as the agents for the revelation of G-d to all the peoples of the world. But Christianity also posits that Israel sinned and was divinely punished by a series of invasions by foreign powers, which demonstrates the need for a new covenant in which the old Mosaic law gives way to the revelation of Jesus Christ as the basis for the covenant between G-d and humanity which creates the "new" or "true" Israel. Hence the Christian Bible comprises two basic components: the Old/First Testament, in which the Mosaic law is revealed to Israel and Israel is punished for not obeying Mosaic law fully, and the New Testament, in which Jesus Christ is revealed as the basis for G-d's relationship to all the world in the forgiveness of sin.

Clearly, the fundamental concerns of Christian theology are expressed in the progression from the Old Testament/Covenant to the New Testament/Covenant as the basic structure of the Christian Bible. Such concerns are not limited to the two-part structure of the Christian Bible, but they appear within the structure and arrangement of books within each major component. Indeed, the four-part structure and arrangement of the New Testament exhibits the Christian belief that the initial revelation of Christ has not yet been accepted by the world at large because of the sinful nature of humanity, but that a second coming of Christ is necessary. In addition, it puts forward a chronological schema of foundations, past history, present concerns, and the future. Hence, the Gospels relate the foundational revelation of Jesus as Christ and his initial rejection and crucifixion; the Acts of the Apostles relate the history of Christianity as it spread from Jerusalem to Rome, the center of the Gentile world; the Epistles take up the timeless or present questions of Church organization and theology as Christianity prepares for Christ's return; and the Apocalypse/Revelation of John points to the future second coming of Christ.

A similar four-part structure informs the Christian Old/First Testament according to the same chronological schema of foundations, past history, present concerns, and the future. This basic four-part structure applies in both the Roman Catholic and Orthodox canons, which contain the Deutero-canonical books, and the Protestant canon, which contains only those books that appear in the Tanak. The Pentateuch or the Five Books of Moses (Genesis; Exodus; Leviticus; Numbers; Deuteronomy) relates the creation of the world and the establishment of the Mosaic covenant between G-d and Israel. The Historical Books (Joshua; Judges; Ruth; 1 Samuel; 2 Samuel; 1 Kings; 2 Kings; 1 Chronicles; 2 Chronicles; Ezra; Nehemiah; Esther) relate Israel's history of failure to live by the Mosaic covenant and its exile to foreign lands as punishment for that failure. The Poetical and Wisdom Books (Job; Psalms; Proverbs; Ecclesiastes; Song of Solomon) take up the timeless questions of the character of G-d and the means by which human beings relate to G-d. Finally, the Prophetic Books (Isaiah; Jeremiah; Lamentations; Ezekiel; Daniel; Hosea; Joel; Amos; Obadiah; Jonah; Micah; Nahum; Habakkuk; Zephaniah; Haggai; Zechariah; Malachi) point to the future beyond the punishment of Israel when G-d will establish a new relationship with Israel and humanity at large. Within the context of the Christian Bible, this of course points to the New Testament. Indeed, the anticipated return of Christ governs the structure and arrangement of the entire Christian Bible, including both the Old/First and New Testaments.

The Tanak is organized according to very different principles which likewise exhibit the fundamental world view of Judaism that the revelation of Torah is the basis for G-d's relationship with Israel and the world at large.[23] Tanak is an acronym for the Hebrew names of the three major divisions of the Bible in Judaism: Torah; Nevi'im; and Ketuvim. The Torah, understood as "Instruction," "Guidance," or "Revelation," includes the books of Genesis, Exodus, Leviticus, Numbers, and Deuteronomy, and relates the creation of the world and G-d's revelation of Torah to Israel at Mt. Sinai as the basis for the covenant with Israel that will lead to the completion or sanctification of all creation. The Nevi'im or "Prophets" includes two sub-divisions. The books of the "Former Prophets" (Nevi'im Rishonim), i.e., Joshua, Judges, Samuel, and Kings, relate Israel's history in the land of Israel from the time of Joshua to the time of the Babylonian exile. The books of the "Latter Prophets" (Nevi'im Ahronim), i.e., Isaiah, Jeremiah, Ezekiel, and the Book of the Twelve (Hosea; Joel; Amos; Obadiah; Jonah; Micah; Nahum; Habakkuk; Zephaniah; Haggai; Zechariah; and Malachi) relate the causes of Israel's exile from the land as a failure to observe G-d's Torah and points to the time when Israel will be restored to the land and the nations will recognize G-d as G-d never abandons the relationship with Israel. Finally, the *Ketuvim* or "Writings" contains Psalms; Job; Proverbs; the Five *Megillot* (or "Scrolls,") i.e., Ruth; Song of Songs; *Kohelet*; Lamentations; and Esther, plus Daniel; Ezra, Nehemiah; and Chronicles. These books take up the various means by which human beings understand and express themselves in relation to G-d as a prelude to the account of the restoration of Jewish life around the Jerusalem Temple based upon Torah. Essentially, the Tanak posits the initiation of Jewish life based upon Torah, its disruption in the period of the Babylonian exile, and its restoration in the aftermath of the exile. Fundamental to the Tanak's presentation is that the relationship between G-d and Israel, indeed with the world at large, is based upon Torah and that this relationship will always stand.

IV

The principle of Torah as the basis for the relationship between G-d and Israel clearly constitutes a central element of the Tanak and must be considered as foundational to Jewish biblical theology. Indeed, the revelation of Torah to Israel through Moses at Sinai provides the basic guidance for Israel to lead a holy life and thereby to become sanctified. Israel's sanctification through Torah provides the means for the rest of the world to recognize G-d and thereby leads to the sanctification or completion of creation at large. Insofar as the Temple provides the center of holiness in both Israel and creation by which G-d's holy presence is expressed and G-d's Torah is revealed,[24] consideration of the Temple, its priesthood, and its rituals is essential in Jewish biblical theology.

Christian Old Testament theology generally understands Torah as "Law" in accordance with its understanding of Paul's use of the Greek term Nomos for the Hebrew Torah.[25] In this conception, "Law" becomes a rigid system of command and obedience, with consequences for those who choose to disobey. Furthermore, in keeping with Paul's critique of "Law" as the foundation of the Mosaic covenant (see Romans; Galatians), inherently sinful human beings are incapable of fulfilling the "Law" completely, thereby necessitating G-d's intervention and forgiveness through the agency of Jesus Christ. According to the highly influential construct offered by Julius Wellhausen and his followers, "Law" represents the spiritual degeneration of Judaism in the post-exilic period as prophecy began to decline and the Temple and its priesthood, the institutional matrix of "Law," emerged as the dominant institutions.[26] In such a conceptualization, "Law" was understood as priestly ritual which lacked efficacy, spirituality, and rationale.

Such a conception of Torah is clearly a very limited theological construct that serves Protestant Christianity's emphasis on the primary role of prophecy and the Spirit as well as its polemics against the Roman Catholic Church and Judaism. A survey of the meaning and use of the term in the Hebrew Bible demonstrates that a very different conceptualization of the term must be recognized. At the philological level, the Hebrew term Torah *(torah)* is a noun derived from the Hiphil form of the root *(yrh),* which means "to guide," "to show," or "to instruct." Torah must therefore be understood and translated as "guidance" or "instruction."[27] The various uses of the term throughout the Hebrew Bible demonstrate this meaning. Torah refers fundamentally to G-d's instruction (Exod 13:9; 16:4; Deut 17:19). It applies to legal instruction for both religious observance (e.g., Lev 6:14; 7:1) and civil or criminal matters (Exod 18:16; Psalm 105:45), and it refers comprehensively to the entire body of legal instruction that stands at the basis of Israel's national, religious, and societal identity (Exod 24:12; Deut 1:5; 28:61; Josh 24:26). Torah also refers generally to the "custom" or "manner" of human beings (2 Sam 7:19), parental instruction (Prov 1:8; 3:1), instruction by a sage (Prov 13:14); ethical, social, or political instruction (Isa 5:24; 30:9; Amos 2:4; Hab 1:4); and G-d's word in general (Isa 2:3; Mic 4:2), and it may be employed as a synonym for the covenant with YHWH (Hos 8:1; Jer 31:33). In post-biblical Judaism, Torah refers to the entire Pentateuch, which includes the narratives concerning creation and the ancestors as well as the revelation at Sinai, so that it embodies the entire tradition of Israel's origins and self-identity. It may also be employed in reference to the entire body of Jewish teaching and tradition or as an epistemological term for the guiding principle of creation at large.

The interrelationship between Torah and Temple must also be considered. Fundamentally, the priests are responsible for the instruction of the people in Torah (e.g., Hos 4:6), which includes cultic matters (e.g., Hag 2:1 1; Zeph 3:4), the arbitration of civil and criminal cases (Deut 17:11; cf. I Sam 7:15-17), and the guidance of the king (Deut 17:19). Indeed, the priestly role in such instruction is indicated by Moses' role as a Levitical priest in communicating Torah to the people of Israel in general (Exodos 19, Numbers, Deuteronomy) and in hearing the people's legal disputes (e.g., Exod 18). Temples are clearly the primary location for such instruction as indicated by Samuel's erecting an altar at Ramah where he built an altar and carried out his judicial function, the prohibition against building an Asherah by the altar in association with instruction concerning judges (Dent 16:21; cf. 16:18-20), the role of the Temple in decisions concerning the status of slaves (Exod 21:6), and the role of YHWH's Temple at Zion in relation to YHWH's judging the cases of the nations (Isa 2:2-4; Mic 4:1-5). Indeed, Levenson points to the correlation between the revelation of Torah at Mt. Sinai and the role of Mt. Zion as the focus of YHWH's revelation and between the wilderness tabernacle that represented YHWH's presence among the people of Israel during the time of the Exodus and wilderness wanderings and the Jerusalem Temple that represented YHWH's presence in the midst of the nation Israel/Judah.[28]

The Temple/Tabernacle serves not only as the primary locus for the revelation of Torah to Israel in the Hebrew Bible, but as a symbol for the stability or completion of the created world order as well. The Temple constitutes an earthly representation of G-d's heavenly court or the manifestation of G-d's presence in the world.[29] Fishbane, citing Buber, notes the correlation between the language of Gen 2:1-3, which relates YHWH's completion of the work of creation and the establishment of Shabbat as a day of rest for all creation with that of Exodus 40, which relates the completion of the Tabernacle as the representation of YHWH's presence in the world and the locus from which Torah is revealed.[30] The interrelationship between Temple and creation is likewise demonstrated in Ezekiel 40-48, which present the reconstruction of the Temple in Jerusalem as the basis for the restoration of creation at large (Ezek 47:1-12) and the twelve tribes of Israel to their land (Ezek 47:13-48:25).[31] The portrayal of Solomon's Temple highlights motifs from the Pentateuchal traditions, such as the sea from creation (I Kings 7:23-26), the cherubim, palm trees, and flowers of the Garden of Eden (1 Kings 6:23-28, 29, 32, 35), and the window of the ark is represented in the windows of the Temple (I Kings 6:4). The references to the two seven-branched lamp stands of the Tabernacle are understood to represent the two trees of the Garden of Eden and the light of creation (Exod 25:31-40; 37:17-24; Lev 24:1-4). The major Temple festivals likewise relate to the stability of creation and the natural seasonal cycles. As noted above, Shabbat sanctifies the seventh day of rest as a fundamental principle of creation. The three major festivals likewise represent the transition of the seasons and agricultural cycle, i.e., Passover inaugurates the year and marks the beginning of the grain harvest and the transition from the rainy to the dry season; Shavuot completes the grain harvest and marks the final transition to the dry season; and Sukkot inaugurates the grape and olive harvest and marks the transition from the dry to the rainy season.

Altogether, the Temple symbolizes the stability and perpetuation of creation, and provides the matrix from which YHWH's Torah proceeds. YHWH's Temple and Torah constitute fundamental expressions of order in creation and the center of Israel's own existence as a people. This points to the need to consider the land and nation of Israel as a fundamental topic in Jewish biblical theology.

V

Although the Hebrew Bible is ultimately concerned with G-d and creation at large, it focuses fundamentally upon the nation of Israel as the primary character by which G-d and creation are to be understood. Israel's identity in the Hebrew Bible is defined by its relationship with and its life in the land of Israel which YHWH grants to the people as part of that relationship.[32]

Israel's central role in a Jewish biblical theology is self-evident. Its origins are related to the creation of the world as presented in the Pentateuch and other biblical writings. following the creation of the world and humanity, the destruction of much of the world by flood, and the continuing attempts of human beings to apply the knowledge gained in the Garden of Eden to attain divine status, the Pentateuch presents the early history of Israel as an attempt by G-d to bring some guidance to the world by using Israel as a vehicle for the revelation of Torah. The elements of the Pentateuchal narrative are well-known. Abram and his wife Sarah are selected for a special covenantal relationship in which Abram is promised that his descendants will become a great nation and that they will possess the land of Israel if Abram will acknowledge YHWH as his G-d and observes commandments. The result is a covenant between YHWH and Abram which YHWH acknowledges in Genesis 15 by the ceremony of passing through the pieces and which Abram acknowledges in Genesis 17 by circumcision. As a result, Abram and Sarah are renamed Abraham and Sarah, and the history of the people of Israel begins. The covenant continues through the various generations of the ancestors, Isaac and Rebekah; Jacob, Rachel and Leah, and the handmaidens; the twelve sons of Jacob who become the ancestors of the twelve tribes of Israel. The Mosaic period, including the Exodus from Egypt, the revelation of Torah at Sinai, and the period of wilderness wandering, are formative events in the identity of the nation Israel. Finally, the land of Israel is granted to the people in return for their continued observance of YHWH's covenant.

Clearly, Israel in the Hebrew Bible is constituted as a nation holy to YHWH and a kingdom of priests (Exod 19:6). This has important implications, particularly in relation to the role that Torah and Temple play in relation to the created world order. As a holy people and kingdom of priests, Israel is selected by YHWH to serve as the holy center of all the nations of the earth, i.e., just as the Temple and priesthood of Israel stands as the holy center of the people in its relationship with YHWH, so Israel stands as the holy center of the nations and all creation in their relationship with. The Bible is careful to specify that Israel was chosen for this role not by any special merit, but merely because YHWH chose to keep the promises to Israel's ancestors (Deut 9:4-7). Israel's experiences thereby become an example for the nations (or all creation) that witness YHWH's power at the Red Sea (Exod 15:13-18), YHWH's punishment of Israel for not observing YHWH's covenant (Isa 1:2-31), and YHWH's restoration of Israel after the punishment is completed (Isa 45:20-25; 49:1-6). Indeed, the Hebrew Bible makes it clear that the nations and all creation will come to YHWH through Israel at the Jerusalem Temple/Zion (Isa 2:2-4; 60-62; Haggai).

To a large extent, the Hebrew Bible presents Israel as a theological construct that is tied to the order of creation and the recognition of YHWH as the creator by the nations. But the socio-historical reality that stands behind and informs that construct must also be considered. In order to establish and maintain this self-conception, the nation of Israel requires all of the normal religious, political, social, and economic characteristics of any nation of its time, and it must implement an ideology that sees these characteristics as divinely ordained in relation to its role as the center of creation. Aspects of the ideology of the Temple and priesthood have been treated above, but "secular" elements, such as the monarchy, the tax system, and the legal system of social justice must be treated as well.

The monarch is obviously a key figure in defining the character of the Israelite or Judean state. Although the Bible provides little information concerning the ideology of the various northern dynasties, it contains a great deal of information concerning the theological character of the Davidic monarchy of Israel and Judah. Like the nation Israel, the royal house of David understands itself to have been chosen by YHWH, and indeed, this sense of royal chosenness may well undergird Israel's general concept of itself as YHWH's chosen people.[33] The Davidic king enjoys a symbiotic relationship with YHWH; just as David and his successors established and maintained YHWH's sanctuary in Jerusalem, so YHWH established and protected the house of David (see esp. Psalm 132). The Davidic king is considered as YHWH's 'son," and YHWH defends the king, the Temple, Jerusalem and nation from foreign threats (see Psalm 2).

The Davidic king rules with the authority of YHWH. He therefore has the right to collect revenues from the people to support the Temple and the monarchy itself in order to ensure the continuity of that rule (cf. 1 Sam 8). As the example of Solomon demonstrates, he also has the responsibility not to abuse that rule by imposing undue burdens upon the people or by abusing his authority (1 Kings 3-11). Overall, the means provided to the king and the priesthood to obtain such support from the people appears in the requirement imposed upon all Israelite males to provide one-tenth of their income, i.e., cattle, sheep and goats, grain, wine, and oil, to the state at the Temple during the three major Temple holidays: Passover, Shavuot, and Sukkot (Exod 23:14-19; 34:18-26; Deut 16:1-17; 26:1-15).[34] Such sacrifices are sanctified as offerings at the Temple to support the Levitical priesthood and the monarchy. Furthermore, Israelite men are required to serve in the army at times of crisis, although newlywed men are exempted from military service for one year so that they may have some time with their wives to begin a family and thereby establish a line of inheritance (Deut 24:5).

The king is responsible for establishing YHWH's justice and righteousness among the people, and he must therefore apply YHWH's Torah in carrying out the rule of the nation. To this end, he reads a copy of YHWH's Torah under the supervision of the Levitical priests (Deut 17:14-20) and serves as the chief judge of the people (cf. 1 Kings 3). It is important to note therefore that the legal corpus in Exodus, Leviticus, Numbers, and Deuteronomy does not take up only ritual or priestly law, but civil and criminal law that is designed to apply YHWH's sense of justice to the social life of the people. The fundamental principle concerning the payment of "an eye for an eye, a tooth for a tooth, etc." (Exod 21:23-27; Lev 24:13-23; Deut 19:21) is designed to establish the fundamental principle of a just punishment for a crime or compensation for a loss and thereby to define the boundaries by which a legal claim may be settled.[35] Furthermore, Israel's legal system can change according to the social realities of the time.[36] For example, the law regulating debt slavery in the Covenant Code stipulates the terms by which an Israelite man will serve as a slave, i. e., he comes in with nothing and goes out with nothing (Exod 21:1-11), but the later Deuteronomic Code stipulates that he is to be paid by his master for his services at the end of his term and that women are to be released on the same terms as the men (Deut 15:12-18). Israelite law treats all manner of situations in social life, e.g., murder, manslaughter, theft, marriage, rape, warfare, commerce, damages, the residency of foreigners, etc., with the goal of creating and maintaining a just, orderly, and viable society defined according to YHWH's Torah or sense of justice.

In general, the Hebrew Bible postulates Israel as an ongoing nation that stands at the center of creation as a well-ordered and just society that embodies the principles of YHWH's Torah at the center of its religious and social life.

VI

The people or nation of Israel is intended to be an ongoing reality that does not come to an end in the Hebrew Bible (see Genesis 15; 17). Nevertheless, the continuity of Israel was threatened at various junctures which required theological reflection and response. The Assyrian destruction of the northern kingdom of Israel in 722/1 B.C.E. and the Babylonian destruction of Judah, Jerusalem, and the Jerusalem Temple in 587/6 B.C.E. challenged the fundamental world view of the people of

Israel that it was their all powerful G-d who offered them security in the land of Israel. Just as the modern experience of the Shoah has provoked a wide variety of responses that seek to come to some understanding of the catastrophe,[37] so the destruction of the Jerusalem Temple and the earlier destruction of northern Israel prompted a wide variety of approaches within the Hebrew Bible to understanding this catastrophe. Overall, the issue must be construed as the Bible's attempts to wrestle with the problems of evil or theodicy.[38]

Perhaps the most fundamental response to the problem of evil in the Hebrew Bible is to maintain that the people of Israel somehow failed to observe their obligations in relation to their covenant with YHWH, and therefore they deserved the punishment that was inflicted upon them. Such a perspective appears throughout the Bible in the Pentateuch, Former Prophets, Latter Prophets, the Psalms, Ezra-Nehemiah, and Chronicles which characterize various disasters that affected the people of Israel as punishment from G-d for Israel's failure to observe G-d's will or to believe in G-d's promises. Such a perspective is especially evident in Deuteronomy, which outlines the blessings that Israel will enjoy if it observes YHWH's covenant and the curses that it will suffer, especially exile from the land, if it fails to observe the covenant. Likewise, the Exodus-Numbers traditions point to Israel's rebellion against YHWH as an explanation for the forty years of wilderness wandering, the Deuteronomistic History points to Israel's idolatry as an explanation for the Assyrian destruction of Israel and the Babylonian exile, Amos points to abuses of social justice, Isaiah points to the failure of the house of David to believe in YHWH's promises, Ezekiel points to Israel's impurity, and the Psalms frequently rehearse Israel's history of sin against YHWH. Although these traditions have frequently been taken as proof that Israel is sinful and that it indeed deserved punishment, it must be recognized that such perspectives do not represent the reality of Israel's sin but only an attempt to explain the problem of evil in the Hebrew Bible. Overall, it reflects a commitment on the part of Israel itself to maintain or protect the righteousness of G-d, to take responsibility for its own misfortunes, and to learn from such experience so as not to repeat the mistakes of the past.

Concomitant with this view of Israel's sin is the argument that Israel's repentance or return to observance of YHWH's covenant will result in the restoration of Israel or the view that Israel will be restored once the punishment is complete. Such a view is evident especially among the prophets. Hosea, Amos, and Jeremiah call for Israel's return to YHWH, and Isaiah, Zephaniah, and Ezekiel envision Israel's restoration once the process of punishment and purification is completed. Isaiah and Ezekiel in particular also emphasize that Israel's punishment and restoration is a means by which YHWH demonstrates sovereignty over all creation and the nations, and Zechariah likewise points to the judgment against Jerusalem as a model for that against the nations at large. Heschel's treatment of divine pathos highlights the responsibility of human beings to undertake righteous action, and points to G-d's sorrow when human beings fail to carry out this responsibility.[39] As before, such explanations attempt to assert the righteousness of G-d by subsuming Israel's very survival and self-identity to some larger divine purpose.

Yet such responses do not represent the totality of the Bible's positions concerning the problem of evil or the righteousness of G-d. Perhaps the best known example is the book of Job, which posits that G-d can be capricious and yet accepts G-d's sovereignty over creation and thus the right to do as G-d chooses.[40] The book portrays Job, a Gentile, as an unquestionably righteous man who suffers affliction as the result of a "wager" between G-d and Satan as to whether or not Job will blaspheme against G-d with sufficient provocation. Through the use of Job's wife, his three friends, and Elihu, the book raises questions concerning the above stated views that posit reward for righteousness and punishment for sin, and it ultimately raises questions concerning the capacity of human beings to understand G-d. Nevertheless, it affirms the human right to question G-d, insofar as Job is judged to be righteous for doing so, although it continues to affirm YHWH's sovereignty and righteousness.

Several of the prophetic books, the Pentateuch, and the Former Prophets raise similar questions about G-d. Habakkuk, for example, demands to know how long G-d will allow violence to continue against Judah (Hab 1:24), only to recognize that it was G-d who brought the violence in the first place as a punishment for Judah (Hab 1:5-6). The issue is resolved to a certain extent when the book posits that the Babylonian oppressors will likewise be judged and punished (Habakkuk 2-3). Isaiah points to a similar scheme of reward and punishment, but it also posits that Isaiah's task is to make the people blind and deaf so that they will not understand and repent of their evil ways, thereby enabling G-d to demonstrate divine sovereignty over the entire world, i.e., Israel is to become a vicarious victim for G-d's greater purposes (see esp. Isaiah 6). Similar perspectives are evident in Exodus where YHWH hardens Pharaoh's heart so that he must be punished (Exodus 1-15) and Ezekiel in which the city of Jerusalem is sacrificed so that YHWH's holiness may pervade the entire earth (Ezekiel 1-11). Indeed, Moses must argue with G-d to prevent G-d from destroying Israel as this will not demonstrate divine power in the world but in fact compromise YHWH's reputation (Exodus 33; Numbers 14). Finally, the Deuteronomistic History blames the destruction of Jerusalem and the Babylonian exile on the sins of Manasseh, and thereby explains the suffering of an entire nation by the actions of one man (2 Kings 21). Such perspectives certainly raise questions about G-d who is willing to sacrifice people, and indeed to prevent their repentance, in order to demonstrate power and to achieve recognition by Israel, the nations, and all creation.

Other perspectives within the Bible accept the fact that evil exists in the world, and focus instead on the human reaction to such conditions and the human responsibility to act despite them. The Psalms, for example, frequently point to YHWH as the cause of evil suffered by the psalmist. Although they frequently posit YHWH's response to resolve the problems, they point to the need of the human being to address YHWH in times of crisis whether YHWH or the psalmist is the party responsible for the situation.[41] The book of Esther is particularly pertinent in that the Hebrew version of the book that is employed in the Tanak, unlike the Greek versions that stand as Christian scripture, does not mention G-d at all, and instead points to human beings as the sole protagonists in the narrative. Despite the many efforts to read G-d into the book by one means or another, the absence of G-d in Esther must be understood as deliberate so that the book thereby asserts the human responsibility to act in the face of evil when G-d fails to do so.[42] Such views of human responsibility may well stand behind the Sodom and Gomorrah narratives in which Abraham challenges G-d's righteousness by arguing that G-d cannot destroy the righteous with the wicked. G-d accepts Abraham's critique, and G-d is vindicated when the cities prove to be so evil that even ten righteous people are not found in them, Indeed, Abraham's acceptance of G-d's righteousness is highlighted when he does not protest G-d's command to sacrifice his son Isaac, even though such a command is inherently evil and risks the destruction of the entire covenant relationship between YHWH and Abraham. The Genesis narrative raises the question of G-d's righteousness and it resolves this question by maintaining that G-d is in fact righteous, but it also highlights the human responsibility to challenge even G-d when G-d is perceived to act wrongfully.

The Tanak asserts a wide variety of responses to the problem of evil or theodicy that range from attempts to explain suffering as a result of human sin to attempts to question G-d's power or righteousness. It stops short, however, in that it never advocates the rejection of G-d altogether.

VII

Finally, the role of later Jewish tradition must be considered in relation to the development of Jewish biblical theology. Throughout the period of the Enlightenment, modern critical scholarship has maintained that the Bible must be interpreted according to objective historical critical criteria and that post-biblical tradition, whether Jewish or Christian, should play little or no role in the interpretation of the biblical text. Such a view presupposes that the Bible must be understood in relation to the ancient setting in which it was written and which determined its perspectives on the world and the questions which it addressed. The rise of post-modernism has challenged Enlightenment modes of interpretation by questioning whether objective interpretation of the Bible is possible at all, given the inherent subjectivity of the interpreter particularly in relation to the religious traditions and world views that shape any biblical reader.[43]

The rise of post-modern interpretation clearly opens the way for the influence of post-biblical Jewish tradition in the enterprise of Jewish biblical theology. The Bible functions as a part of Jewish tradition, and it must continue to interact with the entirety of that tradition. Indeed, the classical sources of Rabbinic tradition, i.e., the Mishnah, the Talmuds, the Midrashim, and the Targums, as well as the various writings of ancient Jewish mystical tradition, the medieval philosophical works, the Kabbalah, the halakhic works, the exegetical writings, the various forms of the prayer book, and other works of Hebrew and Jewish literature throughout the ages are more or less indebted to the biblical literature for their language, ideas, and literary forms of expression. Indeed, the Tanak itself with its three-fold structure of Torah, Nevi'im, and Ketuvim is the product of Rabbinic Judaism.

Insofar as these works grow out of the biblical tradition and develop, extend, reformulate, and even oppose its ideas and language, they must play a role in Jewish biblical theology. Thus, the Mishnah and the Talmud are arranged so that they will provide guidance for the reconstruction of a Jewish state once the period of exile is over.[44] Although they presuppose the destruction of the Jerusalem Temple by the Romans, the pattern for such reconstruction derives from the biblical presentation of the

Babyloian exile and the post-exilic restoration. Likewise, the Rabbinic view of Torah as a comprehensive epistemological concept is derived from the many explicit statements concerning G-d's Torah noted above and the assertion of Proverbs 8 that Wisdom preceded and influenced creation. Likewise, Ezekiel's vision, the creation account, Daniel, Song of Songs, and many of the Psalms influenced the development of the mystical tradition with its concerns for devising means by which human beings could understand and relate to G-d and creation. Similar concerns appear in the philosophical tradition, which owes much to Genesis, Job, and the prophetic books among others.

Modern Jewish movements and experience must also be considered. Indeed, the major branches of Judaism have their respective views concerning the revelation of Torah at Sinai, i.e., Reform posits that G-d's revelation at Sinai calls for continuous innovation and change; Conservative Judaism maintains that Judaism continues to be revealed throughout history in a process that begins at Sinai as the Jewish people define Judaism; Reconstructionist Judaism takes this a step further by asserting that the Jewish people also define the understanding of G-d; and the various branches of Orthodox Judaism maintain that the revelation at Sinai does not change so that process of discovering all of G-d's revelation at Sinai is an ongoing task.[45] The various perspectives of modern Diaspora Judaism, the above-noted discussion of the Shoah, and the modern Zionist movement, among others, require consideration as well.[46]

The problem comes in recognizing what is biblical and what is not, although this issue is perhaps more important to Protestant Christian biblical theology with its concern for basing theology on the Bible alone. Nevertheless, later Jewish tradition cannot be imposed upon the Tanak, although it must always engage in dialogue with it. Indeed, this process of dialogue begins within the Tanak itself as study of the phenomenon of inner-biblical interpretation and exegesis demonstrates.[47] Thus, the laws of Deuteronomy frequently reformulate those of Exodus and Numbers;[48] Jeremiah can oppose Isaiah's assertions that YHWH will protect Zion and the house of David (Jeremiah 27-28); Job can question Proverbs' assertion that fear of YHWH is the beginning of wisdom (Job 28); and Chronicles can reformulate the history presented in Samuel and Kings.

Indeed, Jewish tradition is a process of dialogue, with G-d, within itself, and with the outside world.[49] This essay hardly exhausts the issues and studies that might be included in such dialogue. Nevertheless, it provides some perspective on the emerging field of Jewish biblical theology, which presents another means by which Jews may understand and express Judaism and thereby to continue to make it a living force in the world of the present and the future. ✡

Endnotes

1. See the essays published in Leon A. Jick, ed., *The Teaching of Judaica in American Universities: The Proceedings of a Colloquium* (New York: Ktav, 1970); S. David Sperling, ed., *Students of the Covenant: A History of Jewish Scholarship in North America* (Atlanta: Scholars Press, 1992).

2. E.g., Frederick E. Greenspahn, ed., *Scripture in the Jewish and Christian Traditions: Authority Interpretation, Relevance* (Abingdon: Nashville, 1982); Roger Books and John J. Collins, eds., *Hebrew_Bible or Old Testament: Studying the Bible in Judaism and Christianity* (Notre Dame: University of Notre Dame Press, 1990).

3. At present, only brief surveys of the field of Jewish biblical theology are available. See, for example, Gerhard Hasel, *Old Testament Theology: Basic Issues in the Current Debate* (4th edition; Grand Rapids: Eerdmans, 1991) 34-38; Brevard S. Childs, *Biblical Theology of the Old and New Testaments: Theological Reflection on the Christian Bible* (Minneapolis: Fortress, 1992) 25-26. See also Marvin A. Sweeney, "Reconceiving the Paradigms of Old Testament Theology in the Post-Shoah Period," *Biblical Interpretation* 6 (1998) 142-161.

4. See Hasel, *Old Testament Theology* 10-27; Childs, *Biblical Theology* 3-6; John H. Hayes and Frederick Prussner, *Old Testament Theology: Its History and Development* (Atlanta: John Knox 1985) 1-71. Cf. M. H. Goshen-Gottstein, "Christianity, Judaism, and Modern Bible Study," *Congress Volume: Edinburgh 1974* (VTSup 28; Leiden: E. J. Brill, 1975) 69-88; idem, "Jewish Biblical Theology and the Science of the Religion of the Bible," *Tarbiz* 50 (1980-81) 37-64 (Hebrew); idem, "Tanakh Theology: The Religion of the Old Testament and the Place of Jewish Biblical Theology," in Patrick D. Miller, Jr., Paul D. Hanson, S. Dean McBride, eds., *Ancient Israelite Religion: Essays in Honor of Frank Moore Cross* (Philadelphia: Fortress, 1987) 617-644.

5. Gerhard von Rad, *Old Testament Theology*, trans. by D. M. G. Stalker; New York: Harper and Row, 1962-65).

6. Childs, *Biblical Theology*; see also his *Old Testament Theology in a Canonical Context* (Philadelphia: Fortress, 1986).

7. "Why Jews are not Interested in Biblical Theology," *The Hebrew Bible. the Old Testament and Historical Criticism: Jews and Christians in Biblical Studies* (Louisville: Westminster John Knox, 1993) 33-61, 165-170; originally published in Jacob Neusner, Baruch A. Levine, Ernest S. Frerichs, eds., Judaic *Perspectives on Ancient Israel* (Philadelphia: Fortress, 1987) 281-307.

8. See also Jon D. Levenson, *The Death and Resurrection of the Beloved Son: The Transformation of Child Sacrifice in Judaism and Christianity* (New Haven and London: Yale University Press, 1993), in which he discusses the Church's appropriation of the transformation of child sacrifice in the Hebrew Bible (e.g., Genesis 22) to assert its own sense of chosenness and supersession of Judaism.

9. Julius Wellhausen, *Prolegomenon to the History of Ancient Israel* (Gloucester, MA: Peter Smith, 1973/1885) 1.

10. Walter Eichrodt, *Theology of the Old Testament* (Old Testament Library; 2 volumes; J. A. Baker; Philadelphia: Westminster, 1961-67) 1:26.

11. For fuller discussion, see Marvin A. Sweeney, "Why Jews Should Be Interested in Biblical Theology," *CCAR Journal* 44/1 (Winter, 1997) 67-75.

12. See, for example, Ezekiel 1 with its reticent attempt to portray G-d visually. Cf. mHagigah 2:1, which warns against the exposition of Ezekiel 1 (and Genesis 1; Leviticus 18) except by a sage with full understanding of Jewish tradition. Note its statement, "and whosoever takes no thought for the honour of his Maker, it were better for him if he had not come into this world" (Herbert Danby, *The Mishnah* [Oxford: Oxford University Press, 1977] 213). For a modern attempt to address the nature of G-d without attempting to define G-d visually or otherwise, see Martin Buber, *I and Thou*, trans. by Walter Kaufmann (New York: Charles Scribner's, 1970).

13. For assessments of the role of human beings, both men and women, in Jewish theology, see Joseph B. Soloveitchik, "The Lonely Man of Faith," *Tradition* 7 (1965) 5-67; idem, *Halakhic Man*, trans. by Lawrence Kaplan (Philadelphia: Jewish Publication Society, 1983); Judith Plaskow, *Standing Again at Sinai: Judaism from a Feminist Perspective* (New York: Harper Collins, 1990).

14. E.g., Franz Rosenzweig, *The Star of Redemption*, trans. by William Hallo (Notre Dame: University of Notre Dame Press, 1985/1970).

15. E.g., Buber, *I and Thou*.

16. For examples of work by Christian theologians who accept this premise, see Clark Williamson, *A Guest in the House of Israel* (Louisville: Westminster John Knox, 1993); Paul van Buren, " On Reading Someone Else's Mail: The Church and Israel's Scriptures," in Erhard Blum, Christian Machholz, Ekkehard W. Stegemann, eds.,*Die Hebraische Bibel und ihre zweifache Nachgeschichte* (Festschrift. Rolf Rendtorff; Neukirchen-Vluyn: Neukirchener, 1990) 595-606; Rolf Rendtorff, "Toward a Common Jewish Christian Reading of the Hebrew Bible," *Hebrew Bible or Old Testament?* (eds. Brooks and Collins) 89-108; reprinted in his *Canon and Theology* (Overtures to Biblical Theology; Minneapolis: Fortress, 1993) 31-45.

17. For a study of the continuity of the Jewish people as a civilization, see S. N. Eisenstadt, *Jewish Civilization: The New Historical Experience in a Comparative Perspective* (SUNY Series in Israeli Studies; Albany: SUNY, 1992).

18. See Greenspahn, editor, *Scripture*; Magnee Saebø, editor, *Hebrew Bible/ Old Testament: The History of Its Interpretation, I/1: Antiquity* (Göttingen: Vandenhoeck & Ruprecht, 1996). See also Jon D. Levenson, "Historical Consensus or Historicist Evasion? Jews and Christians in Biblical Studies," *Hebrew Bible or Old Testament* (eds., Brooks and Collins) 109-145; reprinted in his *The Hebrew Bible, the Old Testament, and Historical Criticism: Jews and Christians in Biblical Studies* (Louisville: Westminster John Knox 1993) 82-106, 174-177.

19. See Goshen-Gottstein, "Tanakh Theology"; Rendtorff, "Toward a Cannon Jewish Christian Reading."

20. Goshen-Gottstein, "Tanakh Theology."

21. For a full discussion of this issue, see Marvin A. Sweeney, "Tanak versus Old Testament: Concerning the Foundation for a Jewish Theology of the Bible," in Henry T. C. Sun and Keith L. Eades, with James M. Robinson and Garth L. Mohler, eds., *Problems in Biblical Theology Essays in Honor of Rolf Knierim* (Grand Rapids and Cambridge: Eerdmans, 1997) 353-372.

22. See James A. Sanders, "First Testament and Second," *Biblical Theology Bulletin* 17 (1987) 47-50. For general discussion of the Christian canon, see now Roger T. Beckwith, *The Old Testament Canon of the New Testament Church* (Grand Rapids: Eerdmans, 1986).

23. For discussion of the Jewish canon, see esp. Sid Leiman, *The Canonization of Hebrew Scripture: The Talmudic and Midrashic Evidence* (Hamden, CT: Connecticut Academy of Arts and Sciences/Archon, 1976).

24. See Jon D. Levenson, "The Temple and the World," *Journal of Religion* 64 (1984) 275-298; idem, *Sinai and Zion: An Entry into the Jewish Bible* (Minneapolis: Winston Press, 1985); idem, "The Jerusalem Temple in Devotional and Visionary Experience," *Jewish Spirituality: From the Bible Through the Middle Ages* (ed., Arthur Green; New York: Crossroad, 1988) 32-61; Moshe Weinfeld, "Zion and Jerusalem as Religious and Political Capital: Ideology and Utopia," in Richard E. Friedman, ed., *The Poet and the Historian: Essays in Literary and Historical Biblical Criticism* (HSM 26; Chico: Scholars Press, 1983) 75-115.

25. S.v. "nomos," *Theological Dictionary of the New Testament* (ed., Gerhard Kittel; Grand Rapids: Eerdmans, 1967) 1022-1085.

26. Wellhausen, *Prolegomenon*.

27. BDB 434-436. Cf. Lev 10:11. See also "Torah," *Encyclopaedia Judaica*

15:1235-1246.

28. *Sinai and Zion* esp. 187-217.

29. Levenson, "The Jerusalem Temple in Devotional and Visionary Experience"; see also Israel Knoll, *The Sanctuary of Silence: The Priestly Torah and the Holiness School* (Minneapolis: Fortress, 1995); C. T. R. Hayward, *The Jerusalem Temple: A Non-biblical Sourcebook* (London and New York: Routledge, 1996).

30. Michael Fishbane, *Text and Texture: Close Readings of Selected Biblical Texts* (New York: Schocken, 1979) 3-16, 143-144, esp. 12 (citing Martin Buber, *Die Schrift und Ihre Verdeutschung* [Berlin: Schocken, 19361 39ff).

31. See also Levenson, "The Temple and the World."

32. See Harry M. Orlinsky, "The Biblical Concept of the Land of Israel: Cornerstone of the Covenant between G-d and Israel," *The Land of Israel: Jewish Perspectives* (ed., Lawrence A. Hoffman; Notre Dame: University of Notre Dame Press, 1986) 27-64. Contra many Christian theologians who view the land of Israel as YHWH's "gift" to Israel rather than as part of a binding contract that requires reciprocal action by Israel, e.g., Walter Brueggemann, *The Land* (Overtures to Biblical Theology; Philadelphia: Fortress, 1977).

33. For overviews of the concept of the chosen people or election, see "Chosen People," *Encyclopaedia Judaica* 5:498-502; Dale Patrick, "Election (Old Testament), " *ABD* 2:434-44 1.

34. See "Tithe," *Encyclopaedia Judaica* 15:1156-1162.

35. For the discussion of this principle in the Talmud, see Baba Kamma 83b-86b. For discussion of the Israelite/Judean legal system in general, see Moshe Greenberg, "Some Postulates of Biblical Criminal Law," *Studies in the Bible and Jewish Thought*, (Philadelphia and Jerusalem: Jewish Publication Society, 1995) 25-4 1; Jacob J. Finkelstein, *The Ox that Gored* (Transactions of the American Philosophical Society; Philadelphia: American Philosophical Society, 1981).

36. E.g. Bernard M. Levinson, *Deuteronomy and the Hermeneutics of Legal Innovation* (New York and Oxford: Oxford University Press, 1997).

37. For a survey and analysis of major responses to the Shoah, see Steven T. Katz, *Post-Holocaust_Dialogues: Critical Studies in Modern Jewish Thought* (New York and London: New York University Press, 1985). See also Zev Garber, *Shoah: The Paradigmatic Genocide. Essays in Exegesis and Eisegesis* (Studies in the Shoah VIII; Lanham: University Press of America, 1994); Emil L. Fackenheim *The Jewish Bible after the Holocaust: A Rereading* (Bloomington and Indianapolis: Indiana University Press, 1990); Rolf Rendtorff, "The Impact of the Holocaust (Shoah) on German Protestant Theology," *Horizons in Biblical Theology* 15 (1993) 154-167.

38. See James L. Crenshaw, "Theodicy," *Anchor* 6:444-447.

39. Abraham J. Heschel, *The Prophets* (New York: Harper and Row, 1962).
40. See James L. Crenshaw, *Old Testament Wisdom: An Introduction* (Atlanta: John Knox, 1981) 100-125.
41. See David Blumenthal, *Facing the Abusing G-d: A Theology of Protest* (Louisville: Westminster John Knox, 1993).
42. See Marvin A. Sweeney, "Absence of G-d and Human Responsibility in the Book of Esther," forthcoming in a volume of essays centered around the exegetical methodology of Rolf Knierim, edited by Wonil Kim, Deborah Eliens, Michael Floyd, and Marvin A. Sweeney (Eerdmans).Cf. Emil L. Fackenheim, *G-d's Presence in History: Jewish Affirmations and Philosophical Reflections* (New York: Harper Torchbooks, 1972), who argues that the Shoah obligates Jews to assert Jewish identity so as not to give Hitler a posthumous victory, and Eliezer Berkovitz, *Faith after the Holocaust* (New York: KTAV, 1973), who argues that G-d's hiding of the divine face must be understood as a divine means to prompt humans to assume responsibility for moral action in the world.
43. For an assessment of this shift and its impact upon Old Testament theology, see esp. Leo G. Perdue, *The Collapse of History: Reconstructing Old Testament Theology* (Overtures to Biblical Theology; Minneapolis: Fortress, 1994); cf. Sweeney, "Reconceiving the Paradigms."
44. See Jacob Neusner, *Rabbinic Political Theory: Religion and Politics in the Mishnah* (Chicago and London: University of Chicago Press, 1991).
45. For an overview of the major Jewish movements in America, see Marc Lee Raphael, *Profiles in American Judaism: The Reform, Conservative, Orthodox, and Reconstructionist Traditions in Historical Perspective* (San Francisco: Harper and Row, 1984).
46. See Charles S. Liebman and Steven M. Cohen, *Two Worlds of Judaism: The Israeli and American Experiences* (New Haven and London: Yale University Press, 1990); Shlomo Deshen, Charles S. Liebman, and Moshe Shoked, *Israeli Judaism: The Sociology of Religion in Israel* (New Brunswick and London: Transaction, 1995).
47. See Michael Fishbane, *Biblical Interpretation in Ancient Israel* (Oxford: Clarendon, 1985).
48. Levinson, *Deuteronomy and the Hermeneutics of Legal Innovation.*
49. See esp. Buber, *I and Thou.*

Chapter 5

Approaching the Text:
The Study of Midrash
Herbert W. Basser

In this chapter we offer methods to teach Midrash to students who have no background in the subject and also to students who have some such background. Being teachers we need to reflect upon the precise task our subject demands. In the ancient curricula of the Rabbis, the terms "Scripture" and "Midrash" appear side by side. Here Scripture referred to the teaching of the pronunciation and punctuation of Holy Writ (according to received tradition) and the literal meanings of texts (according to the understanding of the Bible-School master). On the other hand, Midrash referred to the more advanced teaching of the Rabbinic understanding of the Scriptures. This understanding was hidden beneath layers of intricate associations and structures, the very first words of the great *Genesis Rabba Midrash* tell us that the Holy Torah was a work of art which a first tutor could introduce to a child but which also had veiled meanings and hidden secrets. Some said it also contained "Alexandrian" allegories. This initial passage received due attention from the commentators who used these interpretive notions in their writings. The first century historian, Josephus, also introduces his *Antiquities* with similar notions as to how Scripture was written. Some of us may also be familiar with how Jesus began his Sermon on the Mount in Matthew's Gospel by saying he was coming to fill in Scripture; not to destroy it in the least. He then contrasted the way the teachers of tradition pronounced Scripture with his alternate (antithetical) pronunciations. For instance, "Love thy *rei'acha*" could mean *love thy friend,* implying that one could hate his/her enemy. Yet, read differently (but keeping the same Hebrew letters) the verse could say *"ra'echa,"* your enemy too. The reported conclusion must be that both "friend" and "enemy" are to be loved; so *rei'acha* here must mean "your fellow human." In religious Jewish communities Midrash functioned as the uncovering of the intended message of the "divine writings." It was to be separated from the reading of Scripture only in this: the role reading of Scripture (*miqra*) was a learned skill, not an intellectual exercise; Midrash was not only a skill and an intellectual exercise, but also the only conduit to the knowledge of God and His will.

For the professor, the question of how to teach Midrash arises with a peculiar set of problems at hand. The academic setting of the university will not permit the subject to be taught as the definitive sense of Scripture as it has been taught for millennia in the religious academy. It must be addressed as a subject in its own right. Yet the student must never lose sight of the intent of Midrash to uncover the truest senses of Scripture. The student must be taught first to see midrashic literature from the community's perspective and then to view it from an outside perspective. The student should attain some appreciation of the mystery inherent in Midrash by reflecting upon and analyzing some specimens of Midrash. This is a very difficult task. Properly it involves mastery of languages and literatures, an appreciation of the appropriate rabbinic mind-set, and an ability to solve obtuse problems.

The professor who teaches beginning survey courses in Judaism will be faced with introducing students to this very difficult subject matter. The professor will have only a few hours to excite the imaginations of the students. To grasp the nature of Midrash is important for the students of Rabbinic Judaism—Judaism being a religious tradition developed by midrashic imaginations.

Students find their ways into the classes for a variety of reasons. Their life situations have little in common with the scholars who produced Midrash or the modern interpreters of Midrash. The only way I know of dealing with this situation is to plunge the student into translated texts. Which texts? Assuredly, some texts work better than others to introduce students to the genre of midrashic literature. The suggestions which follow are based on one professor's personal experience. The first text was selected, not because it is typical, but because it can engender discussion. I prefer to use a simple Yerushalmi text and ignore a more elaborate parallel in the *Midrash Rabba*. Why select the simpler text to start? I propose that students initially should tackle material that they can appreciate readily. This approach builds confidence in the students' own abilities. The students, unhampered by a plethora of unfamiliar material, can engage in immediate analysis. However, it is important to move quickly along to more sophisticated and normative examples of Midrash. Good teachers try to prevent those barriers which will hinder the student in grasping the rich texture of the material. The intrigue of midrashic puzzle must be transmitted to the students. The religious genius behind the flow of the texts must be allowed to provoke wonder in the imaginations of the students. The instructor who shares this excitement will have solved much of the difficulty involved in teaching the pursuit of this stimulating literature.

I. Introductory Courses

Students sign up for the Introductory Judaism course for a variety of reasons; not the least of which is convenience. Some may find that the hour, location, or subject matter seems "convenient." These students generally have unrealistic expectations, thinking that the course is probably some "Old Testament through Jewish eyes" kind of course. Although these students, for the most part, drop the course after failing an initial test (designed to discourage such types), it is not unusual to receive final papers in which students are still trying to prove that the New Testament is the proper fulfillment of the Old Testament as opposed to the non-Christian view. While this in itself is not a bad beginning point to approach Midrash (with apologies to those NT scholars who see the Gospels as Midrash and may even see one Gospel as Midrash on another Gospel), survey courses in Judaism engender a wider scope of view and the Gospel measuring stick, if left unchecked proves counterproductive. The typical survey course covers the main Jewish political and intellectual movements (perhaps phenomena is a more apt word) from Biblical times to the present.

Four weeks into this course we encounter a topic termed "Rabbinic Judaism." For me this term connotes an ideology whose adherents see and saw their world in definitive structures which are recorded in Mishnaic, Midrashic, Talmudic, Gaonic, Rishonic, and Aharonic literatures. Although the unit follows the unit on the destruction of the Second Temple, no attempt is made to convince students that the ideology of the Rabbis originated after the Destruction in 70. Indeed, the arguments that this ideology in general is as ancient as, or in some cases even more ancient than Scripture, seem to me persuasive.[1] Be that as it may, I refrain from looking at the historical problems and questions in the Introductory course and instead concentrate on an appropriate sampling of the literatures. To cover the Midrash unit we have three one-hour periods. Although students will, at this point, be familiar with selected passages from Philo and Josephus, here too, I generally refrain from speculating on historical connections between various writers. I adopt the attitude that whatever information any piece of Jewish literature produces could be known through some other tradition and that Midrash is not a unique means to derive the new but a creative way to confirm the old. Thus it is not the "what" that is excit-

ing (although it will be new for my students) but the "how."
The teaching plan is drawn up and the game is afoot.

Lesson Plan, Day One:

I introduce the class to the notion of "the wise person," by asking a question like, "What do Joseph, the Soothsayer in Shakespeare's Julius Caesar and Daniel have in common? (The answer I want is "the sage solves riddles, turns the cryptic into the mundane and the curious into the obvious.")

I always plan to stress that the classic riddle is formed by the juxtaposition of items which seem to be so disparate that their mere presence on a given list seems unintelligible.[2] "What is black and white and red all over?" etc., etc. Solutions always find a common thread, and often times the common thread makes use of a pun or paranomasic play. The sage is the one who perceives the intelligible progression in the puzzle and continues it, spelling out the implications of the mysterious, baffling signs and symbols which are being interpreted. In sum, the question I ask concerning commonality between a number of names is fine for opening questions as it, too, is phrased as a riddle.

Next, I put on the board a sample of a riddle found in Rabbinic Literature. This riddle is a "solution" to a cryptic list. The list is given in the Talmud. But the "solution" also has to be explained:

> *"From Mandator to mandator*
> *From Notable to notable*
> *From Zealot to zealot*
> *From Parole to parole*
> *From the Clutch of the Hand of the Holy One, blessed*
> *be He, to the clutch of Moses' hand."* [3]

I show the students that the key to the little verse is found in the last line which identifies the scene of the verse as the *Giving of the Torah at Sinai from God to Moses.* Each line then identifies *God the Giver* and *Moses the receiver* by the same terms to show that Moses was the perfect representative for God. This is so because the same epithets apply to both God and Moses. But what was the list that spawned this verse. It was the list of the letters of the alphabet (Hebrew) which have dual forms and are always stated in a peculiarly unalphabetical order: m, n, z, p, c.[4] The names of the letters are made to yield epithets that can apply to both God and Moses: mem-mem (ma'amar-ma'-amar), nun-nun (ne'eman-ne'eman), zadi-zadi (zadik-zadik), peh-peh (peh-peh), caf-caf (caf-caf). The list in English reads: Mandator, Notable, Zealot, Parole, Clutch. Why does Hebrew have dual forms for these letters? Because they represent the twin terms which identify God and Moses as Divine and human counterparts. The Talmud notes that the children who composed this verse from the list were destined to become great Rabbinic sages.

I keep notes like the above in front of me while I teach. Sometimes I present the list first (as does the Talmud) and then the interpretive poem, and sometimes vice versa. I have found that, at times, one way is more effective and at other times, the other way is more effective. At any rate, by showing that the Hebrew letter *nun* is read as *ne'eman* (notable) or *mem as ma'amar* (mandator), I have begun to draw attention to the technique of paranomasia as an exegetical tool in Midrash. There will be not time for further discussion in this class. I give out copies of the following Midrashim on a prepared sheet and ask the student to work at half the questions on the sheets for the next class.

HOMEWORK SHEET - MIDRASH

A. Let the beloved come
    The son of the beloved
    And build the beloved
    For the beloved
    In the portion of the beloved
    That the beloveds may be purified there   (B.T. Menachot 53a).

B . Let the beloved come
     And build the beloved House
     For the beloved   (Sifrei Deut 352)

> 1. Let the beloved come—this refers to King Solomon as it is written, (the reference is to 2 Sam. 12:_)
>
> The son of the beloved—this refers to Abraham as it is written, ... (the reference is to Jer. 11:_)
>
> And build the beloved—this refers to the Holy Temple as it is written, (the reference is to Psalm 84:_)
>
> For the beloved —this refers to the Holy One, blessed be He, as it is written, ... (the reference is to Isaiah 5:_)

In the portion of the beloved—this refers to Benjamin as it is written,   (the reference is to Deut 33:_)

That the beloveds may be purified there—this refers to Israel, as it is written,... (the reference is to Jer.12:_) (B.T. Menachot 53a)

2.   Then let Israel come who are called the beloveds
    The son of Father (Abraham) who is called "beloved"
    and build the Holy Temple which is called "beloved"
    In the portion of Benjamin who is called "beloved," thus is
    it written,...(the reference is to Deut 33:_).
    For the Holy One,blessed be He,who is called"beloved"(Sifrei
    Deut 352)

3.   Let the beloved come—Let Israel come who are called "beloveds"
    The son of the beloved - the children of Abraham who is called
    "beloved"
    And build the beloved - and build the Holy Temple which is
    called "beloved"
    For the beloved(s)-in the portion of Benjamin who is called
    "beloved"
    In the portion of the beloved - for the Holy One, blessed be He.
        (Yalkut Shimoni Deut. B'racha 955 and compare Sifrei
        Deut 352)

    a.   Match "A" with one of 1., 2.,or 3.,match "B" with one of
        1., 2., or 3.

    b.   Which version do you think is the most original version?

    c.   Compare 2. and 3.Which text seems corrupt? What is the
        nature of the corruption?

    d.   In version "B," who do you think "beloved" refers to:
        Solomon or Israel?

    e.   What is the problem in identifying Solomon as the son of
        Abraham? What is the problem in identifying Israel as the
        builders of the Temple?

    f.   Do you think version "B" is the earliest or latest version of
        all versions given here? Argue the merits of its being the
        earliest version, of its being the latest version.

g. Three looks like the solution to a riddle. Reconstruct the riddle.

h. Which versions are riddles and which solutions?

i. What unstated list of words has generated this cycle of midrashim?

j. In what ways are these midrashim like the verse about the dual letters? In which ways are they different?

k. Fill in the numbers of the verses in the references by consulting a Bible. Why are these verses suitable verses? Describe the exegetical principles involved in each case.

l. Why do some versions omit the verse?

m. In what ways do these versions address Israel's past history, her future history?

n. Are these versions Midrashim or poems? What do you think the best setting for expounding these verse-like Midrashim was: synagogue, temple, school?

o. Who is the supposed speaker of these riddles and when in history would our midrashist think these words were spoken?

p. What is the effect of having God, Israel, the Temple, Abraham, etc. identified by a common, single term?

q. Which text is introduced by the phrase "six are called beloveds"?

Do a. through i. for next class and j. through q. for the following class.

In every section of Midrash that I teach, I try to point out three things: (a) the Rabbinic viewpoint that is being reinforced, (b) how this view is read out of a scripture that seems indifferent to the particular point, and (c) the literary form that identifies the teaching as Rabbinic. In the case at hand I offer the view that #2 provides the best clue to the original, Palestinian formulation which I reconstruct as follows:

Let the beloved come, the son of the beloved.
And build the beloved in the portion of the beloved.
For the beloved.

Thus "the son of the beloved" and "in the portion of the beloved" simply modify Israel and the Temple respectively and do not function as separate units. "B" illustrates the essential teaching of the Palestinian tradition: Israel, Temple, and God function as a unit, as a single term. Even when Israel is castigated, these terms - beloved, beloved, beloved - function. The Palestinian tradition centers upon the renewal of Zion and the Temple and may not necessarily only reflect past history. On the other hand, the Babylonian tradition "A" adds a sixth line such that the builder of the Temple is now identified as Solomon. This forces the focus of the passage to refer to past history and also moves around the lines so that the "purification" line follows immediately after the "portion" line. Thus the "for the beloved" and "in the portion of the beloved" trade places in "A". In Yalkut Shimoni we find the Palestinian text as in Sifre, the explanations of the last two lines are in the Palestinian order, i.e., *Benjamin,* followed by *the Holy One.* However, the beginnings of the lines "for the beloved" and "in the portion of the beloved" are in the reversed, Babylonian Talmud position such that the two halves of each sentence do not match. Sifre texts actually read "Six are called *beloved"* as does the Babylonian tradition. Even so, Sifre lists only five *beloveds* unlike the Babylonian Talmud which lists six *beloveds.* It would appear that copyists have confused the two traditions somewhat. However, it is remotely possible that the Babylonian Talmud actually preserves the oldest of the traditions, dating back to Second Temple times and that the traditions in the Palestinian sources are later (looking to the restoration of Temple). The point is not to solve these issues but to discuss them by using the selected texts in some coherent system of explanation. This is all I distribute for this unit. I know some teachers who give their students lists of the various critical editions of Midrashim and bibliographies concerning Midrash. But I think any survey course becomes entangled in thorny detail if too much is attempted. The teacher must clearly recognize his/her goal and not let any other issues cloud the presentation. I therefore concentrate on these seventeen questions.

Lesson Plan, Day Two:

I expect some students have done work and others have not. I read the question, ask a student to respond, if the answer is what I wanted, I write it on the board, if not, I give my answer and ask who has similar answers and we discuss them for a few minutes pointing out their merits or problems. I spend no more than 5 minutes on each question and at the end of the period I have my answers on the board which represent my opinions and I let the class know this. Next, I assign the reading of the English translation of Bialik's article on "Halakhah and Aggadah" and let the class know that I will take up the remaining nine questions on the last day of this unit, the next class.[5]

The last class requires no specific plan. The class is simply a continuation of day two. If the presentation seems cursory and rushed, it is. Introductory courses are meant to introduce topics for further study, not to settle issues. By following the regimen I have outlined, more or less, I intend to prepare students to respect the study of Midrash as an academic inquiry. One should always aim for intelligent discussion on a limited topic. Examinations and papers reflecting these discussions are necessary to challenge students, to keep them actively engaged in the course, and to insure honest feedback on the effectiveness of the teaching methods utilized by the instructor.

II The Teaching of a Course in Midrash Translation

Such a course presents unique challenges. The selection of materials is important and each teacher may decide upon some personal cluster of Midrashim which he/she senses can be shaped into keys to unravel the corpus in general. Here, I will offer my suggestions, but it must be understood that my preferences hinge upon a personal predilection for Midrashim which bear upon halachic teachings. I like such traditions because they present an added problem for the reader: the question of which halachic text is, in fact, being commented upon.

If Bialik is correct in that *Aggadah,* unrestrained by the practical considerations of *Halakhah,* may give rise to outlandish notions in shaping hope, courage and aspiration, the reverse is also true. Halakhah is a vast literature, each sentence of which interconnects with every other sentence, reaching every nook and corner of possible human behavior. It is an enterprise which has united Jews as a whole, set them apart from others, and led to schisms within Judaism itself. But the student of Halakhah without Aggadah would lack social memory and religious impetus. To follow the dictates of Halakhah, people need story, comprehension, art. We must feel the imperative from within, know its justice and experience its "perfect fit."

I generally begin the first week of a course in midrash in translation by doing just the thing I do in the survey course. However, in the survey course, there is no time to discuss Bailik's essay.[6] After the initial week, in the "translation" course, I discuss Bialik's essay. I then introduce the students to Mishnah Shabbat 2:6 in translation, which presents a list of three items. The relationship amongst these items is not clear and therefore calls for interpretation.

Let us look at this Mishnah in Shabbat(2:6):"Women die in childbirth for die commission of three sins: taking laxities in regard to menstrual laws, dough-offerings and candle lightings." Here we encounter an excellent example of a troublesome statement in the Mishnah. By careful questioning, the teacher will be able to show the students that the statement cannot be lightly dismissed for the simple reason that it is Mishnah (and thus "canonical"). Let us see some midrashic literature on these themes.

(Selection: Tannu Rabbanan, etc., Appendix)

After some discussion as to why the Rabbis understood "delight" to refer to having candles lit, the teacher focuses on the word *man (Adam)*. Does this mean only man? Does it refer to any Jew (man or woman)? Can it refer to a non-Jew? After some discussion of the materials within the context they are found, one may decide that we are dealing here probably with the notion of a *man*, but that the term could possibly refer to a woman. We then turn our attention to how Lam 3:17 implies an obligation for candle lighting.[7] Rashi explains B.T. Shab 25b to mean that a meal is not a delight without light and to mean that Lam.3:17 suggests that light is a delight since one can see to eat or avoid injury through falling. But we have no source showing that the obligation was given to women (the verse is phrased in the masculine form). An early midrashic poem confirms that candle lighting (dough offerings and blood laws) were meant for all, men and women. B.T. Shabbat 31b reads:

(See selection from B.T. Shabbat, Appendix)

Is there anything at all in this poem which suggests that these commandments of blood, offerings, candles apply specifically to women? The poem itself is phrased in the masculine. Let us now examine the poem in detail. What can be said about its use of repetition of sounds, which is apparent even in English translation? What is the significance of the grouping of items in Mishnah which this poem alludes to? Notice the progression of the poem which follows the progression of the Mishnah but here takes on fuller shape:(a) physical life blood,(b) covenantal election, and (c) spiritual life. Body, election and soul are tied together with the obligations outlined in the Mishnah. The Mishnah's grouping is not merely explained, it is given cosmic significance which revolves around human creation, Israel's election, and spiritual existence. Note how the unity of these obligations is stressed by the repetitive cadence of the lines, and half-lines.

The following Midrashim know that some traditions did not speak of these obligations in terms of woman solely and contain the query, "Why were these commandments given to women as implied in the Mishnah (and similar literatures)?"

(See selections from Tanhuma Noah 1, Tanhuma Buber Noah 1, Appendix)

These two texts above should be compared, their differences noted and discussed. Students should be asked to compare these traditions with the text in Gen.R.17 (end) which omits proof texts (or were they later added to the above traditions?). The teacher may wish to compare the texts with those found in Printed Tanhuma Mezora 9 and Buber Mezora 17. The quotation of the Mishnah Shabbat which is found in many of these sources may or may not be the original source for these traditions and that question should also be discussed. Gen.R.17:13 reads:

(See selection from Gen.R.17, Appendix)

These texts should be read and discussed thoroughly by the students and teacher. It is important in each case to see:

(a)   what problems the texts answer,

(b)   how the texts make their points,

(c)   what problems these texts create.

The salient points for discussion here touch upon such issues as the source texts upon which these Midrashim are based (Mishnah, Toseftah, other) and the nature of the recording and the transmission of these Midrashim.

Without too much of a lapse the teacher can now introduce two versions of the Midrash found in Avot de Rabbi Nathan B,ch.9. These texts do not supply proof texts. Is this because the versions with the proof texts were so well known or is it because these texts represent an older version which did not have proof texts? Is the rhyme and meter of the poetic versions (of which the proof texts break the rhythm) necessarily proof that these texts were originally promulgated without proof texts?

The text of Avot de R. Nathan contains Mishnah Shabbat 2:6, and presently functions as a commentary upon it much as the Tanhuma and Yerushalmi texts appeared to. Whether or not these texts are actually based upon our Mishnah or upon some related tradition, not connected with childbirth, is a moot point. David Weiss Halivni, *Mekorot Umessorot* (vol.3,p.94), suggests that the more original traditions of the Mishnaic teaching did not mention death in childbirth, but only death. What can be said in support or in contradiction to his thesis in regard to our Midrashim? Avot de Rabbi Nathan B,ch.9:

(See text in Appendix)

The teacher should then present the Talmud Yerushalmi Shabbat to Mishnah 2:6. The passage bears an obvious relationship to the Midrashim we have just looked at. This Midrash seems to have been cast in rhymed form (perhaps the first line should be amended so that it ends with *haya* - was). The Toseftah is uniquely presented as a rhyme so that it ends with *"hadlakah* (lighting)" and omits the mention of *"ner* (candle)" found throughout the other legal and homiletic traditions. It thereby completes the rhyme.

(See text of Talmud Yerushalmi Shabbat, Appendix)

Now that the student has had a wide view of the texts, a number of pertinent issues can be addressed. The students may be asked to prepare a short essay discussing the philosophic thrust of the various Midrashim. The theology inherent in B.T. Shabbat seems more towards the maintenance of the world through *imatatio dei*. Through specific commandments, e.g., the list found in traditions like Mishnah Shabbat 2:6, Israel preserves, by imitation, the divine act of creation and election. The marked, balanced cadence of the tradition and its poetic phrasing make it especially apt for this message.

The other Midrashim and the Yerushalmi tradition, in the spirit of measure for measure, present the Tannaitic list of commandments given to women as a benevolent remedy for the collective sins against Adam which Eve had originally committed. The form of these Midrashim, with their balanced rhymes of "crime and atonement," is suited for the message.

Whether one likes the one tradition, or another, the artistic interpretations of the apparently incongruent list of female obligations on the Mishnah, cannot fail to make its impression. Some students may feel that these "solution" traditions were created for women and children, the poetic quality not suiting the serious tone of the study halls, but such conjectures (while worthwhile making) cannot be proven or disproven.

A central question must now be asked. Do these "solution" Midrashim explain, in reality, the rationale for Mishnah Shabbat and its related traditions, or were they promulgated after the fact to explain the seemingly incongruent list found in these traditions. Maimonides, Mishnah

Torah *Yad* Sabbath Laws 5:1, tells us that the list, in the Mishnah which mentions the sins for which women die, reflects the sociological pattern that women customarily did these commandments because they were the ones who were home. it is worthwhile discussing Maimonides' view and asking on what basis he dismissed the reasons cited in the midrashim we have looked at. What would Maimonides have thought about these midrashim?

The students should be encouraged to compare the proof texts of the various sources and note their differences. For example, the Yerushalmi text uses a Biblical verse to show that Adam was the blood of the world ("And a mist went up ...") while this very verse is used to show that he was the dough offering of the world in other versions. Do we simply have a scribally misplaced text here, or has something else happened?

Once students begin working with the texts and familiarize themselves with the variations in the sources, they will concoct theories as to why one text differs from another. The wise professor is one who will place obstacles in the path of his students as they proceed, the idea being to get them to study by refining and testing ideas, not to discourage them from offering suggestions (no matter how outlandish).

Other texts can now be looked at and prepared by students.[8] The students will now, know to ask standard questions and should be allowed to expound upon pre-selected texts themselves. Thus seminars can be arranged, with a different student every week presenting a text which is then collectively discussed by the work in translation, the teacher, whose class is class. Since many texts will not work in translation, the teacher, whose class is reading in translation only, will need carefully selected texts where detailed knowledge of Hebrew is not basic to the comprehension of the Midrash. Occasionally, the teacher will have to explain a word play but generally one can either select Midrashim which are not dependent upon such devices or find English editions where the plays are explained in notes. For classes which read Hebrew, it is recommended that they use a scientific edition, if available.What should students read for such a course? Such authors as Alon, Bloch, Bowker, Daube, Finkelstein, Gerhardsson, Ginzberg, Heinemann, Herford, Kadushin, Lieberman, Marmorstein, Moore, and Urbach have done ample work in the field. For those who read Hebrew, two excellent works are: *Darkei Ha'aggadah* and *Toledot Ha'aggadah*.

literature, Hebrew language, comparative religion, modern Hebrew literature. It goes without saying that any student who wishes to proceed to do work in Rabbinic Judaism must be well-grounded in Midrashic texts.

III. Graduate Studies

Finally, a word should be said about students in graduate courses. Graduate students require very careful training. It is not advisable to accept students into a graduate program in Rabbinic literature unless they have demonstrated excellent language facilities and an intense working knowledge of Talmudic literature, medieval commentaries on Talmud, and halakhic process. It is, in my opinion, far easier to teach such a student Hellenistic Jewish Literature than to teach Talmud to one already adept in Hellenistic Jewish literature. The process of studying a Talmudic sentence involves much more technical knowledge than reading even the most difficult passage of Philo. Once the typology of Philo's system is understood, one can read with relative ease. Talmudic literature assumes a detailed knowledge of halakhic constructs on the part of the reader and much of it eludes interpretation even after many readings. The goal of graduate education in Midrash is to expose the student to various types of Midrash, to discuss their theologies and their world views.

No less important is the critical study of the text itself. Teachers have to teach the proper approach, by example, to the selection of better readings amongst variants, the use and misuse of parallels in deciphering texts, and notions of development of textual traditions. Students should be well read in the secondary literature, but they must also develop the skills and intuitions necessary to make decisions concerning the meaning of the texts they study. I think it advisable that students be asked to submit work in both Hebrew and English. Students will be more inclined to read and contribute to the Hebrew specialty journals in Midrash if they have experience with producing this type of material in its own idiom.

Finally, if there is any specific advice that can be offered it is this: classes should reflect concern with texts but also concern for people's feelings. Education at any level is not concerned with progress in a limited area but in the general intellectual development of a student. Students cannot develop properly if they bear hostility toward a subject area, a particular professor, or themselves. The cultivation of proper attitudes in the student, towards his/her own self, colleagues and teachers, and the discipline as a whole is what we mean by good education. A congenial atmosphere, a pleasant emotional climate in the classroom, and the mutual respect of achievements is necessary to promote high standards and excellence without resentment. It is amazing what students will do if they want to and what they will not do if they do not want to. ✡

APPENDIX

Mishnah Shabbat(2:6):

> Women die in childbirth for the commission of three sins: Taking laxities in regard to menstrual laws, dough-offerings and candle-lightings.

Tannu Rabbanan (the Rabbis studied as official tradition):

> From whence do we know that a man *(adam)* is obligated to be extremely punctilious in the obligation of candle lighting? From the verse which states, "And thou shalt declare the Sabbath a delight" (Is 58:13), which refers to the obligation of candle lighting.

> (See Tanhuma Buber Mezora 17, Printed Tanhuma Noah I and Midrash Leqah Tob Beshallah 16:8)

B. T. Shabbat 31b reads:

> A "measure of blood" I have given you
>   Concerning blood I have commanded you
> The "first of all" I have declared you
>   Concerning first offerings I have commanded you
> The soul which I gave you was called a "candle"
>   Concerning candles I have commanded you.

Printed Tanhuma Noah 1:

> Says the Holy one:
> First Adam at the head of my creatures had breath
> And received the order about the Tree of Knowledge
> But the Scripture says of Eve
> That the woman saw the tree ... and gave to her man to whom she

did cleave (Gen 3:6)
And since Scripture says, "Whoever spills the blood of Adam (man)
so within man shall his blood be spilled (Gen. 9:6)
Her blood is spilled as punishment in surety
And she observes the blood of menstrual purity
That it may atone, for the spilling of Adam's blood in perpetuity.
Why was the commandment of the dough offering given to them?
  Since she defiled the dough offering of the world
  As Rabbi Yosi ben Kezarta said just as when the dough becomes
  wet the woman takes her dough offering so did God act in creating
  first Adam, as it is said, "And a mist rose from the earth and wa-
  tered..." (Gen 2:6)
  and afterwards it states,
  And the Lord God created Adam of the dust ... "

Printed Tanhuma Noah I (continued):

Why was the commandment of candle lighting given them?
  She extinguished the candle of Adam (other texts: the world) as it
  is written, "God's candle is Adam's soul" (Prov 20-27), Thus shall
  she be obligated to observe the candle lightings.

Tanhuma Buber Noah I:

Since Adam was the head of His creation of the world and Eve
deceived him bringing upon him that which was said, "for thou art
dust and to dust thou shalt return"
So the Holy One said:
May there be given to her, the commandment of menstrual purity
That there may be atonement, for that blood which she spilled, in
perpetuity.

And why was the commandment of dough offering given to her:
  Since Adam was the dough offering of the world.
  And Eve came and defiled him
  So the Holy One said,
  May there be given her the commandment of dough offerings that
  will atone for her for the dough offering of the world which she
  defiled.

And from whence do we know that Adam was the dough offering of the world? Thus did our Rabbis teach: Rabbi Yosi ben Kezarta said just as when the dough becomes wet the woman takes her dough offering so *as* soon as the Holy One wet the earth be took Adam as the dough offering from it. This is as Scripture states, And a mist rose from the earth...(Gen 2:6) and afterwards it states, "And the Lord God created Adam of the dust..."

And why was the commandment of candle lighting given them?
Since Adam was the candle of the world (of the Holy One)
And Scripture states, "God's candle is Adam's soul' (Prov 20:27)
And Eve came and extinguished him
The Holy One said,
Let die commandment of the candle be given to her
In order to atone for the candle which she extinguished,

Gen.R.17. 13 reads:

And why was the commandment of menstrual purity given to her?
Since she spilled the blood of first Adam
Therefore the commandment of menstrual purity was given to her.

And why was the commandment of the dough offering given to her?
Since she defiled first Adam who was the completion of the dough offering of the world
Therefore the commandment of dough offering was given to her.

And why was the commandment of Sabbath candle lighting given to her?
Since she extinguished the soul of first Adam
Therefore the commandment of Sabbath candies was given to her.

Avot de Rabbi Nathan B, ch9:
For three sins women die in childbirth, because they do not observe carefully the commandment of menstrual purity or the commandment of dough offerings or the commandment of candle lighting.
Why was the commandment of menstrual purity given to women and not to man?

For Adam was the blood of the Holy One Blessed be He
Eve came and shed it
Therefore she was given the commandment of menstrual purity
In order to atone for the blood which she had spilled.

Why was the commandment of dough offering given to woman and
not to man?
For Adam was the pure dough offering of the Holy One blessed be
He,
And she defiled it
Therefore she was given the commandment of dough offerings
In order to atone for the dough offering she had defiled.

Why was the commandment of candle-lighting given to woman and
not to man?
Adam was the candle of the Holy One blessed be He who lit the
way for all who would be born
And she extinguished it.
Therefore she was given the commandment of candle-lighting
In order to atone for the candle she extinguished.

Talmud Yerushalmi Shabbat to Mishnah 2.6:

"When they are not careful about the laws of menstrual purity ... "
First Adam, the blood of the world (he was)
As it is written, "and a mist went up from the earth... "
Eve, of his death, was the cause
Thus was given to woman the menstrual laws.
And about the law of the dough offering:
Adam, the pure dough offering, for the world he was
As it is written, "And the Lord God formed Adam of the dust of
the earth.." And the tradition accords with what Rabbi Yosi ben
Kezarta said: "as soon as the dough becomes wet the woman takes
her dough offering."
Eve of his death, was the cause
Thus was given to woman the dough offering laws.

And about the law of candle lighting:
First Adam the candle of the world he was
As it is written, "God's candle is Adam's soul."
Eve, of his death, was the cause
Thus was given to woman the candle lighting laws.
We learn: Rabbi Yosi says
Three tentacles, which death do cause
There are
And the group of three to woman given was
And these they are
Menstrual laws, dough offering laws, and lighting laws.

Endnotes

1. See Ch. Tchernowitz, *Toledoth Hahalaka* (New York, 1934), pp. 197-223.
2. See A. Wunsche, *Die Rätselweisheit bei den Hebräern* (Leipzig, 1883) and G. *Nador, Jüdische Ratsel aus Talmud and Midrasch* (Köln, 1967).
3. Palestinian Talmud Megillah 1:9.
4. See Babylonian Talmud Megilla 2b.
5. See *Law and Legend* (Tr.J.L.Segal, New York, 1932) and *Halachah and Aggadah* (Tr.L.Simon, London, 1944). The Hebrew text can be found in *kol kitve H. N. Bialik* (Tel Aviv, 5725, reprinted from 5698 edition),p.216. See also "Halakhah and Aggadah," published anonymously in *Contemporary Jewish Record* VII, 1944, pp.663-67,677-80 (copyright 1944 by Commentary); an abridged version of "H and A" is found in *Modern Jewish Thought: A Source Reader,* ed. by Nahum N. Glatzer (N.Y.: Schocken Books, 1977; pp. 55-64).
6. The purpose of assigning this reading is to introduce students to the genre of Midrash through the writings of one of the century's ablest students of the genre. Bialik treats concerns of the artist by showing what the artistic impulse, if left unchecked by the sobering Halakhah, could lead to. He thus glorifies the balance of these two enterprises which largely define the Jewish worldview. Bialik's essay provides a focal point for H. Slonimsky's perceptive work, *Essays* (Cincinnati, 1967).
7. The Hebrew of Lamentations 3:17 reads "shalom nafshi". The Rabbis took "Nafshi" in the sense of "vayinafash" as in Exodus 31:17: "On the seventh day He ceased *(shavat)* and rested *(vayinafash)*." The Rabbis understood Lamentations 3:17 to mean that there should be a peaceful atmosphere and safe surroundings for Sabbath repose. This, they claimed. implied that there had to be Sabbath lights.

8. My purpose in presenting this paper is to offer some samples for study. I have, therefore, kept the texts together to facilitate comparisons. Having presented these texts to a number of different college audiences and Synagogue study groups, I must caution the reader that these texts require much more analysis and introduction than have been provided here. The teacher must supply that approach from his/her own experience and views. It is also advisable to have more texts available if these texts fail to sustain interest. The pace must not be allowed to slacken. Generally speaking, the approach provided here is a good skeletal one which can provide all with fun and insight no matter how many times the material is presented to various groups.

Chapter 6
Honor It and Suspect It:
A Resurgence of Christian-Hebraism
Harris Lenowitz

I.

Ha-megale panim ba-torah

"He who gives a (wrong) interpretation of the Torah"

While scrutinizing the wares on display at the booth of the Dutch publisher, E J. Brill, at the 1997 Annual Meeting of AAR/SBL , I came across M. Pérez Fernández, *An Introductory Grammar of Rabbinic Hebrew* (Leiden, 1997) (hereafter, the *Grammar)* and was immediately struck by the possibility of using it for a course in mishnaic Hebrew I was about to give that winter. I was perhaps over-animated at the prospect of finding, at last, a textbook/grammar that would replace xeroxes of M. H. Segal, A *Grammar of Mishnaic Hebrew* (Oxford, 1927), an outdated work. I looked first at the foreword, which said that the book was a "practical teaching grammar"—what I wanted—and that it had been tested from 1990-1992 in the classroom. I looked next at the table of contents, then at the bibliography, then at the structure of the work in terms of the organization of the material to be covered and the organization of each unit. They seemed fine to me, and I ordered the volume for the students, at the convention discount, of course.

The book calls its approach morphosyntactic, in essence, a practical descriptive grammar. There are 32 units divided among four parts: nouns, verbs, particles and clauses. The units in the first part cover personal pronouns, demonstratives, the article, possessive pronouns and the genitive particle *shel*, interrogatives, indefinite expressions, reflexive and reciprocal structures, the relative pronoun *she-*, noun patterns, gender and number of nouns, absolute and construct [states], Greek and Latin words, adjectives, and numerals. (It may be observed that syntax—for example, the treatment of the relativizer in unit eight—is woven into the treatment of morphemes, i.e., morphosyntaxis.) In the second part, the verb, conjugations [*binyamin*], tenses and moods, the perfect, the imperfect, the participle, the infinitive, and the imperative are dealt with; in the third, particles, prepositions and conjunctions, and adverbs and interjections; the last part makes a painful progress through clauses: Types of clause, interrogative clauses, comparative clauses, temporal clauses, con-

ditional clauses, causal clauses, final and consecutive clauses, conces-
sive clauses, and adversative clauses are the topics. Each unit contains
an introductory text, a section on morphology (including diachronic
matters), a section on grammar and usage, one on phraseology, one on
or of vocabulary, and an exercise section containing twenty brief texts in
rabbinic Hebrew that display features treated in the unit. The linguistic
bibliography is good and up-to-date; the indices are a little peculiar—in
addition to the scriptural index ("Texts"), there is one called "Hebrew
and Aramaic Forms" that includes words, morphemes, whole phrases,
and abbreviations all lumped together and listed alphabetically according to the first letter of the (first) word rather than by root, or the third
person masculine singular perfect form (in the case of verbs) or any
other convention with which I am familiar. The same words may therefore appear several times in this index. This may be helpful to the searching student but is an odd way, perhaps not ultimately to the student's
benefit, to index or lexicalize a Semitic language. The other indices are
not so strange ("Verb conjugations," "Types of verbal root," "Forms of
the paradigm verb *qatal*, "Noun patterns" (only fourteen!), "Forms from
other Semitic languages," "Greek forms," "Latin forms"), but "English
glosses" repeats the system employed for entering lexemes in the "Hebrew and Aramaic forms" index so that, once again for presumed student ease, a methodological principle that is native to the Hebrew language (and its whole family, actually) has been sacrificed.

I was familiar with neither the author, Miguel Pérez Fernández of the
University of Granada, nor the translator, Dr. J. F. Elwolde of the University of Sheffield.[1] Pérez Fernández writes only in Spanish and his
work has appeared, with one exception, in Spanish journals that are not
well-known in Hebrew linguistic circles. Elwolde has published a single
article in the field, which appears in a symposium *Proceedings* volume
edited by him and T. J. Muraoka,[2] in addition to his review of the *Grammar* which appeared in The *Society for Old Testament Study Book List
of* 1993. When the book arrived, I glanced at the indices again, for no
particular reason other than to familiarize myself with the work so that I
could explain to my class how to use it. It was then that I began to pay a
special kind of attention to the tome, for, in the first index, that of Texts,
following a list of the usual suspects—books of the Hebrew Bible—ending with 2Chr, there appeared five abbreviations that I was familiar with
from contexts that I did not readily associate with the study of Hebrew:
Mt, Mk, Lk, Jn, 1 Co. The more familiar abbreviations resumed thereaf-
ter. I don't want to lay too much stress on the alarm I felt at that point,

but I will mention a cartoon by Charles Addams of a man sitting with one mirror behind his head and another in front of his face in a barber shop. The mirrors reflect each other's reflections and about five or six reflections deep, in the location where the man sitting in the barber chair had been appearing, there suddenly came into view the visage of a horned and hairy monster. And then the reflections went on as they had before the surreal interruption, with the man in his place. I decided to order the original edition of the work in Spanish.

While waiting with bated breath for its arrival, I began to learn, and then to teach, the book. What I had thought a simple grammar book turned out to have bigger game in its sights. "The introductory texts," I read, "and short explanations are designed to introduce the student to the language *and the concepts* (my emphasis) of the *tannaim.* Each introductory text exhibits the linguistic feature covered by the unit, although it serves primarily as a starting-point for discussion of literary, theological, historical and methodological issues."[3] This statement, as I will show, is as misleading—perhaps intentionally misleading—as one earlier, "The exercises are generally drawn from tannaitic literature, and the student should find everything required to deal with them in the book."

I hasten to add that I like what Pérez Fernández/Elwolde have gotten wrong in that latter sentence. The truth is that no student, and not many teachers, could be expected to understand the exercise texts without turning to examine them in their original contexts. If a phrase in rabbinic Hebrew is laconic in its context, it is often not to be understood at all outside of it. That meant that the students (and I) would have to do a lot of reading outside the book. We would have to find every exercise text in its original and where possible in a translation, with footnotes, and we might have to look at some commentaries as well, whether in Hebrew, or in translation. The way the exercises are set up would then rejoice the heart of any teacher (but only rare students). Many of the exercise texts in rabbinic Hebrew[4] are easily found, fully developed: the tractates of the Mishna (in Albeck or Blackman or wherever), Finkelstein's *Sifre to Deuteronomy,* Horovitz' *Sifre to Numbers,* Lauterbach's *Mekhilta,* Weiss' *Sifra,* among others. Two texts were used in uncommon editions: the *avot de-rabbi natan* was cited from a 1987 Spanish translation by Angeles Navarro Peiro (and some citations included the number of the page from Schechter's edition); and the *pirke de-rabbi eliezer,* from a Spanish translation by Pérez Fenández. (Both of these are published in the same series as is the *Grammar,* the Biblioteca Midrásica.) Referring to works that are in the same language as the referencing authority—rather than to standard editions—is not uncommon but should be avoided when the work is translated into another language.[5]

Another entry among the list of "Other rabbinic texts" raises a different issue, not whether the book is useful as a practical teaching grammar, but whether it succeeds as a replacement for Segal, 1927. A major problem with the latter work is its dependence on printed texts of the Mishna. Pérez Fernández writes that he will use the Codex Kaufmann[6] Mishna text since it is "unanimously agreed to be the best witness to the language of the Mishna" in his brief discussion on pp. 10-11. True enough. The Kaufmann manuscript reflects the language variety of the period of the Mishna (rabbinic Hebrew, RH) with greater fidelity than do the printed editions, which uniformly seek to harmonize rabbinic Hebrew usages with those of biblical or post-rabbinic Hebrew. Some of the harmonizations (and other sorts of alterations) hide gross differences in vocabulary and in consonantal orthography or in vocalization (which includes phonemic as well as phonetic matters, as we know). The striking point here is that Elwolde's presentation of Pèrez Fernández, which pretends to provide us with a better text of the Mishna as a document faithfully representing rabbinic Hebrew, in fact accords us a document that is so error-ridden, so misspelled, so misprinted that no advance at all is made over the Albeck edition; rather the opposite.[7] A question worth asking here is, "Is it good for the classroom to have a bad textbook?" I will return to that.

On balance, the two largest improvements over Segal are associated with the *Grammar's* purpose (pedagogy) and its time. When Segal wrote his work, he sallied forth to defend rabbinic Hebrew from accusations of ungrammaticality and jargonism or hybridization. Although there had been dictionaries and some scientific articles[8] on the language and literature, there had been no grammar since Sebastian Münster's of 1542, and that was—with all due credit to a great Hebraist of historic importance—not a well-defined product in terms of the texts employed, the language varieties mixed together and the grammatical approach typical of such dawn works. Münster was quite familiar with Aramaic and even wrote the first Aramaic grammar by a Christian, based on Nathan ben Yehiel's dictionary, the *Arukh* (1101). Segal sought to limit recourse to Aramaic in his *Grammar* while establishing mishnaic Hebrew as a language with all the regularity necessary to meet the highest standards of contemporary linguistic science in the west. He was partly reacting to the disesteem to which rabbinic Hebrew, along with many of its texts — as opposed to biblical—had been treated by the *Maskilim*. He overdid his work in this respect and, with the passage of time and the accrual of data as well as methodological improvements, the book needed to be updated and pacified. As a teaching grammar it was quite difficult to use since its arrangement was not very logical, and there was no index to help a student locate discussions of specific points. Pérez Fernández improves on Segal in these respects. From the title—which is a better description than Segal's *Mishnaic*—on, it is more rigorous and, of course, benefits from the mass of new data and scholarship accrued during the last seventy years. Pérez Fernández is well read in that scholarship and his citations are germane.[9]

To return to my narrative: When I got my copy of the original version, *La lengua de los sabios,* my eye fell first on the cover and stuck fast. On the spine above the title appeared the words *"Institución de S. Jerónimo para la investigación bíblica,"* repeated on the back cover over and under a design I will not hesitate to call a logo. This was made up of the letters alef and tav from the right and alpha and omega from the left, the former in the square script, the latter in cursive. The name of the Midrashic Library *(Biblioteca midrásica)* also appears on the spine, is referred to in the back cover copy, and is printed on the front cover below the publisher's logo and name, *Editorial Verbo Divino.*[10] My suspicion (and if this essay has a single purpose it is to teach the proper engendering and control of suspicion in a field of study—religion— where it must be a constant tool, kept sharp and ready to hand) was aroused. Jerome is the patron saint of all who translate. He was a resourceful translator and one who took great pains in his work for all that his translation of the (Hebrew) Bible into Latin was enslaved to Christian dogma. The Hebrew and Greek letters of the Institute's logo recall the original languages of the Bible and the New Testament, but they are composed as a double merismus. The logo is readily interpreted to represent the whole of the two languages (the Greek is a famous designation of the Lord in the New Testament work, Revelations 1:8) as well as to indicate that Hebrew and Greek are equally the languages of Holy Texts. It may be read as declaring that Hebrew represents the ancient way and Greek represents its completion in the new dispensation. "Verbo Divino" recalls the Johnnanine *Logos.* The initial identification of the *Grammar* is not only styled to its purpose of offering instruction in a Jewish language; some of the indicia places it in a "larger" context.[11]

Before beginning to trace the lineaments of this larger context, its impact on the work and the questions associated with that, I must say that my suspicions of works by non-Jews, particularly Christians, on

Jewish topics are always engaged and are certainly not always borne out by further inquiry. In the modern period alone, for every Welhausen and Schürer[12] there have been Stracks and Herfords, Sanders, and, in particular, Dalmans and Delitzsches aplenty. The last two mentioned, Gustaf Hermann Dalman (1855-1941) and Franz Delitzsch (1813-1890) were both important scholars in the field of Hebrew language and literature, rabbinic literature in particular, and were also convinced and faithful Christians who were sincere in their appreciation of Jews and Jewish traditions; though both wrote from Christian viewpoints, they kept the two traditions apart and did not misconstrue that of the Jews.[13] After examining some various sorts of material that appear in the *Grammar* and the purpose or tendency of their inclusion, I will return to deal with the question of anti-semitism and what is known as Christian-Hebraism.

II.

Tzarot ha-aharonot meshakehot et ha-rishonot. (p. 181)

The man who ran from a lion and met a bear, but made it home, leaned on the wall, and was bit by a snake. (Amos 5:19)

Pérez Fernández' *Grammar* is not the same as a grammar of the same variety of Hebrew that might be written by a Jewish scholar of language and literature for use in a classroom situation where the students cannot be expected to possess an intimacy with the New Testament (NT) and its interpretative tradition. It contains references to all manner of things that relate to Christianity, its society, its history, its ideas and its written texts. Some of these references are made more overtly, some less so. I will deal with the overt references first, and first from among them, those that contain NT citations. I will then show how the argument developed in connection with these references may be extended to other cases where no overt citation is made and, as an example, to one case where no direct citation or reference is made.

The first NT scriptural citation is on p. 13 and refers the reader to "John 11:1, etc." The context of the grammatical point is the appearance and disappearance of an initial alef. Alefs sometimes appear as prostheses in RH to break up an initial consonant cluster when foreign words are borrowed; some initial alefs in Hebrew words, especially in proper names, disappear in RH. After mentioning two names, Eliezer and Eleazar, that appear as Liezer and Lazar in "inscriptions, and the presence of which in Palestine is evidenced by the Gospels in the name Lazarus," Pérez Fernández cites the NT text. (Elwolde writes the name as "Lazarus;" the Spanish original has the Greek form.) The name as it appears in the NT does expand the social environment to include Christian Greek texts in which the name occurs without its alef but this raises other questions, a technical phonetic question: What effect does the nominative singular ending— -*os* in Greek, -*us* in Latin—have on the loss of the alef?[14]; and another sort: What is a Hebrew name doing in a Greek document anyway? Did it come there from another document or was it original in some text, whether oral or written, that underlies the canonized text? Who is the author of the document? What was his/her language? What was the language of his/her audience? All these questions— and they are serious ones, as students of the New Testament in its social environs know—are begged. In any case, dealing with them would at best serve to take the student away from the language being studied and towards something else. Is the reference to the NT necessary in the context of a grammar? helpful? to whom? if not, then what is its purpose?

The same questions arise when Pérez Fernández works with ideas rather than sound patterns and cites (p. 134) Mk 4:24 and Lk 6:38 to expand on *Tosefta Sotah 3.1* and *Sota* 1.7. It is true that all these texts speak of the ethical principle of reciprocity, "measure for measure," (Pérez Fernández has brought them together to illustrate the employment of the masculine plural participle to express, among other things, the impersonal nature of a proposition), but so do texts from hundreds of other literatures; the idea is so common that no author can claim it, no civilization escape it. One other case, at least in part, should be included with this and the one preceding. On p. 122, the author compares the social situations described in *Sifre to Deuteronomy,* 48 with Mt 23: 6-8. Both texts decry the employment of education for political or social advantage. The passage from *Sifre* attacks those who employ it to get rich, to be called rabbi, or to receive a reward in the next world; the gospel passage generalizes at the outset—"*everything* (my emphasis) they do is to aggrandize their self-esteem"—and cites their fashions in clothing, placement at feasts, and the forms of address they prefer, including being called rabbi. So far, *grosso modo,* so good. The author concludes his comparison, however, by saying that the "theological message [of the passage from *Sifre*] unambiguously states that the only reason for spending one's life in the study of the Torah is love for God nothing else." This is far from an accurate description; I am not convinced that this passage even contains something that could be called a "theological" message. The passage from the NT, especially in its context (Mt 23:1 is directed against the Pharisees and the scribes and concludes with Jesus admonishing his listeners that he, Christ, alone is to be called Rabbi, he alone is to be called Master) is certainly theological and, by the same token, contains no ethical message, which I take to be the burden of the *Sifre* text.

Of the fourteen uses Pèrez Fernández makes and cites from the NT these three are the least objectionable, the least problematic in terms of what is being compared and how tight the comparison is. They have only the purpose of showing similarity between things said or written by Jesus or his followers and those by some users of RH (who cannot be shown to be these former). The comparisons might serve to make a classroom of students who are intimate with the NT feel that they are on familiar territory with texts in RH. I feel that even these comparisons are so remarkably loose, in terms of the crudeness with which linguistic, rhetorical, generic, social and historical matters are taken into account, as to badly serve both the NT and the RH material. But let me turn now to some real excesses, in which the author's purpose, the state of mind consciously or unconsciously driving such mistreatment, may display itself.

I apologize in advance for traveling rapidly through the other cases where Pérez Fernández provides explicit NT text citations to be compared with the RH passages. (It is further evidence of the audience to whom the *Grammar* is addressed that the NT texts are not quoted; I venture that Pérez Fernández' students would be expected to have the NT in their minds or on their desks while in their RH class.) I will cut directly to the (unargued) claim that the passages cited from the NT testify to an acquaintance (Jesus and) the NT authors had with the society employing RH, that they shared with the latter certain opinions concerning theology and ethics as well as ways of expressing them, and that certain NT texts actually illuminate the RH texts to which they are compared.[15] Aside from the three discussed above and one of those on p. 122 of the *Grammar,* seven of the remaining NT citations are to be found in the "introductory texts and short explanations" sections of the units.

On p. 17 the concept of "tradition" and "transmission"[16] is compared as it appears in Avot 1.1 and in "1 Cor 15:3 cf. 11.23." The NT texts have Paul saying that he passed on what he received from Christ (11:23 is required in order to complete 15:3, where the source of transmission is unclear); Avot has the famous *'ithnad* of the oral Torah "from Sinai to Moses to Joshua to the elders to the prophets to the men of the Great Assembly." "The terminology of the [Hebrew for transmission] is reflected in [the Greek] in New Testament passages that emphasize the faithfulness of the process of gospel transmission." (It is not clear what Elwolde means by "reflected;" Pérez Fernández actually wrote *usada*, "is employed.") The employment of the same terms (in Greek) in the epistle as in the RH text points out the change that Paul seeks to emphasize. Whereas the Avot tradition-chain wants to establish the authority of the text that follows by laying claim to antiquity on its behalf, Paul is presenting a new tradition that breaks with the old and has come to him from God directly. The most important distinction proceeds from this one: the *torah she-be' al pe*— the oral law— is obviously not the written law—*torah she-bikhtav*—is precisely not Holy Scripture and does not have its status. On the other hand, Paul is actually writing letters and claiming exactly that latter status of them.

On p. 34, Pérez Fernández compares Mt 25:35 with a number of RH texts that list deeds of *gmilut hasadim* (in English, "kindness" "benevolence" "lovingkindness"). Though there are similarities among these lists, the one in Matthew differs from those in RH by being set in a judgmental framework (within a parable), where the performance of such deeds will serve as evidence in favor of or against an individual seeking admission to "the kingdom." I think the RH concept, on the other hand, represents such acts, as they appear in the introductory text presented from *avot di-rabbi natan* (ARN) (ed. Schechter p. 21), as mitigating to some degree the sense of desolation and despair RH speakers felt at the loss of the temple and thereby the loss of a central social institution. The passage argues that these acts replace the power of the temple cult to expiate sin with other acts; these latter, though, are primarily atonements for the community's inadequacy, its failure to sustain the temple. In any case, the phrase *gmilut hasadim* impacts first and foremost an immediate situation in the ARN text while that of the NT concept in Matthew achieves its aim by granting or refusing entrance to the Other World in accord with what an authority in that world deems proper.

Since Pérez Fernández goes on to mention some acts of *gmilut hasadim* that received "particular emphasis" in the "Jewish tradition," among them attendance at weddings and congratulating newlyweds, I will turn to p. 104, where *pirke di-rabbi eliezer* (PRE) 12 is compared with John 2:1-11. The PRE text presents a discussion in which God invites some angels to accompany him to do deeds of *gmilut hasadim* for Adam and Eve at their wedding. In contrast to the passage from ARN, these deeds are done in PRE by personages of the Other World. Of course, there was no one else to do these deeds and in some sense God and the angels were all the family and friends Adam and Eve had at the moment. A more interesting possibility is that having God at the wedding—and later, following his example, humans—elevates the importance and prestige and holiness of marriage. Friedlander goes so far as to suggest that the PRE text might actually be "counteracting the attitude of the Church towards marriage" and cites I Cor 7:8 and Mt 19:10,12.[17] Be that as it may, I find Pérez Fernández' reading of John 2:1-11, where "Jesus begins his ministry by attending a wedding and assisting the newly-weds," indeed "significant." This act is the first of the *semeia,* the signs, by which Jesus reveals his glory (v.11). This is the point of the story, not the marriage but the miracle of the provision of the wine — a better wine than the family could provide as well as more generously supplied. This signifies, in John, the beginning of Jesus' mundane career. I don't agree at all with Pérez Fernández' reading of this passage as related to the PRE passage or to the concept of *gmilut hasadim* (and I will return to his treatment of the works/grace problem as he compares it in RH and NT texts, below). I am also not sure that the Cana wedding really "marks the beginning of Jesus' ministry," as Pérez Fernández writes, since he's already been created in his unique character and gained disciples in the preceding chapter.

When Pérez Fernández draws a parallel (on p. 151) between the RH text *Sifre on Deuteronomy,* 49 and Luke 6:36, he says that the gospel passage is "a similar (Spanish, *paralela*) formulation." I can't tell whether the author is referring to the rhetorical or the ideational formulation. In either case, again, the differences between the RH and NT texts are apparent. The treatment of the imitation of God in Sifre attests to the impossibility of imitating him while the NT text does the opposite. The first has to do with how one may achieve a reputation for possessing various qualities, how one may come *to be known* by an epithet which is also an epithet of God's; the second is concerned with how one can become a "son of the Most High." As the *Sifre* text continues, it goes so far as to say that even cleaving to God can only be done through the intermediation of the Sages and that such an encounter will be as direct as possible if one approaches God through the aggadot. Moreover, the two cited passages in their full contexts display a gross conceptual difference (as in their rhetorical judgment surfaces): the NT text again deals with judgment, "Pass no judgment and you will not be judged" (v. 37), "How blest you are if you..." vs. "But alas if you are..." (vv. 20-22 vs. 24-26); the RH text threatens no punishment as one aspires to do worthy deeds. When it comes to speak of the reward if one "does one's duty" we find that it is the usual, this-worldly reward, the basis of the covenant: God will drive out all these nations from before you if you do your duty. The gospel passage speaks of no earthly return for one's struggle to imitate God but only of a rich reward in Heaven.

Earlier I touched on some NT passages that Pérez Fernández brought as parallels to RH texts dealing with faith and works, or words and deeds, or grace and commandments (pp. 34 and 104). Pp. 44, 48 also pertain to the argument Pérez Fernández is making and two other passages in the *Grammar* on pp. 39 and 191, though they do not contain a direct citation, do have a complete NT reference. It will be clearer if I begin the examination of the author's position with an introductory text cum discussion in which no mention of the NT is made at all. On p. 129, the author presents part of the RH text of *Sifre on Deuteronomy,* 329. In the passage it is demonstrated that fathers cannot save their sons nor brothers each other. The examples are Abraham/Ishmael, Isaac/Esau[18] and Isaac/Ishmael, Jacob/Esau. A literal translation of the conclusion of the Hebrew text would read, "the soul is precious and when one sins against it there can be no redemptory payment." Both Elwolde and Pérez Fernández, however, translate *nefesh* here (and in the earlier passage "the redemption of their *nefesh* is very costly") as "life" rather than "soul," though Pérez Fernández never makes an argument for this extension of the meaning of the word, and the idea of "life" doesn't work here since both the sons and the brothers who "cannot be saved" do survive after they leave the family. The Grammar's commentary reads, "With regard to the supreme gift of life, a person is completely in the hands of God— one's personal merits or those of one's parents or siblings count for nothing; it is entirely a matter of God's grace."[19] "One's personal merits"— what one does in conformity to the law and beyond its requirements, *gmilut hasadim*—count for nearly everything in the way RH culture assesses the worthiness of one's social contribution. As Christianity developed during the century after Jesus' death, grace came to supersede works; the religion turned away from the laws of the Torah and toward the testimony of faith in the salvatory agency of Christ as sufficient. As far as the "merits of the fathers' goes, again there is a generous discontinuity between RH society and Christianity. Pérez Fernandez does not cite any NT texts, but he could certainly have in mind 1 Tim 1:4, Titus 3:9, Mt 3.9 and Luke 3:8 which make the devaluation of ancestral ties an essential part of the new faith. The *Sifre on Deuteronomy* text, on the other hand, sees things a bit differently. Comparing ARN 12, y. Ber. 4, and b. Ber. 27b with the Sifre passage, Urbach concludes that Akiba's position is that the merit of the ancestors may help one, but does not affect free will or individual responsibility.[20] Again, free will, the choice made, and the deed done are all important ethical and religious variables in RH society.

In addition to the introductory text and commentary to unit 19, those to units 3 (p. 25), and 6 (39f.), 7 (44), and 8 (49) touch on this same large and difficult topic. On p. 44, Pérez Fernández presents and discusses *Peah* 1.1, a text that lists deeds for which one is rewarded in this world and in the next as well. He writes, "The belief in heavenly reward/punishment also underlies numerous New Testament texts, such as Luke 6:20-38 (the beatitudes), 14:12-14, and 18:28-30 (a further instance of a double reward, both on earth and in heaven)."[21] In fact, there is no punishment involved in the *Peah* list while the beatitudes do speak of heavenly punishment. Luke 18:20-30 are the only verses that touch on rewards on earth as well as in heaven. Setting the virtuous deeds extolled in the RH text alongside those in the last-mentioned parallel is instructive: Where the Mishna speaks of one's unending duty toward one's parents, Luke *rewards* with a heavenly carrot those who give up their homes, wives, brothers, parents and children for the sake of the kingdom of God. The two texts are indeed parallel, but only in the force they put behind their propositions; they are in utter opposition as far as the deeds themselves are concerned.[22]

On p. 49, Pérez Fernández compares Avot 3.17 with Mt 7:24f., where "we read of those who hear and practice what they hear (wisdom with deeds) and of others, who hear but do not put what they hear into practice." Again, there is a fissure between the RH and NT texts. In the former, the choice one makes between learning and not learning is different in two ways from the proposition Jesus offers. First, learning in RH society is not a necessity of the same sort that obedience to the law is. Second, learning (actually *hokhma,* wisdom, the sum of learning) differs from "hearing," *pace* Pérez Fernández; what one learns is that learning is an investigative process that remains open to disputation and is in some sense endless and in some sense pointless, non-teleogical. What one hears from Jesus is the Word, an incarnate deed, so that the NT contrasts a righteous with a sinful, rebellious deed.

The final discussions (that I will present here among the group of overt connections the author makes between RH and NT texts) that deal directly with the topic of works/wisdom/study/faith, etc., do not contain direct NT references, but allude to the whole of one man's work, that of Paul, and to the whole of the work of two other personages, Hanina ben Dosa, a "charismatic miracle-worker from the Galilee," and "another

Galilean," Jesus of Nazareth. The first of these discussions (p. 191) presents, translates and interprets *Sifre to Numbers*, 87.1: "We remember the fish that we ate without charge in Egypt [Num 11:51]. Does it say in the context that the Egyptians had given them fishes without charge?...[If not], how should I interpret, 'Without charge?' Without the commandments!" I do not entirely disagree with Pérez Férnández' comment, "Here we see a contrast between grace and commandments that Saint Paul himself could have put his name to," though I may read that differently than the author intended.[23] In the biblical context and in the interpretation it receives in the RH text it is clear that these words, spoken by the unhappy Israelites, are put in their mouths to indicate their weakness and the contempt in which they hold their leader and their destiny. The fish that they ate in Egypt, before receiving the commandments, are seen in this text as the delights these weak people took pleasure in and failed to see as further instruments of enslavement. Contrasted with the fish, the commandments liberate the Israelites. "To be free" of the commandments here means to be childish, at liberty to disregard judgement and direction.

Last, on this topic, is the introductory text and discussion of Avot 3.9 (p. 39). It is very similar to what the author presented on p. 49. There are two other points to be considered, in addition to the matter of Pérez Fernández' understanding of how the works/grace question plays out in RH texts as opposed to those of the NT. The author describes the "dialectic contrast in which the statement is couched [as] typical of Semitic rhetoric." The statement says that fear of sin keeps one's wisdom real and that deeds do too, and the couching is: IFF fear of sin > wisdom THEN wisdom will endure/IFF deeds > wisdom THEN wisdom will endure. I can't tell that this "couching" is different from that of any other logical proposition. More to the point, I don't know what "Semitic rhetoric" is and I'm afraid I do know what the author means. (The Spanish is even worse, "*La expresion por contraposiciones dialecticas es muy del gusto semitico..*") If Pérez Fernández is implying that the Semitic peoples have their own peculiar rhetoric, I would say that the form of this logical proposition is neither common to all of them nor uncommon among members of other races, the Hittites, say, or the Egyptians, just to stay in the same geographical region. Moreover, how can a proposition be understood as the genetic property of a race? I am, in fact, convinced that Pérez Fernández is stereotyping Jews and the way Jews argue.

At the beginning of this same commentary, the author writes, "Hanina ben Dosa was a charismatic miracle-worker from Galilee. Some authors have compared him to another Galilean, Jesus of Nazareth." The author does not disclose the writers or works where this statement originates, nor is it possible to locate them in the bibliography. The single work mentioned there that deals with the society of that longish period (Second Temple to the end of the second century CE), or its history or with questions of NT authorship, editing, and audience, or with the personalities of RH documents and those of the NT and the employment of these figures in the texts, etc., etc., is Schürer's *History* (n. 12). No names — like those of F P. Sanders, J. D. Crossan, J. Klausner, or D. Flusser — appear in it to enlarge on or support or detail Pérez Fernández' ideas on these subjects as they touch on the several Jesuses; none — like those of E E. Urbach or J. Neusner, or P. Schäfer—are mentioned to shed some light on the historicity of these figures from the NT or from the RH texts; or to provide the amateur with guidance to the texts from experts' scholarship and interpretations. Contrast, if you will, the quotation at the beginning of this paragraph with another like, "Tales about Hanina ben Dosa present him as a charismatic worker from Galilee. These accounts might be compared with tales about another Galilean, Jesus of Nazareth." Pérez Fernández has no authority and makes no argument that would enable him to speak in such an off-handed way of "another Galilean" or "Hanina ben Dosa" and to reach the point of comparing them. (it would in any case be simpler not to take up such matters; this is, after all a *Grammar!)* Is Pérez Fernández merely naive, a person who has neglected to examine his argumentative premises? I don't believe so. The lack of argument and support should make it clear that the reader is being given opinions; the tendency of the opinions—to interpret the RH texts as associated with Christian ideas and Christian ideas as emerging from the schools that produced the RH texts—attests to bias, whether conscious or not.

I will turn now to whether connections like these are made between RH texts and the NT without overt citations. This is a much more difficult matter for me, or for the student reckoning with the *Grammar* or similar works, since one's suspicion arises without proof and has to be justified on circumstantial evidence and the interpretation of the author's intent. In my first example, an item in the vocabulary section (p. 20) and one in the exercises (p. 21) are related to each other, though the author notes an association between the NT and this usage only in the case of its appearance in the vocabulary section. Pérez Fernádez brings two NT texts (Mt 16:19 and 18:18 [24]) to enlarge the student's understanding of the verbs *ntr* and *'asr* (to "bind," "prohibit," and to "release," "permit').

Item #8 in the exercises shows a typical RH use of the pair from *idem* 6.11. The passage deals with a purchaser's determination that a merchant's declaration that he has paid a tithe on certain produce is reliable when the obligation to tithe has itself been confessed by him: If the seller is taken as trustworthy in determining that he is obliged to pay tithe and the buyer depends on him for this he has no reason to assume that the seller has not, as he says he has, done so, the first statement being to the seller's disadvantage. "The one who has confessed obligation is the same one who has released himself from it." The NT texts have Jesus granting judgmental authority to Peter and the disciples, respectively: "What you permit/forbid on earth is permitted/forbidden in heaven." Each of the verbs in the NT text do indeed appear to have the same meaning as each of them in RH; however, the pairing of the verbs in the vocabulary and in the exercise is not the same as in the NT passages and this leads to the more important distinction, that the authority for the RH passage flows from logic and from the statement of the individuals engaged in the act as interpreted, while the authority of the NT passage rests not in the correct interpretation of those acting but in the authority of a higher power, one made not susceptible to logical proof. The world views of the two passages are utterly opposed; the Mishna seeks to instruct its audience in how to arrive at correct deductions; the NT seeks to set logic aside in favor of mystery.

In the last case of what has, I'm sure, proven a tedious exercise to the reader, we come to the affair to which the title of this section of my paper refers. In the introductory text to unit 24 (p. 181), *Mekhilta* 13.2, a parable (similar to the one from Amos, above) concludes, "[After surviving two other attacks] the person was attacked by a snake but was rescued from it and, forgetting both the earlier stories [which he had told] continued the journey, relating [only] the story of the snake. So it is with Israel: their later tribulations make them forget earlier ones." Pérez Fernández concludes his explication of the text, "Given the biblical dynamic, there is the underlying idea not only that the latter replaces the former but also that it is better, that the second liberation will be superior to the first one." Although he cites no NT reference, some at least will provide a background to his understanding and clarify what is otherwise completely unintelligible. In Paul's *Letter to the Hebrews,* 7:28 praises the "oath which supersedes the Law"; 8:6 says, "But in fact the ministry which has fallen to Jesus is as far superior to theirs [i.e., priests of the Law] as are the covenant he mediates and the promises upon which it is legally secured"; v.8f., "I will conclude a new covenant with the house of

Israel and the house of Judah. It will not be like the covenant I made with their forefathers when I took them by the hand to lead them out of Egypt." The author's interpretation of the RH passage simply cannot be understood without a recognition of the Christian position on the replacement of the Law by the person of Christ—the liberation of humanity from the yoke of the Torah —and I have tried to provide the texts from the NT that furnish such an understanding. Yet even knowing what Pérez Fernández means by "the second liberation"—as well as understanding how the giving of the Law constitutes the first liberation—it remains to be said that the RH text does not provide the grounds for the interpretation he gives. As a general principle, suspicions that a text has been misconstrued may be substantiated, even when no direct reference to later texts is present, if the circumstantial evidence is strong enough and if one has evidence of the character of the author and his interpretative tendency based on cases where factual evidence is provided. The circumstantial evidence here is provided by the interpretation of "tribulation" as its antonym, "liberation." The previous pages of this essay will have provided enough evidence on which to reach a conclusion concerning the author's interpretative tendency.

III.

Ma la-nahash be-gan 'eden?

What is a snake doing in the Garden?

I would say that the latest tribulations brought upon Jews and their works by Christians, particularly in the field of the Hebrew language and literature, have not only not "made the earlier ones forgettable" but serve to remind one of them. The modern study of Hebrew begins with the late Renaissance and the Reformation.[25] The path-breaking studies done by Jews, such as that of Hayyuj, as a result of contact with Arabic grammarians were gradually taken into account by Renaissance Christians, who were led back into the classical and then into the far distant past to Eden itself where Adam learned the secrets of Nature and the (Hebrew) Word from God. The resurgence of interest in the Greek original of the New Testament brought a concomitant and determined curiosity to bear on the original language of the (Hebrew) Bible. With increasing rapidity Christian scholars took up rabbinic texts on the Bible as well, assuming that they who were joined through their forefathers to the traditions of the text itself might cast some light on its interpretation. The sixteenth and seventeenth centuries saw the production of brilliant works of grammar that set the Christian understanding of the Hebrew Bible and of the Jews on an entirely new plane. The rapid development of printing and the institution of chairs for scholars of Hebrew at leading denominational institutions of learning made the spread of knowledge unstoppable and that, unfortunately, was a problem. Protestants and Christian Reformers found untrammeled inquiry and the conclusions of linguistic research a stumbling block in the way of their doctrinal absolutism. Due to some political disputes in which the Jews played the pawn's role, their fortunes and that of the study of Hebrew rose and fell with heartstopping velocity. Nor were all the scholars and their works equally beneficial to enlarging the understanding of the language and its contexts. Some rather odd ideas about Hebrew as a magical mystery key to the riddle of existence emerged from the works of both of the premier scholars in the language, Johannes Reuchlin and Pico delta Mirandola, in the very earliest stage of its acceptance into the academy. But in general, placing the language of Hebrew alongside other Semitic languages, and all of them within the compass of European linguistic science, achieved gains that advanced knowledge and method in the study of the Bible and its languages (to include Aramaic) enormously before the whole enterprise fell back into desuetude for a pair of centuries.

Friedman attributes the post-medieval Christian study of Hebrew, as well as of classical texts, to a longing for a simpler time, nostalgia.[26] Positing that time as "the early days" meant a way around present complexities of doctrine and politics as well as a means to regain a view of all creation that would be as complete as it had been in those times when humans lived closer to Nature and knew its secrets or saw things clearly through the Book because they had received it directly from the Creator of secrets. One important Christian Hebraist, Michael Servetus, was burned by Calvin in 1553 for his opinions concerning the orthodox polytheistic doctrine of the Trinity. He drew on the Bible and rabbinica as the source for understanding the New Testament.[27] Another, Paul Fagius, an orthodox scholar, "searched rabbinic sources for descriptions of the Pharisaic milieu from which Jesus and the apostles emerged."[28] He incorporated his findings in *Hebrew Prayers* (Latin, Isny, 1542), which related Jesus' ritual acts at the Last Supper to Jewish mealtime practices. He fled Germany after rejecting the Interim agreement imposed by Charles V, suppressing the Reformation (as did Andreas Osiander, who was an opponent of Luther's anti-Jewish positions), and died there, to be buried, exhumed and publicly burned. These two scholars, perhaps the most well disposed toward Jews and their literature — in principle — until

John Lightfoot in England, still felt free to turn to Hebrew grammar when
it worked, or to theological concepts when grammar would not serve, to
substantiate the arguments for their own Christian theological positions.
Goldish summarizes the history of Christian Hebraism as having been
driven initially by conversionary and disputational aims. From the end of
the fifteenth century, Christian scholars began to see Hebrew, including
post-biblical Jewish texts, kabbalistically—as a way to the *prisca doctrina,*
uniting linguistics and material science—and went on learning the language for the purpose of Bible study. Later scholars found Hebrew useful
for redefining Christianity and politics.[29] For some, Hebrew and Hebrew
texts would unseal the millennium. At least until the end of the seventeenth century, the purposes of Hebrew study for Christians were different
than they were for Jews, and the way they went about them was different.
Since all the reasons for their study had to do with Christianity—
conversionism, disputation, a source among many in creating a melange
of mystic knowledge, contributions to Christian doctrine and politics—
they did not engage in the study of the texts and their part in Jewish life
and thought except as that touched on Christianity. Their contacts with
living Jews were highly limited and in general relatively insignificant,[30]
and their lack of support when Jews' lives were in danger occasionally
reached heights of anti-Jewishness (as in Luther's case). These scholars
might defend Jewish books from the fire but not Jews, their families or
their homes. After all, they made the books serve their own purposes, read
them in their Christian light. In his monograph, and in an important sharp-
ening of the argument in his essay, Heiko Oberman assesses the results of
the movement.[31] In the essay (p. 33) he writes, "Whatever it achieved for
the understanding of biblical Judaism, the Hebrew truth could not escape
the deep-seated Christian disaffection with post-biblical Jews." I cannot
say how much this has changed.[32]

Having never met either Pérez Fernández or Elwolde or read anything
of theirs that directly touches on living Jews and their right—and the right
of their traditions and writings — to be treated like other human beings
and their works, without respect to their (lack of) sympathy with Christian
aims, I cannot take any position on the interesting question of whether the
Grammar has the peculiar nature it does as a result of an intention to
convert Jews and speed the millennium, or to convert Jewish (Hebrew)
literature,[33] or is simply the result of the two of them continuing blindly in
the footsteps of their antecedents, the Christian Hebraists. The work that
has emerged has its uses: it does update Segal's study in many ways. In
the way it goes about its mixed task, it also raises the question of the "bad

textbook." The *Grammar* is filled with misprints that teachers and students may enjoy finding and correcting; thereby a lot may be learned in practice about scribal tendencies, particularly scribal errors. All the exercise texts have to be restored to their contexts so that the grammatical point being illustrated may be made understandable; thereby a good deal of reading in RH texts becomes part of the course. Equally, students and teachers who come to the work with their suspicions ready at hand or engaged by features such as those I have brought out may gain insight into the differences between Jewish and Christian world-views by examining, as I have done in a few cases, how the two may be made to appear alike.

"He who profanes the hallowed things, and despises the festivals, and gives a (wrong) interpretation of the Torah—*ha-megale panim ba-torah* —and makes void the covenant of Abraham our father, and puts his fellow to shame, even though he has good works to his credit, he has no share in the world to come." Avot 3.11 (M. S. Kaufmann) (See Urbach, *op. cit.,* 295-6). ✿

Endnotes

1. I am no longer innocent. This paper will limit itself to this book in Spanish and in English, and deal only with the place of the work in the history of Christian Hebraism. Perhaps, at some later date, Brian Dickman, my student in two courses on mishnaic Hebrew this last year, will continue the work he has done (I am grateful for the help he has been to me in this paper) and extend these investigations to touch on other members of what must be considered a sort of circle. In addition to Pérez Fernández and Etwolde, these would include those working in the field at the University of Granada and those who write for the Institucion de S. Jeronimo or for the Editorial Verbo Divino along with Prof. Dr. Günter Stemberger and Prof. Luis Girón, whom the author mentions in his acknowledgments as having helped him and having read and annotated the first draft of the Grammar.
2. See the Grammar bibliography, pp.256-266.
3. Foreword, p. v.
4. Pp. xxi-xxii
5. Like this are the occasional lapses in translating Spanish orthography to that of English, as where the Spanish *jota* remains, ("Jobab" for Moses' father-in-law, p. 29) though the sound /h/ (het) needs to be transliterated as an aitch of some sort in English spelling.
6. Codex Kaufmann is dated to the period of the 11th-13th centuries. A facsimile edition, *Faksimile-Ausgabe des Mischnakodex Kaufmann A*

30 (1967) was used by Pérez Fernández (The Elwolde version of the Grammar fails to cite this publication.).

7. I am not going to go into all the other sorts of errors, miscitations and so forth, but it seems worthwhile to make this point since it touches on the utility of the Grammar as against Segal. The original edition, in Spanish, is, though hardly free from errors, much more carefully proofed (Etwolde, Anne Lee and Rosemarie Kossov and the Brill typesetters ought to be ashamed. Brill,in particular, shouldn't be selling this book for $113 (!) and presenting us with ca.330 pages replete with inaccuracy); on the other hand, the printing of the Spanish edition is less readable overall; and again, the Brill edition is jam-packed with ink-spots, often appearing to be, sadly, vowel points.

8. The most important dictionaries before Segal were M. M. Jastrow's *Dictionary of the Targumim, the Talmud Babli and Yerushalmi, and the Midrashic Literature* (1886-1903), still the standard in English, and the second edition of G. H. Dalman's *Dictionary ofAramaic and New Hebrew* (in German, 1922).

9. I think the original work is to be preferred in this respect too over the English version. I like the bibliographic survey that precedes each unit, citing the most important works that deal with the topic for comparison and elucidation. Moreover, some of the scholarship the author cites is not well-known, particularly that in Spanish.

10. The cover copy also refers to Pérez Fernández' other publications in the Midrashic library and to the forthcoming volume II of *La lengua de los sabios* (a less accurate title than that of the English version, returning us, in fact, to the undistinguished term *leshon hazal* of yore). The second volume is to deal with genres, *Generos y fórmas, fórmulas y términos*.

11. Nicholas de Lange makes a similar observation, which he writes is "not intended as an accusation of bias, but simply as a reflection that other approaches are possible," in his review (*Journal of Theological Studies* (New Series) 48.2 (October, 1997) 630-633 of M. Saebø, *Hebrew Bible. Old Testament. The History of Interpretation* (Göttingen, 1996), discussing the title of the work and its "compound determination." "Is 'Hebrew Bible' intended to be a well-meaning concession to Jewish readers? ... but surely 'Hebrew Bible' is [like 'Old Testament'] also a Christian term ... Moreover the equation of 'Hebrew Bible' with 'Old Testament' hints at a particular Christian theological orientation which the Editor appears to rebut by mentioning in his Preface that he has enlisted the help of Catholic advisers as well as a Jewish one."

12. E Schürer's prejudiced work, *The History of the Jewish People in the Age of Jesus Christ,* is the single historical volume that appears in the Pérez Fernández bibliography. It has been used in the revision by Vermes,

Millar and Black of 1979.

13. Delitzsch is a particularly interesting case. He was very slow to accept the documentary hypothesis and quite restricted in his use of the theory which had,after all, in Welhausen a noteworthily, anti-Semitic father. Delitzsch was also very conservative in embracing any sort of textual emendations of the masoretic text. Delitzsch was also the author of a Hebrew translation of the New Testament and a pamphleteer, devoted to proselytizing Jews. His son was a rather different matter. Friedrich (1850-1922) was an Assyriologist who found no value in Jews or Judaism; the, "Babylonians" were his preference. His work *Babel und Bibel* (1902-1905, English, 1906) was followed, after the First World War, by *The Great Disappointment* both played important roles in the development of anti-Semitism in Germany.

14. Pérez Fernández is similarly inattentive to the subtleties of large scale linguistic phenomena. On p. 141 he writes that *haya yoshev vedoresh* "implies public or authorized instruction" and compares the phrase to the opening of the sermon on the mount, Mt 5:1. If the linkage of the two verbs *yshv* and *drsh* (compare others like *hlkh* and *s'r,* from Jonah 1:11,13 where the first participle intensifies the action of the second; or *'amd* and *ytsv* in 1 Sam 19:20 where the first participle 'sets' the action of the second) is what makes this meaning then one must note that the Greek of Mt 5:1 has two verbs between "sit" and "preach." (A better case could have been made for Luke 4:20-21, though there is again an interruption in the verb pair).

15. I think it useful to distinguish the two groups of authors/texts by their attested use of RH. The bibliography in the English version of the *Grammar* contains 28 references to articles and monographs that deal directly with the question of the language or languages employed by Jesus and his followers, none of them written in Hebrew, several of them quite antique, a large number having appeared in popular periodicals written for a Christian audience. Notwithstanding the erudition displayed here, no argument is made in the *Grammar* that there is an oral or written RH forerunner to the NT. Again, even to make—if it can be made—such. an argument would distract from the study of RH as a language, sufficient in itself for one book.

16. The topics of the introductory text-with-discussion of each unit are listed in a separate index in the Spanish text. They appear in the table of contents of the English translation: transmission of the Torah; fulfillment(!) and harmonization of Scripture; study and practice; proselytes and Israelites; the temple cult and love for one's neighbor; wisdom and works; eschatological retribution; wisdom and works; the justification of the *halakhah* through Scripture; the exegetical methods of Akiba and Ishmael; the *al tiqra* principle; the midrashic function of parables; rabbinic argumentation in dialogue form; scriptural proofs of

resurrection; the relationship of oral law to Scripture; deeds of mercy; *ma'asiyyot* in the Mishna; the motives for studying Torah; the responsibility of the individual before God, development of the oral law sanctioned by Moses; "Be gracious and merciful just as God is gracious and merciful". human virtues and divine gifts; God's solidarity with his people; the second liberation will be superior to the first; grace and law; a rabbinic "parable of the talents;" the thirteenth rule of Rabbi Ishmael; circumcision; reliving the first Passover (!); uniqueness and interdependence of human beings; the "liberated" tribe; Abraham's love for God. The list inspires one to question the principle behind the selection of introductory passages.

17. Friedlander, *Pirke De Rabbi Eliezer* (London, 1916) 107.

18. The Hebrew text is presented correctly in both the Spanish and the English versions of the *Grammar,* and both of them mistranslate "Isaac cannot save Esau" as "Isaac cannot save Jacob." Sometimes, in this unhappy work, Elwode and company get it wrong even though Pérez Fernández has it right p. 33 of the English version translates *ten lo mishelo* as "Give him of (that which is) yours(!)."

19. I believe that the intent of translating nefesh as "life" in this text is to associate the word and the text with the idea of "eternal life," a basic Christian theological construct, though it might be that some derived Christian doctrine (I think of the position of the Roman Catholic Church on birth control, etc.) is being validated here.

20. There is ample room for differences on this issue in RH texts. See the discussion in E. E. Urbach, *The Sages* (Cambridge, 1987) 258, 500.

21. Elwolde contributes the second parenthetical remark.

22. Of the same order is the comparison drawn on p.167 between the characteristic formula *leshem shamaylm,* "for the highest purpose," and Mt 19:12. The NT text has Jesus praise those fortunate enough to have remained chaste and unmarried or been born or made eunuchs "for the sake of the kingdom of heaven." Pérez Fernández says that this idiom—though actually *leshem shamayim* is not the same as *dia ten basileian ton ouranon*—extols a deed done out of the "purest form of motivation." Again, the force of esteem is sort of parallel in both (see my discussion of the difference between these RH and Greek phrases, above) but the deeds—marrying and having children and not marrying and not having children—are themselves sufficiently different. What is the purpose of drawing a parallel between the phrase "lip-smackin' good" when spoken by a cannibal and when spoken by one who is attentive to the laws of kashrut?

23. In fact, I doubt that Paul would have so mistaken the meaning of the Sifre text.

24. The Spanish edition has the correct citation; the English cites Mt 19:18. The proofreading and typographical errors will not be mentioned again,

but it needs to be said that, in addition to the time-honored *resh/dalet, mem/samekh, vav/nun, he/het* scribal errors and *mis-dageshed* sequences, the work contains wrong references to both RH texts (see, among many, p. 74 where two passages, #4 and #7, are improperly located) and this NT text.

25. The brief bibliographic note in M. Gordish, *Judaism in the Theology of Sir Isaac Newton* (Dordrecht, 1997) l9n5 updates the longest work on Christian-Hebraism, J. Friedman, *The Most Ancient Testimony* (Athens, Ohio, 1983), and the chapter itself ,"The Background of Newton's Jewish Studies," is very instructive. There are several bibliographic additions I would make: the *Encyclopedia Judaica* entries, "Hebraists, Christian," "Linguistic Literature, Hebrew" by James Baff, and "Hebrew Language, Mishnaic" by E Y. Kutscher (the last served Pérez Fernández as the most important guide for his revision of the work done by Segal); Heiko Oberman, *The Roots of Anti-Semitism in the Age of Renaissance and Reformation* (German, Berlin, 1981; English, Philadelphia, 1984); idem, "Discovery of Hebrew and Discrimination Against the Jews: The *Veritas Hebraica* as Double-Edged Sword in Renaissance and Reformation," in Andrew C. Fix and Susan C. Karant-Nunn, eds. *Germania Illustrata: Essays on Early Modern Germany Presented to Gerald Strauss* (Kirksville, 1992) 19-34 and my article, "Hebrew Studies in Institutions of Higher Education in the United States: materials toward an assessment," *Shofar, 9.3* (Spring, 1991).

26. *Op. cit.,* 19.

27. idem, 59-70.

28. idem, 100 (the chapter on Fagius goes on to 118).

29. Goldish, 19-25, esp. 22. ff.

30. *op. cit.,* 35.

31. See n. 25.

32. See my (dated) survey (n. 25) of the teaching of Hebrew in U.S. institutions of higher education which shows that most Hebrew is taught in dispensational settings and that Christian schools treat the biblical variety alone, with one or two exceptions.

33. Another motive to be considered is whether the author and the translator undertook the christianization of RH language and literature in order to provide a reason for their work and a defense of it against claims of judaization. Setting their work in the context of the conversion of the Jews and adding prefaces or missionary tracts to more straightforward works on Hebrew were common practices throughout the sixteenth and seventeenth centuries. See Friedman, *op. cit.,* 214.

Chapter 7

Teaching Modern Hebrew Literature to American Undergraduates
Gilead Morahg

In memory of my mother, who taught

Anyone who has attempted to teach Hebrew literature to American undergraduates knows that this undertaking involves an encounter with a wide variety of problems which often hamper the success of the enterprise. An analysis of the instructional process of teaching Hebrew literature to students who are not Israelis shows that the many difficulties this process must overcome stem from a multi-faceted clash between two divergent contextual frameworks: the cultural context in which the literary text was written and the cultural context in which the literary text is being read. The numerous disparities between these cultural matrixes inhibit the learning process and their range must be significantly reduced if the targeted literary works are to be effectively taught.

Reading a literary text constitutes a communicative act between its sender (the writer) and its recipient (the reader) who are often widely separated by time and place. Like all acts of human communication, successful reading depends on a productive interaction between a basic set of presuppositions held by the sender and a corresponding set of relevant presuppositions held by the recipient. These essential presuppositions fall into three broad categories: (1) presuppositions concerning the *language* in which the message is communicated; (2) presuppositions concerning the *genre* (i.e., the novel, the newspaper item, the business letter) which gives the message its form and enables much of its meaning; (3) presuppositions concerning *previous knowledge* that is shared by the sender and the recipient and thus constitutes the referential context within which the message becomes meaningful. If we apply these concepts to the actual conditions of teaching Hebrew literature outside of Israel, we will find a great gap between the presuppositions of the sender (the Hebrew writer) and the recipient (the American learner) in every one of the critical categories.

The most obvious disparity between writer and reader is in the area of language. This is more apparent in the introductory level of a literature program, when the students first encounter authentic Hebrew literary texts. But the disparity persists through the most advanced levels of undergraduate instruction. The linguistic presuppositions of the Hebrew writer concerning his or her intended reader are radically different from those of the American Hebrew learner who attempts to read the writer's work. The writer assumes a reader with the language competence of a fully educated native speaker of Hebrew. Few American students entering a Hebrew literature course fit this description. Their elementary and intermediate level language courses accustom them to reading the simplified and artificial language of Hebrew textbooks and of the newspapers that are written specially for beginners. But these courses can usually do little to prepare students for meeting the linguistic demands of Hebrew literary texts. Consequently, students find it very difficult to decipher the complex sentence structures of most literary works and their vocabulary falls far short of enabling them to engage the richness and intricacy of Hebrew literary style. Their attempts to comprehend even a short work of Hebrew literature prove to be an extremely difficult, time-consuming and often highly frustrating undertaking.

Presuppositions concerning genre are equally problematic. The literary writer presupposes a reader who is not only proficient in the language but is also truly literate. This intended reader is expected to have at least a basic understanding of the forms and functions of literature as well as a clear grasp of what distinguishes literary art from other forms of human discourse. It is an unfortunate aspect of the American educational system that many students may graduate from high school — and often even from college — without acquiring this necessary knowledge. Having never been taught how to read a work of literature analytically and critically, these students do not know how to approach a story, a novel or a poem. For such naive readers the encounter with a sophisticated literary text is often a bewildering experience that bears little relationship to the intended impact of the work.

The most formidable obstacle in the way of effective learning of Hebrew literature is presented by the disparity in presuppositions concerning previous knowledge that is created when the writer and the learner come from different cultural backgrounds. It is important to recognize that in addition to being a singular act of personal expression, a work of literary art is usually also a product of the immediate historical, cultural and social surroundings of its author. Explicit and implicit references to the world that lies outside the text are a major communicative device which few writers can do without. The effectiveness of almost every work of literature is largely dependent upon the familiarity of its readers with characteristic facets of the time and place in which the work was written. Most writers presuppose such a familiarity and draw upon it as they go about shaping and developing their works. Thus Bialik, in writing his poem *Levadi* ["Alone"], presupposes readers whose previous knowledge includes a familiarity with the concept of the "Shekhina" to which he can assign a central role in his poem without having to explain what it is. Likewise, Tschernichowski, in writing his *'Ani Ma'amin*["I Believe"], can include such verses as:

For my soul still yearns for freedom,
I have not sold it to a golden calf,
For I still believe in man,
And in his spirit, his vigorous soul.

His soul will cast off petty chains,
Will uplift us to the heights sublime,
No worker shall in hunger die,
Freedom — for the soul, bread — for the hungry.

with the assumption that his reader's previous knowledge will include sufficient familiarity with Marxist doctrine to enable an understanding that the poem embodies a defiant repudiation of this doctrine.

The ironic construction of Brenner's story *'Avlah* ["The Slander"], to give one final example, is predicated on the reader's presupposed knowledge of the values and ideals of the Second Aliyah pioneers. Without such knowledge, the ironic intent that underlies the development of the narrative may be easily overlooked, causing its thematic signification to be entirely misconstrued. And this, indeed, is what often happens when American undergraduates are required to respond to this story without having been sufficiently prepared. The teaching of literature outside of its natural cultural context makes one intensely aware of the extent to which each work of literature is, indeed, an intertextual construct — a product of various cultural discourses on which it relies for its intelligibility. Learners cannot truly comprehend the works of such poets as Judah Halevi, Bialik and Yehuda Amichai, or the fiction of Peretz, Agnon and Yehoshua without a basic understanding of the cultural context from which these works emerged. Yet the typical student enrolling in a Hebrew literature course at an American college will not have acquired such an understanding. The detrimental effects of this lack of historical and cultural background are often compounded by the natural inclination of naive readers to impose presuppositions derived from their own cultural context upon works that have little affinity with this context. All of this results in an all too familiar sense of confusion, misunderstanding and even disrespect for the material that is being studied. In view of the impediments that exist at each level of essential interaction between the American learner and the Hebrew text, it seems evident that without systematic corrective action the encounter of the learner with the text will inevitably result in a dismal failure of communication.

The above analysis of the existing disparities between the presuppositions of the writer and the learner may serve to explain many of the difficulties that hamper the teaching of Hebrew literature. But it may also provide us with a useful point of departure for seeking ways to overcome these difficulties. The first obvious step in this direction is the introduction of a mediating figure into the communicative transaction. This, of course, is the figure of the teacher whose role is to facilitate learning by devising and implementing appropriate means of bridging the gaps that exist on each essential level of interaction between the reader and the text. In order to fulfill this role successfully, the teacher must regard the teaching of a specific text as the end-product of a sequence of preparatory stages that precede the actual classroom presentation.

Effective classroom instruction is always preceded by a process of selection and organization which determines the content and structure of the complete schedule of study, or *syllabus,* designated for a particular course. Each of the texts that are selected and arranged within the syllabus should be regarded as an interactive component of a larger pedagogical design. This process of selection and organization should, in turn, be guided by a clear conception of the instructional objectives that are to be pursued within the general framework, or *curriculum,* of an integrated, multi-level program of Hebrew language and literature courses. The notion of an integrated, comprehensive curriculum that encompasses all the courses in the program and determines the substance and organization of each individual course is the mainstay of the approach to the teaching of Hebrew literature that I am about to propose.

The first stage in designing a functional program for teaching Hebrew literature is the determination of a set of basic principles that define the didactic objectives of this program and the methodological means of attaining these objectives. These principles should serve to determine the content and sequencing of all the courses within the program. They should guide the selection and organization of texts in each course and generate the most fitting and productive methods of teaching the selected texts. The primary structural principle for creating an integrated curriculum is the *principle of coherent continuity*. This principle stipulates that a viable curriculum is a sequence of courses in which each course constitutes a direct continuation of the preceding course and a controlled foundation for the course that is to follow. The principle of coherent continuity also applies to the organization of the instructional units within an individual course and it must be sustained on each of the three levels of essential interaction that have been discussed.

The Language of Literature: A Coordinated Curriculum

Coherent continuity of required language competence is an absolute necessity for the creation of a cohesive sequence of interlocking Hebrew language and literature courses. In order to ensure a smooth transition from one course to another, the linguistic starting point of each course must coincide with the level of language competence attained in the preceding course. The previously acquired language skills of students entering a new course should be a critical consideration in determining the textual content of this course. We should never confront students with texts written on a linguistic level that exceed the limits of their previous knowledge of Hebrew. But since the language of the designated texts must become increasingly difficult and complex, the language skills of the students must be continuously enhanced. As their learning of literature progresses, the students must also continue to acquire language skills that will enable them to meet the increasing linguistic demand of more advanced literary texts. This correlation must be maintained on all levels of instruction. At no point in the literature curriculum should the teacher abandon the systematic effort to enhance the students' semantic and syntactic accommodation to the Hebrew literary text by designing and implementing exercises, activities and instructional aids that serve to diminish the disparities between the linguistic presuppositions of the learners of Hebrew literature and those of the Hebrew writer.

The need for linguistic continuity exists on all levels of instruction, but it is particularly apparent at the point of transition from the last course in the language sequence to the first literature course, which is the weakest link in many undergraduate Hebrew programs. The materials incorporated into the lowest level literature course all too often consist of texts that are far too advanced for students who have completed the usual four semesters of elementary and intermediate college Hebrew language courses. This qualitative leap has significant quantitative consequences.

Most students who complete the Hebrew language program do not continue into the Hebrew literature program. The majority of the relatively few undergraduates who enter the literature program are not drawn from the ranks of the learners in the elementary and intermediate language courses. They are usually students who have acquired Hebrew competence outside the university — in Jewish day schools, in high schools that offer Hebrew as a foreign language, in various programs of study in Israel, in homes where Hebrew is spoken and, on rare occasions, in parochial afternoon schools — and whose superior command of the language qualifies them for entering directly into the more advanced levels of the literature courses.

The break in linguistic continuity between the Hebrew language and literature programs causes the sharp decrease in advanced enrollments and accounts for the radical discontinuity between the students completing the language program and those entering the literature program. A curriculum that denies its language students access to its literature courses undermines its viability by stemming the flow from an important pool of potential learners who, with appropriate action, could have been directed to the study of Hebrew literature. The characteristic incompatibility of Hebrew language and literature programs is usually not the result of a calculated policy but rather of a lapse in planning and coordination. The key to redressing this unfortunate situation is a conception of the *entire* Hebrew curriculum as an integrated continuum which maintains constant contact and coordination among all its courses. Maintaining a coordinated continuity is particularly important to the integration of the Hebrew language and literature courses which all too often operate independently of one another and sometimes actually work at cross purposes. One of the more typical instances of such detrimental lack of continuity occurs in the area of reading acquisition.

Many language programs favor an extensive approach to reading. They train and encourage students to combine their previous knowledge of the language with the contextual hints provided by the text in order to arrive at an approximate understanding of the general content of this text. Translation and detailed paraphrasing in the target language. are discouraged. Dictionary use is held at an absolute minimum. This approach may have merit in the reading of textbook passages and newspaper items, but it is inadequate and often counterproductive when applied to all but the simplest literary texts. The complicated and often irregular sentence structures of most Hebrew literary works, combined with their tendency towards idiomatic and allusive language, will quickly frustrate attempts at extensive reading by all but the most advanced Hebrew learners. More-over, the true study of literature will benefit very little from a learner's tenuous grasp of the "general content" of important works of poetry and fiction in which both words and sentences are carefully measured, delib-erately shaped and heavily loaded with signifying implications. The com-petencies that are required for the study of such texts include an array of *intensive* reading skills that will enable the learner to decipher difficult semantic elements and complex syntactic structures.

Prospective students of Hebrew literature must be taught to read in-tensively and analytically—as well as extensively and intuitively — from the earliest stages of their instruction. A Hebrew language curriculum that is oblivious to the specific language skills that are necessary for the study of literature and does not provide for their systematic development will either disqualify many students from making a successful transition to a more advanced literature program or, as is often the case, make it impossible to establish such a program. Ongoing coordination between the language and literature components of a Hebrew curriculum is an essential means of ensuring that the instructional objectives of the lan-guage program will take into account the specific competencies required in the literature courses. It will also ensure that the level of instruction in the first course of the literature sequence will be based on the attain-ments of the prerequisite language course.

The Meaning of Literature: A Supplementary Learning Sequence

Diminishing the disparities between the presuppositions concerning genre that separate the American learner from the Hebrew text involves a second area of instruction in which continuity must be maintained. The typical American undergraduate does not possess the conceptual knowledge and analytical tools that are necessary for progressing be-yond the surface content of a literary text to its deeper levels of structure, meaning and aesthetic expression. Consequently, an effective Hebrew literature curriculum must be supplemented with a clearly defined se-quence of instructional activities that will integrate basic concepts of literary analysis into the general progression of targeted texts. From the earliest stages to the most advanced levels, the teaching of Hebrew liter-ary texts must be accompanied by a corresponding development of the students' analytical and interpretative skills. The objective of this cur-ricular component is not to instruct the students in the latest permuta-tions of the prevailing critical theories but rather to familiarize them with the distinctive features and fundamental structures of the literary genre.

The topics of genre-specific instruction that are to supplement the learning of individual texts should include such basic concepts as the inherent relationship between form and meaning, the elemental structural and prosodic components of poetry and fiction, the distinction between subject and theme, as well as author, narrator and character in fiction. They should also include an active understanding of the more common rhetorical devices in literature such as metaphor, irony and ambiguity. A comprehension of the nature and function of plot development and narrative point of view in fiction is as essential as the familiarity with the role of image, contrast and analogy in poetry. While this list of suggested topics is not definitive, it does offer a general guideline for designing an appropriate supplementary learning sequence.

Since the structural and conceptual elements that are required for effective learning constitute the characteristic attributes of the literary genre, they can be found in many individual works of literary art. Consequently, this aspect of curriculum planning is of secondary importance in the selection and organization of the particular texts that are to be included in a given course or sequence of courses. It should be subordinate to more crucial considerations that are yet to be discussed. But one should never lose sight of the needs that the supplementary learning sequence is meant to serve. Once the appropriate texts for a particular course are collected and the general framework for their organization is determined, consideration must be given to the manner in which the final selection and organization of these texts in the syllabus will advance the acquisition of analytical and interpretative skills. In addition to serving all other objectives of the integrated curriculum, each text must be examined for the opportunities it provides for enhancing the students' cumulative knowledge of basic critical concepts and techniques.

Every Hebrew literature course should include a schedule for introducing relevant generic concepts and activities designed to apply these concepts to the assigned texts. This necessary interaction between concept and text can begin at the earliest stages of instruction, for even the simplest story will lend itself to introducing such concepts as the distinction between subject and theme or the differences between author, narrator and character. The most modest of poems will provide opportunities for learning some basic elements of prosody or the essential characteristics of a metaphor. Once such concepts are learned they can be readily reinforced by systematic application to future texts which, in turn, should serve to introduce additional literary concepts and critical skills. Thus, as the texts become more difficult and complex, the learners become more adept at addressing themselves to the deeper structures and underlying meanings of these texts.

The Reason for Literature: A Humanistic Perspective

The principles I have been discussing so far constitute a merely structural framework for a program of study that is yet to be filled with appropriate content. A determination of the specific literary content of each course requires recourse to yet another set of normative principles that will guide us in the appropriate selection and organization of the target texts. The need for a definitive answer to the question of "What should we teach?" may appear to be self-evident, but an informal survey of various Hebrew literature programs in American universities shows that this question has not always been thoroughly and systematically addressed. Many of these programs operate on a catch-as-catch-can basis. Text selection is determined by a teacher's familiarity with and fondness for certain works, or by considerations of the works' accessibility and appeal to the students, or by what is available in the few existing textbook anthologies of Hebrew literature, none of which are effectively designed to meet the needs of American undergraduates. In some cases texts are grouped into topical or thematic units (i.e., parents and children; friendship and love; childhood; war; kibbutz life; etc.) which are internally cohesive but are not related to other units in the course or to the materials studied in other courses. The transformation of this haphazard manner of teaching Hebrew literature into a cohesive, fully integrated curriculum requires the extension of the principle of coherent continuity to the textual content of the entire literature program.

The practical planning of an integrated curriculum must be preceded by a clear formulation of the ultimate instructional objectives of the literature program as a whole. We must begin designing the means of instruction by questioning their desired ends: Why do we wish to teach Hebrew literature? What are the benefits we intend our students to gain by studying it? What is the purpose of the enterprise? Definitive answers to these cardinal questions will provide an overriding rationale for our program and generate the criteria for selecting our texts, assigning them to functional locations upon the continuum and devising effective methods of teaching them to our students. Of the various possible answers to these fundamental questions, I would like to propose an approach that seems most relevant to the pedagogical realities of teaching Hebrew literature to American undergraduates.

Most American undergraduates who choose to study Hebrew literature have no intention of pursuing a more advanced course of studies that will train them to be professional Hebrew scholars. While our curriculum should certainly provide for the few who may seek a professional career in this field, it must take into account that it is directed primarily towards the education of people who are headed in other directions and whose future contact with Hebrew literature will be, at best, very limited. This is also true of their ongoing contact with the Hebrew language itself. Most of our students will not be going into fields of professional endeavor that require a knowledge of Hebrew language and literature. Even fewer will end up making a life for themselves in Israel. Our curriculum should clearly encourage the former and provide for the latter. But it should not be designed as a teacher-training program or as a preparatory program for prospective immigrants. With few exceptions, a Hebrew literature curriculum should be designed to contribute to the general experience of an education in the humanities which most America undergraduate programs aspire to provide.

A sharper definition of the overriding objective of a viable Hebrew literature curriculum may be arrived at by eliminating some of the more common misconceptions as to what this objective may be. Perhaps the most common misconception in this regard is approaching the study of literature as yet another means of enhancing competence in the language. Such an approach vitiates the very essence of the learning experience that an encounter with literature can provide. The primary objective of a Hebrew literature curriculum should, therefore, not be the advancement of the students' mastery of the Hebrew language. It should also not be providing instruction in the methods and disciplines of literary criticism. It should not even be the pursuit of the singular aesthetic experience offered by select works of literary art. Let there be no mistake: all of these objectives are extremely important. They should be integrated as essential components into every curriculum. But, as such, they must be subordinated to an overriding objective which is to create a broad and dynamic encounter between the American learner and Hebrew culture.

The dynamics of literature are often generated by the encounter of an individual sensibility with the forces of circumstance and, in many cases, the nature of this encounter is defined by the circumstances of a specific historical reality. Of all the humanistic disciplines, literature is unique in its capacity to merge individual experience with cultural context so as to reflect the human dimensions of historical occurrences. An effective undergraduate literature curriculum should be geared towards drawing upon the genre's unique properties of deepening our understanding of human experiences while illuminating the historical and cultural realities that almost invariably contribute to the shaping of these experiences. Expanding the students' knowledge of the historical circumstances, social dynamics and intellectual trends that have shaped the destiny of the Jewish nation, while deepening their understanding of the effects of this destiny upon the lives of individuals and communities within the nation, is the principle purpose of the humanistic approach to a viable Hebrew literature curriculum. This purpose also serves as the primary criterion for selecting the culturally significant materials that are to be incorporated into the curriculum.

The proposed approach assumes a reciprocal relationship between history and literature. It requires that the works selected for inclusion in the curriculum be representative of the historical and cultural contexts to which they belong. Each of these texts should be regarded both as a unique work of individual expression and as a literary reflection of a writer's reaction to a specific social reality. In addition to establishing a normative touchstone for text selection, this approach provides a conceptual framework for relating the selected texts to one another and an orienting perspective for the manner in which each text should be taught. The resulting curriculum will comprise a literary continuum that reflects clear historical and cultural patterns in the life of the Jewish people. Among the guiding criteria for selecting the texts that will comprise the culturally oriented Hebrew literature curriculum are the topical and thematic aspects of these texts. Every work must be considered on the basis of the degree to which its topical concerns and thematic significations reflect a representative range of the central historical characteristics and human issues of the period in which it is set. The selected texts should be drawn from a variety of literary genres. They should gradually cohere into a thematically integrated historical framework, although they need not be taught in strict chronological order or arranged in tight thematic clusters. A modern Hebrew literature curriculum, for example, should contain works that range from the Haskalah, or post-Haskalah period through the pioneering settlement period to the present time of Israeli statehood. The sequencing of these works within the curriculum is determined largely by their ascending levels of difficulty.

Introductory-level courses may consist of simple texts representing a variety of genres, periods and thematic concerns. As instruction progresses, the connections between the various literary aspects will begin to emerge and will serve as a basis for a systematic presentation in the more advanced survey courses. A strictly topical or thematic grouping of texts is appropriate only in the most advanced levels of instruction, after the general contextual framework has been firmly established. The process of establishing this framework begins at the earliest stages of instruction and is made possible by continuously involving the learners with the salient thematic elements in different periods of Hebrew literature as they occur and recur in the designated works.

A critical step in planning a curriculum is the formulation of explicit thematic guidelines for selecting texts and relating them to one another. These guidelines are, to a large extent, subjective and may vary from program to program, but, in all cases, they must be clearly defined and consistently applied. By way of example, it might be useful to present the thematic designations that have been providing coherence and continuity to the modern Hebrew literature program in which I teach:

1. *Modern revolutions in Jewish life: Hasidism, Haskalah, Zionism.*
2. *Diaspora and Zion: A crises of values.*
3. *Experiences of the pioneers: The ideal and the real.*
4. *Holocaust: The human dimensions of a national tragedy.*
5. *Israeli society at war: Consequences and implications.*
6. *Literary perspectives on Israel myths.*
7. *Living in a realized dream: Literary perspectives on social issues.*
8. *Israel and the Israeli: Harmony or conflict?*

Every text included in the curriculum should have a direct bearing on at least one, but usually several, of the predetermined themes and should be taught in relation to other, similarly oriented works.

After they are gradually introduced at the introductory level, these themes will accompany the curriculum through all its stages. As they progress from level to level, the students encounter these themes in different variations, combinations and contexts. They approach them from different perspectives and perceive their interrelations as interlocking manifestations of a dynamic social, historical and cultural reality. The more we involve our students in the deeper levels of works by representative writers, the better they will be able to perceive the human dimensions of the ongoing encounter with the various historical and cultural contexts that these writers represent. Once our students complete the Hebrew literature program they will have acquired a body of humanistic knowledge that may well accompany and enrich their lives in the years to come. An example from one of the learning units in an Introduction to Hebrew Literature course will serve to illustrate this dynamic.

The figure of Hannah Senesh serves as a focus for an instructional unit in our introductory-level course. This unit consists of the following texts: a biographical chapter in simple Hebrew;[1] selections from the diary of Hannah Senesh,[2] two poems by Hannah Senesh,[3] selections from Aharon Megged's play, *Hannah Senesh.* The topical and thematic considerations for this selection should be evident. The events surrounding the life of Hannah Senesh, her prominent place in the pantheon of Israeli heroes, the things that she wrote and those that were written about her, all lend themselves naturally to many of the thematic underpinnings of the extended curriculum. They provide opportunities for addressing such prevalent aspects as the dichotomy between Zion and the Diaspora, the ambivalencies of the pioneering experience, reactions to the Holocaust and to war, the distinctions between literature and myth, the disparities and tensions between the needs of the individual and the demands of society. This selection also satisfies the requirement for generic diversity by presenting elements of essay, confessional writing, poetry and drama. Effectively taught, these texts will enhance the students' knowledge of an important historical period as well as their understanding of some characteristics of the literary response to historical reality.

The biographical text which opens the learning sequence provides the necessary factual context for the later readings. It also provides an example of didactic writing that selects and organizes its factual material in accordance to ulterior ideological motives. A comparison of this text to the selections from Hannah Senesh's diary will reveal the extent to which the didactic text simplifies her character and ignores the complexities of her motives. In addition to illuminating the disparities between popular myth and subjective reality, the diary selections introduce a variety of relevant thematic aspects and constitute a useful transition from the non-literary writing of the biographical text to the literary characteristics of the poetry and the play. Much of what is learned in this unit will be used to inform subsequent stages of the integrated curriculum.

A curriculum based on coherent thematic continuity creates the necessary conditions for diminishing the disparities in communicative presuppositions that separate the reader from the text. But it does not constitute a definitive solution to all the problems that are created by the fundamental incongruity between the essential aspects of the cultural context in which a Hebrew text was written and the different cultural context in which this text is being read by the American learner. The actualization of the learning potential that is inherent in the integrated curriculum must take place within the day-to-day process of overcoming the cultural, linguistic and generic barriers presented by each individual text.

Teaching the Text: Aids and Means
Providing a Context
The relevant meanings that are to be communicated by almost every work selected to serve the objectives of the culturally oriented curriculum are often the function of explicit or implicit references to an extra-textual context with which the writer assumes his reader to be familiar. It is impossible to grasp the meaning of the opening lines of Bialik's "Alone," for example, (They were all carried away by the wind,/The light has swept them away,/Thrilling to a new song of their dawning life;) let alone of the entire poem, without being aware of the conflict between the convictions of traditional Jewish orthodoxy and the new spirit of Enlightenment in which Bialik's generation was caught up and to which his poem was responding. Such knowledge is necessary for the effective learning of all other texts related to the theme of Modern Revolutions in Jewish Life, be they the poems of Saul Tschernichowski, the, fiction of David Frishman or the essays of Ahad Ha'am. A general knowledge of different historical and cultural contexts is similarly necessary for the effective learning of texts related to the other thematic components of the curriculum. Since the knowledge presumed by the writers is typically lacking in many of our students, the teaching of the selected texts must be accompanied by a systematic enhancement of the learners' historical and cultural knowledge. This may be accomplished by a variety of means.

Brief periodic background lectures by the teacher are most useful in placing a text, or group of texts, in the appropriate historical and cultural context. The text itself can serve as a valuable source of historical and cultural knowledge. Preparation for teaching each text should include a search for internal contextual indicators that are most relevant to the period and thematic features this text is intended to represent. A discussion of these contextual references should be incorporated into the teaching plan in such a manner that will enable the teacher to expand upon them and to lead the learners to an understanding of the particular relation of the specific text to its general context.

Another means of bringing American learners into the contextual framework of the assigned works involves the use of visual and audio-visual aids. Occasional in-class viewings of slides and video programs that present salient aspects of the period in which the assigned texts are set provide a valuable visual link between the world of the reader and the unfamiliar world of the text. They create natural opportunities for a discussion of the contextual dimensions that are most relevant to the intended thematic orientation and constitute valuable points of reference for future discussions as well. They also add diversity and texture to the learning process. Such materials are readily available from a variety of sources, many of which are still virtually untapped.[4]

The objectives of an ambitious curriculum must always contend with the constraints of actual time available for classroom learning. Given the diversity of activities that must be carried out during the usual three weekly contact hours, the time devoted to contextual enhancement in class must be rigorously controlled. But this essential aspect of knowledge may be further expanded outside the classroom by assigning background readings (in English and/or Hebrew) that are to be carried out independently by the students. Brief historical background readings in simple Hebrew may be assigned in the early stages of instructions.[5] In the more advanced stages of learning, these basic Hebrew texts may be supplemented by more extensive and more sophisticated background readings in English. The best single source for such readings that I have found is Meyer Waxman's *A History of Jewish Literature.*[6] This comprehensive work is particularly suited for undergraduates. The introductory chapters to each of the historical periods, as well as the biographical and critical discussions of individual writers are lucid, informative, and pleasingly free of jargon. Relevant background readings should routinely accompany the learning process. Students should be expected to demonstrate their knowledge of this supplementary material in class discussions, in their papers and on their exams.

Efficient management of instructional time requires that all learning activities that can be carried out outside the classroom should be assigned as homework. In addition to reading the background materials, these activities include the initial readings of each designated literary text and a systematic preparation for its discussion. In-class instruction should begin only after the students have contended with the linguistic difficulties of the text and addressed themselves to its relevant contextual, structural and thematic dimensions on their own. Yet, in reality, most students need help with each of these textual aspects. If we are to make good use of valuable class time, we must devise effective means of facilitating the students' independent encounter with the linguistic, generic and contextual aspects of the text. These means consist of instructional aids and conceptual guidelines that will orient the learners in their initial readings and assist in their preparation for the class discussions that are to follow.

Guides for the Perplexed

One of the most effective methods of enabling students to accomplish the required preliminary readings of a difficult Hebrew text involves the preparation of a detailed Reading Guide that will accompany every assigned work of literature. The Reading Guide should be written in Hebrew and will typically consist of a brief introductory statement concerning the contextual and circumstantial setting of the work, followed by several sets of questions, each addressing a different aspect of the text. It will also contain a glossary of selected lexical items.

More often than not the most difficult part of a literary work from a different time and place are its opening passages which thrust the reader into an alien environment of obscure references and disorienting authorial presuppositions. The opening to Brenner's "The Slander" may serve as a case in point:

> It happened at the end of that winter, when you on the other side were already under the British while we here continued under the Turks. I will not pause to describe the nervous tension in which we lived day after day. Newspapers and telegrams never came to our commune, and we had no inkling whatever of what was happening in the rest of the world. We were fed by rumors, and by the sound of firing which came from the direction of Kfar Saba. Of one thing we were sure — that things were in a sorry mess. Our liberators were stuck midway between Jerusalem and Nablus. and were not moving. Why didn't they march straight ahead, northwards? The general opinion was that they did not want to pass through our settlements for fear of provoking the Turks, who in their retreat might destroy us.

This passage presupposes a reader who is familiar with the political, social and ideological realities in Palestine during the First World War. A reader who does not possess the presupposed knowledge will quickly become disoriented and have great difficulty in comprehending the Hebrew text. The introductory Statement that opens the Reading Guide is intended to alleviate some of this difficulty by placing the work in its historical context and providing some essential information concerning the immediate setting and circumstances to which the work refers. In the case of "The Slander" this statement may read as follows [in Hebrew]:

> The story takes place during the First World War. The Turks ruled Palestine and the British were trying to conquer the land. The Jewish inhabit-

ants wanted the British to succeed because they believed that British rule would be better for them. At the time of the story the British had succeeded in conquering only the southern part of the country.

The narrator of the story is a member of a small commune of Jewish farmers, not far from a larger Jewish colony in the central part of the country. This area was still in the hands of the Turks and their allies, the Germans. The members of the group are waiting for the British army to reach them but the British advance has been stopped.

The situation in the commune and in the colonies around it is not good. They are suffering from hunger and were also afraid of the Turks.

The Introductory Statement is followed by two sets of guiding questions. The students are instructed to read all the questions before they begin reading the text itself and to refer back to them as their reading proceeds. The first set consists of Content and Context Questions that are designed to assist the learners in understanding the surface meaning of the text and to alert them to the various contextual references that are embedded in it. These questions will usually follow the linear progression of the text and address each textual block — a stanza in a poem, a paragraph in a prose work — in the order of its appearance. The Content and Context Questions for the opening paragraphs of "The Slander," for example, may read as follows [in Hebrew]:

1 . What are the reasons for the settlers' "nervous tension"?
2. Why was it difficult for the settlers to know what was happening on the front and how did they get their information?
3. Who is being referred to as "our liberators" and why?
4. What was the general opinion about the British reasons for not advancing straight to the north?

A preliminary reading of these questions, as well as those that follow, will provide the students with considerable information and necessary orientation concerning the story they are about to read. Once they begin reading, they can continuously check their comprehension of each textual block by attempting to answer all of the questions that are related to it. They may consider their initial reading of a given textual block as being complete only when they can answer all of these questions. The Content and Context Questions also serve the teacher as a quick and effective means of verifying student comprehension without resorting to translation or line-by-line reading and elucidation in class. This allows for the larger portion of the instructional time allocated to each textual unit to be devoted to a more wide-ranging, in-depth discussion based on the second set of questions that accompany the text. These are Discussion Questions that are designed to relate the surface of the text to its underlying structures and significations.

The Discussion Questions included in the Reading Guide for each text are intended to orient the learner towards the interrelated contextual, structural and thematic aspects of the texts that have been targeted for discussion. They provide an informed common basis for such a discussion by requiring a preparatory consideration of predetermined textual elements that are most relevant to this particular juncture in the learning sequence. Once again Brenner's "The Slander" may serve as an example.

"The Slander" is an appropriate textual selection because of Brenner's importance as a writer and because of this story's affinities with several of the curriculum's central themes: Modern Revolutions in Jewish Life; Diaspora and Zion; Experiences of the Pioneers. By the time they encounter this story, the students will have already acquired a basic knowledge of the circumstances, problems and ideals of the Second Aliyah. They will have also been introduced to some of the rudimentary formal attributes of narrative fiction. Our objectives in teaching this story may include:

1 . Enhancing the student's knowledge of the social issues and human dimensions of the Second Aliyah period by identifying the most relevant contextual references.

2. Enhancing the students' awareness of the nature of a literary work's thematic response to a given historical reality by viewing Brenner's work as a realistic antithesis to the then prevailing "Israeli genre" of writing which tended to idealize the pioneering experience.

3. Introducing the function of irony in communicating meaning and advancing thematic signification.

The Discussion Questions that will accompany "The Slander" should be designed to orient the readers towards the designated instructional objectives and to lead them towards discoveries of the interrelationships among the relevant contextual, structural and thematic aspects of the story. They may include the following clusters:

1. When the officer first arrives at the kvutza and encounters the narrator, the following exchange takes place: "He addressed me in fluent German: 'Who lives here? Jews, I presume.'
"'Jewish workers,' I stressed in a Germanic Yiddish."
   a. The narrator's answer reveals an important set of values that he shares with the other members of the group. What are these values and how are they expressed in this brief exchange?
   b. Find three other instances in the story in which these and other related values are expressed.
2. In "The Slander," as in many of Brenner's other works, the values of the pioneers are put to the test of reality. Where do we see this testing taking place and what are its outcomes in:
   a. The relationships among the members of the group.
   b. The attitudes and actions of the group towards the officer.
3. The members of the group feel very badly about what they did to the officer, but at the end of the story their feeling changes. All of them, including the narrator, feel good.
   a. What were the reasons for their bad feelings?
   b. What caused the change in their feelings?
   c. Does the author expect the readers to share in the good feelings of the group, or is the ending of the story ironic?
   d. Irony involves a contrast between an expectation and its fulfillment, or between the appearance of a situation and the reality that underlies it. Do you agree that there is irony in the first exchange between the officer and the narrator?
   e. Can you find any other instances of irony in the story?
   f. How is the author's use of irony related to the central themes of the story?

It may be argued that such a structured approach to the teaching of a text curtails the spontaneity of the reader's response. Eliciting highly subjective responses to the designated texts is not a primary objective of the proposed curriculum. But experience shows that proper direction actually enhances the discovery and pleasure in what may otherwise be difficult and frustrating material.

Breaching the Lexical Barrier

The suggested Discussion Questions are a most effective means of involving learners with the text, orienting them towards the designated instructional objectives and generally enhancing the learning process. But they do not serve to remove the numerous lexical obstacles that usually hamper, and often subvert, this process. Most significant Hebrew literary texts contain numerous lexical items that are not part of the typical students' acquired vocabulary. Many of these are simply words that are unknown to the students and may be found in their dictionaries, But the paperback dictionaries that are most commonly used offer little help in deciphering idiomatic phrases and culture-specific terms. They also omit many words that are infrequently used in all but literary texts. Even students who are very skilled in using their dictionaries will quickly become confused and frustrated when attempting to read a Hebrew literary text which will typically contain key lexical items that are not to be found in their dictionaries, Since we cannot expect undergraduate students to invest in R. Alcalay's expensive *Complete Hebrew English Dictionary,* we must find an alternative way of providing the necessary lexical aid.

One way of closing the gap between the lexical presuppositions of a Hebrew text and the American learner's previous knowledge of Hebrew is to explain the unfamiliar items in class. This is highly undesirable since it requires devoting a considerable amount of valuable class time to a tedious, non-participatory process of translation and/or lexical explication. It also denies the advantages of having the learners do the initial readings of the text on their own. A far more advantageous way of providing the necessary lexical assistance is the preparation of a selected glossary for each of the assigned texts.

The Reading Guide for every text should include a Glossary that is designed to provide learners with immediate access to difficult Hebrew texts without undercutting the ongoing development of general language skills. The Glossary should contain selected lexical items in the order of their appearance in the text for which Hebrew explanations or, when necessary, English definitions are provided. The items selected for glossing are to be drawn from four distinct categories: cultural and contextual references with which the learners are assumed to be unfamiliar; difficult idiomatic constructs; key words that do not appear in the students' dictionaries; randomly selected words that are unknown to the students but may be found in their dictionaries. The reasons for including the first three categories should be evident. The fourth may require further explanation.

A successful Hebrew literature curriculum cannot exclude all but the simplest literary texts. The objectives of the comprehensive curriculum require a continuous introduction of works with increasing degrees of linguistic difficulty. At every level of instruction the students will be confronted with texts that contain numerous words that are unknown to them. Requiring students to look up every new word, or even every unknown word that is essential for their understanding of the test is counterproductive. It involves tedious hours of largely mechanical dictionary work in which little actual learning takes place. Much of this time could be better used for other learning activities. The value of looking up words in a dictionary cannot be wholly discounted since it enhances the learners' grasp of Hebrew morphology and may contribute to increasing their vocabulary. But these benefits are amply provided for by the many lexical items that are not included in the glossary. By incorporating a portion of the unfamiliar words into the glossary, we enhance its effectiveness as a means of facilitating reading comprehension without detracting from the desired learning objectives.

The principles and practices delineated above evolved from the experience gained over the many years in the Hebrew literature program at the University of Wisconsin in Madison. This program was established in 1955 as part of the undergraduate course offerings of the Department of Hebrew and Semitic Studies. The growing strength and effectiveness of this program, the scope of knowledge it provides and the enthusiasm it generates, lead me to believe that the principles and practices on which it is founded constitute a viable basis for a successful approach to the problems of teaching Hebrew literature to American undergraduates. ✡

Endnotes

1. "Hannah Senesh," *Pirkei keri'ah betoldot ha'am veha'arets: 'ishim* ["Readings in the history of the nation and the land: major figures"] ed. Nira Sha'anan. Ministry of Education, Department for Adult Education (Jerusalem, 1979), 131-134.
2. *Hannah Senesh* [Includes diaries and other writings] (Tel Aviv, 1959). Some selections may be found in *Sha'ar lesifrut* ["Gateway to literature: readings for Hebrew learners"] ed. Michal Homsky (Tel Aviv, 1968), pp. 168-171.
3. *Ibid.*
4. The slide Archives of the Shazar Institute in Jerusalem, for example, offer a wide selection of authentic slide programs on various aspects of the modern Jewish experience, i.e., The First Colonies; "Hashomer"; The Second Aliyah; Illegal Immigration 1938-1948; The Holocaust; the Jews of North Africa; Benjamin Ze'ev Herzl; David Ben Gurion; the Jewish Underground. These programs may be obtained from: Slide

Archives of Jewish History, Zalman Shazar Institute, 4 Hovevey Zion St., P.O. Box 4179, Jerusalem, Israel. The PBS television series "Heritage: Civilization and the Jews" which covers a much wider span of Jewish history is available on video cassettes from: Films Incorporated, 1213 Wilmette Ave., Wilmette, IL 60091. Additional information about available visual and audio-visual materials may be obtained from: The Pedagogic Centre for Jewish Education in the Diaspora, The Melton Centre for Jewish Education, Hebrew University of Jerusalem, Jerusalem, Israel.

5. See, for example, Reuven Bar-Sever *Perakim betoldot 'am yisrael laulpanim* ["Chapters in Jewish History for the Ulpan"], Ministry of Education, Department for Adult Education (Jerusalem, 1965).

6. Meyer Waxman, *A History of Jewish Literature* (New York, 1960).

Chapter 8

Integrating Gender Analysis into Jewish Studies Teaching

Judith R. Baskin

To design a syllabus and teach a course in virtually any area of Jewish Studies without including course content and illustrative materials indicating how constructions of gender have shaped the subject matter is to disregard an essential category of academic analysis. In previous generations, scholars in most disciplines tended to assume that the lives, activities, and intellectual achievements of men constituted the norm for all human behavior. In recent decades, however, feminist scholars have created new analytical frameworks that convincingly demonstrate that gender, as much as race, ethnicity, and social class, is an integral consideration in studying human endeavors. Investigating the ways in which cultural and religious systems apportion not only roles and responsibilities but essential human qualities and capacities between the sexes tells us a great deal about those traditions. Similarly, determining what defines and constitutes appropriate and inappropriate male and female behaviors is crucial in delineating the assumptions and values of any given society. Moreover, in many cultures, including Jewish societies in virtually all times and places, women's lives, concerns, and spiritual and creative endeavors have differed from those of men and are deserving of study on their own terms. In this essay I explain why both the implications of gender and the specific experiences of women should be incorporated into Jewish Studies teaching, offer some bibliographic suggestions to further these goals, and suggest some of the ways in which they can be fulfilled.

The discussion that follows is informed in part by the thirty-five course syllabi collected in my co-edited volume, *Gender and Jewish Studies: A Curriculum Guide*[1] in which prominent North American and Israeli scholars suggest a variety of ways to incorporate Jewish gender issues into a broad range of academic courses. While some of the teaching strategies delineated in *Gender and Jewish Studies* are for courses which center attention on specific topics connected with women and the Jewish experience, others systematically incorporate women's experiences and contributions into general Jewish Studies instruction. Building on the work of these colleagues,[2] my essay discusses some of the reasons why studying the often neglected perspectives and experiences of the female half of the Jewish people and considering the implications of gender in Judaism and in Jewish cultures is central to understanding and teaching the Jewish experience.

Methodological Premises

The perception that women's lives and experiences in any particular historical epoch may differ from men's has profoundly affected the ways in which many scholars approach and interpret their subjects of study.[3] Introducing gender as a factor in the study of human societies, endeavors, and achievements has revealed a persistent pattern of limiting women's access to public activities and the status they confer, and has highlighted the ways in which women have frequently been excluded from the education and empowerment which would allow them to function and achieve in the culturally valued spheres of public communal life and discourse.[4] Attentiveness to gender differences focuses attention instead on issues of family life and the activities of the private domestic domain. Raising questions about age of marriage, dowry endowments, tolerance of polygyny, and attitudes about spousal abuse, for example, discloses important information about the status of women in specific Jewish communities, and provides measures of the influence of contiguous cultures on Jewish social life as well. Similarly, studying the gendering of economic enterprises is also revelatory of a Jewish social polity in which women have always played an essential role as wage earners and entrepreneurs. And examinations of Jewish education which compare curriculum for boys with how and what girls were taught provides another way of defining how Jewish societies have designated different skills and functions between the sexes and illuminates what qualities and abilities were seen as most valuable in each gender and in Jewish society in general.

Using gender as a category of scholarly analysis also demonstrates new ways of evaluating cultural innovation and tradition. While women have rarely been a part of the events and accomplishments which have been valued and taught as part of a culture's intellectual heritage, investigation can sometimes reveal contemporaneous and alternative women's histories and cultures. Where women have been excluded from "sanctioned" male cultural activities or religious observances they have often created their own artifacts and rituals, a phenomenon which anthropologist Susan Starr Sered has defined as the "little tradition." This body of spiritual practices and often interpersonally oriented ceremonies will frequently differ profoundly from the "official religion" shaped and practiced by men.[5] In the Jewish realm one can point to such phenomena as women's prayer groups and other activities in the medieval synagogue,[6] the development of devotional literature intended for women and sometimes written by women,[7] women's needlework or other donations to the synagogue as forms of communal participation,[8] as well as the contemporary sometimes extra-halakhic spiritual practices of Jewish women documented by Sered and other authors.[9] And, as scholars like Marion Kaplan and Paula Hyman have demonstrated, gender analysis also demonstrates that in times of rapid social change and political turmoil women are frequently the culture bearers for their group, preserving the essentials of cultural identity both in the domestic setting and the public sphere.[10]

The resurgent feminist movement beginning in the early 1970's has brought both religious renewal and bitter controversy to contemporary Western Judaism, especially in North America. Significant numbers of Jewish women, linking feminism's mandate for female equality in all areas of human endeavor with an explicit commitment to Jewish identification and the Jewish community, have sought full participation in and access to a tradition which rarely considered women as central figures in its history, thought, religious practice, or communal life. Academic study of present day Judaism must, perforce, document how American Jewish feminists are re-visioning their roles in an environment in which American Jews in general are facing previously unimagined challenges in the areas of family formation; unprecedented higher education and career opportunities; increased communal acceptance of homosexuality and other alternative life-style choices; and a wide range of options in religious and spiritual expression, and in political and civic activism. The consequences of the Jewish feminist movement for Jewish religious practice, including the increasing prevalence of egalitarian worship, the ordination of female rabbis and cantors in liberal forms of Judaism, the introduction of liturgical change recognizing women as part of the communal worship congregation, and new rituals sacralizing life cycle events that are particular to women's lives are all phenomena of contemporary Judaism which cannot be ignored by responsible teachers of the Jewish tradition.

For those who question the value of presenting a gender-oriented perspective on Judaism as a religious tradition or on any aspect of Jewish history, literature or thought, it is useful, as well, to observe the parallels between the academic study of women and the study of the Jews. For one thing, the experiences and histories of both women and Jews have often been quite different from the experiences of the dominant or majority groups from whose points of view history has generally been written. Moreover, the consequences of major historical events and transformations have often been profoundly different for marginalized groups including Jews and women, while the periodizations that characterize general historical studies are not always meaningful for women's or Jewish history.[11] Similarly, recent efforts to introduce Jewish Studies into the mainstream liberal arts curriculum are analogous to similar endeavors vis-à-vis Women's and Gender Studies. In each instance the passage from marginal and parochial to an accepted place in the academic pantheon has been hesitant and halting, even in an academic atmosphere celebratory of cultural diversity.[12]

Despite these correspondences, however, introducing research which incorporates gender as a category of analysis into the Jewish Studies curriculum has been a slow process. Judaic scholarship has almost always been written and taught from the point of view of the male Jew, and has accordingly documented male intellectual concerns and achievements. The classical Jewish literary tradition was overwhelmingly, if not wholly, produced by men. Scholarly references to Jewish women have generally assumed that activities connected with the realm of the female are secondary; extrapolating from women's position in most aspects of halakhah, many Jewish scholars have portrayed women, if they considered them at all, as objects of male authority rather than as independent actors in their own lives. The reality that few Jewish women before modern times possessed the skills or authority to preserve their own reflections for posterity has also played a part in the absence of women's experiences in studies of the Jewish past. An early modern exception, of course, is Glückel of Hameln (1646-1724), whose readily available autobiography is an essential accompaniment to any study of early modern Jewish history.[13] Its female voice and particular concerns with household and children, as well as business and the synagogue, set it apart in Jewish literature up to its time.

Glückel and most other Jewish women from previous eras whose activities are recorded or whose words survive were generally elite women who came from wealthy families able to give their daughters educations and opportunities far beyond what most Jewish women were ever offered. Their lives demonstrate an additional essential pedagogical point:

that social class can be as central as gender in determining human destinies. However, even women like Glückel or other prominent wealthy women like Doña Gracia Nasi were not learned in traditional Jewish scholarly texts. Until recent decades, few Jewish women were empowered to become scholars and interpreters of the authorized versions of Jewish history and intellectual achievement. While the growth of Women's Studies as a field of scholarly endeavor has led to increased academic study of both women in Judaism, and of Jewish women and their experiences and accomplishments, there are still very few works of general Jewish history which take into account the lives and experiences of Jewish women of previous eras, as opposed to and as compared to those of men. As scholars within the field of Judaic Studies continue to actively encourage the inclusion of Jewish history and intellectual and cultural achievements in the general liberal arts curriculum, there must also be a commitment to recognizing the diversity of the Jewish experience — geographic, ethnic, religious, and social, including the ramifications of class and gender — in teaching content and materials.

New Research

During the past two decades there has been a flourishing of scholarly research on the lives and experiences of Jewish women in Jewish cultures and societies from ancient to modern times. Similarly, investigations of Jewish constructions of gender and the ramifications of Judaism's traditions of engendering specific roles and activities as male or female have also resulted in the establishment of an ongoing scholarly discourse. The fruits of this research are slowly entering the mainstream of Jewish scholarship and responsible teachers of Jewish Studies courses should be aware of it and able to share it with their students. Accessible points of entry include the course syllabi in *Gender and Jewish Studies* which list primary and secondary sources other Jewish Studies professors have found useful in their teaching. The eleven essays by prominent scholars in *Feminist Perspectives on Jewish Studies* survey and situate the impact of feminist research on a variety of areas of Jewish Studies scholarship and teaching including biblical studies, rabbinics, history, theology, philosophy, sociology, anthropology, Hebrew literature, American-Jewish literature, and film studies, while also providing bibliographic information and desiderata for future research. My first edited anthology of essays, *Jewish Women in Historical Perspective*, second edition (1999), provides scholarly essays by experts in their fields on women's experiences in a variety of historical and cultural settings, while the second, *Women of the Word: Jewish Women and Jewish Writing* (1994) explores female literary representations and expressions in languages including Hebrew, Yiddish, Italian, English, and Spanish, from medieval times to the present.[14] The essays are written to be accessible to undergraduate and general audiences while the notes provide detailed references to both primary and secondary sources relevant to this growing field of Jewish study. Many instructors use *Jewish Women in Historical Perspective* as required reading in Jewish Studies survey courses alongside more traditionally oriented history texts as a way to integrate women's experiences into the curriculum.

My extensive essay, "Women and Judaism," forthcoming in *Encyclopaedia of Judaism* (Leiden and New York, 2000), provides an historical overview based on recent scholarship and provides a full bibliography. Recent important scholarly work on the ramifications of gender construction in Judaism and Jewish history include *Judaism since Gender*, edited by Miriam Peskowitz and Laura Levitt (New York, 1997); Paula Hyman, *Gender and Assimilation in Modern Jewish History* (Seattle and London, 1995); and Daniel Boyarin, *Unheroic Conduct: The Rise of Heterosexuality and the Invention of the Jewish Man* (Berkeley, 1997). *Women in the Holocaust*, edited by Dalia Ofer and Lenore J. Weitzman (New Haven, 1998), provides a major resource for understanding the implications of gender in the horrific context of Nazi genocide, while *Pioneers and Homemakers: Jewish Women in Pre-State Israel*, ed. Deborah S. Bernstein (Albany, 1992) collects essays discussing women's roles in Jewish settlement of the Yishuv. *Calling the Equality Bluff: Women in Israel*, ed. B. Swirski and M. Safir (New York, 1991) discusses Jewish women in contemporary Israel. Works which discuss the ramifications of feminism on the contemporary Jewish community include various readings in *On Being a Jewish Feminist: A Reader*, ed. Susannah Heschel, (New York, 1983; rep. 1995), and Sylvia Barack Fishman, *A Breath of Life: Feminism in the American Jewish Community* (New York, 1993).

A number of excellent collections have illuminated our knowledge of Jewish women's contemporary concerns. Anthologies that address a variety of issues connected with women and Judaism include *On Being a Jewish Feminist* and *The Tribe of Dina: A Jewish Women's Anthology*, eds. Melanie Kaye/Kantrowitz and Irena Klepfisz, (1986; rep. Boston, 1989); other useful sources are referred to elsewhere in this essay. Among bibliographies that deal with women in Judaism are *The Jewish Women: 1900-1981.. Bibliography*, ed. Aviva Cantor (Fresh Meadow, NY, 1981);

Jewish Women and Jewish Law. Bibliography, ed. Ora Hamelsdorf and Sandra Adelsberg (Fresh Meadows, NY, 1990); and *The Jewish Woman. An Annotated Selected Bibliography, 1986-1993*, ed. Ann S. Masnik (New York, 1996).

Using Primary Sources about Gender in General Courses

Every Jewish Studies course, from the elementary survey to the graduate seminar, regardless of topic, makes uses of primary documents. An initial step in integrating gender concerns into a Jewish Studies syllabus is to include primary documents which teach something about gender at the same time as they illuminate the topic of the course; the possibilities are boundless: all that is required is a desire on the part of an instructor to choose to include relevant texts and to address appropriate questions to them. In a course which studies the Hebrew Bible, for instance, a focus on the two creation stories in Genesis can illustrate competing points of view embedded in biblical texts and the need to decipher their redactional histories while also generating examinations of differing biblical traditions about the origin of human beings and of the relationship of women to men. Considerations of biblical narratives centering on family tensions and dynastic struggles can also demonstrate the range (and limits) of female options in a patriarchal society at the same time as patterns of succession are revealed. A gender analysis approach to figures like Sarah, Rebecca, Rachel, Deborah, Yael, Ruth, Abigail, Bathsheba, or Esther can demonstrate how women achieved their ends of protecting themselves, the larger community, or advancing favored offspring in what the biblical authors portray as "female" ways. Delineating biblical women's diverse strategies in realizing their goals in different times and places is also a way of pointing out how gender roles could be rigid or fluid depending on the vicissitudes of Israelite history. Asking why militant female figures like Deborah and Yael appear in transitional times of political struggle and why polished and beautiful women like Bathsheba and Esther are successful in royal courts can also highlight the very different social settings portrayed in biblical literature, and the adjustments in gender style that diverse environments require. Similarly, study of Levitical laws of ritual purity can reveal priestly concepts of separation of kinds and of ways of achieving holiness; they also demonstrate ways in which women can be construed as different from men and categorized as dangerous in certain circumstances. These are just a few examples of the rich possibilities biblical literature offers to discuss themes connected with women and relationships between women and men. Rabbinic literature offers analogously abundant opportunities. It is simply a matter of an instructor believing that inclusion of texts centered on women's experiences and varying Jewish constructions of gender are essential to a comprehensive presentation of his or her area of instruction.

In many cases, primary documents which pertain to Jewish women are either present in long available anthologies or are rapidly being made accessible in new collections. For late antiquity, for instance, both *Maenads, Martyrs, Matrons, Monastics: A Sourcebook on Women's Religions in the Greco-Roman World,* ed. Ross S. Kraemer (Philadelphia, 1988), and *Texts and Traditions: A Source Reader for the Study of Second Temple and Rabbinic Judaism,* ed. Lawrence Schiffinan (New York, 1997), contain a variety of texts from Second Temple, Rabbinic, and Hellenistic Jewish literatures which comment on women's lives and on gender expectations in post-biblical Judaism. For the medieval and early modern periods, *The Jew in the Medieval World. A Sourcebook,* ed. Jacob R. Marcus (New York, 1938, rep. 1969) contains a number of useful passages; *Judaism in Practice: From the Middle Ages through the Modern Period,* ed. Lawrence Fine (Princeton, 1999) includes a number of primary texts which are informative about women's lives. For the modern era, *Four Centuries of Jewish Women's Spirituality: A Sourcebook,* ed. Ellen M. Umansky and Dianne Ashton (Boston, 1992), is extremely useful. *The Jew in the Modern World: A Documentary History.* Second edition, ed. Paul Mendes-Flohr and Jehuda Reinharz (Oxford, 1995) provides some documents connected with women. Rachel Katznelson Shazar, *The Plough Woman Memoirs of the Pioneer Women of Palestine,* contains a number of interesting readings from the Yishuv period.

Similarly, literary works such as memoirs, poetry and fiction are not only stimulating additions to any syllabus but also may offer profound insights into Jewish women's lives; again, many of the syllabi in *Gender and Jewish Studies* offer a number of sources of this kind, including an extensive bibliography of women's Holocaust accounts. Among the memoirs I have taught which have been most successful with undergraduates are *The Memoirs of Glückel of Hameln* and Bella Chagall's *Burning Lights* (New York, 1944; rep. 1996). Other good choices include Mary Antin, *The Promised Land*; Rebekah Kohut, *My Portion;* Kate Simon, *Bronx Primitive*; and Faye Moskowitz, *A Leak in the Heart: Tales from a Woman's Life.*

Novels and short stories are also an accessible way to enter the lives and experiences of Jewish women. Anzia Yezierska's *Bread Givers* is always a great success with undergraduates who identify with the protagonist's struggle to find her place in the world, come to terms with her parents' expectations, and become "a person." It is also a powerful statement of entrenched patriarchy in traditional Judaism and of the very different ways in which women's achievements were valued as compared with those of men. E. M. Broner's *A Weave of Women* tends to be disturbing for some students, but its powerful critique of women's disabilities in traditional Judaism and in present day Israel, and its faith in the power of women to repair their own worlds, expressed in poetic and liturgical language, provides excellent themes for class discussion. *Follow My Footsteps: Changing Images of Women in American Jewish Fiction*, ed. Sylvia Barack Fishman, provides well-chosen excerpts from a variety of novels by female and male authors that illumine diverse aspects of Jewish women's experiences in the United States; *America and I: Short Stories by American-Jewish Women Writers*, ed. Joyce Antler, is also an extremely useful source. The articles and bibliographies in *Gender and Text in Modern Hebrew and Yiddish Literature*, eds. Naomi B. Sokoloff, Anne Lapidus Lemer, and Anita Norich (Cambridge, MA and London, 1992) offers thoughtful articles and annotated bibliographies on women's writing in Hebrew and Yiddish.

Although I am wary of using the "Great Jewish Women" approach in teaching about women in Judaism, attention to the biographies and autobiographies of Jewish women of outstanding achievements can certainly be a valuable teaching gambit. Surely these women's lives are primary texts of the first order. At the same time as we honor these accomplished Jewish women, however, it is the questions we ask about them that are crucial in connecting their experiences to the lives of Jewish women in general. The most central inquiries have to do with social class and gender. Most famous Jewish women came from elite families, unusual in wealth or in learning. Many were daughters of scholarly fathers who had no sons. Certainly the unusual educations and sense of personal empowerment most received, which often made their achievements possible, were a consequence of their social privilege. Other less advantaged women of talent sometimes found the strength and courage to forge unusual destinies as a result of their anger and rebellion at their limited opportunities as women in oppressed Jewish communities. However, regardless of their social origins, all of these women had to deal with the constraints their societies imposed by virtue of their sex. Whether it is Rebecca Graetz or Golda Meir, Emma Lazarus or Henrietta Szold, students must learn to ask how Jewish gender constructions shaped the choices these exceptional women made and how their lives might have been different had they been men. Why was marriage mostly incompatible with public roles and accomplishments for Jewish women, as for most women, before the second half of the twentieth century? What were the painful choices between family and accomplishment in the worlds of arts and letters, political activism, or scientific research that these women were compelled to make? In what ways did Jewish traditions further female achievement and how did it present roadblocks? These are the kinds of queries that I encourage my students to bring to their study of famous Jewish women's lives.

Teaching "Women in Jewish Life and Literature"

For the past decade I have been teaching Judaic Studies 248, "Women in Jewish Life and Literature" (see Appendix for a recent version of the course syllabus). The course generally enrolls from thirty to sixty students of whom three-quarters are usually women. Since the course is cross-listed with the Department of Women's Studies it attracts a diverse audience; the class always includes a broad cross-section of Jewish students from yeshiva graduates to those with minimal Jewish educations, as well as Christian students from a wide range of backgrounds. While many students have taken previous courses in Judaic Studies and have a working knowledge of Judaism and Jewish history, others do not. Some of the students are traditional in their religious orientations and their worldviews; others are radical in their feminism and in their espousal of alternate life-styles. Two significant challenges throughout the course are to present primary texts and course readings in their historical and cultural contexts for those with scant previous background and to maintain an atmosphere of respectful tolerance for widely differing viewpoints.

As an historian I have chosen to organize the course chronologically, proceeding from biblical texts to contemporary concerns and dilemmas. This comprehensive framework is becoming increasingly unwieldy because of the volume of material to be covered and I am considering dividing the course into two separate courses; perhaps one would deal with the period up to the end of the Middle Ages and the second would concentrate wholly on Jewish women in the early modern and modern eras. The assigned readings for the course are built around my edited collection *Jewish Women in Historical Perspective* and the articles in *On Being a Jewish Feminist*. In addition, the students are required to read *The Memoirs of Glückel of Hameln*, Bella Chagall's *Burning Lights*, Anzia Yezierska's *Bread Givers*, and E. M. Brener, *A Weave of Women*.

There is also a reading packet with additional articles and primary sources for specific class sessions. Student requirements include a midterm, a take home final, and two short papers out of three possibilities. In addition each student must work with a fellow student in preparing a ten minute oral report based on one of the assigned readings.

I find the oral report component of this course to be an extremely effective pedagogical method for helping students to learn about the rewards of close reading of texts, the need to organize and digest what is read in order to present it coherently to others, and what techniques are effective in oral presentation. The reports, which generally take place at the beginning of each class, vary widely in quality, imagination, and panache; however, regardless of the strength or weakness of the presentation, it becomes a platform for that day's teaching. I see it as my responsibility to build on what the students have presented by providing context, supplementing weak areas and correcting misunderstandings, and returning in more depth to the central themes that have been raised. Because I never know exactly what the reports will be like, I find that my responses in each class are more lively and spontaneous than if I were simply presenting prepared lecture notes; I must listen carefully for what is said and for what is missing and frame my teaching that day accordingly. Sometimes the reports move from the assigned reading to the personal as students respond to what they are learning out of their own life experiences; occasionally students respond negatively to what they have read and offer their own points of view. As long as the presentation is essentially text-based such digressions are acceptable and also help to make the session more exhilarating and thought provoking for the class as a whole.

Before embarking on our chronological journey through Jewish history, the course begins with two introductory classes. Here I preview some of the issues involved in studying women's position in Judaisms of various eras and suggest what we will be looking for when we study texts and documents having to do with Jewish women's lives in many different times and places. I share with the class a definition of feminism as a political movement which aims to transform society so that gender does not define behavior or limit opportunities, and I read the statement of the 1974 Jewish Feminist Organization which expressed a shared commitment to the development of its members' full human potential and to the survival and enhancement of Jewish life. The signatories of this statement sought the full, direct and equal participation of women at all levels of Jewish life—communal, religious, educational, and political—and looked forward to being a force for creative change in the Jewish community. It is Jewish women's historic unequal status in these areas and their desire, both past and present to participate fully in an active and inclusive Judaism, I tell the students, which will form the substructure of the course throughout the semester.

I spend time in the first class providing an overview of the development of Judaism in its contemporary forms in North America and in Israel, and I also raise the topic of the different ways in which people might look at religious systems and at male-female differences. Someone who believes that a religious system reflects divine commandments and a divine blueprint for humanity, for example, will have a very different view of the possibilities for change within a religion than someone who understands religious systems as human designs continually adapting themselves to changing human needs. Similarly, someone who believes that differences in human qualities, capacities and abilities between males and females are intrinsic to each gender's specific biological functions and reflect the Creator's will would likely disagree about the potential for and desirability of changes in women's status with a person who believes that gender, like religion, is a human construct based more on cultural and societal determinants than on inherent female/male differences. These are new ideas for many of the students, some of whom have never considered such issues seriously before; suggesting how varying presuppositions affect attitudes and behaviors about gender, as other topics, thus becomes an essential beginning to the course.

The second class session is spent viewing "Half the Kingdom," an excellent documentary film about a variety of Jewish women in the United States, Canada, and Israel directed by Francine E. Zuckerman[15] which covers virtually all of the issues of women's status in Jewish communal, religious, educational and political life raised in the first class session. The greatest virtue of the film is its multivocal quality as it highlights a broad variety of articulate Jewish women from a Reform Rabbi to an Orthodox feminist activist and teacher, and from a female member of Israel's Knesset to the travails encountered by the writer E. M. Brener in trying to say *kaddish* for her father each day in an Orthodox *minyan*. It includes moving footage of the naming of an infant daughter in a newly developed ritual as well as a graphic portrayal of the hostility faced by women when they attempt to pray publicly with a Torah scroll at the Western Wall in Jerusalem, and is in every way a powerful witness for why courses such as this should be taught.

The course continues with several classes based on biblical material. As the syllabus indicates, I start with examples of active Jewish women like Rahab, Ruth, and Abigail, who acted independently and took risks to determine their own fates, and those of their loved ones, within the framework of a patriarchal society. We also read from the matriarchal narratives to see how women's lives were shaped by the demands of matrimony and motherhood in polygynous households. Further classes focus on the Song of Deborah, which again presents strong women acting on their own and in traditionally male-gendered ways at a time of crisis in early Israel's history. Only then, do we approach the two creation narratives and contrast the two very different visions of women which emerge from them. Our final foray into biblical texts is an examination of some of the priestly documents which impose separations of various kinds between women and men. After reading about so many strong and active female figures, these legal prohibitions highlight the differences between biblical glimpses of life as it was lived and priestly efforts to impose a ritually based hierarchical framework on the Israelite community.

Although it is all but impossible to enter into the complexities of rabbinic literature and the formation of halakhah in a course like this, the class does read a survey and analysis of the many attitudes expressed concerning women in the Mishnah and Talmud. Then we concentrate on the issue of divorce, using a chapter from Rachel Biale's *Women and Jewish Law* (New York, 1984) as our source for a discussion of the evolution of biblical and rabbinic social policy on this particular topic. Such a study demonstrates the ways in which the rabbis improved women's situations in many areas beyond the possibilities offered in biblical law, and highlights, as well, where rabbinic legislation fell short, as indicated by the problems in medieval and modern times as a result of women's inability to initiate divorce or end a marriage when a husband has disappeared or is unwilling to cooperate in dissolving the union.

I also devote a class to representations of Jewish women's lives in late antique Jewish documents in Greek and Aramaic, which offer evidence of alternative models for Jewish social life in the period in which rabbinic Judaism was evolving. Awareness of women who owned and managed property independently, who served as synagogue leaders, and whose marriage contracts state the unilateral right of a wife to dissolve an unsuccessful marriage, teaches students that there were contemporaneous options to the decisions rabbinic Judaism chose to privilege; such texts demonstrate, as well, that throughout its historical development Judaism has provided a range of possibilities for women.

Several classes on the medieval period contrast the lives of Jewish women in the Muslim and Christian worlds. Here we raise issues of the degree of influences from contiguous cultures on Jewish social life and customs. We inquire, too, why the status of Jewish women was so much higher in the Christian world of Northern Europe than in Muslim territories. Why was polygyny outlawed for Ashkenazic Jewry in the eleventh century and why were dowries so high? Why did women frequently become independent businesswomen and sometimes even support their scholar husbands? And why do we hear of a significant number of women learned enough to teach other women and to lead women in prayer? Was it only influence from a monogamous Christian culture in which women's work, independence, and access and participation in communal religious life were valued to a high degree, or were there also factors particular to the small and precariously situated Jewish communities of this environment that allowed for more latitude for at least some women? We also examine some of the evidence of Jewish women's spiritual lives in the early modern period through study of some *tkhines*, the supplicatory vernacular devotional prayers of Central and Eastern European women, some of which were written by learned women. *The Memoirs of Glückel of Hameln*, an ethical will whose remarkable author wrote the story of her joys, sorrows, and piety as a moral testament for her children, provides insight into the day to day activities of an active Central European women of the seventeenth century at the same time as it illumines numerous aspects of Jewish social, economic, political, and religious life at the dawn of the modern mercantile age.

The second half of the course deals with the encroachments and challenges of modernity for Jewish life in general and for Jewish women in particular. Following the order of the chapters in *Jewish Women in Historical Perspective*, the class considers Jewish women in Enlightenment Germany, including the Salon Jewesses of Berlin; in nineteenth century Eastern Europe; in Victorian England; Imperial Germany; the Middle Eastern teachers of the Alliance Israelite; women in the Yishuv; and the experiences of female Jewish immigrants to the United States. Reading for this segment of the course includes Bella Rosenfeld Chagall's *Burning Lights*, illustrated by her husband, Marc Chagall. Told from the point of view of a precocious child and following the cycle of the Jewish calendar, *Burning Lights* is a vibrant and beautifully written memoir of a prosperous Hasidic family's life and religious observance in Vitebsk, the

White Russian city where both Bella and Marc Chagall were born. It is also a significant historical document illuminating aspects of Eastern European women's lives. Chagall's focus on women behind the shop counter and in the kitchen, in the women's section of the synagogue and in the bathhouse, and her depiction of her complicated relationship with her harried businesswoman mother, sheds new light on aspects of everyday female Jewish life and spirituality. Written in Yiddish in the late 1930s, *Burning Lights* is an elegaic look at a past which its author had long ago left behind, yet the book has a sense of urgency prompted by Bella Chagall's despair at the deterioration and almost certain destruction of the communities and patterns of life in which she had been nurtured.[16]

From *Burning Lights*, the course syllabus moves to some of the issues connected with discussion of women and the Holocaust. In some years, I have assigned memoirs or literary works that reveal aspects of women's experiences during the Shoah. We also read an essay by Sara Horowitz which demonstrates that women have been marginalized in much of the writing about the Nazi genocide. Horowitz believes that women's experiences during this historical nightmare, and their mediation through memory and literature, reveal different patterns of experience and reflection, intrinsic in women's physical differences from men and in their particular orientation towards family relationships.[17]

In the final weeks of the semester, we return to the themes raised at the outset of the course: the impact of contemporary Jewish feminism on Judaism at a time when western society as a whole is being radically transformed by rapid social and technological change. We speculate how women in the rabbinate, gender sensitive innovations in liberal Jewish liturgies, the formation of new rituals for women, and women's prayer groups and calls for change in the traditional community, will affect Jewish women's lives and Judaism itself in the future. At this point in the course we also listen to the voices of women who often feel on the margins of the contemporary Jewish community: impoverished and elderly women, single mothers, women who are lesbians, women who are childless, and women who are unmarried.

The final assigned reading, *A Weave of Woman*, E. M. Broner's poetic novel set in Israel, is highly controversial among the students, who either love it or hate it. This moving, often painful fiction crystallizes many of the themes of the course in its vision of a highly diverse group of Jewish women, and the men in their lives, who are woven together by tragedies and shared healing rituals into an ephemeral tapestry that momentarily transcends the sense of disconnection experienced by so many contemporary Jewish women and Jewish men.

Needless to say, this brief overview gives only a partial and superficial view of this course and what happens in it, but I hope that my description here will encourage colleagues to find their own ways in which to initiate and teach courses which pay attention to the experiences of Jewish women as well as Jewish men, and which raise profound questions about gender and engendering in Judaisms past, present, and future. ✡

Appendix

JST 248/WSS248   **Fall, 1997**

Women in Jewish Life and Literature

This course explores the various roles women have played in Jewish life and literature from the biblical period through the twentieth century.

Required Texts:

J. R. Baskin, ed.	*Jewish Women in Historical Perspective JWHP*
S. Heschel, ed.	*On Being a Jewish Feminist JF*
E. M. Broner	*A Weave of Women*
Bella Chagall	*Burning Lights*
Glücke	*The Memoirs of Glückel of Hameln*
Anzia Yezierska	*Bread Givers*
Reading Packet	**RP**

Schedule of Lectures and Assignments:

Sept. 2:   Introductory Class.

Sept. 4:   Women and Judaism: What are the Issues?.
             JF xiii-xxxvi; *JF* 3-1 1.

Sept. 9:   Film: *"Half the Kingdom."*
             Film review to be completed in class.

Sept. 11:   The Hebrew Bible and biblical women 1. *JWHP* 25-40;
             RP #1: Joshua 2; Ruth; 1 Samuel 25;
             RP # 2: Genesis 16-18, 28-30.

Sept. 16:   The Hebrew Bible and biblical women III. *JF* 40-50;
             RP #3: Judges 4-5; Judges 11; Genesis 1-3.

Sept. 18:   Women in the Priestly Code:

P.P #4: Deuteronomy 21-22, 25; Leviticus 15, 18, Numbers 22:1-11, 30, 36.

Sept. 23: Women in Rabbinic Judaism I. *JWHP* 68-89; *JF* 12-18.

Sept. 25: Women's status in rabbinic law: Marriage, Divorce, Levitate marriage. **P.P #5:** Rachel Biale, *Women and Jewish Law*, Ch. 3 "Divorce."

Sept. 30: Jewish women in non-rabbinic Judaisms. *JWHP* 43-67.

Oct. 7: Medieval Jewish women: the Islamic and Sephardi spheres. *JWHP* 94-102; *JWHP* 115-134.

Oct. 9: Medieval Jewish women in Christian Europe. *JWHP* 102-114.

Oct. 14: *** *Glückel of Hameln* . **Paper I Due.**

Oct. 21: Jewish women's religious lives in Eastern Europe. *JWHP* 159-181.

Oct. 28: **Midterm Exam.**

Oct. 30: Women and Jewish Modernity in Central Europe. *JWHP* 182-201; *JWHP* 202-221.

Nov. 4: Jewish women's daily lives in Eastern Europe. **RP #6:** Paula E. Hyman, "Seductive Secularization," from her *Gender and Assimilation: in Modern Jewish History.*

Nov. 6: *** *Burning Lights* (including introduction). **Paper 2 Due.**

Nov. 11: Women and the Holocaust I. *JWHP* 243-264.

Nov. 13: Women and the Holocaust II. **RP #9:** Sara R. Horowitz, "Memory and Testimony of Women Survivors of Nazi Genocide," from *Women of the Word: Jewish Women and Jewish Writing*, ed. J. R. Baskin.

Nov. 18: Women in Israel I. **RP #10:** Rachel Katznelson Shazar, *The Plough Woman: Memoirs of the Pioneer Women of Palestine*, selections.

Nov. 20: Women in Israel 11; Sephardi Jewish Women. *JF* 65-87; **RP #11:** Susan Starr Sered, "Toward an Anthropology of Jewish Women: Sacred Texts and the Religious World of Elderly, Middle-Eastern Women in Jerusalem," from *Active Voices: Women in Jewish Culture*, ed. Maurie Sacks.

Nov. 25: Jewish women in America: the immigrant generation. *JWHP* 222-42; **RP #7:** Anzia Yezierska, *Bread Givers.*

Dec. 2: Religious Change and American Jewish Women. *JWHP* 265-288; *JF* 120-51; *JF* 223-233; 177-181; 207-209; 96-104.

Dec. 4:   Jewish women's lives today I: Alternative life style choices
in the Jewish community. *JF* 88-95; 167-176; **RP #8:** Sylvia
Barack Fishman, "Triple Play: Deconstructing Jewish
Women's Lives," from *Gender and Judaism: The
Transformation of Tradition*, ed. T. M. Rudavsky; **RP #12:**
Rebecca T. Alpert, "Coming Out in the Jewish Community";
Pamela Hoffman, "On Being Single"; Rose L. Levinson,
"Standing Alone at Sinai: Shame and the Unmarried Jewish
Woman," all from *Lifecycles: Jewish Women on Life
Passages and Personal Milestones.* Volume1,
ed. Debra Orenstein.

Dec. 9:   *** *A Weave of Women.* **Paper 3 Due.** *JF*, 186-206.

Endnotes

1. Judith R. Baskin and Shelly Tenenbaum, eds., *Gender and Jewish Studies: A Curriculum Guide* (New York, 1994).
2. Other indispensable resources for this discussion include the essays in *Feminist Perspectives on Jewish Studies*, eds. Lynn Davidman and Shelly Tenenbaum (New Haven, 1994); and *Judaism Since Gender*, eds. Miriam Peskowitz and Laura Levitt (New York and London,1997).
3. That historical changes of all kinds, including those driven by scientific and technological innovation, may affect men and women differently is an important insight. See Joan Kelly, "The Social Relations of the Sexes," reprinted in idem, *Women, History and Theory. The Essays of Joan Kelly* (Chicago and London, 1984), 3.
4. For discussions of the distinctions between public and private domains, and the realms of nature and culture and how they pertain to women, see Michelle Zimbalist Rosaido, "Woman, Culture," reprinted in idem, *Women, History and Theory*, 1950 and "Society: A Theoretical Overview;" and Sherry Ortner, "Is Female to Male as Nature is to Culture?" both in *Women, Culture and Society*, ed. Michelle Zimbalist Rosaldo and Louise Lamphere (Stanford, CA, 1974). For applications of these insights to the Jewish realm, see Maurie Sacks, "Introduction," in her edited collection, *Active Voices: Women in Jewish Culture* (Urbana and Chicago, 1995), 1-16; Judith R. Baskin, "The Separation of Women in Rabbinic Judaism," in *Women, Religion and Social Change*, ed. Yvonne Yazbeck Haddad and Ellison Banks Findly (Albany, NY, 1985) and idem, "Silent Partners: Women as Wives in Rabbinic Literature," in *Active Voices*, ed. Maurie Sacks, 19-37.
5. Susan Starr Sered, *Women as Ritual Experts: The Religious Lives of Elderly Jewish Women in Jerusalem* (Oxford, 1992); idem, "Toward an Anthropology of Jewish Women: Sacred Texts and the Religious

World of Elderly, Middle-Eastern Women in Jerusalem," in *Active Voices*, ed. Sacks, 203-218.

6. See Judith R. Baskin, "Jewish Women in the Middle Ages," in Baskin, *Jewish Women*; and Emily Taitz, "Kol Ishah—The Voice of Woman: Where was it Heard in Medieval Europe," *Conservative Judaism* 38 (1986): 43-61; and essays in *Daughters of the King: Women and the Synagogue*, ed. Susan Grossman and Rivka Haut (Philadelphia, 1992).

7. See Chava Weissler, "The Traditional Piety of Ashkenazic Women," in *Jewish Spirituality. From the Sixteenth Century to the Present*, ed. Arthur Green (New York, 1987); and idem, "Prayers in Yiddish and the Religious World of Askenazic Women;" and Ellen Umansky, "Spiritual Expressions: Jewish Women's Religious Lives in Twentieth Century America," both in *Jewish Women in Historical Perspective*, ed. Judith R. Baskin (Detroit, 1991).

8. See Cissy Grossman, "Womanly Arts: A Study of Italian Torah Binders in the New York Jewish Museum Collection," *Journal of Jewish Art* 7 (1980); and *Treasures of the Jewish Museum*, ed. Norman E. Kneeblatt and Vivian B. Mann (New York, 1986), 56, 72, 80,116.

9. See essays in *Active Voices*, ed. Sacks, and *Gender and Judaism: The Transformation of Tradition*, ed. T. M. Rudavsky (New York and London, 1995).

10. On this topic, see, for example, Marion Kaplan, *The Making of the Jewish Middle Class: Women, Family, and Identity in Imperial Germany* (Oxford, 1991); and Paula Hyman, *Gender and Assimilation in Modern Jewish History: The Roles and Representation of Women* (Seattle and London, 1995). On women breaking gender taboos and leading movements for change in Judaism through their literary activities, see Michael Galchinsky, *The Origin of the Modern Jewish Woman Writer: Romance and Reform in Victorian England* (Detroit, 1996).

11. For a discussion of the varying effects of historical events on Jewish men and Jewish women see Paula Hyman, "Feminist Studies and Modern Jewish History," in *Feminist Perspectives on Jewish Studies*, ed. Davidman and Tenenbaum, 120-139.

12. On the effort to introduce gender studies into the liberal arts curriculum in general, see Marilyn Schuster and Susan Van Dyne, "Placing Women in the Liberal Arts: Stages of Curriculum Transformation," *Harvard Educational Review* 54 (1984) 413-428; and into Religious Studies, in particular, see Carol P. Christ, "Toward a Paradigm Shift in the Academy and in Religious Studies," in *The Impact of Feminist Research in the Academy*, ed. Christie Farnham (Bloomington, IN 1987), 53-76.

13. *The Memoirs of Glückel of Hameln*, transl. Marvin Lowenthal, intro. Robert Rosen (1932; rep. New York, 1960, 1977).

14. *Jewish Women in Historical Perspective.* Second Edition, ed. Judith R. Baskin (Detroit: Wayne State University Press, 1998) contains fifteen essays discussing Jewish women's lives from the biblical period to the contemporary United States; *Women of the Word: Jewish Women and Jewish Writing*, ed. Judith R. Baskin (Detroit: Wayne State University Press, 1994) has seventeen essays dealing with Jewish women and Jewish literatures.

15. "Half the Kingdom," directed by Francine E. Zuckerman and Roushell N. Goldstein (Kol Ishah Productions, Inc. in cooperation with the National Film Board of Canada; produced by Direct Cinema Ltd., Los Angeles, 1989).

16. Bella Chagall, *Burning Lights,* Intro. by Judith R. Baskin (New York, 1996).

17. Sara R. Horowitz, "Memory and Testimony of Women Survivors of Nazi Genocide," in *Women of the Word,* ed. Baskin, 258-282.

Chapter 9

Teaching Jewish Ethics and Morals:
Making Sense of Jewish Moral Theory and Practice
Elliot N. Dorff

Moral issues confront us every day. They always have, of course, but now they are considerably more numerous and perplexing. That is partly because we live not only among Jews like ourselves—with non-Jews seen as "other" or even as "enemy"—but rather in a multi-cultural society in which we are accepted as full citizens and partners. As a result, Jews no longer rule out moral guidance from non-Jewish traditions and perspectives; on the contrary, Jews routinely encounter a plethora of varying moral views, and they unabashedly learn from them and adopt parts of them in their own lives. Even Jewish society has become much more pluralistic in Jewish belief and practice than it ever was. It will no longer do, then, simply to ask the community's rabbi and assume that whatever he says is what Jews should do. I now must ask why I should ask the rabbi for moral guidance in the first place—and if so, which rabbi! I must also determine what role the rabbi's opinion will have in my own moral judgment.

Moreover, rabbis themselves must decide how they can reasonably apply the Jewish tradition to the new issues that confront us in our day—and to some of the old ones in their new guises. For modern Jews not only have a dizzying array of new Jewish and non-Jewish options in the *methods* they use to decide what is moral; they also are confronted by new *issues* in either kind or degree. Contemporary technological inventions are responsible for some of these. That is because when one cannot do x, there is no moral question as to whether one should; but as soon as one can do x, one must ask whether one should. The advances in medicine are especially noteworthy as the source of such new dilemmas (e.g., organ transplantations, surrogate motherhood, the proper limits of the use of artificial nutrition and hydration, genetic screening and engineering, the distribution of effective, but costly, medical care), but biotechnology is not the only area of our new power and hence our new responsibility. Outside of medicine, technology has brought us other blessings—and moral questions. Where, for example, are the limits to the right to privacy in a world of e-mail, cellular phones, and electronic banking? Where does an employer's right to supervise employees end and the right of employees to private communications begin? What are the rights of authors to works that are distributed instantaneously over the internet?

Some of the new issues stem not from technological advances, but from the broader world of which Jews are now a full part. When Jews were ghettoized and treated as second-class citizens, they were usually not consulted about whether the nation should go to war, how to balance the conflicting needs of the national budget, or the goals of public education (if it existed at all)[1] Within their own autonomous Jewish communities they faced some of those social questions, but most of the moral problems they faced were restricted to their own private lives and to the issues within the local Jewish community. Now Jews living as full citizens in free countries must take on the responsibilities of citizenship in determining broad social policies—and of balancing their own special interests as Jews with those of the nation as a whole. In the modern State of Israel, Jews are even more directly involved—and responsible—for moral questions affecting all of society, including some excruciating dilemmas of war and occupation that Jews have not faced since the time of the Maccabees.

The field of Jewish studies rightly encompasses the many other aspects of Jewish religion, culture, and society treated in this volume, but Jewish approaches to ethics and morality must surely be part of any adequate Jewish studies curriculum. As the paragraphs above briefly indicate, it is certainly not easy to define a proper method to access the Jewish tradition for moral guidance or to use such a method to resolve the new moral issues that confront us. Nevertheless, these tasks are crucial to any adequate understanding of Jewish thought, practice, and culture, for a significant part of the meaning of the Jewish tradition—and a major reason why contemporary Jews are interested in it in the first place—is that they presume that Judaism can educate and guide them morally. Morality is certainly not the sum total of the Jewish tradition, nor its only lure; but the moral sensitivity and instruction that Jewish religion, law, and history can provide are surely part of what the Jewish tradition has meant historically and must mean in our day as well.

Jewish Ethics

The Jewish tradition can have major implications for Jews' moral thinking and action, but only if important theoretical issues are addressed, the issues of Jewish *ethics*. While the terms "ethical" and "moral" are often used interchangeably in common parlance—or even to reinforce each other, as in "He is unquestionably a moral and ethical person"—in philosophy the two terms denote different things.

"Morals" refers to the concrete norms of what is good or bad, right or wrong, in a given situation. Thus whether abortion is right or wrong, and under what circumstances, is a *moral* question. Similarly, the extent to which life support mechanisms should be used on dying patients, the degree to which an employee's privacy must be maintained, and the norms that should govern sexual relations among unmarried people are all moral questions.

"Ethics," in contrast, refers to the *theory* of morals. Ethics, in other words, is one level of abstraction higher than moral discussions. (That does not mean that ethical questions are more important than moral ones; they just occupy a different level of thought.) Thus in a university course in Ethics one would examine *questions of meaning, knowledge, justification, and comparison* such as these: How should you define the terms "good" and "bad," "right" and "wrong," and why? How are judgments of "good" different from judgments of "right?" Are there universal, absolute standards of moral norms, or do they extend only to given societies (or perhaps only to individuals)? Whatever the scope of moral norms, how do you *know* what is right or wrong, good or bad? (Do you, for example, take a vote, ask an authority figure, decide what pleases you, use your conscience, seek God's will in some way, or do something else?) How do you know that that is the proper method to determine what is moral? To what factors do you appeal in *justifying* your moral judgments? (Some possible answers: the act designated as good provides the most happiness for the greatest number of people; or it fits the requirements of conscience; or it follows from some previously justified principles or decisions; or it obeys an authority figure, whether divine or human; or it is what most people in my community think is right; or it is what the law requires; or it is what pleases you personally; etc.) And how is morality *related* to law? to religion? to custom? to politics? to police or military power? to economics? to art? to education? etc.

While all of these ethical questions can be addressed from a distinctly Jewish point of view, Jewish ethicists have concentrated on methodological issues. That is because the Jewish tradition, perhaps more than any other, has treated moral issues primarily in legal categories. That, in turn, derives from Judaism's fundamental belief that moral norms derive from God's will, and God's will is to be discerned through God's commandments. That, however, is no longer taken for granted. Some modern theorists have challenged the nexus between God's will and Jewish law, and some humanistic Jews have even denied that we should look to God's will in any form to define the right and the good. Even those who believe that Jewish moral norms are to be defined in terms of God's will and that Jewish law is the proper vehicle for knowing what God wants of us cannot rest with Jewish law alone, for the Talmud itself declares that the law is not fully sufficient to define morality, that there are morals "beyond the letter of the law" (*lifnim m'shurat ha-din*).

Beginning, then, with Abraham's challenge to God, "Shall the Judge of all the earth not do justice?" (Gen 18:25), one ethical question addressed throughout Jewish history has been the relationship between moral norms and God's word. Another, more modern question, is this: assuming that God's will defines that which is morally right and good, how shall we discern that now? By Jewishly informed, autonomous choices, as Reform theorists maintain? By straightforwardly applying Jewish legal precedents, as some Orthodox theorists say and most Orthodox rabbis do? Or should we follow the lead of Conservative and some Orthodox theorists and the practice of most Conservative rabbis? They use Jewish law as much as possible to know God's will (and hence the right and the good), but they interpret it in terms of its historical setting as against ours and recognize that contemporary rabbis have both the right and the duty to make changes when that seems morally necessary to the community of rabbis.

To give readers an idea of how to teach these questions, I will reproduce below the essence of two syllabi that I myself have used recently. (I will omit office hours and the like.) The first was an undergraduate course in Value Theory, with attention to both secular and Jewish moral theories. The second was a Masters seminar on Jewish ethics. Following each syllabus, I will discuss some of the ways I teach this material.

PHILOSOPHY 203: Value Theory
Tuesdays and Thursdays, 2:30-3:45

Goals: There are two goals to this course, one of content and one of method. I hope to introduce you to some of the most important issues in moral theory, both general and Jewish, and to some of the major responses to those issues taken by general and Jewish thinkers over the ages down to our own time. While doing that, I also hope to teach you how to analyze an argument philosophically, identifying its strengths and weaknesses and seeing its implications. Quite a tall order!

The content goal requires that this be a survey course, covering a number of topics and as many approaches as possible. The second goal, though, requires that we not only describe the argument in our readings accurately, but that we evaluate them too. This will provide a model for you as to how to proceed in your examinations and papers for this course.

Format:
1) Students will be expected to read the material assigned for each session, as listed in this syllabus, and to come to class prepared to discuss the appropriate readings. Please bring the readings assigned for each session to class since we will be referring to them during our discussion.
2) There will be a take-home midterm examination (taken on the honor system).
3) There will be a (cumulative) final examination.
4) Students will also be expected to write two brief papers (approximately 5 double-spaced pages each).

Books:
Students should buy the following books:
1) Brooke Noel Moore and Robert Michael Stewart, *Moral Philosophy: A Comprehensive Introduction* (Mountain View, CA: Mayfield Publishing Company, 1994). Indicated in the syllabus by "MP."
2) Elliot N. Dorff and Louis E. Newman, *Contemporary Jewish Ethics and Morality* (New York: Oxford University Press, 1995). Indicated in the syllabus by "CJEM."

Topics and Schedule:
I) Concepts and Problems of Ethics
    A) Philosophy, Ethics, and Practice (January 16)
          MP Chapter One
    B) Some Basic Distinctions (January 16)
          MP Chapter Two
    C) Facts, Values, and Moral Knowledge (January 21)
          MP Chapter Three
    D) Theories of Well-Being (January 23)
          MP Chapter Four
    E) Theories of Moral Conduct (January 23, 28)
          MP Chapter Five

F)   Problems of Agency (January 30)
      MP Chapter Six
      First Paper Topic Distributed -- Due February 13

II) History of Jewish and Western Moral Philosophy
A)   Traditional Jewish Ethics
   1)   The Structure of Jewish Ethics (February 4)
         CJEM Chapter One
   2)   The Content of Traditional Jewish Ethics (February 4, 6)
         CJEM Chapters Two, Sixteen and Seventeen
   3)   The Theory of Traditional Jewish Ethics: Natural Law
         and/vs. Covenant (February 11, 13)
         CJEM Chapters Three, Four, and Five
         First Paper Due -- February 13
B)   Greek Moral Philosophy
   1)   Socrates (February 18)
         MP Chapter Seven, pp. 105-124.
         Midterm Examination distributed -- Due March 6
   2)   Plato (February 20)
         MP Chapter Seven, pp. 124-140.
   3)   Aristotle (February 25)
         MP Chapter Seven, pp. 141-168.
   4) Epicureanism and Stoicism (February 27)
         MP Chapter Eight
         Midterm Examination Due
C)   Early Christian Ethics
         Augustine and Aquinas (February 27, March 4)
         MP Chapter Nine, pp. 180-189, 195-221.
D)   Modern Moral Philosophy
   1)   Hobbes (March 6)
         MP Chapter Ten, pp. 219-234.
   2)   Hume (March 11)
         MP Chapter Ten, pp. 234-269.
   3)   Kant (March 13)
         MP Chapter Ten, pp. 269-286.
   4)   The Utilitarians (March 18, 20)
         MP Chapter Ten, pp. 286-329; Chapter Eleven,
         pp. 380-389, 450-461.
   5)   Nietzsche (March 20)
         MP Chapter 10, pp. 330-339.

E) Recent Moral Philosophy
   1) Intuitionism (March 25)
      MP Chapter Eleven, pp. 339-361.
   2) Emotivism and Prescriptivism (March 27)
      MP Chapter Eleven, pp. 362-379.
   3) Naturalism (March 27, April 1)
      MP Chapter Eleven, pp. 390-412.
   4) Existentialism (April 1)
      MP Chapter Eleven, pp. 462-480.
   5) Recent Jewish Moral Theory I (April 3)
      CJEM Chapters Six, Seven, and Eight.
   6) Recent Jewish Moral Theory II (April 8)
      CJEM Chapters Thirteen, Fourteen, and Fifteen.

III. Selected Moral Issues

A) Sex and Family Life (April 10, 15)
      MP Chapter Fourteen.
      CJEM Chapters Eighteen, Nineteen, Twenty, and
      Twenty-One.
B) Medical Ethics I: Methodological Concerns (April 17)
      CJEM Chapters Nine, Ten, Eleven, and Twelve.
C) Medical Ethics II: Abortion (May 1)
      MP Chapter Twelve, pp. 494-517.
      CJEM Chapters Twenty-Seven and Twenty-Eight.
D) Medical Ethics III: Euthanasia (May 6)
      MP Chapter Twelve, pp. 475-493.
      CJEM Chapters Twenty-Five and Twenty-Six.
E) Helping Others in Need (May 8)
      MP Chapter Thirteen.
      CJEM Chapter Twenty-Three.

One distinct advantage of a course like this is that it integrates the study of Jewish ethics into the study of general philosophical ethics. Students thus learn the problems and methods of the field of ethics directly from the non-Jewish philosophers who created this thought, and they are then prepared to apply what they have learned to the Jewish treatment of the same issues. This approach has the historical advantage of accurately presenting the Jewish discussions in the context of the general Western world, for the Jewish materials in medieval and modern times were most definitely influenced by what non-Jews were writing. Integrating the study of general and Jewish ethics also has several educational advantages: it hones students' minds for ethical thought on the materials used by general philosophers so that Jewish ethics are not seen as uninformed or fuzzy by comparison. Moreover, Jewish ethics are then seen as not the only possible choice for intelligent and morally sensitive people; on the contrary, students who learn both the general and Jewish materials together come to appreciate the distinct choices that the Jewish tradition has made.

The exams ask the student, in Part A, to remember, compare, and analyze the materials we have covered and then, in Part B, to analyze a specific case that raises a moral problem from several of the theoretical stances we have studied. Since the latter task is more likely to be new to students, the short papers give students some practice in analyzing specific cases from a variety of theoretical stances, both general and Jewish.

The next syllabus is for a Masters Seminar. It does not assume a background in general ethics or in Jewish studies, but either or both, of course, would help.

PHL 501: Masters Seminar
Jewish Ethical Theories
Mondays, 7:00-9:30 p.m.

This seminar is intended to introduce students to methods of philosophic research by considering a variety of methods by which one topic has been approached within the Jewish tradition—namely, ethics. The readings and discussions in the course will inevitably touch on some matters of defining the content of Jewish ethics, for there is no way to disentangle questions of method from concrete applications of proposed methods on matters of substance; but the emphasis of this course will be on the methodological questions that arise from the specific issues we treat.

Methodological questions in Jewish ethics include, but are not limited to, the following: How does a given interpreter of the tradition understand the substance of Jewish ethics? What are the theoretical and practical implications of interpreting the tradition's ethical message in that way? What assumptions underlie such an interpretation of the tradition? How, if at all, does the interpreter justify those assumptions? What other arguments for and against such an approach—coming from logic, the history and content of the tradition, or the pragmatic implications of such an interpretation—can you pose? What does this form of understanding and applying the tradition share with other approaches, and how is it different? What are the strengths and weaknesses of this way of interpreting the tradition, and how do those compare to the strengths and weaknesses of other modes of interpreting it?

In asking such questions as applied to a variety of approaches to Jewish ethics, students will hopefully gain a sense not only of the methods of Jewish ethics, but also the methods by which any philosophic question can be analyzed. Specific approaches may fare better or worse with other subjects (e.g., God, prayer, salvation) than they do with ethics, and the substance of those other questions may make some methodological issues more or less significant than they are in ethics; but once one learns how to ask methodological questions and how to look for answers, the basic skills can be applied to any subject in Jewish or general philosophy.

Course Requirements:
1. Assigned readings to be done in advance of class sessions.
2. Participation in class discussions.
3. A final paper of 15-25 pages on one of the following topics:
    a. A theoretical analysis of the structure of Jewish ethics, in which you analyze and evaluate several other people's understandings of how Jewish ethical decisions should be made and suggest a methodology of your own; OR
    b. An analysis of the methodological assumptions, ramifications, strengths, and weaknesses of a specific application of Jewish sources to a contemporary moral problem.
    Students should discuss the specific plan for the paper with the instructor before beginning work on it.
4. Leading one session of the seminar.
5. A final examination, based on the readings and class discussions.

Books:
Students should buy the following books:
1) Eugene Borowitz, *Exploring Jewish Ethics.*
2) Joseph Dan, *The Teachings of Hasidism*
3) Elliot Dorff, *Mitzvah Means Commandment.*
4) Elliot Dorff and Louis Newman, eds., *Contemporary Jewish Ethics and Morality: A Reader* (hereinafter "CJEM").
5) Marvin Fox, ed., *Modern Jewish Ethics.*
6) Robert Gordis, *The Dynamics of Judaism.*
7) Ronald M. Green, *Religion and Moral Reason.*

8)   Shubert Spero, *Morality, Halakha, and the Jewish Tradition.*
Except for the Dorff and Newman reader (CJEM), references to these
books in the syllabus below will be by last name of the author. In addition, we will use a compendium of readings, available in the UJ book-
store, which has obtained copyright permissions to reproduce this for
you. Articles included in the compendium are marked by an asterisk in
the syllabus, and the page number on which the first page of the article
is found in the compendium is listed in square brackets.

Course outline:
I.   Philosophical and Biblical Foundations. (Sessions 1 and 2)
    A.   Definition of terms: morality, ethics, law, religion, Jewish
        1.   Borowitz, Chs. I and 2 (pp. 17-36).
        2.   Spero, Ch. 1 (pp. 1-20).
    B.   Biblical sources on the definition of good and bad, the reasons
        the Bible gives for living one's life according to that definition,
        and the ways in which the Bible portrays the relationship of God
        and God's commandments to morality.
    *1.   Three biblical definitions of the goal of life: [7]
        a.   Following God's commands: Deuteronomy 4:1-8,
            32-40.
        b.   The moral call: Isaiah 1:1-2:4.
        c.   The wise course: Kohelet 1:12-3:22; 6:10-12; 7:15-17.
        2.   Some major features of the form and content of biblical
        ethics.
        a.   Spero, first part of Ch. 21 pp. 21-43.
        b.   Dorff, Introduction and Chs. 1-5 (pp. 1-182).
        c.   Gordis, Chs. 1-3 (pp. 13-68).

II.   The Rabbinic Development of Jewish Ethics. (Sessions 2 and 3)
    A.   The methods and justifications for rabbinic exegesis of the Bible.
        1.   Fox, Part One (pp. 3-26).
        2.   Spero, second part of Ch. 2 (pp. 43-63) and skim Ch. 9
        (pp. 275-334).
        3.   Dorff, Ch. 6 (pp. 183-240).
    *4.   Elliot Dorff, "Judaism as a Religious Legal System,"
        The Hastings Law Journal, 29:6 (July, 1978),
        pp. 1331-1360. [14]

5. Gordis, Chs. 5 (pp. 86-99), 6 (pp. 100-120), 8
(pp. 130-137) and 9 (pp. 138-144).
B. Some major tenets of rabbinic ethics.
1. Spero, Chs. 5 (pp. 119-165) and 7 (pp. 201-235).
2. Jospe and Schulweis, in CJEM, pp. 251-258 and 25-37.
3. Ernst Simon and Harold Fisch in Fox, pp. 29-61.
*4. Will Herberg, *Judaism and Modern Man,* Ch. 6. [45]
*5. Joseph Klausner, "Christian and Jewish Ethics,"
Judaism 2:16-30. [51]
6. Borowitz, Ch. 36 (pp. 437-449).

III. **Some Medieval and Modern Theories of Jewish Ethics**
(Sessions 4, 5, and 6)
A. Rationalism (Session 4)
*1. Saadia Gaon, *Book of Doctrines and Beliefs,*
Ch. III, Sections 1-3, 5. [66]
*2. Maimonides, *Laws of Ethics* (Hilkhot De'ot.
Chs. 1-3; selections from Chs. 4-7. [75]
*3. Maimonides, *Guide for the Perplexed,* Part III,
Chs. 8, 10, 11, 26-28, 31, 33, 35, 49, 51, 54. [83]
B. Pietism (Session 4)
*Bahya ibn Pakuda, *The Duties of the Heart,* selections
from the Introduction, Gate II, Gate IV, Gate IX,
and Gate X (as selected by Jacob B. Agus, *The Vision
and the Way,* pp. 128-135.) [144]
C. Mysticism: the Zohar; Lurianic Kabbalah; Hasidism
(Sessions 5 and 6)
*1. Moses de Leon, *Zohar,* Daniel C. Matt, trans. [148]
a. How to read the Torah: pp. 43-45; 121-126.
b. Ethical interpretations: pp. 84-90; 148-152.
*2. Moses de Leon, *Zohar,* in David R. Blumenthal,
Understanding Jewish Mysticism [160]
a. The Tree of Life and the Tree of Knowledge of
Good and Evil, pp. 143-145.
b. Sacrifice and the Heavenly Union, pp. 149-157.
*3. Daniel C. Matt, "The Mystic and the Mizwot," in
Arthur Green, ed., *Jewish Spirituality I* (New York:
Crossroad, 1987), pp. 367-404. [170]
*4. David R. Blumenthal, *Understanding Jewish Mysticism,*
pp. 169-170, 177-180. [190]

  *5. Arthur Green, "Teachings of the Hasidic Masters," in
    Back to the Sources, pp. 373-374. [196]
  6. Joseph Dan, *The Teachings of Hasidism:*
    a. Introduction, pp. 1-36.
    b. Selections, pp. 39-51; 56-57; 59-64; 68-80, 104-105,
     113-114, 124-126, 138-145.
 D. Mussar (Session 6)
  Immanuel Etkes, "Rabbi Israel Salanter and His Psychology of
  Musser," in Arthur Green, ed., *Jewish Spirituality II,* pp.
  206-244. [198]

IV. Religion and Ethics: Twentieth Century Understandings
  (Session 7)
    1. David Sidorsky, "The Autonomy of Moral Objectivity," in
     Fox, pp. 153-173.
    2. Borowitz, Chs. 16 (pp. 204-225) and 30 (pp. 359-374).
    3. Ronald Green, *Religion and Moral Reason,* Chs. 1, 4, 5, 6,
     7, and 8 and Conclusion (pp. 3-23, 77-232).
   *4. Robert Gordis, *A Faith for Moderns,* Chs. 1 (pp. 13-24) and
     13 (pp. 213-225). [218]

V. Jewish Law and Ethics: Twentieth Century Understandings
  (Sessions 8 and 9)
    1. Review Gordis, Ch. 3 (pp. 50-68).
   *2. J. David Bleich, "Halakhah as an Absolute," *Judaism*
     29:1 (Winter, 1980), pp. 30-37. [232]
   *3. David Weiss Halivni, "Can A Religious Law Be Immoral?"
     in *Perspectives on Jews and Judaism,* Arthur Chiel, ed. [236]
    4. Articles by Aharon Lichtenstein, Nachum L. Rabinovitch,
     and Jakob J. Petuchowski in *Fox,* pp. 62-118.
    5. Spero, Ch. 6 (pp. 166-200).
    6. Borowitz, Chs. 15 (pp. 193-203), 24 (pp. 308-319). and 26
     (pp. 332-336).
   *7. Elliot N. Dorff, "The Interaction of Jewish Law with
     Morality," *Judaism* 26:4 (Fall, 1977), pp. 455-466. [240]
   *8. Louis E. Newman, "Ethics as Law, Law as Religion:
     Reflections on the Problem of Law and Ethics in Judaism,"
     CJEM, pp. 79-93.

*9. Louis E. Newman, "Law, Virtue, and Supererogation in the Halakha," *Journal of Jewish Studies* 40 (1999), pp. 61-88. [275]

VI. Twentieth Century, Non-Halakhic Approaches to Jewish Ethics (Sessions 9 and 10)
  A. Existential (Session 9)
    *1. Martin Buber, *Between Man and Man,* pp. 6-19, 65-71, 104-126, 199-205. [290]
    2. Borowitz, Chs. 6, 19, 20; review Ch. 16.
  B. Narrative (Session 9)
    *1. Michael Goldberg, "The Story of the Moral: Gifts or Bribes in Deuteronomy?" *Interpretation* 38:1 (January, 1984), pp. 15-25. [320]
    *2. Richard Lischer, 'The Limits of Story," *Interpretation* 38:1 (January, 1984), pp. 26-38. [332]
  C. Feminist (Session 10)
    *1. Carol S. Robb, "A Framework for Feminist Ethics," *The Journal of Religious Ethics* 9:1 (Spring, 1981), pp. 48-68. [344]
    *2. Carol S. Robb, "Introduction," to *Making the Connections: Essays in Feminist Social Ethics* by Beverly Wildung Harrison, pp. xi-xxii. [355]
    *3. Judith Plaskow, *Standing Again At Sinai,* pp. 60-74. [362]
    4. Laurie Zoloth-Dorfman, "An Ethics of Encounter," in CJEM, pp. 219-245.
  D. Covenantal (Session 10)
    1. Elliot Dorff, "The Covenant: The Transcendent Thrust in Jewish Law," in CJEM, pp. 59-68.
    *2. Daniel Gordis, "Wanted—The Ethical in Jewish Bio-Ethics," *Judaism* 38:1 (Winter, 1989), pp. 28-40. [383]
    3. Articles by David Ellenson, Louis Newman, Elliot Dorff, and Aaron Mackler on appropriate methods to gain guidance from the tradition in Jewish medical ethics in CJEM, pp. 129-193.

Sessions 11-13: Student presentations

This graduate seminar was far more theoretical than the undergraduate course described above. The readings focused on the general goals, philosophical underpinnings, and methods of Jewish ethics rather than on specific cases. While one of the paper topics allowed students to apply ethical theories to a specific case, even that topic asked students to probe the methodological assumptions of several possible approaches to the case. The other paper topic remained completely on the theoretical level. Thus while the course did not assume specific knowledge of secular philosophical theories, it does presume the ability to think in abstract categories.

Jewish Morals

In the 1960s, when I was doing my undergraduate and graduate work, most philosophy departments did not "stoop" to dealing with real-world moral problems like abortion and war. That has changed radically in the last two decades. Virtually all good philosophy departments still concentrate on ethics rather than on specific moral questions—to the extent that they treat these issues at all—but a large number of them now also have courses devoted to moral issues in contemporary society. Moreover, undergraduates often are required to take courses in logical reasoning, and moral issues are commonly the grist for that particular mill. Finally, Jewish studies students (and rabbinical students) are often interested in the specifically Jewish approaches to contemporary moral problems, and so they provide yet another source for students of these issues.

In centuries past, Jewish morals were taught almost exclusively to Jews, primarily in the form of the study of biblical and rabbinic writings, rabbinic rulings, and books of ethical maxims, such as the biblical Book of Proverbs and mishnaic *Ethics of the Fathers*. English translations of many of those now exist, and they still represent a good insight into Jewish moral convictions. These materials generally lack, however, a synthetic presentation of the Jewish tradition's approach to given matters (with the exception of some rabbinic rulings, but they are usually in Hebrew and untranslated). The Jewish tradition is simply too long-standing and too rich to enable a few sources to stand for the Jewish tradition as a whole. Teaching Jewish morals in the university setting therefore is best done by combining some contact with original Jewish sources with some more general, synthetic essays.

I have taught courses in moral problems at the University of Judaism to undergraduate and graduate students in Jewish studies, in not-for-profit management, and in rabbinical school. If the curriculum of the school does not require a course in Value Theory as a prerequisite for a course in aspects of Jewish morals, some brief introduction to the various kinds of general and Jewish moral theories should precede treatment of specific issues. That was true for the graduate course whose syllabus I will reproduce below.

My own predilection is to integrate Jewish treatments of these issues with those in the secular world. Doing that brings the best of secular thinking to bear on the discussion, and it demonstrates where Jewish thought is, and where it is not, distinctive on these matters.

In courses on Jewish morals, I use concrete cases much more heavily than in courses on Jewish ethics—although specific cases are useful in the latter setting too. Often, in fact, I use one specific case to begin the discussion and bring in the various perspectives of the readings as they would apply to that case. This makes the issues involved much more immediate and tangible -and therefore much easier to understand and much more significant in students' minds.

While books on moral problems have been produced for a variety of professions (medicine, law, business, engineering, education, etc.) and for a variety of social issues, there are not very many good books in English with Jewish materials on these issues. What is especially hard to find is non-Orthodox approaches to these matters. Moreover, the vast majority of the Jewish writings on moral issues have focused on medical topics. The syllabus below, taught in Summer, 1998, will provide at least one example of trying to balance the various approaches within Judaism while also addressing issues beyond those within medicine.

PHL410: Issues in Jewish Morality

Goals of This Course:
1) Gain some knowledge of Jewish and general ethical theories.
2) Learn about the problems and methods of deriving moral guidance from the Jewish tradition.
3) Analyze some specific moral issues from the standpoint of the Jewish tradition.
4) Develop the skills to carry out a Jewish analysis of a moral issue on your own.

Requirements:
The Ziegler School of Rabbinic Studies requires class attendance—and so do I! There will be a final examination and a paper required. In the paper, you should provide a Jewish analysis of a moral issue, using comparative material from the world of secular ethics. You should also indicate and explain which movement in Judaism espouses an ideology and methodology closest to the one you used and how representatives of the other movements would have approached the matter differently (if indeed they would).

Books:
Students should buy the following books. The abbreviation that refers to each of them in the syllabus below is listed immediately after the book here:

1) John Arthur, ed., *Morality and Moral Controversies,* 4th edition Upper Saddle River, NJ: Prentice-Hall, 1996). ("Arthur")
2) Barry D. Cytron and Earl Schwartz, *When Life Is In the Balance: Life and Death Decisions in Light of the Jewish Tradition* (New York: United Synagogue, 1986). ("Cytron")
3) Elliot N. Dorff and Louis E. Newman, *Contemporary Jewish Ethics and Morality: A Reader* (New York, Oxford, 1995). ("CJEM")
4) Basil F. Herring, *Jewish Ethics and Halakhah for Our Time: Sources and Commentary* (New York: Ktav, 1984). ("Herring I")
5) Basil F. Herring, *Jewish Ethics and Halakhah for Our Time: Sources and Commentary, Volume II* (Hoboken, NJ: Ktav, 1989). ("Herring II")
6) Gary Rubin, ed., *The Poor Among Us: Jewish Tradition and Social Policy* (New York: American Jewish Committee, 1986). ("Rubin")

Topics and Assignments:
June 4: Introduction to the Field of Ethics
    The distinctions between morals and ethics, laws, customs, religion, and sentiment. Moral absolutism, relativism, pluralism. Morality as consequences; morality as act and intention; morality as character.
        Arthur, pp. 13-29.
        CJEM, pp. 79-93.

June 9: Jewish Ethics: Methods to Derive Moral Guidance from the Jewish Tradition I
        CJEM, pp. 129-193.

June 11: Jewish Ethics: Methods to Derive Moral Guidance
from the Jewish Tradition II
JEM, pp. 106-128, 219-245.

June 16: Euthanasia I
Arthur, pp. 161-182.
Herring I, pp. 67-90

June 18: Euthanasia II
Cytron, pp. 133-156.
CJEM, pp. 363-381.

June 23: Triage and Suicide
Cytron, pp. 43-73; 99-132.
Statement of the Committee on Jewish Law and Standards
on Assisted Suicide.

June 25: Abortion I
Arthur, pp. 183-211.
Cytron, pp. 75-98.

June 30: Abortion II
Herring I, pp. 25-46.
CJEM, pp. 382-402.

July 2: Self-Defense
Herring II, pp. 129-175.

July 7: War I
Arthur, pp. 212-226, 232-234.
Cytron, pp. 193-216.

July 9: War II
CJEM, pp. 403-421, 441-454.

July 14: Poverty I
Arthur, pp. 276-306.
CJEM, pp. 336-343.

July 16: Poverty II
  Rubin, entire.

July 21: Parents and Children I
  Arthur, pp. 442-457.
  Herring I, pp. 197-220.

July 23: Parents and Children II
  Herring II, pp. 177-220.

July 28: Drugs and Smoking
  Arthur, pp. 326-350.
  Herring I, pp. 221-243.

July 30: Truth and Deception in the Market Place
  Herring II, pp. 221-274.

August 4: Environmental Ethics
  Arthur, pp. 148-160.
  CJEM, pp. 327-335.

There are, of course, many other topics that one might choose, but materials, especially of the non-Orthodox sort, are hard to come by. United Synagogue Youth has published a number of source books on various topics (of which the Cytron book is one), some of which are moral issues. Even though they are ostensibly for teenagers, they present classical Jewish sources in a readily understandable and interesting way with a commentary attuned to Conservative ideology. On sexual morals, one can also use the Rabbinical Assembly's rabbinic letter, *'This Is My Beloved, This Is My Friend': A Rabbinic Letter on Intimate Relations.* The Rabbinical Assembly is also now in the process of preparing a rabbinic letter on poverty. To order the United Synagogue or Rabbinical Assembly publications, contact the United Synagogue Book Service, (212)-533-7800, Ext. 2003. See also *Conservative Judaism,* the publication of the Conservative rabbinic organization.

Reform publications on moral issues include the publications of the Reform Action Commission in Washington, D.C. and of the Union of American Hebrew Congregations. Consider, in particular, Albert Vorspan and David Saperstein, *Tough Choices: Jewish Perspectives on Social*

Justice (New York: UAHC Press, 1992) . Consult, also, the *CCAR Journal,* the publication of the Reform rabbinic organization.

Orthodox writers have been quite prolific on moral issues (but not, interestingly, on ethics). J. David Bleich and Fred Rosner have written or edited a number of volumes on medical ethics, and Bleich has published several volumes of his rabbinic rulings on a whole range of issues; the series is entitled *Contemporary Halakhic Problems,* published by Ktav. In addition, I would call readers' attention to *Tikkun Olam: Social Responsibility in Jewish Thought and Law,* David Shatz, Chaim I. Waxman, and Nathan J. Diament, eds (Northvale, NJ: Jason Aronson, 1997) . See also *Tradition,* the publication of one of the Orthodox rabbinic organizations, and *The Journal of Halakhah and Contemporary Problems,* published by another Orthodox rabbinic body.

Finally, one might also consider using books by specific authors on given topics. For example, consider David Novak, *Jewish Social Ethics* (New York: Oxford, 1992) and, if I may be so bold, Elliot N. Dorff, *Matters of Life and Death: A Jewish Approach to Modern Medical Ethics* (Philadelphia: Jewish Publication Society, 1998).

Epilogue

Jewish ethics and morals constitute critical parts of the Jewish tradition. Simply from an historical perspective, then, an adequate and accurate presentation of the Jewish tradition must include attention to these components of it. Since contemporary times raise many new moral issues in either degree or kind, and since contemporary theorists have expanded our understanding of the moral plane of life immensely, the Jewish responses to these developments are especially important to teach. In doing so, professors of Jewish studies can accurately present the Jewish tradition as one that grapples in an ongoing way with what it means to be a moral person and a moral society. ✿

Chapter 10

Theological Education and Christian-Jewish Relations
Eugene J. Fisher

Introduction

Since the publication of my book on *Seminary Education and Christian-Jewish Relations,*[1] interseminary programs have been put on across the country devoted to the issue of integrating better understandings of Christian-Jewish relations in theological curricula. These have taken place in such diverse areas as Dallas, Boston, Chicago, Los Angeles, and Washington, D.C.[2] A distinctive feature of all of these colloquia is their ecumenical as well as interreligious structure. In several cases, students and faculty of various Christian denominational institutions have been brought together for the first time to work together on a theological and methodological challenge that confronts all Christian denominations equally.

At one time it may have been popular to view the rise of the concepts of civic tolerance and religious pluralism as solely and directly the result of the Protestant Reformation or, alternatively, of the "secular" Enlightenment. Such a simple view of Western history, recent work has shown,[3] is no longer acceptable. Antisemitism, the teaching of contempt against Jews and Judaism, can be found in the works of the Reformers and Enlightenment philosophers no less than in their medieval scholastic forebearers.[4] Shared theological anti-Judaism, then, remains a sort of inverted symbol of the unity of Christians. The first great schism experienced by the Church came with its split from the Jewish people. Understanding that split, and the tragic implications of the violent rhetoric with which the early generations of Christians interpreted the meaning of the Church's break with Jews and Judaism, therefore, is of central, not peripheral, importance to the Church's self-understanding today. Ecumenism and Christian-Jewish dialogue are two sides of a single coin.[5]

The thesis raised by this paper is that the question of the relationship of the Church to the Jewish people is integral to every area of the core theological curriculum, from sacred scripture and liturgy to systematics and Church history. The reason for this can be found in the fact that the Church in the first instance (i.e., from New Testament times) defined its identity against its understanding of the identity of the Jewish people as "people of God" (covenant/election).

Though the question of reformulating the relationship challenges Christian theology "at the very level of the Church's own identity," to cite the words of Pope John Paul II, it has seldom surfaced, except in a negative way, in Christian theological curricula.[6] The methodological implication of this view, if correct, is not merely that courses in rabbinics need to be added to the traditional Christian theological curriculum. This is a necessary step, since so much of what we say about Christianity depends on what we say about Judaism. So our traditional ignorance of rabbinic Judaism is an increasing problem methodologically. Beyond such additions to the curriculum, however, the argument is made that each course as currently taught must face a series of challenges raised from within by the contemporary reassessment of the relationship between the Church and the Jewish people, both "people of God."

Such a reassessment of the basic grounding of Christian theological enterprise in the light of its Jewish origins and present dialogue with Jews and Judaism, it is maintained, is a necessary ingredient of the theological renewal called for "in our age."[7] It would seem appropriate, then, to indicate at least some of the challenges raised in the various core areas of the theological curriculum.[8]

1. Sacred Scripture

The immediate and most central question facing biblical theology (and with it systematic theology, of course) is the relationship between the Scriptures. The classic Christian position, heavily influenced by Marcionism, is embedded in the very terminology used to name the two major collections of the Christian canon: "Old Testament" and "New Testament." This terminology in itself implied a theology of discontinuity between the Scriptures, and leans heavily toward a theory of supersessionism (Christianity has superseded Judaism in God's favor and plan for sacred history) if not necessarily abrogationism (God has canceled the "old" covenant with the Jews in favor of a "new" one in Christ Jesus). The distinction between the two is that in the supersessionist theory one can, albeit only with difficulty, preserve the testimony of such texts as Romans 9-11 by arguing that God's covenant with the Jews has not been abrogated or canceled, but merely subsumed into that of the Church as the new people of God. The abrogationist model, however, is compatible only with the ancient Christian "teaching of contempt"[9] that viewed the Jews as "accursed" by God and relegated them to the scrapheap of sacred history. Such a view, of course, implicitly eviscerates the Christian claim to covenant at the same time as it denies that of Judaism. For if God could abrogate His/Her covenant with the Jewish people for their sin (in "rejecting" Jesus), the continued sinfulness of Christians equally questions any Christian claim to covenant.

To reject flatly the Hebrew Scriptures or God's covenant with the Jewish people, therefore, is to destroy the essence of Christianity, which is one good reason why the early Church rejected Marcion when he took the abrogationist model to its logical conclusion. Marcionism, however, proved not so easy to defeat. Supersessionism, while more subtle, maintains a great deal of its dynamic. Thus modern scholars can speak of Second Temple Judaism as "late Judaism," implying that Judaism "died" for all practical purposes with the coming of Christ and the destruction of the Temple in 70 C.E.

The tendency to dichotomize the relationship between the Scriptures remains a strong one: "old" vs. "new," "law" vs. "grace," "love" vs. "mercy," etc. Many New Testament scholars, such as Rudolf Bultmann,[10] can speak of the Hebrew Scriptures as a mere "propaedeutic" to the New Testament,[11] as if they have no intrinsic value as God's Word save as a background paper or proof text for the New Testament. Others can maintain, seemingly with a straight face, that any sayings of Jesus which are congruous with those of contemporary Judaism or rabbinic dicta are, *by that very fact,* eliminated from consideration as authentic *logia* of Jesus. Though he cautions against taking the principle too far, Reginald Fuller, for example, can affirm this strange-sounding *a priori* as a "valuable" criterion:

> We can eliminate any material [in the Gospels] which can be paralleled in contemporary Judaism, for here too the presumption is that the sayings in question have, historically speaking, been erroneously attributed to Jesus. This material would include sayings which we paralleled in Jewish apocalyptic and in Rabbinic tradition.[12]

Christian New Testament scholarship has the tendency as often as not to place both biblical and rabbinic Judaism in the procrustean bed of its own internal Christian dichotomies, as E. P. Sanders has shown so effectively in his analysis of Christian use of rabbinic sources.[13] One example here will stand for many more.[14] It is common, Sanders points out, for Christian scholars to juxtapose divine mercy and justice, using the contrast to "prove" that rabbinic Judaism subordinated the former to a legalistic view of the latter. But the actual rabbinic pairings, as Sanders notes, are between God's "quality of punishing" *(middat pur'anut)* or "quality of justice" *(middat ha-din)* and God's "quality of rewarding" *(middat tobah),* or "quality of mercy" *(middat rahamin),* with the latter greater than the former.[15] Sanders summarizes, counter the notion of rabbinism as a system of "works of righteousness" so often imposed on it by Christians:

> The statements of reward and punishment [in Rabbinic] literature do not indicate how one earns salvation. Their opposite would not be that God is merciful and saves, but that there is no correspondence between God's rewards and man's behavior: that God is arbitrary ... Mercy and justice are not truly in conflict, nor is strict reward and punishment for deeds an alternative soteriology to election and atonement.[16]

In a remarkable essay in the Stimulus volume, *Biblical Studies,[17]* Joseph Blenkinsopp points out the critical difficulties experienced by Christian scholars seeking to develop an adequate "Theology of the Old Testament." His conclusion is that the endeavor as a whole has reached a point of crisis: "If the general impression given in this essay is overwhelmingly negative, and if we have said little positively about the relation between Old and New Testament, we can only plead that we are as yet nowhere close to knowing how to write an Old Testament theology."[18] Again, underlying theological *a prioris* and an essentially apologetical stance *vis à vis* the Hebrew Scriptures surfaces as the *bete noir* of Christian efforts.

Blenkinsopp discerns a depressingly deep strain of anti-Judaism even in the best of Christian experts on Jewish biblical writings, such as Julius Wellhausen, (whose meaningful effort framed much of the methodology for succeeding generations of scholars), Gustav Friedrich Oehler, Wilhelm Vatke, Hermann Schultz, Walter Eichrodt and Gerhard von Rad. The methodological manifestations of this are several, but curiously unified in rhetoric. Wellhausen, for example, writes of Second Temple Judaism (which he identifies with "Early Catholicism," thus writing off Roman Catholic tradition at the same time) in the following way:

> The Creator of heaven and earth becomes the manager of a petty scheme of salvation... The law thrusts itself in everywhere, it commands and blocks up access to heaven; it regulates and sets limits to the understanding of the divine working on earth. As far as I can see, it takes the soul out of religion and spoils morality.[19]

Schultz, who can speak blithely of "the petty Pharisaic view of life," sees in the Second Temple period the victory of "unhealthy" over the "healthy" elements of religion, by which he means of externalism and legalism over the "inward religious assurance which is the gift of prophecy."[20] Schultz is even capable of inventing a socio-psychological analysis: "the consciousness of inward emptiness, and the feeling that the Spirit of Jehovah had departed, kept on increasing."[21] The writers of this period, Blenkinsopp notes, tended to structure their approach to Jewish history "on the procrustean bed of Hegelian dialectics,"[22] following the philosophical fashion of the times, Social Darwinism.

A generation later, and following a philosophical trend less Hegelian but no less strictly formed by *Heilsgeschichte,* Walter Eichrodt can state of Second Temple Judaism (of which early Christianity was a part):

> Thus at the very heart of the desire for salvation we find once again that inner disintegration of the structure of the Jewish faith.[23]

Psychology still seemingly in vogue, Eichrodt speaks of "the inner schizophrenia of Jewish piety" which was overcome in Jesus.[24]

The enterprise of Old Testament theology, as Blenkinsopp has shown, has proven incapable of overcoming its own sense of the discontinuity between the Scriptures save through "a typological linking of Old and New Testament and a virtual bracketing of post-biblical Judaism" as well as of the wisdom writings which form the bulk of the third part of the canon.[25] Theories which cannot encompass large sections of the biblical canon and which are forced to rely on a reed as thin as typology to achieve any sense at all of the continuity between the Scriptures are, from a Christian point of view, very seriously flawed. In learning how to write biblical theology, Blenkinsopp concludes:

> It seems that first we must take Tanakh seriously on its own terms which... involves coming to terms with the Second Temple period inclusive of early Christianity... It involves further, as a necessary consequence, coming to terms historically and theologically with Judaism which, far from declining or disappearing at the time of early Christianity, only reached its most characteristic expressions several centuries later.[26]

One could add, as another way of saying the same thing, that the problem of discontinuity is heightened by the tendency to define the biblical-theological endeavor solely in Christological terms. Christian scholars often look, whether in biblical or rabbinic Judaism, only for parallels to the New Testament, allowing the categories of Christian theology to determine what they find and thus missing or even distorting central elements of sources which they are attempting to understand. Such a reductionist approach to the sources impoverishes Christian thought even today, and has led to some odd pairings in the standard lectionary.[27] Samuel Sandmel once lamented the tendency of the Christian scholar "to create his own categories and to superimpose these on Judaism or else make Judaism fit into them."[28]

2. Systematic Theology

The attempt to form an adequate biblical theology is intimately linked with the conceptual attempt to formulate a way of articulating in positive terms the relationship between the Church and the Jewish people as people of God. Pope John Paul II succinctly frames the issue in a 1980 address:

> The first dimension of this dialogue, that is the meeting between the people of God of the old covenant *never retracted by God* (Rom 11:29), on the one hand, and the people of the new covenant, on the other, is at the same time a dialogue within our own Church, so to speak, a dialogue between the first and second part of its Bible.[29]

This statement effectively challenges both the abrogationist and the supersessionist approaches to the relationship that have dominated so much of Christian thought historically. The abrogationist approach, on the basis of Romans 9-11, is clearly rejected as inadequate: the Jews are in a covenant "never retracted by God." The latter theory, which might be interpreted broadly to avow some sort of notion that the Jewish covenant has been "subsumed" into the Christian covenant, is challenged by the introduction of the notion of dialogue at this level. Jews, the Pope states, clearly exist as a people, whole and integral unto themselves. This very real, historical people, in continuity with their biblical forbears, just as clearly exists in covenant-relationship with God.

Since being "people of God," with a divine mission in and for the world, is likewise the essence of the Church's own claims concerning itself, the Church must listen with care to the Jewish witness to the world in order to develop an adequate ecclesiology for itself. Rabbinic Judaism, which developed alongside early Christianity and reacted in its own unique fashion to many of the same events and pressures (i.e., the destruction of the Temple, the need to respond to Hellenistic philosophy and culture without accepting its pagan elements the crisis of faith and reason, etc.), clearly has much more to say to us spiritually than simply becoming a backdrop for better understanding the New Testament. Israel's struggle with the One God has direct, not indirect or ancillary relevance to the Christian struggle to remain faithful to the God of Israel.

In its divergencies as well as in its parallel solutions to common dilemmas the spiritual riches of the Tannaim and the Amoraim, the medieval Jewish philosophers and the Hasidic masters witness directly, on the level of faith to faith, to Christian thought today. As the Vatican's 1974 Guidelines for Catholic-Jewish relations pregnantly suggest, "the problem of Jewish-Christian relations concerns the Church as such, since it is when 'pondering her own mystery' that she encounters the mystery of Israel."[30]

Not only the mystery of the Church (ecclesiology), but the mystery of Christ itself is centrally affected by the reformation of attitudes toward Jews and Judaism currently under way. A full appreciation of the Incarnation, for example, requires coming to grips with the fully Jewish particularity of Jesus' humanity rather than glossing it over as we have tended to do in the past.

Along with Christology, traditional eschatology will need to accommodate on a more radical level the "not yet" aspect of the New Testament kerygma. It is this aspect that Christians have most been tempted to ignore in their proclamations of the gospel to the world, sliding, at times, to the point of identifying the Church and the Kingdom.[31] The Jewish "no" to Christian claims about Jesus must be seen as a continuingly valid (and necessary) witness to us to avoid the dangers of triumphalism. Theologian David Tracy articulates succinctly both challenge and hope for future theological research:

> For myself, the suspicion which the Holocaust discloses for traditional Christological language is this: does the fundamental Christian belief in the ministry, death and resurrection of Jesus Christ demand a Christology that either states or implies that Judaism has been displaced by Christianity?... For Christians to retrieve the reality of the not yet as a historical reality is to recall that the concept Messiah cannot (by being spiritual-

ized) be divorced from the reality of Messianic times... However influential in later Christian history, theologically pure fulfillment models and a-
historical Messiah models are not only New Testament models that can
be employed... The always/already/not yet structure of belief pervading
Israel's covenant with God and Israel's expectation of Messianic times
remains the fundamental always/already/not yet structure of Christian
belief as well.[32]

The challenge, as this passage illustrates extends into all areas of
Christian doctrine. The promise/fulfillment model, so popular as a frame
for interpreting the fundamental thrust of the Bible, needs to be re-cast
more accurately along the lines of a "promise/confirmation" assertion,
as Paul van Buren has suggested. Christians, no less than Jews, await
the fulfillment of the Messianic times. And Jews, no less than Christians, are filled with the spirit of God's grace in and through Israel's
covenant with the One God. To dialogue with Jews is not, then, to encounter a people who can be adequately counted among the "un-evange-
lized" or the "pre-evangelized." The Jews *are* God's people, and as such
are *already* "with the Father" even as they (no less than we) await the
End Time in divinely inspired hope and expectation.

Missiology, then, needs to take seriously the implications of the renewal of covenant theology in our time. As Daniel Harrington has shown,
the key phrase of the risen Lord's commission to the disciples in Matt
28:16-20, *Matheleusate panta ta ethne* (Matt 28:19) may perhaps most
accurately translate as "make disciples of all the gentiles (*goyim*)."[33]

A number of works by Protestant and Catholic scholars have begun
the task of systematically reformulating Christian teaching. These should
be required reading in all theological schools, since they are among the
truly pioneering efforts of our times. A handy overview of the field can
be found in John Pawlikowski's *What Are They Saying About Christian-
Jewish Relations* (New York: Paulist Press, 1980).

Solid contributions to this growing field of renewed Christian thought
have recently been made by the following. These do not necessarily resolve all the myriad questions that will emerge as the effort progresses.
But, together, they establish a new *status questions* for contemporary
Christian theological efforts. Clemens Thomas' *A Christian Theology
of Judaism* (New York, Paulist Press, Stimulus Books, 1980) assesses
biblical and doctrinal theology to the present, noting where further work
is necessary. John Pawlikowski in *Christ in the Light of the Christian-
Jewish Dialogue* (Paulist Press, Stimulus Books, 1982) develops a solid
Christological model which avoids the pitfalls of past triumphalist ex-

cesses while maintaining (and, in a number of ways enriching) traditional creedal claims. Joseph E. Monti's *Who Do You Say That I Am?* (Paulist, 1984) seeks to develop a "non-negating" Christology based on a dialogic model of theological methodology.

Finally, Paul M. van Buren's A *Christian Theology of the People Israel* (New York: Seabury) undertakes the ambitious task of rethinking all the basic categories of classic theology: creation; covenant; religious anthropology; evil and hope; election; the people of Israel; Land and Torah; Jesus and Torah; and Jesus and Israel. In the process he carefully reconsiders the implications of the writings of St. Paul, which remain crucial to the discussion.

3. Liturgy

Retrieval of the Jewishness of Jesus and the covenantal validity of Judaism has enabled scholars today to see more clearly the roots of Christian liturgy in Jewish practice and the living spiritual bonds that link the Church to the Jewish people. Jesus, again, was a Jew who prayed as a Jew, and who taught his disciples to pray as Jews. Each of the elements of the Our Father ('Avinu) finds close parallels in biblical and especially rabbinic literature.[34]

The Christian order of the Eucharist takes its form by combining elements of the traditional synagogue service (readings from Scripture, Psalms and homilies on the text) with elements from the Passover meal (bread and wine, berakhot, hallel, etc.).[35] Likewise, it is not difficult to discern the Jewish origins of much of the Christian liturgical cycle.[36]

But it is not simply a matter of historical understanding to study the interdependence of the parallel developments of Jewish and Christian liturgies over the centuries. It is equally a matter of surfacing immense spiritual riches within the present age that is the potential of a dialogical approach to the seminary curriculum. Some of this potential is illustrated in the essays included in the volume, *Spirituality and Prayer: Jewish and Christian Understandings,* edited by Leon Klenicki and Gabe Huck (Paulist Press, Stimulus books, 1983).

4. Church History

Several very important new works have come out since the publication of my *Seminary Education* text which have greatly expanded our knowledge of the history of Christian-Jewish relations, which is to say our knowledge of the history of the Church. John Gager's *The Origins of anti-Semitism: Attitudes Toward Judaism in Pagan and Christian Antiquity* (Oxford University Press, 1983), for example, reveals the surprisingly positive attitudes of many pagans toward Judaism and their attraction to it. This corrects the notion that Gentile Christians simply brought anti-Judaism from the pagan world into the Church when they entered. One must, then, look to specifically theological Christian motivations to understand fully the phenomenon of Christian anti-Jewishness. Gager's concluding portion on St. Paul (pp. 174-264) is extremely helpful in understanding the precise character of the 'Apostle to the Gentiles' "argument" with Jews and Judaism. No New Testament course can any longer afford to ignore these new insights, and those of other scholars such as Stendahl,[37] Sloyan,[38] Sanders,[39] Koenig,[40] Gaston,[41] and Davies.[42] It may not be too great an exaggeration to state that the present re-evaluation of a key theme of the Pauline corpus may be viewed in the years to come as the most significant in Christian history since Martin Luther.

Robert L. Wilken's *John Chrysostum and the Jews: Rhetoric and Reality in the Late Fourth Century* (University of California Press, 1983) sets Chrysostum's justly infamous anti-Judaic polemics into the context of the inflated rhetorical style of the time. Once again, as with Gager, we see the attractiveness of Judaism and not only for pagans but for Christians as well. Chrysostum's invectives may well have been aimed not primarily at the Jews as such but at the members of his own Christian community attracted to the synagogue.

Jeremy Cohen's *The Friars and the Jews: The Evolution of Medieval Anti-Judaism* (Cornell University Press, 1983) likewise clarifies our historical understanding, pointing out the radical shift that took place in the Christian ideological stance toward rabbinic Judaism from the relative tolerance that characterized the Augustinian and classical papal legislation on the Jews to a form of intolerance which justified in theological terms the efforts made from the 13th to the 16th centuries to "cleanse" Europe of its Jewish population. This shift in attitudes, Cohen argues, was coincident with, but by no means coincidental to the rise of the mendicant orders.

Heiko Oberman's *The Roots of Anti-Semitism in the Age of Renaissance and Reformation* (Philadelphia: Fortress, 1984) picks up almost exactly where Cohen's study leaves off in the 16th century. He shows convincingly the continuity between the negative attitudes of the later medieval period sketched by Cohen and the equally negative polemics (and actions) of the great Reformers and humanists of the age. The Reformation challenged many aspects of its medieval heritage, but not its virulent anti-Judaism. It was only in a later period, when Christians too began to see themselves in exile, Oberman concludes, that they were able to see in Israel's exile any other than "the marks of a God-sent punishment"[43] and were therefore able to glimpse the notion that a state of diaspora did not necessarily mean the ending of God's covenant with the Jewish people — or with themselves as Church.

Finally, Alice and Roy Eckardt in *Long Night's Journey into Day: Life and Faith After the Holocaust* (Detroit: Wayne State University Press, 1982) grapple with the implications of Nazi genocide for contemporary Christian theology.

Conclusions

It is hoped that the above survey, by no means complete (even on those four issues it does pick up), will serve to whet the appetites of faculty and students for the tasks ahead—and the spirited riches to be gained through them. Again, the point has not been simply to suggest the addition of another elective or hiring a Jewish faculty member, though such advances are by no means eschewed. Rather, it is up to teachers and students alike to seize the opportunities offered in every course in the core curriculum and ponder together what that course would be like if it truly sought to take seriously God's covenant with the Jewish people, and Christian treatment of God's people up to the present age.

Update: Catholic Church Documents Relevant to Theological education, 1985-1998

Zev Garber has graciously invited me to update my original article. Bibliographically, this has over the past decade and a half become a gargantuan task. Biblical, historical, liturgical and theological literature relevant to the study of Jewish-Christian relations has burgeoned. This is, of course, a most positive development, indicating the "mainstreaming" of the dialogue, even if it means that no single individual, certainly not myself, can claim to be on top of all the pertinent literature that has poured out in the various areas of study.

In 1990, for a volume marking the 25th anniversary of the Second Vatican Council's declaration, *Nostra Aetate*, I put together a rather extensive bibliography compiling and bringing up to date earlier efforts. [44] In 1994, I updated that bibliography in a lengthy article for the Journal of the Central Conference of Reform Rabbis, [45]organized into sections roughly corresponding to those in this paper. Even these bibliographies, which combined came to some 80 printed pages, were not exhaustive of the fields they hoped to cover at the time, but merely illustrative of works I considered particularly noteworthy and useful for those engaged in the dialogue or in teaching its fruits.

Similarly, a number of statements issued by Catholic and Protestant church bodies have significantly changed the framework in which denominationally-oriented theological education takes place. This appears to be particularly true of my own Roman Catholic tradition. In what follows, I shall focus on three sets of documents: those of the Holy See, those of Pope John Paul II, and implementing statements issued by the U.S. National Conference of Catholic Bishops (NCCB). With the exception of the most recent, the NCCB and Vatican documents can be found in the second edition of my *Faith Without Prejudice* (New York: Crossroad, 1995). Documents with commentary and extensive bibliography up to 1990 are to be found in E. Fisher and L. Klenicki, eds., *In Our Time: The Flowering of Jewish-Catholic Dialogue* (Mahwah, NJ: Paulist Press, Stimulus Books, 1990). Papal texts have been compiled by E. Fisher and L. Klenicki, eds., *Spiritual Pilgrimage: Pope John Paul II, Texts and Addresses, 1979-1990* (Crossroad, 1995).

In 1985, I gave a paper for a meeting of the International Catholic-Jewish Liaison (ILC) Committee entitled, "The Evolution of a Tradition." The paper was subsequently included in a collection of papers presented to the ILC over the years, *Fifteen Years of Catholic-Jewish Dialogue 1970-1985* (Rome: Libreria Editrice Vaticana and Libreria Editrice Lateranense, 1988). My argument was that from a Catholic point of view no ecumenical council before the Second Vatican Council's declaration, Nostra Aetate (October 28, 1965) had taken up the doctrinal issues that lie at the heart of the Church's understanding of its relationship with God's People, the Jews. Certainly, there had been restrictive decrees, such as those of the Fourth Lateran Council, but these had been purely disciplinary in nature and had long since, given the way Roman Catholic canon law works, fallen into the canonical category of "desuetude," which is to say that when new codes were issued over the centuries without them they ceased to have canonical force. Today, they are of historical interest only.

Thus, I reasoned, the Second Vatican Council began for the Catholic Church its first official look at the relationship since the closure of the New Testament canon. Significantly, the teachings of the Fathers of the Church, which Jules Isaac had aptly called, "the teaching of contempt," and which current Catholic documents tend to call, less dramatically but no less accurately, "theological anti-Judaism" was nowhere appealed to by the Council in *Nostra Aetate*. Rather, they went back directly to the New Testament, especially to St. Paul's reflections in Romans 9-11, using solid biblical scholarship to retrieve the rather more positive theological appreciation of Jews and Judaism that Paul actually embedded therein.

Since that article is available, I will not repeat it here, save to point out what I consider to be the ongoing, evolutionary impact of the Conciliar declaration on subsequent official Church teaching. Nostra Aetate, it is helpful to recall, received mixed, even negative reviews from many Catholic as well as Jewish commentators. It was not as strong as earlier drafts, it was said. It did not even mention the term, "deicide" (which in my view was a good thing because the term has disappeared from the Catholic vocabulary whereas a Conciliar reference to it, even to condemn it, would have kept it alive). It merely "deplored" and did not "condemn" antisemitism. Nowhere did it mention the "teaching of contempt," the centuries of Christian abuse of the Jewish people, or the Holocaust.

I could go on, but I think the point is clear, What was of most interest to the critics of the text was what it did not say. But this, it turned out, was to underestimate what the text did say, and the ongoing theological reflections it launched in its sparse fifteen Latin sentences. For it uttered a definitive biblical interpretation that has revolutionized Catholic thought: "(The Jews) must not be presented as rejected by God or cursed, as if this followed from Sacred Scripture." In rejecting the collective guilt charge against the Jews as a people and insisting on using the present tense to translate Romans ("Theirs are... the covenants and the promises..."), Nostra Aetate destroyed the theological base of the entire edifice of the teaching of contempt. Subsequent Church documents have worked to complete the demolition and to erect in its place a theologically positive understanding of the continuing role of the Jewish People in God's plan of salvation for all humanity.

The 1974 Vatican Guidelines and the 1980 Mainz statement of Pope John Paul II, discussed above, were significant building blocks for this effort. They also, as I argued in my paper for the ILC, went a long way toward filling in each and every theological "hole" pointed out by the critics of *Nostra Aetate*. The 1985 *Notes on the Proper Presentation of Jews and Judaism in Catholic Teaching and Preaching of the Holy See's Commission for Religious Relations with the Jews* similarly took into account and responded to criticisms which greeted the 1974 text. So what is going on here is anything but an example of the old adage, *Roma locuta est, cause finite est*. Rather, what we see, when we look on these developments over time, is a rather stately dialogue in which the Holy See, step by cautious step, is building an official tradition of biblical interpretation, liturgical renewal, and, yes, encounter with the long, ambiguous history of its treatment of Jews and Judaism over the centuries.

Biblically, the 1985 *Notes*, for example, attempted to distinguish between Scripture's use of "fulfillment" theology (which is also basic to much of the Church's liturgy) and "replacement" or "supersessionist" theology (the underlying theory of the teaching of contempt). While admitting that the former presents theology with still "unresolved" problems, it asserts that Christian theology can affirm what is necessary to affirm in fulfillment and typological references in the New Testament, while yet clearly denouncing supersessionism as a theological dead end for the Church.

Historically, the *Notes* flesh out what was meant in the 1974 document's assertion that Jewish history considered as sacred history did not end with the coming of Christ. Thus, the 1985 text affirms the ongoing nature of Jewish witness to the revelation imparted to them, a witness that quite often (and often, tragically, at Christian hands) became "heroic." This is to say, for example, that the Jews who refused the forced conversion that the Crusaders sought to impose on them in 1096, died as true martyrs to their true faith. And the *Notes* calmly reinterpreted even the Jewish diaspora, which the teaching of contempt had seen as a sign of divine punishment, following the destruction of the temple, and therefore a sort of inverted proof of the triumph of Christianity. Now, the diaspora is to be understood as an opportunity for Jews to spread their witness to the one, true God, the God of Israel, throughout the world. It is to be noted that the *Notes* at this point do not go into the patristic tradition of seeing Jewish witness as *preparatio Christi*, but instead turn their reflection back to the "longing for Jerusalem" so cen-

tral to Jewish faith over the centuries and therefore give theological validity to the religious impulse that underlies modern Zionism, albeit with
a strong caution against getting carried away and confusing any modern state with what is divinely willed. (Here, the Church's own long
struggle with *caesero-papism* and divinely willed kingships provides a
context for understanding this caveat, I believe.)

If the Church acknowledges, and it does, the ongoing validity of Jewish tradition (the *Notes* urge that Christians can profit "discerningly"
from rabbinic and later Jewish interpretations of the Bible, for example),
it can only see itself as standing next (and not as having replaced) to
Jews and Judaism in giving witness to divine revelation in the world.
Hence the theological significance of the prayerful visit of the Bishop of
Rome to the Great Synagogue of Rome in 1986 — the first such visit
since the time of St. Peter. Pope John Paul II, in an address to the rem-
nant of the Jewish community of Warsaw in 1987, carried his theological reflection on the theme of joint witness one step further. There, he
spoke of the Jewish People's witness to the Shoah as a "saving witness"
for the entire world today, a witness in continuity with the ancient prophetic voices, and a witness for the Church itself. The Church, the Pope
declared, can only join her voice to that of the primary witness, the Jews.
This is remarkably bold language, theologically, in my opinion, since it
acknowledges not only the validity of Jewish witness to Tanak as divine
revelation, but the validity of Jewish witness to truths necessary for salvation which are post-Christian as well.

The U.S. hierarchy responded to the 1985 *Notes* by developing two
documents to implement it on the local level. The first, issued by the
Bishops' Committee for Ecumenical and Interreligious Relations in 1988,
presented *Criteria for the Evaluation of Dramatizations of Christ's Passion*, which gives detailed guidelines for avoiding the pitfalls of the past
in such depictions. The second, issued by the Bishops' Committee for
the Liturgy also in 1988, is entitled, *God's Mercy Endures Forever:
Guidelines for Preaching on Jews and Judaism*. This develops ways of
understanding and articulating the relationship between the Testaments,
fulfillment and other difficult themes in the lectionary, and Jesus' relations with his own people (e.g. the Pharisees) as depicted in the New
Testament. With regard to the latter, *God's Mercy* details many of the
implications of the 1985 Vatican *Notes* crucial statement that "some references (in the New Testament) hostile or less than favorable to the Jews
have their historical context in conflicts between the nascent Church
and the Jewish community. Certain controversies reflect Christian-Jew-

ish relations long after the time of Jesus. To establish this is of capital importance if we wish to bring out the meaning of certain Gospel texts for Christians of today." Those interested in pursuing this theme in the context of theological education might wish to read David Efroymson, et al, eds., *Within Context: Essays on Jews and Judaism in the New Testament* (Collegeville, MN: Liturgical Press, 1993).

In 1995, on the occasion of the fiftieth anniversary of the liberation of Auschwitz, there began a series of statements of local Catholic Church hierarchies confronting head on the history of their own local Church communities during the Shoah. To date there have been statements by the Hungarian, German, Polish, American, Dutch, Swiss, French, and Italian bishops. In March of 1998, the Holy See issued a document promised in 1987, themes for which had been discussed with Jewish representatives at length in ILC meetings in Prague (1990), Baltimore (1992), and Jerusalem (1994). It is entitled, *We Remember: A Reflection on the Shoah.* It is, I believe, another step along the way of evolution of official Church teaching sketched above. Not surprisingly, Jewish reaction, much like that to *Nostra Aetate* in 1965, the *Guidelines* in 1974, and the *Notes* in 1985, was mixed. Since the document attempted a brief survey of the teaching of contempt and of Christian mistreatment of Jews over the centuries, much was made of events — often very tragic ones that are seared into the Jewish memory — that were not included in the listing. And much has been made of the distinction the document draws between Christian theological anti-Judaism (which also was used over the centuries to rationalize anti-Jewish oppression) and the modern, racial and genocidal antisemitism of the Nazi regime. Since the document stressed the distinction, but did not elaborate the historical relationship between the two, some came to the (as it turns out, erroneous) conclusion that the document intended to deny any relationship between the two.

But as with the earlier documents of the Commission, in which expressions of disappointment precipitated later clarifications, so it will be with this one. Indeed, the President of the Commission, Cardinal Edward Idris Cassidy, has already begun this process. In a very important address to the American Jewish Committee in Washington, DC, in May of 1998, Cardinal Cassidy filled in many of the historical events not covered in the document itself, thus in effect extending its mandate for holocaust education and the teaching of Church history to include a full and balanced account of Christian deeds and misdeeds alike.

Cardinal Cassidy also established the relationship between the Church's teaching of contempt and the ideology of the Shoah. The distinction, he pointed out, is vital to understanding. For the ideological base of the genocide drew its source not on Church teaching but on pseudo-scientific racialism, a doctrine antithetical to core Jewish and Christian understanding that all human beings are created in the image and likeness of God. But while the ideological underpinnings of the Shoah, and of the Nazi regime were "neo-pagan" and fundamentally anti-Christian, it is historically inconceivable that the Holocaust could have taken place without the centuries of Christian anti-Judaic teaching. It was this teaching that pinpointed the Jews in Christian Europe as targets of opprobrium and oppression and, the Pope John Paul II's forceful phrase (referred to also in the document), "lulled the conscience" of many Christians so that they became frighteningly easy prey for Nazi propaganda against their Jewish neighbors. Some years ago, historian Yosef Yerushalmi summed up the relationship between Christian anti-Judaism and the Holocaust by noting that the former was a "necessary cause" of the latter, but not a "sufficient cause." One cannot explain the Holocaust without acknowledging the role played by the teaching of contempt. But one cannot be adequate to the complex realities of the Shoah by simply stopping there. Other causes and factors must also be acknowledged. On the one hand, one needs to explain why nothing approaching the Holocaust happened in Christendom over the long centuries when the Church actually held real political power. Only when that power and the moral restraints implicit in it were broken was the Holocaust conceivable. And one needs to explain why, given the fact that Christians in Germany, Italy, Denmark and France received the same religious teaching about Jews and Judaism, the reaction of various national and regional cultures to Nazi ideological racism was so very different from place to place. Analyzing this hugely complex set of realities, as *We Remember* notes, will be a task of historians, theologians, sociologists and other scholars for some time to come. All of the statements of Catholic hierarchies mentioned above, along with the Vatican document on the Shoah and Cardinal Cassidy's definitive clarification of the document, are to be found collected in the booklet, *Catholics Remember the Holocaust* published by the Bishops' Committee for Ecumenical and Interreligious Relations in September of 1998.

Endnotes

1. Eugene J. Fisher, *Seminary Education and Christian-Jewish Relations* (Washington, D.C.: National Catholic Education Association, 1983).
2. With the exception of the Boston efforts, sponsored by the Boston Theological Institute (and spearheaded by Krister Stendahl of Harvard Divinity School and Daniel Harrington, S.J., of Weston School of Theology), these programs have been co-sponsored by the theological schools involved and the American Jewish Committee (AJC). Reports on the AJC co-sponsored workshops can be found in the 1983-84 issues of AJC's Interreligious Affairs Department *Newsletter.* Reports on the progress of the B.T.I. efforts can be found in the "Ecumenical Events" section of the *Journal of Ecumenical Studies* (Vol, 20, 3, Spring, 1983), 358-360.
3. E.g., Heiko A. Oberman, *The Roots of Anti-Semitism in the Age of Renaissance and Reformation,* transl. by James I. Porter (Philadelphia: Fortress Press, 1984), and Arthur A. Hertzberg, *The French Enlightenment and the Jews.. The Origins of Modern Anti-Semitism* (N.Y.: Schocken,1970).
4. Cf. Jeremy Cohen. *The Friars and the Jews* (Cornell University Press, 1983).
5. Eugene J, Fisher, "Jewish Christian Relations and the Quest for Christian Unity," *Journal of Ecumenical Studies* (Vol. 20:2, 1983), 235-244.
6. Jacob Petuchowski eloquently argues the case for inclusion of rabbinics in Christian theological curricula in "Judaism in Christian Theological Education," *Harvard Divinity Bulletin.*(April-May 1984) 10-12.
7. Reference to *Nostra Aetate,* no. 4, the Second Vatican Council's Declaration of the Jews which, in 1985, celebrated its 20th Anniversary.
8. These are developed more fully, and with bibliographic reference, in my book, *Seminary Education,* cited in note 1, above. This paper will update rather than repeat that bibliography. The curriculum model I have followed is that typical of Roman Catholic seminaries. Some adjustments may have to be made to the particular academic divisions pursued in Protestant and Orthodox theological seminaries.
9. For a definition of this term, cf. Jules Isaac, *Jesus and Israel* (N.Y.: Holt, Rinehart, Winston, 1971).
10. For a spirited discussion of Bultmann's theory on the relationship between the Scriptures, see the essays in B. W. Anderson, ed., *The Old Testament and Christian Faith* (London: SCM Press, 1963).
11. E.g., W. Vischer's essay, "Everywhere the Scripture is About Christ Alone," in *ibid.,* 90-101.
12. Reginald H. Fuller, *The New Testament in Current Study* (N.Y.: Charles Scribner's Sons, 1962) 33.
13. E. P. Sanders, *Paul and Palestinian Judaism* (Fortress, 1977).
14. Other examples are given in Eugene Fisher, "From Polemic to Objectivity? A Short History of the Use and Abuse of Hebrew Sources by Recent Christian New Testament Scholarship," *Hebrew Studies* vol. 20-21 (1980) 199-208.

15. Sanders, *Paul and Palestinian Judaism,*123.
16. Sanders, *Paul and Palestinian Judaism,*182. Sanders' treatment of Pauline theology, included in the last section of the cited volume, is expanded and, to my mind, helpfully clarified in his more recent *Paul, the Law, and the Jewish People* (Fortress, 1983).
17. L. Boadt, H. Croner, L. Klenicki, eds., *Biblical Studies: Meeting Ground of Jews and Christians* (N.Y.: Paulist Press, Stimulus Books, 1980).
18. Joseph Blenkinsopp, "Tanakh and New Testament: A Christian Perspective," *ibid.,* 113.
19. Julius Wellhausen, *Prologomena to the History of Ancient Israel* (1878, Engl. transl. by Robertson Smith, New York: Meridian Books, 1957), 509.
20. Hermann Schultz, *Old Testament Theology* (1869, 1896; Engl. transl. of the fourth German edition, Edinburgh: T. & T. Clark, 1892), vol. 1, 321-331.
21. *Ibid.,* 1, 406.
22. Blenkinsopp, "Tanakh and New Testament," *cit.,* 103.
23. Walter Eichrodt, *Theology of the Old Testament,* transl. by J. A. Baker in two volumes (Philadelphia: Westminster, 1 1961, 11 1967) pp. 11, 464.
24. *Ibid.,*II, 315.
25. Blenkinsopp, "Tanak and New Testament," *cit.,*113, refers to Gerhard von Rad's *Old Testament Theology* (New York: Harper and Row, 1962), G. Ernest Wright, *God Who Acts* (London: SCM Press, 1952) and R. E. Clements, *Old Testament Theology: A Fresh Approach* (London: Marshall, Morgan & Scoft, 1978). Von Rad, he notes, simply ignores the Second Temple period, while Wright and Clements omit entirely treatment of the Wisdom writings.
26. Blenkinsopp, "Tanakh and New Testament," *cit.,* 113.
27. Cf. E. Fisher, "Continuity and Discontinuity in the Scriptural Readings," *Liturgy* (May 1978) 30-37. This reductionist approach to Hebrew sources is particularly striking in H. Strack and P. Billerbeck, *Kommentar zum Neuen Testament und Talmud und Midrash* (Munich: 6 Vols., 1922-61).
28. Samuel Sandmel, *Two Living Traditions* (Detroit: Wayne State University Press, 1972), 230. For an overview of other relevant questions and opportunities facing biblical students as a result of the Jewish-Christian dialogue, see Eugene Fisher, "The Impact of Christian-Jewish Dialogue on Biblical Studies" in Richard Rousseau, S.J., *Christianity and Judaism: The Deepening Dialogue* (Ridge Row Press, 1983), 117-138.
29. John Paul II, "Dialogue: The Road to Understanding," *Origins* (12/4/80).The talk was originally given to representatives of the Jewish community in Mainz, West Germany on November 17, 1980. Italics added
30. Vatican Commission for Religious Relations with the Jews. "Guidelines and Suggestions for Implementing the Conciliar Declaration, *Nostra Aetate* (no.4)," Rome, December 1, 1974.

31. New Testament scholar Daniel Harrington works through these and related points in illuminating fashion in his two recent works, *Light of all Nations: Essays on the Church in New Testament Research* (Wilmington, Delaware: Michael Glazier, Inc., 1982) and *God's People in Christ: New Testament Perspectives on the Church and Judaism* (Fortress, 1980).

32. David Tracy, "Religious Values After the Holocaust," in Abraham J. Peck, ed., *Jews and Christian After the Holocaust* (Philadelphia:Fortress Press, 1982).

33. Daniel Harrington, "Make Disciples of All the Gentiles," in *Light of All Nations,*111. On the missiological issues in general, see Martin A. Cohen and Helga Croner, eds., *Christian Mission — Jewish Mission* (New York: Paulist Press, Stimulus Books, 1982).

34. Cf. M. Brocke and J. Petuchowski, *The Lord's Prayer and Jewish Liturgy (New* York: Seabury, 1978) and A. Finkel and L. Frizzell, *Standing Before God: Studies in Prayer in Scriptures and Tradition* (New York: KTAV, 1981).

35. Sofia Cavalleti, "Christian Liturgy: Its Roots in Judaism," *SIDIC* (Rome: Vol. 6:1, 1973) 10-28; Asher Finkel, "The Passover Story and the Last Supper," in M. Zeig and M. Siegel, eds., *Root and Branch* (New York: Roth Publ., 1973,19-46; and Anthony Saldarini. *Jesus and Passover* (New York: Paulist Press, 1984).

36. L. Bouyer, "Jewish and Christian Liturgies," in L. Sheppard, ed., *True Worship* (Baltimore: Helicon Press, 1963), 29-44; W.O. Oesterley, The *Jewish Background of the Christian Liturgy* (Oxford: Clarendon Press, 1925); and Eric Warner, *The Sacred Bridge: Liturgical Parallels in the Synagogue and the Early Church* (New York: Schocken, 1970).

37. Krister Stendahl, *Paul Among the Jews and Gentiles* (Fortress, 1976).

38. Gerard Sloyan, *Is Christ the End of the Law?* (Westminster, 1978).

39. E. P. Sanders, *Paul, the Law and the Jewish People* (Fortress, 1983).

40. John Koenig, *Jews and Christian in Dialogue: New Testament Foundations* (Westminster, 1976).

41. Lloyd Gaston, "Paul and the Torah," in Alan T. Davies, *Anti-Semitism and the Foundations of Christianity* Paulist Press, 1979). CF. also Harrington and others mentioned above.

42. W. D. Davies, *Paul and Rabbinic Judaism* (N.Y.: Harper & Row, 1984).

43. Heiko A. Oberman, *The Roots of Anti-Semitism* (Fortress, 1984), 141.

44. Eugene J. Fisher, "A New Maturity in Christian-Jewish Dialogue: An Annotated Bibliography," in E. Fisher and L. Klenicki, eds., *In Our Time: The Flowering of Jewish-Catholic Dialogue* (New York/Mahwah: Paulist Press, Stimulus Books, 1990) 105-161.

45. Eugene J. Fisher, "Jewish-Christian Relations 1989-1993: A Bibliographic Update," *CCAR Journal* (Winter, 1994) 7-35.

Chapter 11

Dialogue:
An Infusion Method for Teaching Judaism
James F. Moore

A decade ago I wrote about in-class, team-taught dialogue as an especially satisfying method for teaching Judaism especially in small, church-related colleges and universities which have a significant number of Christian students and few Jewish students.[1] That approach was and is still a very promising approach for teaching Judaism, but in the decade since, university education has faced both an increasing pressure on faculty with cutbacks in full-time staff as well as increased need to reduce courses outside of the normal spectrum required for core field studies. Thus, the in-class, team-taught dialogue is no longer very practical even in the setting such as my own at Valparaiso University. Other approaches have become the norm and will likely remain so in the future. As a result, I have been attracted to another approach that seems even more promising, especially given the current pressures. This model is an infusion model much like is often suggested for teaching core skills within a variety of courses at the university. The point is to infuse the teaching of Judaism into other courses that are already part of the teaching of the department very likely by using the same model for dialogue I proposed a decade ago but applied now to a portion of an existing course or to the whole flow of a course. My guess is that such a model is already applied by many of us, but I would suggest the contours of such a model together with a couple of examples so as to open the conversation on what we are already doing in many cases. The model I propose incorporates both the dialogue approach with a thematic integration of Jewish history, culture and/or thought within a course.

I would be clear at the outset that this model does not replace the free-standing courses that often presently comprise programs in Jewish Studies. In fact, an infusion model needs such free-standing courses precisely because Jewish Studies cannot be done on an infusion model alone, and courses that follow this infusion model will benefit from other specific Jewish Studies courses both in providing essential information for students as well as linking students who are especially inspired by their exposure to Jewish Studies in these courses with a specific direction of study to deepen their work. That is, courses working with an infusion model can be feeder courses for courses in Jewish Studies.

Dialogue as a Strategy

In order for the idea of infusion to work, a dialogue strategy needs to be employed since the development of Jewish culture and thought takes place within a larger cultural context in most cases. No course could effectively integrate Jewish ideas as "Jewish" rather than as simply part of the larger culture without a dialogue strategy. This is surely the case at small church-related institutions like Valparaiso University. Of course, Jewish thinkers such as Spinoza have long been incorporated into the study of Western philosophy, but as another thinker in the history of philosophical thought and not as part of a history of Jewish philosophy. The latter can be accomplished only if the notion of "Jewish philosophy" can be given credibility by putting Jewish thought into dialogue with other specific, even religiously specific, philosophical traditions. The same can be said of theology classes like those I teach. Thus, a dialogue strategy can be employed to move toward an infusion model for teaching Judaism. I will turn to some examples below, but let me develop just such a strategy first giving some judgments as to benefits and drawbacks for this strategy.

In my essay in the first volume on teaching Judaism, I developed a structure to a dialogical approach that can be applied to this discussion as well. The model for teaching is a broad model for dialogue that may be a useful way of conceiving all theological work. This model has four basic points that are separate yet integrated, important on their own but also part of a leveled, developing process of inter-religious communication. Those points are:

1. Openness to listen to another view
2. Openness to accept truth in another view
3. Openness to learn about one's own tradition
4. Openness to risk change [2]

In fact, the last of these points may well be a presupposition for all dialogue preceding the other three basic points. The experience of the class setting, however, tends to show that students and, even, professors are unaware of the risks involved prior to becoming engaged in dialogue. The risks may range from a jumbling of views, to doubt about any truth, to challenges and judgment of peers. For the undergraduate student, all of these risks as well as others are real and can be devastating; nevertheless a student may tend to enter a dialogue class with a certain amount of naive confidence, a confidence that change can be warded off if necessary, that the student can remain aloof.

There are some university settings in which the instructors may also wish to give the appearance of remaining aloof. Attempts to conduct class in a sterile, analytical fashion, however that may satisfy certain images of religious studies on the undergraduate level, is ultimately dangerously naive in the context of a dialogue class. Perhaps the instructors can maintain such an objective relationship to their subject matter, but they must realize that many students cannot. In a class designed to use this strategy to infuse Jewish Studies into the class, the very particularity of the ideas introduced is the most significant factor of presenting the materials. Thus, it is precisely the specific bias of any particular set of ideas, or any tradition of ideas, that must be emphasized in order to allow a legitimate dialogue between traditions to develop.

The belief that even the instructors can remain fully objective in this context may also be a myth. Either the instructor will force objectivity robbing the class setting of the dynamic of true dialogue (and thereby the risks that accompany dialogue) or the instructor will remain unaware of his/her own personal prejudice, how that view affects the communication of the material and the course of the dialogue, and how instructor's views affect the attitudes of students toward the material and toward the dialogue. There is a thin line between forcefully expressing the views of a tradition and actually seeking (at the very least) the intellectual conversation between different particular cultural traditions.

Nevertheless, the main intent of a dialogue may be simply the passing on of information (point one of the dialogue aspects given above). The instructor may aim to do what he/she can to remove barriers to understanding so that students can actually listen to another view. Among Christian students at Valparaiso, views of Jews and Judaism are formed by Christian teaching and Christian teachers with varying degrees of sensitivity to Judaism. Our students are undoubtedly representative of Christian students elsewhere. Thus, a seemingly simple matter such as the use of "scripture" not only produces surprises for our students as they are confronted by the views of Jewish thought but also makes obvious the stereotypical Christian interpretations of specific scriptural texts that make a genuine understanding of Jewish views on the same text most difficult. For example, how is it that Christians read Genesis 3?

Our Christian students will learn and be surprised that many Jews (if not most) do not read Genesis 3 as a fall of humanity. Unless treated with sensitivity to these matters and even if treated with sensitivity, discussion on a single chapter such as this reveals the spontaneous dynamic that occurs in a dialogue setting and, of course, the potential confusion and struggle among students who are trying to grasp a new, even foreign, viewpoint.

Of course, for the student to meet the confusion of the moment, the student must be capable of reflective thinking. The student must be able to step away from his/her own view in order not only to hear someone else speaking but also to recognize how that different view challenges or supports one's own view. Perhaps this requires classes that are limited to upper-division students (juniors and seniors). In addition, classes would work better if they are limited in size to allow for the necessary time for in-class discussion and reflection.

Usually if the student can move to the point of reflection, he/she has already become open to possible truth in another viewpoint — truth that is not solely based on perceived agreement with one's own view. Such a step is difficult since most students (especially if they are not theology or religious studies majors) lack the capability of making sound judgments on truth claims. Rather, most students experience moments of brief insight, have a sense of accommodation for views similar to or not in contradiction to their own, and operate on opinion or some limited level of awareness of facts (i.e., attitudes toward ancient Judaism based solely on the Christian Gospels). Thus, the dialogue class can be an especially sensitive tool which could help students make clear distinctions, recognize differences that actually exist, and challenge oversimplifications with both real data and the personal contact with a representative from another religious tradition. For this reason, even though an ongoing in-class dialogue may not be possible, the infusion of real dialogue can be enhanced by inviting guest speakers to address especially important features of the material. Also assignments can be used to enhance this type of student development. Our classes have utilized short reflective essays to zero-in on typical trouble areas enabling students to see more clearly where stereotypes are mistaken and more sensitivity and awareness can lead to a better judgment. We could hardly expect students to completely resolve truth claims; however instructors can by their own modeling lead students toward a greater openness and, thereby, a fairer judgment of the facts. Of course, the whole matter of dealing with truth claims may only be a by-product of a dialogue course. Perhaps the most satisfying aspect of such courses has been observing students re-learning their own tradition simply by being exposed to alternative points of view. This re-learning process is bound to be an integral part of Jewish-Christian dialogue since beginning students will inevitably discover that Judaism clearly presented gives insight into much of early Christianity. Of course, the role that instructors play in this process of re-learning is significant since the dialogue format of the class can model for students the kind of openness to another that is required in dialogue or for the student to be opened up to genuinely new insight about his/her own tradition. Though our experience is limited in this regard, Jewish students may discover some things about their own tradition by simply being opened up to the fact that early Christianity was in fact an outgrowth of the Judaism of that time.

Despite the satisfying experience just described, we also know from our classes that students experience frustration and, even, anger during a transition from a more exclusivist view toward a more inclusive view. In addition, dialogue produces many gray areas in which the distinctions between views and, thus, truth claims is difficult to determine. For most undergraduate students the likely response is a relapse into a hard-line, exclusivist position (a more comfortable position to inhabit). Although the upheaval may be a long time coming, every class we have taught has experienced a mid-stream, watershed discussion experience in which students express their frustrations and then experience the possibilities of the kind of open discussion and thinking that the instructors have set as a primary objective. While the initial frustration may be directed at instructors (students hope that the instructors will "settle" things), the movement toward new openness depends upon the instructor's willingness to model the struggle that must take place in dialogue (e.g., if the dialogue presumes that a perspective of covenant as perceived from each tradition may also each be legitimate, then the struggle becomes how can different views of the same truth claim be legitimated and made understandable).

The pattern of the development of feelings has been consistent for us. What usually transpires through the latter half of a course is a new form of discussion raised to the level of dialogue simply because the frustrations of the students has been met in the open and new possibilities for open dialogue have been discovered by the students, themselves. Because of this new-found solid ground, we have found in most cases that our students are made more firm in their own tradition while at the same time more open to the views of others. In order to assure this development toward more open dialogue, instructors will have to build into the course schedule that possibility for open expression of frustrations. Of course each instructor will be faced with a decision on course objectives. We would suggest by our experience that the objectives include this effort to enable students to broaden their understanding of their own tradition (a very personalized objective, to be sure) and to appreciate more fully another tradition, even struggling with the possible truth in that view (for most of our students this means a Christian gaining more appreciation and sensitivity toward Judaism but in another setting the situation could be reversed as has been shown in the programs at Hebrew Union College mentioned in my "Team-Taught, In-Class Dialogue" cited above).

Of course, using dialogue as a strategy for infusion will, if this model is followed, mean transforming the class and its objectives to a certain extent. Surely, most courses can be made inter-religious in this sense and with some effort produce this form of dialogue. I would contend that only in this way will full appreciation of the other as other be gained and, thus, an honest infusion achieved. The strategy would work much more effectively if the class were team-taught, but this can work as we have all sensed if a single instructor conducts the class as if the dialogue partner is actually present at all times. Naturally this reality can be achieved through the presence of guest lecturers, but even with that there is a necessity to conduct dialogue with the effort to make as real as possible the presence of the other. This might be managed with the selection of texts for the course but really needs the commitment of the instructor to a strategy of dialogue.

Advantages and Disadvantages

So long as this approach to teaching Judaism in a church-related college or university is not a replacement but an enhancement of Jewish Studies offerings, there are significant advantages to an infusion model. First, this approach will center Jewish Studies in the curriculum uncovering the role that Jewish culture and thought has played in the mainstream of various cultures. As we said above, the incorporation of Jewish thought into various courses has long happened but not really as Jewish thought. By infusing Jewish thinkers and thought into courses through this dialogue strategy, we can center Jewish Studies as such in the heart of the curriculum. In addition, this infusion will effectively relocate Jewish Studies in such a way as to make the focus on Jewish culture and thought a part of the wider effort to globalize the curriculum as well as to incorporate multicultural studies into a broad range of courses. That is, this approach more effectively weds Jewish Studies with current major emphases in curricular reform. Finally, approaching this infusion with an infusion model not only teaches multiculturalism in the most effective way, it is especially helpful to lead Christian students into a model for full appreciation of the richness of other cultures.

Naturally, there are disadvantages lurking. An approach that is only half-hearted can be disastrous as a way of introducing other traditions like Judaism is for many Christian students. The limitation on time can possibly lead to charicatures of Judaism that are hardly responsible in the teaching of Judaism as it would be irresponsible in the teaching of any cultural tradition. In this way, specific courses in Jewish Studies would be preferable. In addition, some approaches that focus on issues cannot possibly give the sense of the fullness of another tradition. Such efforts would give an alternative perspective on various issues but not a sense of another culture as a whole. The same might be said of simply using a text or two that are thought to be "representative" of Jewish thought. Thus, I argue again that only a real effort at a dialogue strategy can lead to a minimizing of these disadvantages. Naturally, the possible trivializing of a cultural tradition cannot be fully avoided, but if dialogue as model is achieved, then the advantages I have seen in making the effort are enormous.

The Vision of Infusion: Some Examples

We can provide more detail of this approach by looking at sample courses in which such an approach can be applied. The approach I have outlined above was developed mostly as a result of teaching the Holocaust course. Since that course has a history that is especially linked to the setting of our university, I must say from the outset that offering courses in a theology department with a requirement in general education in theology gives me certain advantages over other settings. It is this setting of the private religious institution that I am especially anxious to describe, but I am convinced that the approach can be offered from other departments and in public institutions as a way to infuse Jewish Studies into the larger curriculum even though the curricular strategy would have to be different. Let me describe initially the development of the infusion/dialogue strategy as it arose in my teaching and re-shaping of the Holocaust course.

Our version of the Holocaust course began first of all as an independent course taught by a local rabbi as a part of our general education theology offerings. As such, the focus was on both the Holocaust and general literacy in the history of Judaism and Jewish thought. That format is what I inherited when I started teaching the course and with the assistance of the rabbi and others continued to emphasize both the Holocaust and Jewish thought. As I developed my own comfort with this course, however, the shape of the course shifted to emphasize the interaction between Christianity and Judaism as a primary feature of Holocaust Studies. Thus, the course naturally followed the path of the dialogue strategy that I have given above. That strategy is enhanced each time the course is taught by inviting a series of guest speakers who can give insight both into the Jewish Holocaust experience and the history of Judaism. Thus, the course has been a model for the strategy I am suggesting for the infusion model.

Let me emphasize key features of the development of the Holocaust course that will be important for examining how this approach is taken from the setting of the Holocaust course into other courses in my teaching. First, my approach is not a history of religions approach but rather is a theological approach. I am not involved usually in examining the full structure of religious traditions (ritual, practice, organization of institutions, etc.) but am rather focused on religious thought and how interpreters of religious traditions explain the meaning of key beliefs and practices. This is what I call theology and it is this approach that shapes what I am calling the dialogue approach to teaching Judaism. I am isolating what might be called religious ideologies and these ideologies (both in terms of their logic and history) are key to understanding the role of religions in the events of the Holocaust. Even more, the discussion of the shaping of ideologies becomes key for understanding the events in Judaism and Christianity that are a result of the events of the Holocaust at least in part.

I would modify this approach by saying that the theological approach I use can be called post-modern. I generally call this approach post-Holocaust in that I am interested ultimately in the way the Holocaust has affected religious practice and belief and how this effect has been interpreted by the leading thinkers in both Judaism and Christianity on the Holocaust. I have given details of this post-Holocaust approach to theology in other essays, but for our purposes let me push my normal descriptions further by acknowledging that my approach is also post-modern in certain specific ways. First, I assume that all religions, Christianity and Judaism included, are pluralistic in their theologies (or whatever their thought traditions might be called). That is, I start with the assumption that there is no single view that can characterize either post-Holocaust Judaism or post-Holocaust Christianity. Second, I assume that religious traditions often hold views that are seemingly contradictory without rejecting either (they manage to maintain at least ambiguity and probably often real paradox without much difficulty). Third, I assume that ethics becomes central for religions after the Shoah and not belief. In this case, attending to beliefs becomes a way for gauging potential courses of action or understanding the way that beliefs have led to certain actions (particularly as a source for antisemitism) in the past and not for the sake of settling matters of belief. Finally, I assume that religions and religious traditions are able to change and have done so consistently throughout history. The aim for responses to the Shoah are essentially dependent on the belief that religions can and do change.

Four Courses as Examples

I will describe briefly three types of courses that can serve as examples of the infusion model I am suggesting. I have applied this model rather directly to my teaching in our introductory theology course and in another course on Christians in dialogue. In addition, the model can be used effectively given the structure and reading list of our new freshman core course (a multi-staff, inter-disciplinary year long course for our first year students). I will also use as example a sociology course taught at another small private university, which can serve as an alternative case for infusion in a course other than a theology course. That course, which I was privileged to participate in, also showed me several things about the impact of this infusion model on students, primarily because of the instructor's excellent course plan and teaching approach. I have learned much from her about what I am presenting here.

My two courses build on my experience in the Holocaust course and simply apply the lessons learned from that course to teaching a unit of each of the courses devoted to Judaism and Christians' relation to Judaism. That is, I attempt to lead students, in the brief time available in the course, to accept that Judaism is a living, changing and pluralistic religion that differs in most ways from usual stereotypes that Christian students are likely to have. I can enhance this process by bringing in guest speakers again and in the dialogue course by sending students on an assignment to interview a representative of the local community, usually a Rabbi, and writing a reflection paper on that interview. In addition, I aim to lead students to see that the history of Christian thinking about Jews has included antisemitism. By pointing to specific events and Christian beliefs and teachings, this lesson can be easily demonstrated. Even more, they are led to see that Christianity is also a living, changing and pluralistic religion in which such antisemitic beliefs do not need to continue. That is, in a theology course I can help students to see alternative theological positions that are genuine Christian perspectives. My own setting enables this process well, but the same can be accomplished in other departmental or institutional settings simply by inviting me or another theologian of the same approach to the classroom.

It is clear that the infusion model as I have developed it is possible in a theology class, especially in private church-related colleges and universities. I believe that the same can be done in courses of other departments and my examples are an inter-disciplinary core course and a sociology course. The core course represents a new development in our curriculum although the idea has a significant history in American education. The notion of a full year inter-disciplinary course as a core for all beginning students is gaining a new following and may very well be a model for many institutions both public and private. The difference in these new examples of inter-disciplinary courses is, in part, the need for most schools to incorporate both multi-culturalism and global perspectives into general education courses. While this can be done in any number of ways, the most prominent approach is something like an infusion model like I have been discussing.

Our particular version of the core course is issue centered and enables the staff to select a wide range of course materials and assignments that help to focus student attention and thinking on these issues. In courses trying, like ours, to build in multi-cultural and global perspectives, the approach can lead to great advantages and major pitfalls. The pitfalls are fairly self-evident. Without extensive historical background, first year students can easily develop distorted views of any culture assuming far too readily commonalities between cultures that do not exist. This is especially problematic when texts are used to address so-called "common human experiences." The danger is that the particular cultural context and historical context for any text will be ignored for the sake of addressing such human concerns. In the same vein, individual texts will easily be assumed as "representative" of a particular culture.

These pitfalls suggest that teachers trained in Jewish Studies (as well as any other specific cultural studies program) be in the forefront of training and teaching in these core courses. There is likely to be a certain superficiality at any rate that will lead to distortions, but at least the presence of Jewish Studies people will help to minimize these distortions. For example, our course includes texts that are taken from a wide range of Holocaust materials including the diary/journal by Etty Hillesum.[3] Most of our students will lack both the necessary background in Holocaust history as well as Jewish history to be able to see what might be distinctively Jewish about this diary or more importantly how Etty Hillesum is and is not representative of European Jews of that time. At least the presence of teacher/scholars of the Holocaust, especially those trained in Jewish Studies can be of great assistance to other staff teaching these materials.

If such core courses are likely to re-emerge with the challenge of multi-cultural/global education, then it is seemingly mandatory for specialists in Jewish Studies to both take part in the teaching as well as work with the whole concept of infusion of cultural studies into general education curriculum. Given that mandate (as I now face myself), the advantages may now be apparent. The current emphasis on multi-culturalism and globalism in education is a great opportunity for those teaching in a variety of inter-disciplinary studies programs (Women's Studies, East Asian studies, African American studies, Jewish Studies, etc.) to create a place for their teaching in the center of the university's work, that is, in the core general education program. To do so requires these faculty to take on the vision of a model of infusion such as I have been developing. Moreover, this also gives an opportunity for the faculty, in particular, to gain a voice in shaping the core education of all students and not just a select few as is the case with most Jewish Studies courses at the present. Such efforts require adjustments in goals but the opportunities are too great to pass up.

The second course is one that fits the mold of the first since the course was designed as a sociology course but functioned as a senior inter-disciplinary seminar, that is trying to accomplish the same goals as the core course but as a capstone to a student's education rather than an introduction.[4] The potential of this sort of course is greater if the students are appropriately prepared to read, write and think critically about a variety of issues in the humanities and social sciences. This particular course had the significant advantage of also involving serious reflection on developments in the natural sciences as well. It is a perfect capstone course meeting much of the interest of administrators in achieving yet another of the currently hot trends in higher education. That is, courses of this sort will also become more and more common in most institutions in the United States.

I suggest this course for two more reasons. First, the course was designed and taught by another professor. That the structure of the course followed a basic sociological approach also allows me to look at a model that is outside of the theology department completely. The setting of a private formerly church-related institution also gives a good comparison to show how such courses are especially valuable in settings where a great majority of the students come from backgrounds essentially if not explicitly formed by Christianity. The profile of the students is similar to that of my university with many students having a general, often superficial understanding of their own Christian tradition and almost no background in studying Judaism (not to mention any other religious/cultural tradition).

The success of this course precisely in the ways that I have emphasized as important goals of the model of infusion led me to a great deal of insight into the possibilities of this model. The general focus of a sociology of knowledge (both religion and science are forms of knowledge acknowledged as institutions in societies) allowed for a framework within which to incorporate and think about different religious traditions as examples. The comparative framework followed in this course (which included a series of guest lecturers invited for a public lecture series) set into the sociological perspective allowed for an honest dialogue to develop between students and guests, between students and a wider range of course readings and between students and instructors (I was invited to be an ongoing consultant for each class on the religions). What ensued was not only a greater appreciation and knowledge of each religious tradition but also the recognition of the complexity and plurality of any one religious tradition. Above all, the plurality of views finally broke the normal tendency to view all other cultures from the vantage point of one's own giving instead points of comparison within each separate tradition that allowed for a perspective beginning to develop independently from any one religious point of view. Thus, the treatment of Judaism finally was moving toward being able to treat Judaism on its own terms, defined by a variety of thinkers from different viewpoints. This latter objective seems to be a central goal for many Jewish Studies courses and the success of this course in reaching toward this objective, obvious in the comments, performance and evaluations by the students, shows that the infusion model if it is truly multi-dimensional dialogical strategy, can be an effective way to teach Jewish Studies.

Naturally, the other goals of in-depth study and more detailed historical context also important for Jewish Studies is more difficult to achieve in a course designed to be an infusion of Jewish thought into a multi-cultural, inter-disciplinary course. I was amazed at how much depth of insight students managed to achieve in this setting, however. Perhaps the results can be largely attributed to the instructor who has an extraordinary talent at pushing students toward rich learning as well as leading them into highly productive, in-class interactions. Perhaps the setting of a course in a private, church-related institution also allowed the freedom to pursue religious questions in ways difficult for other settings. Perhaps the context of a sociological framework also sets up a certain kind of analysis that will clearly be different for courses in history or literature or political science. In fact, I would agree that all of these factors led to the success of this particular course, most especially the talent of the instructor. Even so, I am convinced that this course shows that such an infusion model aimed at a multi-dimensional dialogical strategy does work beyond what I might have thought possible before, even with my long-standing commitments to the dialogical strategy.

Conclusions

My aim in this essay is to set before the reader a model for teaching Judaism that is both a continuation of the teaching approach I wrote about in the first edition of this volume as well as a strikingly new approach that has emerged mostly because of developments in education since I wrote that earlier essay. In suggesting this dialogical infusion model I am only outlining an approach that many of these readers have already applied in many ways. I believe, however, that the dialogical strategy that I have added to this mix does lead in a direction distinct from many notions of infusion that help to safeguard against the most obvious forms of superficiality and distortion. In addition, I believe that my experience as described in the variety of courses given above does show both that this model for teaching Judaism and the additional idea of moving Jewish Studies into the wider curriculum and not just isolated to particular courses or in a separate department is both successful and necessary for the health of Jewish Studies in university curriculum of the twenty-first century.

This approach may be especially helpful in approaching and teaching Christian students who are especially steeped in distorted stereotypes of Judaism and Jewish history. Of course, I have said previously that we all teach such students even if the religious identity of our students is for many both unknown and irrelevant to their teaching. Still, this sort of approach does work well in moving students with preconceptions of Judaism toward a new and exciting appreciation for the diversity and creativity of Jewish thought and history. I would argue even more strenuously that the setting of a dialogical approach strategy that sets Judaism into a course designed to study a variety of religious traditions is even more effective in moving students away from a closed point of view to a more flexible and adventuresome approach to learning about traditions other than their own. This possibility is bound to be pleasing to teachers and administrators looking for ways to do multi-cultural and global general education. Of course, this approach must be taken as an addition to current Jewish Studies courses and programs, but the gains are significant enough to make the effort exciting and realistic.   ✡

Endnotes

1. James Moore, "Team-Taught, In-Class Dialogue: a Limited but Promising Method in Teaching Judaism," in Zev Garber, ed., *Methodology in the Academic Teaching of Judaism* (Lanham, MD: University Press of America, 1986), 201-211.
2. *Ibid.* p. 202.
3. Etty Hillesum, *An Interrupted Life* (New York: Washington Square Press, 1983).
4. This course was designed and taught by Prof. Barbara Strassberg of Aurora University in the Spring of 1998.

Chapter 12

Teaching Shoah in the Contexts
of Sacred Texts and Teachings

David Patterson

"At Auschwitz," Elie Wiesel has written, "not only man died, but also the idea of man."[1] A key point of conflict characterizing the Shoah as Shoah lies in the opposition between two views of the human being. According to Nazi ideology, the human being is an accident of nature whose essence is determined by race and who therefore has no fundamental connection to anyone outside the race. According to the testimony signified by the very presence of Jews in the world, the human being is a child of G-d created in the image of the Holy One; and since G-d begins His creation of humanity with one human being, all are essentially connected to one another. In its metaphysical dimensions, then, the Shoah is characterized by an assault not only on a people but on a teaching and tradition concerning the essence of a human being.

The usual study of "the history of the Holocaust," therefore, does not provide a sufficient understanding of what was slated for destruction; the Event eludes the chronicle of events. Characterized as an annihilation of the holy within the human —of the holy through the human — the Shoah is the calculated destruction not only of Jewish bodies but of Jewish souls and Jewish prayers, of Jewish teachings and traditions, of Jewish homes and families. These are the elements that go into the Jewish view of humanity, and the fundamental constituents of that humanity are the mother, the father, and the child. It is the relationship of these human beings to one another that attests to the status and the essence of a human being. Undertaking their assault on the very notion of a human being, the Nazis murdered not only mothers, fathers, and children but the very idea of a mother, a father, and a child. At this definitive core of the Event, the teaching of Shoah in the contexts of sacred texts most significantly comes into play.

In the pages that follow we shall examine the sacred texts and teachings on the mother, the father, and the child. Those who embark on the teaching of the Shoah with these sources in mind will penetrate deeper into the metaphysical dimensions of the greatest catastrophe in the long history of the Jewish people.

The Mother

If we understand the significance of the mother in Jewish tradition, then we may better understand what is targeted for annihilation in the Shoah. What, then, do the sacred texts and religious thinkers teach us about the significance of the mother in Jewish tradition? In his commentary on the *Sefer Yetzirah*, an ancient work of Jewish mysticism, Aryeh Kaplan points out that the Feminine Essence—the essence of the mother—belongs to the domain of Understanding or *Binah*,[2] a word that derives its root from *bein*, which means "between." Understanding arises from the difference *between* two, and, as the highest manifestation of the Feminine Essence, the mother transforms the radical difference that characterizes understanding into the absolute non-indifference of love. The mother, then, is the closest tie that we have to the Creator, to that absolute Other who is revealed in the absolute non-indifference of love. Since this Other who is the Creator of the world is the one who is ultimately targeted for extermination in the Kingdom of Night,[3] the obliteration of the mother is among the first principles that rule in that Kingdom, where the essence of Israel was under assault.

"The greatness of Israel," we are told in the *Midrash Rabbah*, "is compared. . . to a woman bearing child."[4] For a woman bearing child is the embodiment of the origin, of the love, and of the home that constitute Israel. The *Zohar*, in fact, suggests a connection between the mother and the origin of humanity, declaring, "The [Supernal] Mother said: 'let us make man in our image.'"[5] If we may allow ourselves a moment of midrashic association, then we can see why the concept of the mother appears not just at the origin of the individual's life but in the midst of the six days of creation. Jewish tradition teaches, for example, that the Torah not only precedes the Creation,[6] but it is the basis of all that is born, as though from a womb, in the Creation. The *Zohar* expresses it rather cryptically, saying, "First came *Ehyeh* (I shall be), the dark womb of all. Then *Asher Ehyeh* (That I am), indicating the readiness of the Mother to beget all."[7] G-d as loving and merciful—G-d as Creator—is G-d as the Supernal Mother. In this connection Emmanuel Levinas points out, "*Rakhamim* (Mercy). . . goes back to the word *Rekhem*, which means uterus. *Rakhamim* is the revelation of the uterus to the other, whose gestation takes place within it. *Rakhamim* is maternity itself. G-d as merciful is G-d defined by maternity."[8] And since maternity is defined by the capacity for creation, it forms the basis of Torah itself.

This point becomes more clear if we recall that the first letter in the Torah is the letter *beit*, which is also the word for "house," the place where human life first makes its appearance in the world. The notion of a house, moreover, is associated with the Patriarch Jacob, as Rabbi Yitzchak Ginsburgh points out: "At the level of Divinity, the house symbolizes the ultimate purpose of all reality: to become a dwelling place below for the manifestation of G-d's presence. Not as Abraham who called it [the Temple site] 'a mountain,' nor as Isaac who called it 'a field,' but as Jacob who called it 'a house.'"[9] Since, according to the Talmud, "blessing is only found in a man's house on account of his wife" (*B. Mes* 59a), the sanctity of the house is linked with the Jewish woman, the wife and mother, who sees to all of the affairs of the house.[10] Thus the women, the wives and mothers, of Israel are known as the House of Jacob. This being the case, we see that, if the Torah is the foundation of Creation, the mother, through her tie to the *beit* in which the Torah originates, is the foundation of the Torah itself; she is the origin of the origin.

This position is further reinforced if we bear in mind the mothers who constitute the House of Jacob when in the *Midrash Rabbah* we read, "The Holy One, blessed be He, said to His world: 'O My world, My world! Shall I tell thee who created thee, who formed thee? Jacob has created thee, Jacob has formed thee.'"[11] The interconnections linking Torah, Creation, and women may explain why tradition holds that at Sinai "the Torah had to be accepted *first* by the women (the 'house of Jacob') before it could be accepted by the men (the 'house of Israel')."[12] If the Torah is the basis of Creation and the mother lies at the origin of the Torah, then one understands why the Torah enters the world through the women of the House of Jacob. First among those women are the mothers; according to Jewish tradition, the mother is the consummate form of woman. Why? Because the mother is the consummate manifestation of love.

In the sixteenth century Rabbi Yitzchak Luria, the Ari, asked the question: "If *Binah* or Understanding, which is associated with the Mother, is a mental process, why is it said to be in the heart, and not in the head?" To which Aryeh Kaplan answers, "The heart is actually the Personification of Imma-Mother, which is Binah-Understanding, where She reveals herself."[13] In the *Shema's* injunction to love G-d, the first thing with which we are called upon to love is the heart, *b'kol levavkhah* (Deut 6:5). One also recalls that the *lamed* and the *beit* of the Hebrew word for "heart," *lev*, are the last and the first letters of the Torah. The heart, therefore, contains all of the Torah: it is on the heart, indeed, that the Teaching is to be inscribed (Deut 6:6). The mother whom the *beit* situates at the origin of the Torah thus includes the sum of the Torah in her personification as the heart, or the *lev*. Personified as the heart, the mother signifies not only the origin of life but the center of life. The heart bears this significance because it is the seat of the love and the teaching of G-d. And the lovingkindness shown by one human being toward another is the highest expression of that love and teaching centered in the heart and personified by the mother.

Hence, Rabbi Ginsburgh reminds us, "lovingkindness is the means through which G-d's presence is ultimately revealed,"[14] and it is originally revealed through the mother. In the *Tanya*, moreover, Rabbi Schneur Zalman of Liadi maintains that lovingkindness in the form of charity is feminine and, by implication, maternal, for "it receives a radiation from the light of the *Ein Sof* that [like a womb] encompasses all worlds."[15] From a Jewish perspective, therefore, maternal love is not just a feeling or a state of mind, not simply a natural or psychological phenomenon, but is the manifestation and revelation of the Most High. When that love is targeted for extermination, as it was in the Shoah, the light of all there is to hold dear, the light that was in the beginning, is assailed. Hence the ontological assault that is manifested in the assault on the mother moves to a metaphysical level in the annihilation of maternal love. Like the light created upon the first utterance of G-d, the mother's love is the mainstay of life, even and especially during the reign of death; she is the one who reveals to the individual that he is still a human being and that his life *matters*. As the one who reveals to us the dearness of life, she is the one who makes it possible to *dwell* in the world. For dwelling is made possible only where life has value. And the center of that value is the home.

This brings us back to the *beit*. If, according to Jewish tradition, the letter *beit* situates the mother at the origin of all life, the meaning of the letter *beit* places the mother at the center of the home. "The feminine aspect of the soul," Rabbi Ginsburgh points out, "and, in general, the woman in Judaism is symbolized by the house."[16] The reverse is also the case: the home, which houses life within its walls, is symbolized by the woman, who also houses life within her womb. Other associations and explanations also come to mind; one recalls, for example, Rashi's commentary on the Torah, where he writes, "The decree consequent upon the incident of the spies had not been enacted upon the *women*, because they held the Promised Land dear. The men had said, (Num 24:4) 'Let us appoint a chief and return to Egypt,' whilst the women said, (Num 27:4) 'Give us a possession in the Land.'"[17] It is the women, in other words, who seek out a home and who thus signify the home. The House of Jacob, whose reception of the Torah made it possible for the House of Israel to receive the Torah, embraces the promise of a place to dwell. The sum of the Torah lies in the commandment to love, and the commandment to love opens up a dwelling place, a place where children and families may come into the world. As we have seen, the mother is the incarnation of that love; hence the mother is the personification of the home. And the Nazi Reich is precisely the opposite of the home.

The Kingdom of Night instituted by the Nazis is the Kingdom of Exile. If, as Martin Buber has said, "'Good' is the movement in the direction of home,"[18] then we see that this height of evil is the movement away from home and into exile, into ghettos, camps, and hiding places. It was not for nothing, then, that the language of extermination included terms such as "resettlement." It was not enough to kill the Jews. Waging an ontological war, the Nazis had to annihilate their homes and their concept of home; they had to drive them from their homes and thus render them homeless prior to killing them, since the ontological onslaught was aimed directly at the destruction of all being that inheres in dwelling. In the Nazi assault on the mother we see the fundamental human problem of dwelling manifested in its most extreme form: the murder of the maternal love that distinguishes the origin of life is engineered by the devastation of the home. Once the mother is eliminated, the reign of exile and homelessness is inaugurated. Of course, there is no mother without a father: with the assault on the Supernal Mother comes the assault on the One we call, "*Avinu, Malkenu*—our Father, our King." And, as with the mother, this assault is articulated through the murder of the human father.

The Father

We have seen that the mother embodies the origin of life, the love of what is most dear in life, and the home that establishes a center for life. In the father we have the truth that provides a ground for life, the wisdom that underlies all thinking about life, and the order that constitutes the reality and substance of life. From an ontological standpoint, then, when the father's existence is rendered illegitimate, truth, thought, and reality come under attack. In Jewish terms, these entail the truth of tradition as an avenue of revelation; the wisdom and the intellect that thinkers such as Maimonides[19] and Gersonides[20] identify with G-d; and the order of reality as it continually issues from the hand and the mouth of the Creator. All of this is lost in the loss of the father, so that the memory of the father entails far more than a mournful reminiscence surrounding the head of a household. The attack on the father is, indeed, an attack on memory itself. For, according to Jewish tradition, memory belongs to the father, who is responsible for handing down the tradition, just as the nurturing of life belongs to the mother. Regarding the *zachor v'shamor* that pertain to the Sabbath, for example, the *Bahir* teaches that "'remember' (*zachor*) refers to the male (*Zachar*). 'Keep' (*shamor*) refers to the bride."[21] The male is the bridegroom, he who is to become a father in the observance of the first of all the commandments, namely to be fruitful and multiply (Gen 1:28).

In the project to exterminate the Jews, the Reign of Nothingness begins with the undoing of this commandment, and it is this commandment that makes the father who he is. The father contains the seed of Israel, and what befalls him reverberates throughout the nation. In the ontological assault on Jewish being it is not enough simply to murder the father. The killing of his body must be preceded by the annihilation of his image, for in his image lies the Jewish being that the father symbolizes. Now the attack on being is effective only if it is felt. And it is felt only if it is introduced as an imposed absence,[22] that is, as a sense of have been abandoned. When the father is in his place, being is itself in place: truth, thought, and reality are in place. Here truth is not simply a matter of fact. According to the Jewish tradition, it is an avenue of return to the Most High and lays claim to us before we stake any other claims.

Like the father, the truth that lays claim to us commands us to pursue the good prior to our own choosing. This pre-originary *having been chosen already* links the memory of the father to the good that distinguishes truth. An illustration of this idea can be found in the *Pirke de Rabbi Eliezer*, where we find a comment on Joseph that states, "In all his wisdom a certain woman enticed (him), and when he wished to accustom himself to sin, he saw the image of his father, and repented concerning it."[23] From a third position, between the self and the other, the father emerges as the figure of the good and therefore as a figure of truth. In the murder of the father the good itself is targeted for extinction. And the eclipse of the good—the disintegration of truth—characterizes the condition of absolute evil, which, according to Jewish tradition, occasions the coming of the Messiah. In the *En Jacob*, for instance, we are taught that in the generation of the Messiah, "the wisdom of the scribes will be corrupted. Men fearing sin will be hated. The leaders of that generation will have the nature of dogs. And the truth will be lacking." In short, the father will be annihilated.[24] Thus it came to pass.

In the tractate *Avot* of the Mishnah, Rabbi Shimon ben Gamaliel teaches that truth is one of the foundations of the world (1.18). "Speaking falsehood, then," writes Moshe Chayim Luzzatto, "is comparable to removing the foundation of the world; and, conversely, if one is heedful of the truth it is as if he maintains the world's foundation."[25] With the disintegration of truth, when words are torn from meaning as families are torn apart, the world's foundation crumbles and with it collapses the ground of tradition. It is not enough to kill the father; a father killed is still a father, still the one who signifies the truth affirmed in the teachings and traditions of Torah and Talmud. In the ontological assault not only the person of the father but all he signifies must be destroyed. Indeed, comprehension itself must be destroyed.

In *Legends of Our Time* Elie Wiesel recalls, "In dying, my father looked at me, and in his eyes where night was gathering, there was nothing but animal terror, the demented terror of one who, because he wished to understand too much, no longer understood anything. His gaze fixed on me, empty of meaning."[26] As the father, however, it falls to him to understand, that is, to comprehend and to *think* what the world poses for thought. According to Jewish tradition, the *Sefirah* of *Chokhmah* or Wisdom is associated with the father; further, among the connections between the ten *Sefirot* and the parts of the body, *Chokhmah* belongs to the skull or to the mind,[27] that is, to the seat of thought. The night that gathers in the eyes of the dying father darkens the mind that constitutes the father, darkens not only the mind of this particular father but the mind as such. From a philosophical standpoint, the love of wisdom that is philosophy itself is the key to every conception of the human being and his world. Looking to the Jewish tradition, we find that the eleventh-century sage Bachya ibn Paquda, for example, expresses this notion by saying, "Sages declared that philosophy is man's knowledge of himself, that is, knowledge of what has been mentioned in regard to the human being, so that through the evidence of divine wisdom displayed in himself, he will become cognizant of the Creator."[28] But the cognition that characterizes our thinking about creation is obliterated upon the murder of the father, for the father is the embodiment of that cognition.

To the extent that the human being struggles to remain human, he or she struggles to understand; one cannot decide not to understand any more than one can decide not to breathe—or not to have a father. In the Shoah it is not that the reasons for the extermination are obscure or complicated; rather, the "reasons" do not belong to reason or to the rational and the thinkable, for, again, that is just what the evil of the anti-world sets out to destroy. In the words of Charlotte Delbo, those sent to the anti-world "expect the worst—they do not expect the unthinkable."[29] They do not expect the nullification of thought itself, which defines the parameters of expectation and the operations of the mind. The fact that thinking does continue—something that ordinarily enhances life—now serves to further undermine the life of the human being. Intelligence and thought themselves become the enemy.

As a tradition of thought, the Jewish tradition is a tradition of commentary, not only on the text of the Torah but on the world created from the blueprint of the Torah. Here the function of thought is to read the text of the world, as one might read the letters of the alphabet. Yitzchak Ginsburgh explains, "Each of the twenty-two letters of the Hebrew alphabet possesses three different creative powers, which in the teaching of *Chassidut* are termed: energy (*koah*), life (*hayot*), and light (*or*). . . . In the creative process, the Hebrew letters appear at each of these three levels: as the energy building-blocks of all reality; as the manifestation of the inner life-pulse permeating the universe as a whole and each of its individual creatures ('pulsing' every created being, instantaneously, into and out of existence); and as the channels which direct the influx of Divine revelation into created consciousness."[30] Just as the father teaches his child the *alef-beit* by which the Torah is read, so does he signify the reading of the world and its symbols through a process of thought. In the anti-world, however, the alphabet of the world is turned on end, so that energy, life, and light are swallowed up rather than released in the effort to read the revelation. There is no burning bush. There is only the burning.

Contrary to what many have claimed, the breakdown of reality that follows in the wake of the collapse of thought, then, is not a problem posed for the imagination. On the contrary, once thought collapses— and with it the measures and limitations of reality—imagination itself becomes unlimited; after all, everything the Nazis did was imagined before it was done. The result of this loss of limits is a perversion that renders the real unreal. "Existence as such," Jean Améry states it, "became definitively a totally abstract and thus empty concept. To reach out beyond concrete reality with words became before our very eyes a game that was not only worthless and an impermissible luxury but also mocking and evil."[31] Where reality happens, Levinas reminds us, "the *appearing* of a phenomenon is inseparable from its *signifying*. . . . Every phenomenon is a disclosure or a fragment of a discourse."[32] But in the anti-world of Auschwitz, where existence *as such* becomes an empty concept—that is, where there is no signifying of anything, where the phenomenon does not speak but rather overwhelms with indifferent silence—there unreality happens. And it happens because the father, who is the sign of giving signs, no longer happens.

If the appearing of a phenomenon is inseparable from its signifying, it is because the father has made an appearance and has thus rooted the human being in the real. In the concentrationary universe it is not that one universe or world has replaced another; rather, the real has broken down, so that there is no place where a world can make its appearance. That place, or that space, emerges in the midst of the relation that makes the father who he is. With the loss of the father all relations that go into the structure of the real are overturned. Having already noted the father's association with the *Sefirah* of *Chakhmah*, we may recall that, according to the same tradition, "Wisdom is the conduit of G-d's essence."[33] As the guardian of tradition, the father is the guardian of one of the avenues of G-d's revelation. There is no murder of the father, then, that does not entail a murder of G-d the Father. And one profoundly horrifying way in which the status of G-d and man as father is obliterated is through the obliteration of the child. For a mother and father need a child in order to be a mother and father.

The Child

On 5 May 1942 Adam Czerniakow, head of the Jewish Council of the Warsaw Ghetto, took care to note, "Today [is the] Jewish children's holiday: *Lag B'Omer.*"[34] *Lag B'Omer* is the thirty-third day in the counting of the *omer*, which numbers each day of the seven weeks from the second night of Passover to the Sixth of Sivan, the holy day known as *Shavuot*, when we celebrate the Revelation at Sinai. Why is the thirty-third day of the omer the Jewish children's holy day? Perhaps because it is eighteen days away from the giving of the Torah, with the number eighteen signifying *chai*, or life. When the Torah was given at Sinai life was given to the world: in the Jewish tradition the Torah is life itself, and our children are the guarantors of that life. For in the *Midrash Tanchuma* it is written, "In the hour when the Holy One, blessed be He, was to offer the Torah to Israel, He said, 'Preserve My Torah.' They told Him, 'We shall.' He said to them, 'Give Me a guarantee that you will keep it.' They said to Him, 'Abraham, Isaac, and Jacob will be our guarantee.' He told them, 'Your fathers themselves need a guarantee. . . . They told Him, 'Our children will be our guarantee.'"[35] And, the Midrash on Psalms adds, G-d "asked the sucklings and the embryos: 'Will you be sureties for your fathers, so that if I give them the Torah they will live by it, but that if they do not, you will be forfeited because of them?" They replied: "Yes."[36]

This teaching that affirms the dearness of our children is so strongly embraced among the Jewish people that when Czerniakow was ordered to personally turn over the children for deportation to Treblinka, as he indicates in his suicide note written on 23 July 1942, he chose instead to take his own life. Perhaps he knew on some level that to participate in this murder of the children would amount to becoming an accomplice in the murder of G-d, if one may speak in such a manner. The association between the murder of G-d and the murder of the child is made all too clearly in a haunting and horrifying scene from Elie Wiesel's *Night*. When the prisoners of Buna were forced to witness the hanging of a child, a man standing behind Eliezer whispered, "Where is G-d now?" And, we read, "I heard a voice within me answer him: 'Where is He? Here He is—He is hanging here on this gallows.'" [37]

How deeply ingrained is the status of the child in the Jewish soul we begin to realize when we recall a passage from the *Midrash Rabbah* attributed to Rabbi Yehudah ha-Nasi: "Come and see how beloved are the children by the Holy One, blessed be He. The Sanhedrin were exiled but the *Shekhinah* did not go into exile with them.[38] When, however, the children were exiled, the *Shekhinah* went into exile with them." In the *Zohar* we read, "Who is it that upholds the world and causes the patriarchs to appear? It is the voice of tender children studying the Torah; and for their sake the world is saved."[39] And, in the name of Rabbi Yehudah, the talmudic sage Resh Lakish said, "The world endures only for the sake of the breath of the school children" (*b. Shabb* 119b). Why? Because on the breath of the children, both at prayer and at play, vibrates the spirit of the *Shekhinah* herself. Thus, says the *Zohar*, "From the 'breath' which issues out of the mouth the voice is formed, and according to the well-known dictum, the world is upheld only by the merit of the 'breath' of little school children who have not yet tasted sin. Breath is itself mixture, being composed of air and moisture, and through it the world is carried on. Esoterically speaking, the breath of the little ones becomes 'voice,' and spreads throughout the whole universe, so that they become the guardians of the world."[40] Not by might but by spirit, the world endures as long as it attends to the "voice" that speaks from within the breath of the children.

That voice is just what the Nazis set out to silence; that breath is just what they aimed to suffocate, consciously and deliberately. At the core of the Nazis' assault on G-d and creation, on the mother and the father, is the calculated attempt to suffocate the breath and to silence the voice arising from the mouths of Jewish children. The suffocation of the children that characterizes the Shoah lies not only in the destruction of the bodies of the little ones but also includes the perversion of their very being. The children of the Shoah know only fear. The paralyzing effect of knowing only fear suggests a *rigor mortis* that takes over the soul before the body is laid into the earth or reduced to ashes. And so the children do not move; they do not speak and they do not play—they are not children but only the vanishing shadows of children. "One never sees even one child playing," says the sculptor Rivosh, for example, writing from the Riga Ghetto. "All of them, like beasts at bay, cling timidly close to their mothers or sit in the gateways."[41] Ridden with fear, their bodies are all but emptied of life's spirit, which is the spirit of the child, who in turn sustains the spirit of a people and a world. Indeed, dwelling along the edge of the origin, the child is our link to the earth itself. But the edge of the origin has been transformed into the edge of annihilation. With the assault on the being of the child the status of the origin is obliterated. For the child is an emanation of the origin, which consists of a compassion that is the opposite of the cruelty to which these children are subjected.

The ontological status of the child whose being now lies in being suffocated, however, is established long before any children are marched or shipped off to a camp. Indeed, establishing this condition of the child is one of the aims of prohibiting children to attend schools in the ghetto. "Children were old, and old men were as helpless as children," Wiesel puts it,[42] a statement illustrated by the image of two children in a ghetto pushing an old man in a baby carriage in Ka-tzetnik's *House of Dolls*.[43] If time is a fundamental horizon of human being, then this collapse of time in children robbed of a future fundamentally alters their being. It steals their life away from them before they are sent to their death, making them more ancient than the Ancient of Days. These little ones are forced into an awareness of every breath sucked forth from their young souls.[44] The days they live are not the days of their lives but the days of their death. Robbed of their time, they are robbed of their place, so that any place they occupy is a non-place, and their presence is out of place. Thus the ontological condition to which the Nazis relegated the child exemplifies an ontological aspect of the assault on the people of Israel. As the Jews are cut off from the world, the children are cut off from the Jews. Throughout the ghettos of the Shoah the condition of the child is such that he has been removed from the care of all. This absence of care is a manifestation of the absence of the holy, so that the assault on the child becomes an integral part of the assault on the Holy One. Paradoxically, in the ghettos it is an absence as omnipresent as the Holy One Himself. This absence of children and childhood is the death before death, the slaughter before the slaughter, which is a slaughter of the innocents in their innocence. If the essence of the Nazi empire is the murder camp, the essence of that murder is the murder of the children, which transcends the barbed-wire boundaries of the camps. The Nazis were not merely murderers—they were child murderers who relentlessly tracked down their prey. They were murderers of the dimension of height that ordains and sanctifies all of being. They were the murderers of redemption.

Echoing the tradition's teachings on the significance of the child, Wiesel's character Moshe from *The Oath* asserts, "The Messiah. We seek him, we pursue him. We think he is in heaven; we don't know that he likes to come down as a child. And yet, every man's childhood is messianic in essence."[45] One of the texts from the Jewish tradition that articulates this view of the child as savior is the *Even Sheleimah* of the Vilna Gaon, the renowned sage of the eighteenth century. There he writes, "The child redeems his parent from Gehinom and causes him to be brought to Gan Eden."[46] The Maggid of Dubno, a contemporary of the Vilna Gaon, illustrates this significance of the child with a parable about a family that lived in a house in the forest. Every evening the father of the family would barricade the windows and doors of the house to protect his wife and children from danger. One night, however, a fire broke out in their home. And somehow a heavy stone had fallen outside to seal the door, so that they could not get out. Since the windows were locked from the outside, they had no way of crying out to their neighbors for help. One of the youngest of the children, however, discovered the dormer window, and, because he was so small, he was able to climb outside and go for help. The villagers came and rolled away the stone from the entrance to the house. And so the family was saved thanks to the courageous efforts of a small child. "Even as this one little boy triumphantly flung open the door of his father's house and thereby saved his family," says the Maggid, "so, too, the study, prayers and tears of our children can open the lofty gates of Heaven and thus bring about the deliverance of their elders."[47] What is slaughtered with the slaughter of the innocents is salvation itself.

Perhaps more than anywhere else, in the figure of the child we encounter what is at stake both in the sacred texts and in the teaching of
the Shoah. What is at stake in the sacred texts is redemption; what is at
stake in the teaching of Shoah is the salvation of redemption. Because
the Shoah is about the assault on the human being through the murder of
mother, father, and child, teaching Shoah entails a testimony to the infi-
nite dearness of what was slated for destruction. Indeed, the project of
Shoah studies is about more than study: it is about recovery—the recovery of a sacred teaching and of the human image sanctified by that teaching. That is why those of us who teach and study Shoah are implicated
by our subject matter, even—or especially—when we retreat to the relatively comfortable confines of "the history of the Holocaust" rather than
collide with the fate of mother, father, and child. Where do those colli-
sions take place? In the testimony of those who speak from the core of
the Event.

From Sacred Contexts to Shoah Texts

In this last section we shall point out some examples of testimony from
diaries and memoirs that illustrate the assault on mother, father, and child
discussed so far. Considering first the mother, we note that, since the
crime of the Jews was being, the one who brought Jews into being was
by that very act the worst of criminals. Making pregnancy a criminal
condition, and not just a criminal act, the Nazis demonstrate the totality
characterizing the ontological scope of their assault on humanity as it
unfolds in their assault on the mother. And the Holocaust diarists thoroughly attest to this assault.

On 5 February 1942 Vilna Ghetto diarist Herman Kruk, for example,
wrote, "Today the Gestapo summoned two members of the Judenrat and
notified them: No more Jewish children are to be born. The order came
from Berlin."[48] In his diary from the Kovno Ghetto, on 24 July 1942,
Avraham Tory notes, "From September on, giving birth is strictly for-
bidden. Pregnant women will be put to death."[49] And in November of
1941 Emmanuel Ringelblum, reported that in the Lodz Ghetto "Jews
had been prohibited from marrying and having children. Women pregnant up to three months have to have an abortion." [50] The is why Vittel
diarist Yitzhak Katznelson cries out, "These Jewish mothers with babes
in their wombs! This murderous German nation! That was their chief
joy! To destroy women with child!"[51] It was their chief joy because it
was an expression of their primary aim; it was the joy of those who bask
in the satisfaction of a job well done.

Turning to some examples from Holocaust memoirs, one recalls the terrifying power of Charlotte Delbo's memory of her arrival at Auschwitz: "My mother / she was hands / she was a face / They set our mothers before us naked / Here mothers are no longer mothers to their children."[52] We are overwhelmed by the realization that a people and a world are ontologically orphaned, their essence redefined as the essence of the orphan. In many cases—and, from an ontological standpoint, in every case—these memoirs are the memoirs of orphans. Sara Zyskind's memoir, for example, begins with the memory of the last Mother's Day that her mother enjoyed,[53] before the destruction of all days. Soon she loses her mother to the slow death of ghetto life, and the memory of an outcry rises to the surface of her page: "I don't want to be an orphan, Mother!"[54] In Isabella Leitner's memoir we see what becomes of infants—and of mothers—in a realm where motherhood is a capital crime. Relating how the women were forced to destroy babies born in Auschwitz in order to save the mothers, Leitner addresses the child, saying, "You belong to the gas chamber. Your mother has no rights. She only brought forth fodder for the gas chamber. She is not a mother. . . . And so, dear baby, you are on your way to heaven to meet a recent arrival. . . your father,"[55] whose destruction in this case, precedes the murder of motherhood.

Of course, the mothers and fathers of a community are not just among those of childbearing age, as we see from an entry in the Warsaw diary of Abraham Levin: "In Pabianice," he reports on 6 June 1942, "all men of 60 and over were shot."[56] By now we realize that when diarists such as the sculptor Rivosh of Riga relate that "the street is strewn with the corpses of old men,"[57] they offer much more than a report on casualties. When Ringelblum writes that "they put old folks in prison, even Jews over sixty,"[58] he files much more than a report on arrests. And when Éva Heyman says, "Today they arrested my father," adding that "at night they came to him and put a seal on his door,"[59] she implies that what is sealed off is much more than the entrance to a room. It is the center of home and family, the entrance to a life in the world, that is sealed off like a tomb. Just as Jewish souls were crushed before their bodies were destroyed, very often the image of the father was broken before he himself was taken away to death. We find an example of this breakdown of the paternal image when, after she and her family had been forced into the Varad Ghetto, Éva remarks, "I saw Grandpa cry for the first time in my life. From the gate arch you can see the garden, and the garden never looked so beautiful, even though no one had taken care of it for some days now. I will never forget how Grandpa stood there looking at the garden, shaking from his crying."[60] If her grandfather is broken, what becomes of the ground that the grandchild Éva stands on? With the collapse of this center of her home and family, all of life, an entire world, collapses; Éva herself loses all sense of herself, so that in turning to her diary, she struggles to retrieve the pieces of what is broken in the convulsions of her grandfather.

Similar examples abound in the memoirs of the Shoah. Sara Zyskind, for example, recalls a moment of gazing upon her father as he prayed, wrapped in the *tallis* of ancient tradition. "It struck me," she relates, "that there was something very strange about Father's praying form, as if it were an apparition from another world. Another world? What am I thinking? I mustn't think of such things. Father was still part of this world, and he was all that I had left here. I gazed at him again. There was nothing about him that recalled the image of my once young and exuberant father."[61] Another example of the fragmentation of the image of the father is found in Gerda Klein's description of her father's reaction on the occasion when her brother Arthur was forced to leave their home: "Now he was as helpless as I. An overwhelming feeling of pity and pain swept over me. I embraced Papa. The touch of my arms made him shiver, and a suppressed and terrible sobbing cry rose from his throat, a cry which I will never forget, which had no resemblance to the human voice; it sounded rather like the cry of an animal when it has been stabbed and is dying."[62] He who had been the heir to the word—who had conveyed the word to his children—loses the word in the loss of his image. For the word, the human voice, is just what constitutes that image. Gerda Klein remembers that her father "had changed so much."[63] Leon Wells notes that his father's hair "had turned gray and he was very thin."[64] And in the opening pages of her memoir Livia Jackson recalls, "My father seemed to grow somewhat slack as winter wore on. His silences became longer."[65] In the ontological assault on Jewish being it is not enough simply to murder the father. The killing of his body must be preceded by the annihilation of his image, for in his image lies the Jewish being that the father symbolizes.

While the mother and father signify an origin and a tradition, the child represents the future from which every present and past derive their meaning. What becomes of that future-oriented meaning we see in an entry from the diary of Aryeh Klonicki-Klonymus. "How many times," he writes on 5 July 1943, "would I look at my little child, so handsome and full of life, and it would seem to me that it is not a child I am looking at but a box filled with ashes."[66] This undoing of the image of the child is the first manifestation of the undoing of his essence; where the child is concerned, image and essence are of a piece. And in the Shoah their essence is fear. Says Hanna Levy-Hass in her Bergen-Belsen diary, "The children know no joy. They know only fear, nothing but fear. These poor, humiliated little creatures stand erect for hours on end, with fear racking their bodies, as they stare in paralyzed anticipation of things that will surely befall them."[67] And in his Warsaw Ghetto diary Hersh Wasser comments on the fate of the children, saying, "The soul of the child grows more and more tainted. The lack of schools, the gutter, absolute demoralization, leave their terrible mark. What sort of generation will grow out of all this?"[68] The answer, of course, is that no generation will grow out of this: these children belong to a generation consigned to the gas chambers. And the authors of the memoirs bear the memory of that generation.

In the memoirs of the Shoah the G-d beseeched to heed the cries of the children is Himself reduced to their outcry. Says Issahar's wife, the woman in Wiesel's *A Jew Today* who sees dead children everywhere, "they are G-d's memory."[69] Because the child is the vessel of all meaning harbored by a living future, the death of the child renders the future dead, turned back on the child himself. Here the child is no longer the flower of youth but the broken shoot of old age, forced into a category robbed of all meaning. "For them days were months," Simon Wiesenthal remembers. "When I saw them with toys in their hands, they looked unfamiliar, uncanny, like old men playing with childish things."[70] In the child the Promise from a past goes out to meet us in the future. But when the child collapses into old age, time and eternity collapse with him, and the Word of the Promise is lost. Another symptom of the mutilation of the child's image, then, is the loss of the child's word. "Little Bina," Leon Wells says of his sister, "whom I remembered as a lively child, had completely altered. She went about sad and unhappy, and hardly spoke. . . . She would neither talk nor laugh nor play."[71] In the play of the child lies the play, the movement of life, a celebration of the life and meaning signified by the child. When that play ceases, being loses its significance. With this in mind we recall a passage from Alexander Donat's memoir, where he says of his three-year-old son, "The lively child whose nature had been movement and playfulness now sat for hours at a time without moving. Whenever I seemed to be leaving him, his only reaction was to tighten his grip on me, uttering only the single word: '*Daddy*.'"[72] This single word not only undoes the father; it announces the ontological undoing of being, for it is a word that both demands a response and makes all response impossible.

Which returns us to the problem of teaching the Shoah. If teaching the Shoah entails responding to it, then it must include a response to those mothers, fathers, and children who put to us the question put to the first man: Where are you? Answering them—answering to them and for them— we answer to a voice that commands us to answer, the Voice that speaks to us through the sacred texts and teachings of Jewish tradition. If we lose the context of the holy in our effort to respond to the Shoah, we may not lose the voices that cry out to us; but we lose the Voice that commands us to care. If what Emil Fackenheim terms "the commanding Voice of Auschwitz" indeed commands Jews to be Jews so as to refuse the Nazis a posthumous victory,[73] the we must draw that Voice and its commandment into our study of the Shoah. And if non-Jews are to fathom the signifi- cance of the Shoah to the Jews, then they too must incorporate Jewish religious teachings into their study of the Shoah. And one way to do that is to undertake the teaching of the Shoah in the contexts of sacred Jewish texts and teachings. Without that context we soon grow deaf to the Voice that commands us both from the sacred texts and from Auschwitz. And once we grow deaf to the Voice, we grow worse than deaf to the voices of the murdered mothers, fathers, and children: we grow indifferent.

Endnotes

1. Elie Wiesel *Legends of Our Time* (New York: Avon, 1968), p.230.
2. *Sefer Yetzirah: The Book of Creation,* tr. with commentary by Aryeh Kaplan (York Beach, Maine: Samuel Weiser, 1990), p. 16.
3. Recall passages such as the one from Judith Dribben's memoir, where a Nazi beholds a synagogue in flames and declares, "The Jewish G-d is burnt to ashes!" In Judith Dribben, *And Some Shall Live* (Jerusalem: Keter Books, 1969), 24.
4. *Midrash Rabbah,* Vol. 9, tr. H. Friedman, Maurice Simon, et al. (London: Soncino, 1961), 327.
5. *The Zohar,* Vol. 1, tr. Harry Sperling and Maurice Simon (London: Soncino, 1984), 92.
6. *Midrash Rabbah,* Vol. 1, 6.
7. *The Zohar,* Vol. 5, 57.
8. Emmanuel Levinas, *Nine Talmudic Readings,* tr. Annette Aronowicz (Bloomington: Indiana University Press, 1990), 183.
9. Yitzchak Ginsburgh, *The Alef Beit: Jewish Thought Revealed through*

the Hebrew Letters (Northvale, New Jersey: Aronson, 1991), 46.

10. It should be noted that "seeing to the affairs of the house" entails a responsibility for three of the most sacred realms of Jewish life: adherence to the laws of kashrut, the observance of the laws of family purity, and ushering in the Sabbath, all of which are in the care of women.

11. *Midrash Rabbah,* Vol. 4, 460.

12. Adin Steinsaltz, *Biblical Images: Men and Women of the Book,* tr. Yehuda Hanegbi and Yehudit Keshet (New York: Basic Books, 1984), p. 8. See also Rashi, Commentary on the Torah, Vol. 2, tr. M. Rosenbaum and N. M. Silbermann (Jerusalem: The Silbermann Family, 1972), 97.

13. Aryeh Kaplan, commentary on *The Bahir* in *The Bahir,* tr. with commentary by Aryeh Kaplan (York Beach, Maine: Samuel Weiser, 1979), 127-28.

14. Ginsburgh. 88.

15. Schneur Zalman, *Likutei Amarim Tanya,* tr. Nissan Mindel *et al.* (Brooklyn: Kehot, 1981), 593.

16. Ginsburgh, 45.

17. Rashi, Vol. 4, 131.

18. Martin Buber, *Between Man and Man,* tr. Ronald Gregor Smith (New York: Macmillan, 1965), 78.

19. Maimonides, *The Guide for the Perplexed,* tr. M. Friedlaender (New York: Dover, 1956), 74.

20. Gersonides, *The Wars of the Lord,* Vol. 1, tr. Seymour Feldman (Philadelphia: Jewish Publication Society, 1984), 157.

21. *The Bahir,* 70.

22. Compare to Alvin Rosenfeld's remark that those who struggle with the Holocaust are "forced to acknowledge the emptiness and silence of an imposed Absence," in Alvin Rosenfeld, *A Double Dying: Reflections on Holocaust Literature* (Bloomington: Indiana University Press, 1980), 14.

23. *Pirke de Rabbi Eliezer,* tr. Gerald Friedlander (New York: Hermon Press, 1970), 305.

24. *En Jacob: The Agada of the Babylonian Talmud,* Vol. 5, tr. S. H. Glick (New York, The Hebrew Publishing Co., 1921), 39.

25. Moshe Chayim Luzzatto, *The Path of the Just,* tr. Shraga Silverstein, 3rd Ed. (New York: Feldheim, 1990), 147-49.

26. Wiesel, 18.

27. *The Bahir,* 145.

28. Bachya ibn Paquda, *Duties of the Heart,* Vol. 1, tr. Moses Hyamson (New York: Feldheim, 1970), 151.

29. Charlotte Delbo, *None of Us Will Return,* tr. John Githens (Boston: Beacon Press, 1968), 6.

30. Ginsburgh, 2-3.

31. Jean Amery, *At the Mind's Limits,* tr. Sidney Rosenfeld and Stella P. Rosenfeld (Bloomington: Indiana University Press, 1980), 19.

32 . Cavities, *Collected Philosophical Papers*, tr. Alphonso Lingis (Dordrecht: Martinus Nijhoff, 1987), 112.

33 . *The Bahir,* 92.

34. Adam Czerniakow, *The Warsaw Diary of Adam Czerniakow,* ed. Raul Hilberg, et al., tr. Stanislaw Staron, et al. (New York: Stein and Day, 1979), 350.

35. *Midrash Tanchuma,* Vol. 1 (Jerusalem: Eshkol, 1935), 170-7 1. My translation.

36. *Midrash on Psalms,* Vol. 1, tr. William G. Braude (New Haven, Conn.: Yale University Press, 1959), 125.

37. Wiesel, *Night,* tr. Stella Rodway (New York: Bantam, 1982), 62.

38. *Midrash Rabbah,* Vol. 7, 106.

39. *The Zohar,* Vol. 1, 4.

40. *The Zohar* Vol. 3, 121.

41. Rivosh, "From the Diary of the Sculptor Rivosh (Riga)" in *The Black Book,* ed. Ilya Ehrenburg and Vasily Grossman, tr. John Glad and James S. Levine (New York: Holocaust Library, 1980), 324.

42. In David Patterson, *In Dialogue and Dilemma with Elie Wiesel* (Wakefield, NTH: Longwood Academic, 1991), 21.

43. Ka-tzetnik 135633, *House of Dolls,* tr. Moshe M. Kohn (New York: Pyramid, 1958), p. 44.

44. "She was six years old," Wiesel tells the tale of a little girl who embodies the ontological condition of all these children, "a pale, shy and nervous child. Did she know what was happening around her? How much did she understand of the events? She saw the killers kill, she saw them kill-how did she translate these visions in her child's mind? One morning she asked her mother to hug her. Then she came to place a kiss on her father's forehead. And she said, 'I think that I shall die today.' And after a sigh, a long sigh: 'I think I am glad.'" The child who is glad of dying has been robbed of her life before that life has been extinguished. See Wiesel, *A Jew Today,* tr. Marion Wiesel (New York: Random House, 1978), p. 128.

45. Wiesel, *The Oath* (New York: Avon, 1973), p. 132.

46. Vilna Gaon, *Even Sheleimah,* tr. Yaakov Singer and Chaim Dovid Ackerman (Southfield, MI: Targurn Press, 1992), p. 45.

47. Benno Heinemann, *The Maggid of Dubno and His Parables* (New York: Feldheim, 1967), pp. 200-01.

48. Herman Kruk, "Diary of the Vilna Ghetto," tr. Shlomo Noble, Y*IVO Annual of Jewish Social Sciences,* 13 (1965), 20.

49. Avraham Tory, *Surviving the Holocaust: The Kovno Ghetto Diary,* tr. Jerzy Michalowicz, ed. Martin Gilbert (Cambridge: Harvard University

Press, 1990), p. 114.

50. Emmanuel Ringelblum, *Notes from the Warsaw Ghetto,* tr. and ed. Jacob Sloan (New York: Schocken, 1974), p. 230.

51. Yitzhak Katznelson, *Vittel Diary,* tr. Myer Cohn, 2nd ed. (Tel-Aviv: Hakibbutz Harneuchad, 1972), p. 109.

52. Delbo, p. 15.

53. Sara Zyskind, *Stolen Years,* tr. Margarit Inbar (Minneapolis: Lerner, 198 1), p. 11.

54. *Ibid.,* p. 44.

55. Isabella Leitner, *Fragments of Isabella,* ed. Irving Leitner (New York: Thomas Crowell, 1978), p. 32.

56. Abraham Levin, "Extract from the Diary of Abraham Levin," *Yad Vashem Studies,* 6 (1967), 316.

57. Rivosh, 340.

58. Ringelblum, 64-65.

59. Eva Heyman, *The Diary of Eva Heyman,* tr. Moshe M. Kohn (Jerusalem: Yad Vashem, 1974), 73.

60. *Ibid.,* 85-86.

61. Zyskind, 100-01.

62. Gerda Weissmann Klein, *All But My Life,* (New York: Hill and Wang, 1957), 20.

63. *Ibid.,* 8.

64. Leon Wells, *The Death Brigade* (New York: Holocaust Library, 1978), 103.

65. Livia E. Bitton Jackson, *Elli: Coming of Age in the Holocaust* (New York: Times Books, 1980), 3-4.

66. Aryeh Klonicki-Klonyrnus, *The Diary of Adam's Father,* tr. Avner Tornaschaff (Tel-Aviv: Hakibbutz Hameuchad, 1973), 24.

67. Hanna Levy-Hass, *Vielleicht war das alles erst der Anfang: Tagebuch aus dern KZ Bergen Belsen* 1944-1945, ed. Eike Geisel (Berlin: Rotbuch, 1969), 15. My translation.

68. Hersh Wasser, "Daily Entries of Hersh Wasser," tr. Joseph Kermish, *Yad Vashem Studies,* 15 (1983), 223.

69. Wiesel, *A Jew Today,* 81.

70. Simon Wiesenthal, *The Sunflower,* tr. H. A. Piehler (New York: Schocken, 1976), 47.

71. Wells, 107.

72. Alexander Donat, *The Holocaust Kingdom* (New York: Holocaust Library, 1978), 94.

73. See Emil L. Fackenheim, *G-d's Presence in History* (New York: Harper and Row, 1970), 84.

Chapter 13

TEACHING ZIONISM:
THE INTRODUCTORY COURSE
Zev Garber

Our essay on "Teaching Zionism: The Introductory Course" is an invitation to study the Zionist movement from origins to the three thousand year declaration of Jerusalem, called the city of God, as one of contemporary Jewry's most successful responses to the Jewish predicament: the Jewish People as the victim of world history. The student is exposed to a brief historical background, beginning with episodes from the Pentateuch, Psalms and pharisaic literature, dealing with the development of Zionism as it is related to an exposition of its central affirmations. The goal is to familiarize the student with what the Zionist tradition regards as its essential genius and to provide an opportunity for an appreciation of the similarities and differences between ideologies and divisions within greater Zionism. Among the class topics that are seen as beneficial in this quest are the following: (a) the theory of Zionism (nationalist messianism): political, cultural, religious, mystical, socialist, synthetic; and (b) the practice of Zionism: the State of Israel as pinnacle or aberration of Zionism, politics of statehood, social problems, the diversified and competitive role of religion-tradition and secularism, contemporary values, and the present state of Zionist belief, e.g., partition or retention of Land for peace, the morality of Jewish power, etc.

Students are required to do three papers of uneven length and varied methodology: (1) an 8–10 page critical discussion of how Laqueur, Hertzberg, Avineri, and O'Brien approach and analyze Zionism; (2) a 12–15 page standard research project intended to examine in some depth one of the ideologies, platforms, institutions, or problems of contemporary Zionism introduced in class. The student examines the topic in whatever manner he or she deems most productive (historically, philosophically, theologically, socially, or any combination of several of these), evaluates the vital issues, points out faults, merits, etc., and makes constructive comments. The structure of the paper is construed from the viewpoint of writing college quality work, using Kate L. Turabian's *A Manual for*

Writers of Term Papers or the *MLA Style Sheet;* (3) a 10–12 page creative writing exercise in problem solving, which is designed to engage
the student in ethical decision making and moral development, the twin
pillars of a role-playing sequence. Problem-solving activities can be enacted in almost every phase of Zionist Studies, from Sinai-Zion, zealot-
pacific-messianic confrontations in the biblical and rabbinic periods, respectively, to the different Zionist and non-Zionist debates of today, from
learning about the outlook and mentality of the *Yishuv* during the Palestine Mandate to understanding Israelis, 1948–present, and the different
replies to Israel under siege. Individuals develop sensitivity, learn empathy, and see values, commitments, aspirations differently when they
enact various roles. If done properly, a simulation project can simplify
complex and variegated material, and make the course content more
particular and personal.[1]

What follows is a maximal but not exhaustive, learning-focused and
not research-intended, outline for an introductory course on Zionism. It
is stimulated by though not restricted to our class on this subject taught
at Los Angeles Valley College, one of the nine public colleges of the Los
Angeles Community College District. What is presented is a set of four
sections containing 21 units concerning the intellectual history, culture
and challenges of classical and modern Zionism. For each unit we have
suggested (1) a thematic approach to relevant data in the making of
Zionism, (2) recommended readings, and (3) a description of what is
presented and, within a conceptual framework, why it is presented. Books
suggested for purchase are:

Walter Laqueur, *A History of Zionism* (1972)
Arthur Hertzberg, *The Zionist Idea* (1975)
Shlomo Avineri, *The Making of Modern Zionism* (1981)
Conor Cruise O'Brien, *The Siege* (1986).

Also recommended:

Martin Buber, *On Zion* (1973)
Amos Elon, *The Israelis: Founders and Sons* (1983).

Needless to say, all works are placed on reserve in the university library
and reading selections can be made available for purchase.

OUTLINE OF THE COURSE
I. WHENCE ZION?

1. Defining Self-Determination for the Jewish People

Is the definition of Zionism different only in degrees, not in kind, from the Age of Abraham to the Age of Autonomy? Does Zionism differ from previous and contemporary statements of self-rule and self-determination?

Readings

Nahum N. Glatzer, "Forward," in Martin Buber, *On Zion: The History of an Idea* (New York: Schocken Books, 1973), vii–xiv.

Martin Buber, *On Zion,* "Introduction," xvii–xxii.

S. D. Goitein, *Jews and Arabs, Their Contacts Through the Ages,* 3rd. rev. ed. (New York: Schocken Books, 1974), 3–45.

Yigal Yadin, "What is Zionism?," in Mordechai S. Chertoff (ed.), *Zionism: A Basic Reader* (New York: Herzl Press, 1975), 75.

Louis D. Brandeis, "Our Jewish Pilgrim Fathers," in M. S. Chertoff (ed.), *Zionism: A Basic Reader,* 55–60.

Marie Syrkin, "Zionism Today," in M. S. Chertoff (ed.), *Zionism: A Basic Reader,* 3–8.

Yosef Tekoah, "Zionism: From the Rivers of Babylon to Lake Success," *In the Face of Nations: Israel's Struggle for Peace* (New York: Simon and Schuster, 1976), 65–67.

Bernard Lewis, "Semites," *Semites and Anti-Semites* (New York/London: W. W. Norton and Company, 1986), 42–57.

2. Understanding Zionism in Terms of "The Land," Religion and Nationality

Readings

Martin Buber, *On Zion,* 1–57.

Harry M. Orlinsky, "The Biblical Concept of the Land of Israel: Cornerstone of the Covenant Between God and Israel," in Lawrence A. Hoffman, ed., *The Land of Israel: Jewish Perspectives* (Notre Dame, Indiana: University of Notre Dame Press, 1986) 27–64.

Charles Primus, "The Borders of Judaism: The Land of Israel in Early Rabbinic Judaism," in L. A. Hoffman, ed., *The Land of Israel: Jewish Perspectives,* 97–108.

Richard S. Sarason, "The Significance of the Land of Israel in the Mishnah," in L. A. Hoffman, ed., *The Land of Israel: Jewish Perspectives,*109–136.

Arnold M. Eisen, Galut: *Modern Jewish Reflection in Homelessness and Homecoming* (Bloomington/Indianapolis: Indiana University Press, 1986), 3–56.

3. The Lessons of the *Golah:* Medieval Judaism

Reflecting on the Land of Israel/Zion in philosophical and mystical thought is a continual process of unconditional correlation of opposite but related elements (Land/Exile, particular/universal, national/messianic, and so forth).

Readings

Isaak Heinemann, ed., "Judah Halevi: Kuzari," in *Three Jewish Philosophers* (Cleveland/New York/Philadelphia: Meridian Books and JPSA, 1961), 7–42, and especially, 64–75, 80–84, 132–142.

Gershom Scholem, *Major Trends in Jewish Mysticism* (New York: Schocken Books, 1967), 244–324.

Charles B. Chavel, *Ramban: Commentary on the Torah* (New York: Shilo Publishing House, 1971), passages listed in the Index under "Land of Israel."

Martin Buber, *On Zion,* 59–108.

R. J. Zwi Werblowsky, *Joseph Karo: Lawyer and Mystic,* 2nd rev. ed. (Philadelphia: JPSA, 5737/1977), 38–147.

4. Prolegomena to the Rise of Modern Zionism

Readings

Walter Laqueur, *A History of Zionism,* (New York/Chicago/San Francisco: Holt, Rinehart and Winston, 1972), 3–39.

Arthur Hertzberg, ed., *The Zionist Idea, A Historical Analysis and Reader* (New York: Atheneum, 1975), 15–32.

Shlomo Avineri, *The Making of Modern Zionism: The Intellectual Origins of the Jewish State* (New York: Basic Books, Inc., 1981), 3–13.
Conor Cruise O'Brien, *The Siege: The Saga of Israel and Zionism* (New York: Simon and Schuster, 1986), 25–80.

II. EMANCIPATING ZION: MOVERS AND MOVEMENTS

5. Nationalism and Socialism: Moses Hess

Readings

Martin Buber, *On Zion*, 111–122.
Walter Laqueur, *A History of Zionism*, 46–54.
Arthur Hertzberg, ed., *The Zionist Idea*, 36–40, 116–139.
Shlomo Avineri, *The Making of Modern Zionism*, 36–46.

6. Critique of Emancipation—Enlightenment to Jewish Nationalism: P. Smolenskin, M. L. Lilienblum, L.P. Pinsker

Readings

Walter Laqueur, *A History of Zionism*, 61–75.
Arthur Hertzberg, ed., *The Zionist Idea*, 40–45, 143–157, 167–177, 179–198.
Shlomo Avineri, *The Making of Modern Zionism*, 56–64, 65–72, 73–82.

7. Hebrew Horticulture: Seeding the Exotic Flower of Modern Jewish Nationalism

A. *Literature and Language: Abraham Mapu and Eliezer Ben-Yehudah*
B. *Hovevei Zion*

Readings

Robert St. John, *Tongue of the Prophets* (Beverly Hills, CA: Hal Leighton Printing Co., 1952), selections.
David Patterson, *Abraham Mapu, The Creator of the Modern Hebrew Novel,* (London: East and West Library, 1964), 3–11, 13–25.

Arthur Hertzberg, ed., *The Zionist Idea*, 158–165.
Shlomo Avineri, *The Making of Modern Zionism*, 83–87.
B. *Hovevei Zion*

Readings

Walter Laqueur, *A History of Zionism*, 75–83.

8. Political-Practical Zionism: Theodor Herzl

Readings

Theodor Herzl, *The Jewish State* (New York: American Zionist Emergency Council, 1946), all.
Martin Buber, *On Zion*, 123–142.
Walter Laqueur, *A History of Zionism*, 84–135.
Arthur Hertzberg, ed., *The Zionist Idea*, 45–51, 201–245.
Amos Elon, *Herzl* (New York/Chicago/San Francisco: Holt, Rinehart and Winston, 1975), selections.
Shlomo Avineri, *The Making of Modern Zionism*, 88–100.

9. Cultural-Spiritual Zionism: Ahad Ha-Am (Asher Zvi Ginsberg)

Readings

Leon Simon, *Ahad Ha-Am* (Oxford: East and West Library, 1946), selections.
Martin Buber, *On Zion*, 143–147.
Walter Laqueur, *A History of Zionism*, 162–166.
Arthur Hertzberg , ed., *The Zionist Idea*, 51–72, 249–277.
Shlomo Avineri, *The Making of Modern Zionism*, 112–124.
Jacques Kornberg, ed., *At the Crossroads: Essays on Ahad Ha-Am* (Albany: SUNY Press, 1983), selections.
Steven J. Zipperstein, *Elusive Prophet: Ahad Ha-Am and the Origins of Zionism* (Berkeley/Los Angeles: University of California Press, 1993), selections.

10. Labor Zionism: N. Syrkin, B. Borochov, A. D. Gordon

Readings

Samuel Hugo Bergman, *Faith and Reason: An Introduction to Modern*

Jewish Thought, translated and edited by Alfred Jospe (New York: Schocken Books, 1968), 98–120.
Martin Buber, *On Zion,* 154–161.
Walter Laqueur, *A History of Zionism,* 270–277.
Arthur Hertzberg ,ed., *The Zionist Idea,* 72–80, 331–386.
Shlomo Avineri, *The Making of Modern Zionism,* 125–138, 139–150, 151–158.

11. Religious Zionism: Y. Alkali, Z. H. Kalischer, A. I. Kook, J. L. Magnes, M. Buber

Readings

Samuel Hugo Bergman, *Faith and Reason,* 81–97, 121–141, 142–151.
Martin Buber, *On Zion,* 147–154.
Walter Laqueur, *A History of Zionism,* 54–55, 166–169.
Arthur Hertzberg ,ed., *The Zionist Idea,* 32–36, 99–100, 103–107, 109–114, 417–431, 441–449, 451–465.
Shlomo Avineri, *The Making of Modern Zionism,* 47–55, 187–197.
William A. Brinner and Moses Rischin, eds., *Like All the Nations? The Life and Legacy of Judah L. Magnes* (Albany: SUNY Press, 1987), selections.

III. THEORY AND PRACTICE OF ZIONISM

12. From Basle, 1897, to World War I and the Balfour Declaration: Zionist Congresses, Diplomacy, Trends, Critics

Readings

Walter Laqueur, *A History of Zionism,* 136–162.
Conor Cruise O'Brien, *The Siege,* 81–131.

13. From the Balfour Declaration, 1917, to State: Recognition—Birth

Readings

Walter Laqueur, *A History of Zionism,* 171–205.
Conor Cruise O'Brien, *The Siege,* 132–195, 196–227.

Anita Engle, *The Nili Spies* (Jerusalem: Phoenix Publications, 1989), selections.

14. The Legacy of the Left: The Redemptive Power of Jewish Labor

Readings

Martin Buber, *Paths in Utopia* (Boston Beacon Press, 1949), 139–149.
Walter Laqueur, *A History of Zionism,* 270–337.
Arthur Hertzberg , ed., *The Zionist Idea,* 389–395, 605–619.
Shlomo Avineri, *The Making of Modern Zionism,* 198–216.
Amos Elon, *The Israelis: Founders and Sons* (New York: Pelican Books, 1983), 82–105, 106–147.

15. Reign from the Right: "In Blood and Fire Judea Will Arise": Zev Jabotinsky and Revisionism

Readings

Walter Laqueur, *A History of Zionism,* 338–383.
Arthur Hertzberg, *The Zionist Idea,* 557–570.
Israel Eldad, "Jabotinsky Distorted," *The Jerusalem Quarterly,* No. 16 (Summer 1980), 27–39.
Shlomo Avineri, *The Making of Modern Zionism,* 159–186.
Alice Stone Nakhimovsky, *Russian Jewish Literature and Identity* (Baltimore/London: The John Hopkins University Press, 1992), 45–69.

16. Perpetual Conflict: The Arab Factor in the Basle Slogan, "A Land Without a People for a People Without a Land"

Readings

Aaron Cohen, *Israel and the Arab World* (New York: Funk and Wagnalls, 1970), selections.
Walter Laqueur, *A History of Zionism,* 209–269, 505–545.
S. D. Goitein, *Jews and Arabs,* 217–234.
Yosef Tekoah, *In the Face of Nations,* 145–169.
Y. Harkabi, *The Palestinian Covenant and its Meaning* (London: Valentine, Mitchell and Co., 1979), selections.

Conor Cruise O'Brien, *The Siege,* 333–361.

Bernard Lewis, *Semites and Anti-Semites,* 164–191, 191–235.

Paul R. Mendes-Flohr, ed., *A Land of Two Peoples: Martin Buber on Jews and Arabs, (Oxford/New York/Toronto/Melbourne: Oxford* University Press, 1983), selections.

Rosemary Radford Ruether and Herman J. Ruether, *The Wrath of Jonah: The Crisis of Religious Nationalism in the Israeli-Palestinian Conflict* (San Francisco: Harper and Row, 1989), 92–130, 131–161, 220–246.

17. Yishuv and the Politics of Mandatory Palestine

Readings

Ephaim Dekel (Krassner), Shai: *Historical Exploits of Haganah Intelligence* (New York: Thomas Yoseloff, 1959), selections.

Gerald Frank, *The Deed* (New York: Berkeley Publishing Corp., 1963), selections.

Yehudah Bauer, *From Diplomacy to Resistance: A History of Jewish Palestine* 1939–1945 (New York: Atheneum, 1973), selections.

Menachem Begin, *The Revolt: The Dramatic Inside Story of the Irgun* (Los Angeles: Nash Publishing, 1972), selections.

Walter Laqueur, *A History of Zionism,* 505–545.

J. Bowyer Bell, *Terror Out of Zion: The Shock Troops of Israeli Independence* (New York: Avon Books, 1978), selections.

Eli Tavin and Yonah Alexander, eds., *Psychological Warfare and Propaganda: Irgun Documentation* (Wilmington, Delaware: Scholarly Resources, Inc., 1982), selections.

Conor Cruise O'Brien, *The Siege,* 227–256, 256–286.

IV. ZIONISM AND THE STATE OF ISRAEL

18. From Ideological Dream to Territorial Reality

Readings

Amos Elon, *The Israelis: Founders and Sons,* 222–255, 256–289, 290–320.

Abba Eban, *My People,* rev. ed. (New York: Random House, 1984), 430–466, 486–521.

19. The State of Religion in Israel: (Dis)Continuity of an Identity?

Readings

Emile Marmorstein, *Heaven at Bay: The Jewish Kulturkampf in the Holy Land* (London/New York/Toronto: Oxford University Press, 1969), selections.

Simon N. Herman, *Israelis and Jews: The Continuity of an Identity* (New York: Random House, 1970), selections.

Oscar Kraines, *The Impossible Dilemma: Who is a Jew in the State of Israel?* (New York: Bloch Publishing Co., 1976), selections.

Zalman Abramov, *Perpetual Dilemma: Jewish Religion in the State of Israel* (Rutherford/Madison/Teaneck: Fairleigh Dickinson University Press, 1976), selections.

Charles S. Liebman and Eliezer Don-Yehiya, *Civil Religion in Israel* (Berkeley/Los Angeles: University of California Press, 1983), selections.

20. 1967 Six-Day War: Israel and the Territories

Readings

Henry Near and Avraham Shapiro et al., eds., *The Seventh Day: Soldiers Talk About the Six-Day War* (Harmondsworth/Middlesex, England: Penguin Books, 1970), selections.

Walter Laqueur, ed., *The Israel-Arab Reader: A Documentary History of the Middle East Conflict,* 3rd. rev. ed. (New York: Bantam Books, 1971), selections.

Arie Bober, ed., *The Other Israel: The Radical Case Against Zionism* (Garden City, New York: Anchor Books, 1972), selections.

Yosef Tekoah, *In the Face of Nations,* 170–175, 176–199.

Itamar Rabinovich and Jehuda Reinharz, eds., *Israel in the Middle East: Documents and Readings on Society, Politics and Foreign Relations, 1948–Present* (New York/Oxford: Oxford University Press, 1984), selections.

21. Evaluating Zionism: Has Zionism Emancipated the Jewish People?

<u>Readings</u>

Walter Laqueur, *A History of Zionism,* 589–599.
Zev Garber, "Rethinking Jewish Peoplehood," *Forum:* On the Jewish People, Zionism, and Israel, No. 39 (Fall 1980), 149–154.
Amos Elon, *The Israelis, Founders and Sons,* 321–335.
Abba Eban, *My People,* 522–539.
Conor Cruise O'Brien, *The Siege,* 642–662.

CONCEPTUAL FRAMEWORK OF THE COURSE

I. WHENCE ZION?

1. Defining Self-Determination for the Jewish People

Ravaged and reviled by Arab Moslem nations in the name of a beneficent and merciful God, Zionism's enduring vision by Jews is two-fold: the religion of Jewish nationalism no less than a pivotal core in the religion of Jewish faith. Whether the resolution declaring "Zionism is racism," introduced by the UN-sponsored Women's Conference in Mexico and subsequently accepted by 72 member nations of the General Assembly (35 against with 32 abstentions and three delegations absent) in 1975, is antisemitism and/or anti-Israel, Zion as the plank of the ship of State (Israel) cannot be denied.[2] The winds of war and the currents of peace nowadays have affected the national character and outlook of the Jewish State. Undeniably, Zionism today is undergoing significant intellectual and cultural change.

2. Understanding Zionism in Terms of "The Land," Religion and Nationality

The function of Zion in early Israelite religion and later Judean nationalism as reflected in the biblical age. From the Abrahamic cycle of self-dependency ("Not a thread or a sandal strap lest you [the Nations] shall say: 'I [we] have made Abram rich'") (Gen 14:23) to the Covenant at Sinai by which a priest nation was born ("You shall be unto Me a kingdom of priests, and a holy nation") (Ex 19:6) to the settlement of the Land under Joshua and the Judges to the destruction of the First Temple under the Babylonians (587 B.C.E.). Sinai and Zion (Jerusalem): divine plan and religious idealism vs. political realism and earthly sanctuary (Ex 25:8, 9, 40; I Chron 28:19). The First Exile ("By the rivers of Babylon, there we sat and wept, as we thought of Zion" and "If I forget thee, O Jerusalem") (Ps 137:1, 5) and the hope of return ("Let us go up to the Mount of the Lord [Zion] to the House of the God of Jacob") (Is 2:3; Mic 4:2). The rise and fall of the Second Jewish Commonwealth (164–63 B.C.E.). First- and second-century Eretz Israel in turmoil. The Great Revolt against the Romans, fall of Jerusalem, and Second Temple, Masada suicide (66–73 C.E.), and Bar Kochba Rebellion (133–135 C.E.): triangular nationalism (zealot-pacific-messianic). Golah (diaspora, dispersion, "Off-the-Land") vs. Galuth (exile, banishment, captivity). Beyond nationalism, the ascendancy and triumph of rabbinic Judaism: Torah as a portable homeland.

3. The Lessons of the *Golah:* Medieval Judaism

Varying medieval views on the attachment to the Land of Israel in the writings of universalists (Maimonides), particularists (Judah Ha-Levi), mystics (Isaac Luria and Kabbalists of Safed), and legalists (Joseph Karo).

4. Prolegomena to the Rise of Modern Zionism

Enlightenment and Emancipation brought a radical departure from traditional thought patterns and aspirations. Emancipation destroyed the authority of the Jewish community, and Enlightenment offered an ideological justification of surrendering the authority of Jewish tradition. The organic relationship of God-Torah-Israel (religion, culture, peoplehood) was not challenged by reason and equalitarianism. Count Clermont Tonnerre's declaration to the French National Assembly in 1791: "To the Jew as an individual—everything; to the Jew as a nation—nothing," and the positions adopted by the French Great Sanhedrin in February 1807, though bestowing equal civic rights upon Jews, began the process of redefining Jewish doctrines and values.

Unlike the national-religious identifying Jews in the Arab world and in Eastern Europe, Jews of the West now saw themselves as nationals of their countries of citizenship and worshippers in the "Mosaic faith." However, what Jews as individuals may have gained by Emancipation, Jews as a group lost. By leaving the Ghetto and attaining the status of citizens, the Western Jews loosened the bounds of Jewish group identity, which in many cases led to total assimilation. Fin-de-siècle Zionism provided an alternative to the reverential on-your-knee responses before European assimilation, nationalism and modern antisemitism.

II. EMANCIPATING ZION: MOVERS AND MOVEMENTS

5. Nationalism and Socialism: Moses Hess

Moses Hess, Karl Marx's "My Communist Rabbi," never considered his Jewishness in the heyday of his cosmopolitan socialism until he was aroused by the Damascus Affair (1840) and was offended by the limited results of the 1848 revolution. Hess now struggled with his Jewish problem in terms of nationalism, albeit religious minority, to wit a revolutionist, socialist state in Eretz Israel as the answer to antisemitism. Thus, the publication of *Rome and Jerusalem: The Last National Problem* (1862). His teaching that the Jews are a messianic people and only in their historic homeland could they discharge their divinely assigned task of bringing about a proper social order, described by him as "the historical Sabbath" of mankind, is the beginning of modern Zionist thought. His views of the Yishuv (Jewish population of Eretz Israel) as a socialist commonwealth, whose infrastructure is the Jewish masses of Eastern Europe and the Moslem world, is influential in pre- and post-Herzlian debate and prophetically forecast a future reality.

6. Critique of Emancipation-Enlightenment to Jewish Nationalism: P. Smolenskin, M. L. Lilienblum, L. Pinsker

Haskalah was the magnet which drew Jewish intelligentsia of the Pale of Settlement in mid-19th century Russia. From ghetto-restricted heder education, Peretz Smolenskin (1842–1885) and Moshe Leib Lilienblum (1843–1910) travelled the road to Jewish Enlightenment in Odessa. The son of an "enlightened" Hebrew savant, Leo Pinsker (1821–1891) was there at the start. However, Russian pogroms and May Laws 1881–1882 raised serious doubts about whether the teachings of Jewish tradition and Enlightenment can guarantee serenity and security in Czarist Russia.

Smolenskin is the Hebrew Dickens. His novels are charged with a reformer's zeal and idealist passion; their bite is reserved for scoundrels, adventurers, and obscurantist "pillars of society"; and their love is allocated for the weak, humble, and oppressed. As a founding editor of the Hebrew monthly, *HaShahar* (*The Dawn*, 1868), he wrote that Jews are citizens of their respective countries but are united as a people in spirit. His declaration of "spiritual nationalism" was among the first to awaken Jewish intellectuals to the idea of Jewish nationalism.

The 1881–82 pogroms were decisive in the thinking of Moshe Leib Lilienblum: Jews may be divided along ideological, doctrinal, and religious lines, in theory and practice, but in times of stress, they are fated as one people. Contra religious and secular orthodoxies, Lilienblum advocated a pluralistic, nondoctrinaire interpretation of Jewish existence. His answer to the catastrophe of 1881–1882, "[I]nitiate our efforts for the renaissance of Israel in the land of its forefathers, where the next few generations may attain, to the fullest extent, a normal national life," was central to the activity of a movement in which he played a major role, *Hovevei Zion* ("Lovers of Zion").

Describing antisemitism as an incurable pathological disease and relating it to the socioeconomic infrastructure of the kehillah (Jewish community) is the focus of Leo Pinsker's *Auto-Emancipation* (1882). Pinsker's Zionist manifesto proclaims that "Judeophobia" springs from the homelessness of the Jew who, for the living is dead, for the native-born a stranger; for the long settled a vagabond, for the wealthy a beggar; for the poor a millionaire and exploiter, for citizens a man without a country, for all classes a hated competitor. Jewish religion without Jewish nationalism is a soul without a body, and this abnormality mystifies and terrifies European non-Jews. Once Jews acquire a territory of their own, the Gentiles will relate to them as a normal people and "Judeophobia" will wither away. In his pamphlet, Pinsker saw the territory as "one single refuge" from antisemitism in North America (United States) or in Asiatic Turkey (a sovereign *pashalik* in Mt. Lebanon), but his later activity in behalf of *Hovevei Zion* pushed him in the direction of Palestine for a homeland.

7.   Hebrew Horticulture: Seeding the Exotic Flower of Modern Jewish Nationalism

A. Literature and Language: Abraham Mapu and Eliezer Ben-Yehudah
B. Hovevei Zion

The role played by the founding pioneers of modern Hebrew literature, language, and settlement in Eretz Israel. Abraham Mapu (1808–

1867) conceived the first modern Hebrew novel, *'Ahavat Ziyyon/Love of Zion* (Vilna, 1853), which casts attention on the Holy Land by focusing pride in the national past. Eliezer Ben-Yehudah's article, "She'elah Lohatah"/"A Burning Question" (published in P. Smolenskin's *HaShahar* in 1879), the first clear proposal of Eretz Israel as a spiritual center, takes issue with the elitism of maskilim, i.e., that Hebrew is only a medium of the intelligentsia; Hebrew should be the language of all, and to accomplish this, there must be a "nation and a land."

Hovevei Zion was founded at the conference of Kattlowitz in 1884 and headed by Pinsker until his death. Mikveh Israel, first agricultural school, founded in 1870; Petah Tikvah, first agricultural settlement, established in 1878; and the beginning of the agricultural colonization of Eretz Israel by immigrants from Eastern Europe (*Biluim* from B.I.L.U., Hebrew acronym of *Beit Ya'akov Lechu ve-Nelchah*/"House of Jacob, come ye and let us go up [to the Land]," Isa 2:5) and Yemen. Settlements Rishon leZiyyon, Nes Ziona, Zichron Ya'akov, Rosh Pina, Gedera (historically *the* Bilu colony).

8. Political-Practical Zionism: Theodor Herzl

Theodor Herzl (1860–1904), the man and his fame. His herculean undertakings as the organizer of the Jewish People on the way to statehood. The emergence of political Zionism; Dreyfus Affair (1894), Basle Congress (1897), and following World Zionist Congresses; the Uganda controversy. His conviction ("The Jewish State is essential to the world; therefore it will be created," from *Der Judenstaat,* February 14, 1896) to concern ("Today, as in every moment since I began to write, I am conscious that I always used my pen as a decent person. I never sold my pen, I never used it to mean ends, and not even for the purpose of winning friends. This will may be published. There will not be any man after my death who will contradict me," from his literary testament, February 12, 1897) to vision ("In Basle I founded the Jewish State. If I said this aloud today, I would be answered by universal laughter. Perhaps in five years, and certainly in *fifty,* everyone will agree," from his *Tagebocher,* September 1897) to victory ("If you will, it is no fairy tale," from *Altneuland,* 1902) to triumph ("I truly believe that even after we have obtained our land, Eretz Israel, Zionism will not cease to be an ideal. For Zionism, as I understand it, includes not only the aspiration to secure a legally recognized territory for our downtrodden people, but also an aspiration towards moral and spiritual integrity," from his message to youth, April

1904). His last will (". . . I wish a funeral of the poorest class, without eulogies and without flowers. I wish to be buried in a metal casket in a grave next to my father and to lie there until the Jewish People transfers my remains to Palestine," March 5, 1903) and the lasting will of a "down-trodden people":

Theodor Herzl

Farewell, O Prince, farewell, O surely tried
You dreamed a dream and you have paid the cost:
To save a people, leaders must be lost;
By foes and followers be crucified,
Yet 'tis your body only that has died.
The noblest soul in Judah is not dust
But fire that works in every vein and must
Reshape our life, rekindling Israel's pride.

So we behold the captain of our strife
Triumphant in this moment of eclipse;
Death has but fixed him to immortal life,
His flag upheld, the trumpet of his lips,
And while we, weeping rend our garments' hem
"Next year," we cry, "next year, Jerusalem."

Israel Zangwell[3]

9. Cultural-Spiritual Zionism: Ahad Ha-Am (Asher Ginsberg)

Ahad Ha-Am (1856–1927), classical Zionism's most important essayist and moralist, and political Zionism's most persistent critic. His literary debut at age 39, *Lo'zeh ha-derech/This Is Not the Way* (1889), and his essay, "Moses" (1904), show why. Ever since Emancipation-Enlightenment, there has been the victimization of Jews and Judaism in exile. Yet the road back from exile is not the present (antisemitism; Zion as a refuge political state) but past-future (past Jewish glory renewed as the secular and literary culture of a majority in Eretz Israel; Zion as a cultural center) conceptualization. For Ahad Ha-Am, national autonomy, not necessarily statehood, is crucial; and this is not to be achieved by a mass movement of a purely political nature, but by the evolvement of a modernized cultural and intellectual life. Thus, the *Yishuv* is not merely a refuge for oppressed Jews, or an historical memory, but the sine qua non center for the spiritual health of the Jewish People on the Land and in the far-flung Diaspora and the preservation and development of its heritage. Not a state of Jews but a Jewish state of mind. Disciples of Ahad Ha-Am: Chaim Weizmann, Chaim Nachman Bialik, Judah Leib Magnes, Martin Buber, among others. Influence and continuity of Ahad Ha-Amism in American Zionist and religious (Conservative, Reconstructionist, Reform) thought.

10. Labor Zionism: Nachman Syrkin, Ber Borochov, and Aaron David Gordon

The ideals of Labor Zionism, rooted in nineteenth-century national liberation movements and general socialist thought, are expressed differently by Nachman Syrkin (1867–1924), Ber Borochov (1881–1917) and A.D. Gordon (1856–1922). Syrkin's brochure, *The Jewish Problem and the Socialist Jewish State* (1898), is the first systematic attempt to formulate messianic tradition within a socialist context. Borochov's first major study, *The National Question and the Class Struggle* (1905), integrates Jewish nationalism with orthodox Marxist thought, and a year later, *Our Program* (1906) speaks of a proletarian Zionism that "will be consummated by *political territorial autonomy in Palestine*" (italics added; against Marx' striking phrase, "The proletarians have no homeland"). Gordon asserts that nations are cosmic phenomena, the results of the interaction between man and nature in a given geographical area; thereby, the Jew in exile is stunted, and by returning and working the soil of his/her natural habitat the marginal Diaspora Jew can be restored to physical and spiritual wholeness. Like the Kabbalists before him, Gordon stipulates a metaphysical bond between the Jew and the Land of Israel. Also, he insists that a "living culture," embracing the whole of life, takes precedent over "high culture" (science, art, poetry, ethics, religion): "[I]s it possible to make butter without milk or will man make butter from milk belonging to others, and will the butter then be his very own?" The impact of the "Triumvirate" on Labor Zion, from the Second Aliya (1904–1913) and continuum.

11. Religious Zionism: Yehudah Alkali, Zvi Hirsch Kalischer, Abraham Isaac Kook, Judah Leib Magnes, Martin Buber

The Rabbinical Hebrew writings of the Sephardi Rabbi Yehudah Hai Alkali (1798-1878) and the Ashkenazi Rabbi Zvi Hirsch Kalischer (1795-

1874). Alkali spent his early years in Eretz Israel and then returned to his native Serbia in 1825, from where he advocated the preparation of the land for the later redemption. As early as 1834, he argued for Jewish settlement in Eretz Israel, which became an obsession for him following the Damascus Libel (1840). His book *Minhat Yehudah (The Offering of Judah,* 1845) posits the rabbinical dual messiahs, Mashiah ben Yosef (Messiah of [the House of] Joseph) and *Mashiah ben David* (Messiah of [the House of] David), in modern garb. The First Messiah is the process (philanthropic, military, political) that acquires and sustains the Land, the *'atchalta di-geula/* "the beginning of the redemption," which sets the stage for the ingathering of the exiles by the divinely appointed Second Messiah. For Alkali, the revival of spoken Hebrew as the language of instruction (teachers and students) and of the streets (boys and girls) is the condition *sine qua non* for the dawning and the eschatological fulfillment of the messianic age.[4]

Kalischer's book *Derishat Ziyyon (Seeking Zion,* 1862) propounds the theory, by reference to scriptural and talmudic sources, that the messianic era must be preceded by the establishment of Jewish colonies in Eretz Israel through the cooperation of willing governments, the benevolence of wealthy Jews (the Rothschilds, the Montefiores, the Baron de Hirschs, etc.) and "agricultural self-help." The latter inspired the Alliance Israélite Universelle to establish the Mikveh Israel agricultural training school near Jaffa and Petah Tikva, a Jewish agricultural colony.

Like a soul ablaze, the revolutionary religio-mystical philosophy of Rav Abraham Isaac Kook (1865–1935), first Chief Rabbi of Mandatory Palestine, is grounded in kabbalistic particularity ("The People of Israel, the Torah, and the Land of Israel are One") but soars to heights of universality (the whole earth, and all therein, is His creation). In Kook's *Weltanschauung,* the love of God is fully demonstrated in the love for all God's creation; the impurity of the Exile, a cosmic distortion, is corrected by the return to Zion, a cosmic restoration; no longer to cast our sight on a heavenly Jerusalem, but rather to look to our own (religious and secular alike) efforts here below to make the earthly Jerusalem a fit place to live in, an outpouring of Divine "Light unto the Nations," perfecting the world (tikkun 'olam) through reconciliation, harmony, and peace. Rav Kook's intellectual sincerity and piety was one giant step in bridging the chasm between secular Zionism and the religious tradition.

Less philosophy and theology and more history and politics characterize the rabbinic calling (Reform), community service, and Zionist orientation of San Francisco-born Judah L. Magnes (1877–1948). Orator and writer, socially and religiously committed, a pioneer of American Zionism, who is best known as a founder of the Hebrew University in Jerusalem (1925, chancellor; 1935, president) and for his humanistic, pacifistic plans of reapproachment between Arabs and Jews. However paradoxical and controversial were his positions, and sometimes misunderstood and misjudged, he remained his own dogged servant for his brand of Zionism in Judaism: His self-imposed distance from American Reform and departure from the American Zionist establishment; his unswerving pacifism, uncritical faith in cultural enlightenment and progress, and commitment to prophetic Judaism embarrassingly abated by events in World War II; and the opposition that greeted his founding of '*Ihud*/ "Unity" (with Martin Buber in August 1942) that called for the establishment of a binational state in Eretz Israel. He taught as he lived—"A dissenter in Zion."

Martin Buber (1878–1965)'s religio-cultural-mystical approach to Zionism, having its roots in Hasidism, which he discovered and interpreted for the West, is interlaced with his viewpoint on the nature of Man. His central question of the meaning of humanness is expressed in his recurring word *Wessen* (essence, being, nature), as understood in terms of two primary word-pairs: "I–You" and "I–It." The I–You relationship is total involvement of self and other in intimacy, sharing, empathy, caring, openness, and trust. The I–It relationship consists of self viewing other in abstract terms, resulting in possession, exploitation, and distrust. The I–It pair permits the self to objectify the other, creating a state of manipulative dependency, and the I–You pair encourages an atmosphere of interdependence, permitting growth and respect. Only through genuine I–You encounters do people discover their humanity and, by mutually affirming and confirming one another, come face to face with the Eternal Thou. Thus, for Buber, Zionism is fundamentally social, consisting of interpersonal relations between "self and other," and the result is the nation's communal experience as expressed in righteousness, justice, and moral action. The faith in Buber's strand of national religion gives rise to a new type of Jewish personality, in which the ideals of a nation and the interests of humanity coincide. For Buber, the deepest motive for Jewish presence in the homeland is in the religious-social arena, invoking and involving the cooperation of Israel and her neighbors on the basis of equality and brotherhood.

III. THEORY AND PRACTICE OF ZIONISM, 1897–1948

12. From Basle, 1897, to World War I and the Balfour Declaration: Zionist Congresses, Diplomacy, Trends, Critics

Background of the World Zionist Organization and the six Conferences presided over by Theodor Herzl until his death. The trials and tribulations of the official policy of the WZO, endorsed by the First Congress (1897), and known as the Basle Program ("Zionism strives to establish a homeland for the Jewish People in Palestine secured by public law") in Zionist diplomacy: Turkey, Germany, Italy, Vatican, England. The Kishinev (Bessarabia) Pogrom (Passover-Easter 1903) and the Uganda, East Africa response which resulted in conflict and near-split in WZO. Zionist trends to gain statehood: diplomatic activity (political); small-scale settlement policy (practical); promotion of the Hebrew renaissance (cultural); and the suggestion to combine the three (synthetic), proposed by Chaim Weizmann in a speech delivered at the Eighth Zionist Congress (1907).

Rivals of Zionism: *Galuth* Nationalism (Simon Dubnow, 1860–1941) and Territorialism (Israel Zangwell, 1864–1926). Dubnow, among the greatest Jewish intellectual historians, articulated in his "Letters on Old and New Judaism" (1897–1907) the creativity of the Diaspora and the belief that Jews are a nation (against the assimilationists and socialists) who aspire to spiritual and cultural—but not territorial—independence. He saw value and disadvantage in the positions of political and cultural Zionism:[5] Supported the rebuilding and the revival of culture in the *Yishuv* but opposed the negation of the *Galuth* and the centuries-long contribution of Diaspora Jewry. Zangwell, great English Jewish man of letters and protégé of Herzl, abandoned official Zionism when the Seventh Zionist Congress decided not to continue the Uganda project (1905). He and other seceders from the Congress formed the Jewish Territorial Organization (I.T.O.), perhaps the best-known Jewish movement to proclaim an autonomous Jewish territory somewhere in the Diaspora.[6]

Selected opponents of Zionism, Classical Reform conferences: "A messiah who is to lead back the Israelites to the land of Palestine is neither expected or desired by us; we know no fatherland except that to which we belong by birth or citizenship" (1843); "The messianic idea would receive some prominent mention in the prayers, but all petitions for our return to the land of our fathers and for the restoration of a Jewish state should be eliminated from our prayers" (Frankfort, 1845); "We consider ourselves no longer a nation, but a religious community, and therefore, expect neither a return to Palestine nor a sacrificial worship under the administration of the sons of Aaron, nor the restoration of any of the laws concerning the Jewish state" (Pittsburgh, 1885). Samson Raphael Hirsch (1808–1888), foremost advocate of Modern Orthodoxy in nineteenth century Germany: "Land and soil were never Israel's bond of union" *(19 Letters on Judaism,* 1836). Agudah (Agudath Yisrael) founded in 1911 on the platform that "the solution of all problems of contemporary Jewry (be done) in the spirit of Torah." "Zionism" is tolerated by Agudah but is seen as dangerous: Zionism can point the "assimilationists" toward the Torah, but its prevailing secular spirit contaminates holiness and may wean the pious away from Torah.[7]

13. From the Balfour Declaration, 1917, to State: Recognition—Birth

Aspirations and position of Zionism in the First World War. Positive contributions to the British war effort: Weizmann's scientific experiments making acetone needed by the munitions industry; Zion Mule Corps; the Jewish Legion (the 39th Regiment of the Royal Fusiliers); Jewish intelligence network Nili (acronym for *nesah yisrael lo' y'shakker*/ "The Eternity of Israel will not die," I Sam 15:29), and the role played by the Aaronsohns (Aaron and Sarah; brother and sister) and Absalom Feinberg. Zionist lobby and the British connection. The obscure McMahon letter and Sykes-Picot Agreement, and the equally vague wording and intent of the Balfour Declaration (November 2, 1917). The twisted road to the Mandate: negotiations between Weizmann and Faisal; San Remo Conference (Spring 1992); the American King-Crane Commission report; the Paris Peace Conference; Herbert Samuel, First High Commissioner in Palestine; White Paper of 1922; Churchill-Emir Abdullah talks; Transjordan separated from Palestine; League of Nations. The legacy of the 1930's and 1940's, and the impact of the Shoah. End of the British Mandate and the War of Liberation (1948).

14. The Legacy of the Left: The Redemptive Power of Jewish Labor

Three faces of Labor Zionism: (1) Economic regeneration and class normalization; (2) return to soil and the making of a socialist society; and (3) redemption of the Land by Jewish Labor. Major Labor Zionist Aliyot: Second Aliya and Third Aliya (1919-1923). The Labor parties, Poalei Zion and Hashomer Hatzair, camaraderie and differences. "Conquest of Labor": The kvutza, *Gdud Ha'avodah*/"Legion of Labor" (founded in 1920 at a memorial meeting for Yosef Trumpeldor, who was killed defending Tel-Hai against Arab marauders), the Kibbutz movement, Moshav, and Histadrut (General Federation of Jewish Workers). HaShomer (Hebrew defense). Impact of Berl Katznelson (1887–1944), prolific writer on matters between tradition and revolution (socialist), who founded *Davar* and *'Am 'Oved,* the newspaper and publishing house of Histadrut; and David Ben-Gurion (1886–1973), socialist visionary and overseer of the birth of the modern State of Israel.

15. Reign from the Right: "In Blood and Fire Judea Will Arise": Zev Jabotinsky and Revisionism

Bio-capsule of the titan of the Zionist Right, Zev Jabotinsky (1880–1940), a leader of startling talents, polyglot orator and multi-genre writer, whom Laqueur calls "the *Wunderkind* of Russian Zionism" and Hertzberg describes as "the most controversial figure in Zionism." No man in its entire history, except Herzl, was as adored by his disciples; the passion with which Jabotinsky's enemies hated him was unique. His followers rallied to him as the Garibaldi of the Jewish revolution; his foes reviled him as its "would-be Mussolini."

Jabotinsky's militarism and political programs, called by his adamant opponents "fascism," and by his loyalist supporters "maximalist Zionism": (1) Revitalizing the Herzl-Nordau[8] tradition of state-Zionism (so the name "Revisionism," i.e., returning to Herzl's primary vision, the Jewish State) (2) obsession with security within Zionism (firstly, *Yishuv* self-defense, then the Jewish Legion in World War I, and then the fighting underground for statehood): (3) rescue of European Jewry by all means and routes available, including accords with antisemitic leaders and regimes; (4) the establishment of the Betar youth movement committed to the sole idea of a Jewish State on both sides of the Jordan; (5) opposition to the expanded Jewish Agency of 1929, whose policy is viewed as a renunciation and compromise of primary Zionist goals; and (6) leaving the World Zionist organization over its apparent resolve *not* to define the Zionist *Endziel* in the present time as a Jewish State.

In 1925, Jabotinsky convened the first conference of the ZoHaR (Zionism-Hadar/"Honor"-Revisionism) party, which in retrospect, was the beginning of the end of his affiliation with the World Zionist Organization. Ten years later, in 1935, he seceded and founded the New Zionist Organization as an alternative to the Socialist-dominated Jewish Agency and its platform of "minimalist Zionism." Strong support for the Jabotinsky revolution came from young Jews and the intelligentsia especially of Poland and other East European countries. Still his appeal, "Liquidate the Diaspora," for many was silenced by the Shoah. The legacy of Revisionism: Unadulterated Zionism.

> From the pit of decay and dust
> Through blood and sweat
> A generation will arise to us
> Proud, generous, and fierce
> —Song of Betar

16. Perpetual Conflict: The Arab Factor in the Basle Slogan, "A Land Without a People for a People Without a Land"

For the greater part of the twentieth century, Jewish-Arab disputes have agitated the Middle East and have shaken the foundations of global balance. Efforts to end these discords depend largely on a full understanding of how this historic conflict originated, developed, and intensified. Part of the problem is the approach that sees the history of the Middle East in the form of a tapeworm which grinds forth period after period, as well as the theory which considers Middle East culture self-contained with a life-cycle as predetermined as that of a eucalyptus tree. Also reactionary are viewpoints obsessed by images of Arab and Jewish nationalism driven along a collision course toward a no-return summit. The errors are attributed to chauvinism, lack of sensitivity, and the inability to understand the Middle East and its culture.

By reviewing the history of communal conflict ("the Arab revolt," Peel Commission and Report, the partition controversy) and the attempts to achieve a reapproachment between Arabs and Jews in Mandate Palestine (e.g., Ihud), we propose, inter alia, the following questions: What is the origin of the Arab-Jewish "dispute" and has it historical basis? Are the national goals of two peoples irreconcilable? After 1948, is Israel a Western state planted by Zionism or is it a Middle Eastern country? What are the Palestinian ideological claims to Palestine-Israel? Are Israel and the Arab nations exerting themselves to end belligerence so as to bring about peaceful coexistence?[9]

Honest, no-holds-barred answers to these searching questions may help to understand (and make a dent in) the question of Zionism in the Arab world.

17. Yishuv and the Politics of Mandatory Palestine

A critical examination and analysis of British governance during the Mandate period and Jewish and Arab reactions to influence policy. *Yishuv* politics and exercise of authority, with special emphasis on the Fourth and Fifth Aliyot (1924–1932, 1933–1936); the 1929 riots and "the Arab revolt" (1936–1938); and the 1939 White Paper, where sections on land and immigration restrictions represented for the Zionists a repudiation of the Balfour Declaration. The *Yishuv* during the Second World War: *Havlagah* (restraint in self-defense): "We shall fight the War (against Nazism) as if there was no (1939) White Paper," and *Ha'palah* ("daring" rescue of "illegal" Jews to Palestine): "We shall fight the White Paper as if there were no wars" (policy of Aliya Bet). The rise and decline of the Hebrew underground (1939–1947): Haganah/Palmach—Etzel (Irgun Zvai Leumi)—Lehi (Lohamei Herut Yisrael): Personalities, ideologies, organization, military operations, and psychological warfare; internal and external division(s), leading to near civil war (e.g., "the Season," 1944–45); and the inevitable, the days of the official Jewish underground ended with the birth of the State of Israel, 5 Iyar 5708 (14 May 1948).[10]

IV. ZIONISM AND THE STATE OF ISRAEL

18. From Ideological Dream to Territorial Reality

29 November 1947—15 May 1948—7 January 1949: Three irrevocable dates on the way to statehood. November 29, 1947: the United Nations General Assembly passed a resolution calling for the establishment of a Jewish State in Eretz Israel; two days later, this was greeted by repeated Arab attacks against Jewish settlements and lines of communication. May 15, 1948: The morning after the Provisional Government of the Jewish State declared its independence and pronounced the birth of the State of Israel, a united armed Arab response was launched to abort it. The War of Liberation ended on January 7, 1949, when fighting between Egypt and Israel was halted and both combatants entered into armistice negotiations. The State of Israel as the fulfillment of Zionist self-determination. Between State and People: unwritten constitution; territorializing democracy; government and politics; immigration policy; ethnic, religious-secular, minorities integration; changing demography; economic development; and national security. Israel and world Jewry.

19. The State of Religion in Israel: (Dis)continuity of an Identity?

Synagogue and State: evaluating the role of religion and traditional values in developing a collective Israeli identity in light of a polity governed by the nonreligious and a rising secularism; the appropriation of "Homeland as Holy Land" by the religious right; judicial decisions on "Who is a Jew?" and what "being Jewish" entails; and the continued public inroads made by state religious politics and the dominance in the private domain by the state religious establishment. Israeli civil religion: creating a moral community by infusing Zionist and Jewish myths, symbols, beliefs and practices into state and society. The result is a community life more ethnic than religious, with more democracy and less theocracy.

20. 1967 Six-Day War: Israel and the Territories

Zionism and the (Palestinian) Arabs: Two intellectual patterns and a personal opinion.

Centralist-Left, Shalom Achshav ideology. The historical model of the past provides the basis of Aaron Cohen's suggestion, "(R)eviving that collaboration through which both peoples produced such splendid achievement in the past, to the benefit of themselves and of all mankind." For this to happen, Arabs must recognize Israel, as the United Nations did in 1948, and agree to the integration of Israel into the political, cultural, and social setting of the Middle East. But Israel, militarily superior as well as dominant and successful, must make the first move toward peace. Such a move will be evidence of strength and good statesmanship, not of weakness. Israel must realize that her insistence, "only at the negotiation table will we show our cards," is too rigid and has borne no fruit. While protecting the June 1967 cease-fire lines, Israel should offer to withdraw from most of the conquered territories and aid in the search for solutions to the personal and national rights of the Palestinian Arabs, the permanent population and the refugees. Responsible leaders of the Palestinian Arabs must participate in all peace negotiations; there is no hope for a lasting peace in the area without consideration for their demands.

The Centralist-Left envisions the possibility of an Israeli-held territory with an Arab majority, and a territorially smaller Israel where Jews will be a majority. This will make possible the development of a distinctive Jewish way of life. Further, it sees an Arab-Jewish federal union, as delineated by some of the best thinkers of both peoples. Israel must demonstrate that it is a "Jewish" State by living up to the ethical teachings of Judaism, including those pertaining to the "strangers" who are citizens of the State.

For some, the above may be seen as academic and theoretical. What cannot be denied, however, are the facts on the ground. From the Six-Day War, and beyond, over a million (and growing) Palestinians are now in close contact with Israel, and this presents, for the State, a challenge and opportunity. Israel must assure the Arabs of the West Bank that she is not planning to annex them but is holding the West Bank in trust, trying to develop it economically, politically, and socially.

Payments to the refugees for lost properties are an important step toward this goal. Internally, the West Bank Palestinians must be given home rule. Tension on all fronts should be reduced by refraining from establishing new settlements in the territories taken in the Six-Day War. Finally, Israel should encourage and support the establishment of a Palestinian Arab state.

Right ideology, Gush Emunim, the Greater Land of Israel Movement. "Occupied" territories and "West Bank" are misnomers; the area is Judea-Samaria and Gaza *(YeSHa')*, historically founded and correctly understood. There is a potential military threat to Israel by an autonomous Palestinian state. It is an historical fact that the *Yishuv* has offered to live in peace with the Arab community in a shared state or in a partitioned state, but the Arabs vehemently opposed both. After the wars of aggression against Israel, they have forfeited a legitimate claim to pre-war boundaries, including the "occupied" West Bank. There were Jewish settlements on the Golan Heights and in Hebron centuries ago. Even if these areas are to become part of a Palestinian Arab state, Jews must be able to live there in peace, just as Arabs live in Israel.

True, the Great Powers are the problem-perpetuators of the Mideast crisis, and it is a mistake to speak of the Arabs as if they are one united people. However, it is wrong to ignore the spuriousness of a "democratic" Palestine, as proposed by Palestinian leaders in such manifestos as "Palestinian National Covenant" (July 1968), "The United Command of the Palestinian Resistance Movement" (May 1970), "The Fifth (Fatah) General Congress" (August 1989), and "The Hamas Covenant" (ongoing). Can Israel engage in dialogue with such "partners"?

An end thought which is construed as a beginning comes from the penultimate paragraph in my review of B. Lewis, *Semites and Anti-Semites:*

If the prospects for Arab-Israeli dialogue are not bright, then it is the business of responsible intellectuals and thinkers among the combatants to make them bright. Learning the complexity of the historical, religious, cultural, psychological and political factors of the Palestinian national movement is imperative for Jews. Similarly, Arabs must come to realize that Jewish self-pride as expressed in peoplehood, religion and the statehood of Israel are answers to Jewish identity, survival and antisemitism. And both Semitic peoples must learn that blatant immoral acts by individual or state can never be condoned, and prejudicial, passionate ideology which feeds these atrocities must never be tolerated.[11] The alternative is frightening: a genocidal end of all that Judaism and Islam have sought, taught and wrought.

> *Holocaust and Genocide Studies*, vol. 2.2 (1987), p. 326.

21. Evaluating Zionism: Has Zionism Emancipated the Jewish People?

The view of Zionism as a success story is often postulated by the role it played in bringing about the State of Israel as the fulfillment of Jewish self-determination. Notwithstanding this popularly accepted view, three observations are in order:

(1) Gershon Schocken's remarks that the fathers of Zionist ideology (Moses Hess, Leo Pinsker, Theodor Herzl, etc.) did not want "to establish a Jewish state, teach Hebrew, build a powerful army, or build a productive economy based on agriculture and industry."[12] They worked to abolish the Jewish problem, i.e., the inability of Jews in Diaspora to live safely as equals among equals. Their assumption was that a majority of world Jews, given the chance, would opt to live in an independent Jewish-controlled territory, established by public acclaim and recognized by international law. The goal "a secure refuge" for the majority not a protectorate for a minority of Jews who prefer to lose their identity by living the ways of Gentiles (ergo no Jewish problem). But the Zionist ideologues are in error. Despite the worst period of Diaspora history and its aftermath, the existence of the State of Israel, and despite the full emancipation of Jews in the West, many of the Chosen People, like their forebears, voluntarily choose not to settle in the Promised Land. Why so?

(2) In the worst pre-Hitlerian days of East European suffering, the Jewish People survived due to a combination of factors, including acts of Gentile philo-Semitism and Jewish religious and moral resistance. Philo-

Semitism is complex. It is found in religious, racial, nationalist expressions by a plethora of individuals and groups for a variety of reasons and gains. Yet not all actions by a supposed philo-Semite are intended to benefit Jews. Cases in point, "Edict of Tolerance" by Joseph II (February 2, 1782) and the benevolence of the Russian Czar Alexander II, who abolished the Cantonist system (1859) in his liberal policy of Russification of the Jews. Also it can be argued that an action initially meant to harm Jews, in the long run had beneficial results for them. For example, the Ghettos of Europe were created to restrict Jews from social contact with Christians, but the forced separation from Christian society enabled Jews to develop their own system of values and beliefs. However, the Dreyfus Affair (1894) in France, the birthplace of liberalism and Jewish emancipation, changed forever the agenda for Jewish survival. A few years later, Zionism declared its aim to create a Jewish homeland in which the Jewish People would be free to make decisions independent of the good will of its friends or the animosity of its enemies.[13]

In terms of Realpolitik, this Zionist ideal has fallen short. It started with the illusion that Great Britain gave the Jewish People a ready-made Jewish State, it continued in a much more extreme way by the United Nations' partition of Eretz Israel, and it is being pursued today by the parsing of Judea-Samaria and the call for the internationalization of Jerusalem, visible and undivided capital of Israel. Alas, Israel's political fortunes are not fashioned by the vision of Ben Gurion, nor the posturing of Golda Meir, nor the statesmanship of Menachem Begin, nor the expansionism of Yitzhak Shamir, nor the handshakes of Yitzhak Rabin. They are fashioned, paradoxically, in the final analysis on the whims of diplomacy with Israel's staunchest ally, the United States of America. How come?

(3) As the road to peace widens, Israel is faced with an identity problem: *Kedushat Ha-Aretz* (Security of the Land) or Kedushat Ha-Am (Security of the People). Is Israel a sovereign state reaching its decisions in terms of different religious and social orientations and diverse power structures? Or are Israelis a *Bnei Yisrael*, a family, bound to habits of solidarity and harmonious movement? The truth is that both factors, fueled by the ashes of Shoah memory, are the engines that drive the State at different times.[14] Now that Israel appears to stand at the threshold of peace and prosperity, it requires a new Zionist order. To define it is the challenge of all who "pray for the peace of Jerusalem" (Ps 122:5a).

Endnotes

1. Additional comments on role-playing and a simulation game, "Yom Kippur 5735: The October War, One Year Later," are found in my "Alternative Teaching Methods in Teaching Introduction to Judaism." Paper presented at the Annual Meeting of the American Academy of Religion, Washington D.C., October 24–27, 1974. Offprint is available from ERIC Document Reproduction Service (ED 094 077).
2. To equate Zionism with racism, see my article, "The Absent Israelis," *Los Angeles Jewish News* (October 1992).
3. Zangwell's sonnet to Herzl is cited in Jacob de Haas, *Theodore Herzl, A Biographical Study* (Chicago/New York: The Leonard Company, 1927), vol. 2, 334.
4. Alkali on Joel 2:28: "I will pour out my spirit upon all flesh and your sons and daughters shall prophesy."
5. Though critical of Ahad Ha Am's restricted affirmation of the Diaspora, Dubnow admired and respected the father of "spiritual Zionism," and called him more than once not "Ahad Ha-am" ("One of the People") but "Meahed Ha-Am" ("Unifier of the People," i.e., Diaspora and Zion branches of nationalism). A declarative issue for Ahad Ha-am is that in the age of modernism the Jewish People must decide whether its future lies in continual dispersion and assimilation or in ingathering and national renaissance. This and related topics are brought out in his magnum opus, '*Al parashat derachim/ At the Crossroads* (4 vols., 1894–1913). "At the Crossroads" for Dubnow is the French-based Yiddish periodical by that name (*Oyfn Sheydveg*), where he published one of his last writings in August 1939. In it, he admonished the Ahad Ha-am-like quest and declared that in the midst of catastrophe, basic survival is the only event that matters: "First Jews—then (after the crisis) Judaism." Shades of Theodor Herzl? Lamentably, the great Jewish savant was murdered in Riga on December 8, 1941.
6. Zangwell was president of I.T.O. from the start until the dissolution of the organization in 1925. The one notable success of I.T.O. was the "Galveston Movement," which brought over ten thousand Jews to an assembly-point in Galveston, Texas whence they were assisted to settle in western and southern United States.
7. The inference that Zionism both sanctifies and defiles the Jewish People is based on the paradox of *parah adumah/*"The Red Heifer" (Num 19).
8. Max Nordau (1849–1923) was Herzl's most important colleague and disciple. His position paper at the Basle Congress (1897), and subsequent writings and speeches, are perceptively critical of Emancipation's impact on Jewish life in European culture and society. His brand of political Zionism is akin to the position later taken by Zev Jabotinsky.
9. On this point, consider the 1979 Egypt-Israel treaty; the September 1993 Israel-PLO pact; and the July 1994 historic declaration between Israel and

Jordan which closed an official state of war. The latter is particularly noteworthy since Israel and Jordan, carved out of the British Mandate for Palestine, have been blocked by almost half a century of hostility from developing cooperative economic projects that their similar geography seems to demand. In the words of US Secretary of State Warren Christopher (at the Washington signing between Jordan and Israel on July 25, 1994), "Each one of these historic breakthroughs that happens makes it slightly easier for the next one to happen"—say a mediated peace between Syria, Lebanon, and Israel, and the ultimate goal of ending the legacy of war between belligerent neighbors.

10. For the record, the Irgun Organization in Diaspora formally disbanded on January 12, 1949. The Irgun's Paris headquarters became the official European address of the Herut Movement, civilian successor of Etsel, whose party was led in the First Knesset by Menachem Begin: Commander of Etsel, Herut-Likkud leader, and Prime Minister.

11. After the massacre of Muslim worshippers in Hebron's "Cave of Machpelah" on Purim day 1994 by a follower of Rabbi Meir Kahane, Israel immediately outlawed two Kahanist groups as terrorist organizations. Subsequently, Israel and Jordan vow an end to "bloodshed, sorrow" (July 25, 1994), but suicide martyr groups linked to Hezbollah, and its connections with Iran and Syria, have been formed "to confront and combat Zionism everywhere." How long might it be for Syria, Iran, and other Islamic states, reactionary and fundamentalist alike, to condemn the bombing of Jewish organizational offices and Israeli embassies/consulates "around the world"?

12. Gershom Schocken, "Revisiting Zionism," *The New York Review* (May 28, 1981), 41.

13. See above, the Abrahamic reference, section I unit 2.

14. See my review of Y. Zerubavel, Recovered Roots: Collective Memory and the Making of Israeli National Tradition (1995), *Modern Judaism* 18.2 (1998) 197-200.

Chapter 14

Primary Sources Revisited:
Methodology in the Study of Jewish History
In Jewish Secondary Schools
Gill Graff

Introduction

As the 21st century draws near, the flowering of Jewish day schools in the United States, a phenomenon which gained momentum in the years following World War II, is very much in evidence. There are, in 1998, approximately 200,000 students, grades K-12, in all day Jewish schools. The greatest growth in the past decade has been in the number of schools and students at the high school level. While yeshiva high schools under Orthodox sponsorship have long been available, the emergence of Jewish "community" high schools serving expanding populations of Jewish adolescents, many of them graduates of elementary Jewish day schools, is striking. In September, 1997, 10 new day high schools opened their doors, from Atlanta to Boston to Orange County, California. In 1997-98, the Jewish Education Service of North America (JESNA), a national, umbrella organization for the enhancement of Jewish education, reported that it had been engaged by five communities to undertake feasibility studies arising from serious interest in launching additional community day high schools.

Several years ago, I visited classes at a day high school, the students of which had been in all day Jewish schools since kindergarten. I observed one section of students discussing passages of Maimonides' *Guide to the Perplexed* (in Hebrew translation) and a second section discussing love versus infatuation, based on various (Hebrew) Biblical texts; in both cases, the discussion itself was conducted in flawless Hebrew. While this level of conversational Hebrew facility is exceptional, familiarity with classical Jewish texts is, increasingly, a *sine qua non* within the upper divisions of Jewish day high schools. This chapter is informed by more than two decades of professional contact with secondary Jewish day school education, including several years of teaching upper division students Jewish history.

By the eleventh and twelfth grades, Jewish day school students have studied substantial sections of Tanak and varying amounts of Rabbinic literature (Midrash, Mishnah, Gemara, Codes, Responsa). Jewish thought and Jewish history are also "staples" of day high school curricula. Increasingly, except in those Orthodox schools which view rabbinic works as, somehow, impervious to the influence of history, educators are recognizing the desirability of including primary source texts in the study of Jewish history. The text skills of the learners and the intensive use of primary documents in the students' historical studies, generally, lend themselves to an appreciation of classical sources as vehicles for better understanding the experiences of the Jewish people.

This chapter begins by describing the state of the field, in terms of the study of Jewish history in Jewish day high schools. Through specific examples, it explores the emerging trend of enhancing the Jewish history curricula of Jewish day high schools by the use of primary sources. The examples selected are from three distinct historical periods, reflecting the usefulness of this methodology for the study of various eras. Despite the difference of mission underlying the teaching of Jewish Studies in Jewish day high schools and in universities, there is, increasingly, methodological similarity in the approaches of the two systems to the study of Jewish history.

State of the Field

The goals associated with the study of Jewish history at the secondary school level are broadly defined. Among the more commonly indicated objectives are nurturing a deeper understanding of the Jewish past, developing a keener appreciation of and identification with the Jewish present and recognizing the interplay between Jewish history and western civilization. While schools use a variety of textbooks as instructional tools, most curricula are teacher-produced. With the escalating numbers of day high schools and students, it is to be anticipated that textbooks especially designed for this population will, soon, be created. Given the background of increasing thousands of students who enter high school already reading classical rabbinic sources, it is not unusual to find Responsa literature, Talmudic texts or medieval commentaries incorporated into courses of study at the secondary school level.

In some schools, instruction in Jewish history is integrated into courses in world, European and U.S. history and the instructor (generally, not a specialist in Judaica) is expected to integrate the "Jewish experience" into the various units of study. In other instances, the teacher of Judaica (e.g., Bible, Rabbinics) is expected to integrate Jewish history into the course of religious studies. Increasingly, however, the trend is to develop discrete courses in Jewish history, taught by persons whose expertise is Judaica and whose interest and training includes familiarity with classical Jewish texts.

There are two tensions in evidence in the teaching of Jewish history which are parallel to similar tensions sometimes found in the university teaching of Jewish Studies. In the university setting, there are proponents of "separation" (i.e., encouraging the placement of Jewish Studies within a distinct department) and of "integration" (placing Jewish Studies within such departments as history, religious studies, sociology, etc.). Those who teach about Jews or Judaism at the university level, bring substantial knowledge to their field of study regardless of the departmental placement of given courses. The incidence of high school instructors well rooted in European or American history and in the texts and experiences of Jews and Judaism and their interplay with these settings is, as yet, an unusual phenomenon. It is from this reality that the tendency to develop courses focusing on Jewish history, taught by persons whose primary focus is Judaic studies, has emerged.

A second tension inherent in the study and teaching of Jewish history in the secondary Jewish day school relates to the assumptions underlying the course of study and the nature of the questions to be asked. Is Jewish history to be studied by way of the same tools of analysis as are commonly applied to any people's historical experience, or are the rules (and tools), somehow, different? The mission of the Jewish day school includes nurturing an identification with and internalization of Jewish teachings. Typically, each school has a certain notion of Judaism and what it expects of its adherents; all Jewish day schools share the objective of encouraging identification with Jews and Judaism.

The tension between this ideological objective and the pursuit of academic knowledge generates a degree of ambivalence. In some traditionalist (Orthodox) schools, the study of Jewish history is avoided altogether, as it is deemed to represent a relativizing tendency-subjecting Torah and its interpretation to the realm of contextual influence and critical scrutiny. In the many traditionally oriented secondary schools which do provide courses in Jewish history, it is common to begin formal study of the subject with the Second Commonwealth, avoiding the study of ancient Israel and the challenging questions associated with it. Common to all streams of Jewish ideology, often reflected in the curricula of Jewish schools, is the view of Judaism in linear progression. For some Jews and Jewish schools, the prophetic ideal has been and continues to be the sustaining vision of Jewish life, while, for other schools the dynamic application of Jewish law by the people of Israel to changing conditions of life holds a pre-eminent place in understanding the Jewish present.

Notwithstanding different emphases, the study of Jewish texts informs the course of study of Jewish history in all school types. Indeed, it is a remarkable phenomenon that a "common language" is, today, being developed, as thousands of Jewish teenagers recapture texts which speak of Jews' experiences through several millennia. This will not only create a "pool" of interesting and interested students for university courses in Jewish Studies and related disciplines, it may have significant implications for discourse among and between Jews of varying perspectives in decades to come.

Methodology

Twenty years ago, I enjoyed the opportunity of teaching students in their junior and senior years at a "community" secondary Jewish day school a course in modern Jewish history. Consistent with the school's commitment to openness in the pursuit of Jewish learning and to serving as a college preparatory institution, I structured the class around texts drawn from a broad range of primary sources, while encouraging students to read a general textbook for background information. Two decades later, as the parent of a junior in high school at another Jewish day school, I read with interest my son's syllabus for a course in Jewish history of the Second Temple, Mishnah, and Talmudic Periods. It was prefaced by the following description:

> This is an introductory course focusing on the history of the Jewish people during the Second Temple, Mishnah and Talmud period. The course is designed to survey and critically analyze the major social, religious, political, military, and intellectual events and developments relating to Jewish history during this period. It should be noted from the outset that this is not a course in religion, rather it is a history course. This means that our studies will involve the same methods of critical analysis one would find in a general history course.
>
> Class meetings will not be oriented around chronology or historical facts and figures. Each meeting will focus on a particular issue relevant to this period in history, and the issue will always be studied through the critical analysis of primary sources and texts.[1]

The emphasis on "methods of critical analysis one would find in a general history course" is particularly interesting in light of the twin facts that (a) the instructor is a recently ordained rabbinic graduate of an Orthodox seminary and (b) the school defines itself as an Orthodox yeshiva high school.

Readings for the course so described include such Biblical texts as Deuteronomy, Chronicles and Ezra, along with selections from the Books of Maccabees, Philo, Josephus and the Talmud. Clearly, each text approaches the events it recounts or about which it speculates with a particular bias, and that orientation is subjected to close and comparative scrutiny. Students do not view any of these texts as definitive records of historical verities. The school *does*, however, consistent with its mission of nurturing a deeper understanding of the Jewish past, developing a keener appreciation of and identification with the Jewish present and recognizing the interplay between Jewish history and western civilization, analyze such sources with an eye to their implications for achieving the above-referenced outcomes. Such study takes seriously what has been described as "the four sequential steps of a learning experience: *Confrontation*, where the student experiences the idea, behavior or object superficially; *Analysis*, where the student seriously probes the occasion or text in light of previous experience and knowledge; *Interaction*, where the students' mutual or reciprocal communication with others helps him/her benefit from their feelings, ideas, and experiences with the reality under discussion; and *Internalization*, where by turning the new experience and sharing of ideas upon oneself, the student reacts meaningfully to the new reality as it relates to him/her as an individual and as a member of society as a whole."[2]

To illustrate the application of this process to the study of Jewish history at the high school level, I shall probe three sets of sources from each of three periods, examining briefly the types of issues and considerations they evoke, as studied in the context of Jewish history courses offered at secondary Jewish day schools. Such sources are likely candidates for inclusion in Jewish history textbooks which will, surely, be created to meet a growing need. Today, such materials are culled by classroom teachers and included in the variety of courses of Jewish history commonly offered.

The sources presented, below, relate to the first generation of rabbinic leadership at *Yavneh*, Jewish life in the *middle ages*, and the onset of *modernity*. The ideology of each Jewish school and, ultimately, of each teacher, significantly shapes the learning experience. However broad the span of ideological diversity in Jewish schools, the study of Jewish history nurtures Jewish "belonging" through a continuing dialogue with texts which have informed the thinking of Jews and Judaism(s) for centuries.

YAVNEH

The Texts:

(A) Abba Sikra the head of the *biryoni* ("strong ones") in Jerusalem was the son of the sister of Rabban Yohanan b. Zakkai. [The latter] sent to him saying, Come to visit me privately. When he came he said to him, How long are you going to carry on in this way and kill all the people with starvation? He replied: What can I do? If I say a word to them, they will kill me (note: The Judaean zealots [*biryoni*] were committed to fighting "to the last man"). He said: Devise some plan for me to escape. Perhaps I shall be able to save a little. He said to him: Pretend to be ill, and let everyone come to inquire about you. Bring something evil smelling and put it by you so that they will say you are dead. Let then your disciples get under your bed, but no others, so that they shall not notice that you are still light, since they know that a living being is lighter than a corpse. He did so, and R. Eliezer went under the bier from one side and R. Joshua from the other. When they reached the door, some men wanted to put a lance through the bier. He said to them: Shall [the Romans] say, They have pierced their Master? They wanted to give it a push. He said to them: Shall they say that they have pushed their Master? They opened a town gate for him and he got out.

　　When he reached the Romans he said, Peace to you, O king, peace to you, O king. He [Vespasian] said: Your life is forfeit on two counts, one because I am not a king and you call me king, and again, if I am a king, why did you not come to me before now?....

　　At this point a messenger came to him from Rome saying, Up, for the Emperor is dead, and the notables of Rome have decided to make you head [of the State]. He had just finished putting on one boot .... He said: I am now going, and will send someone to take my place. You can, however, make a request of me and I will grant it. He said to him: Give me Yavneh and its Wise Men.... (*Git.* 56a-b)

(B) [In the course of a debate over an issue of Jewish law, at Yavneh] ... R. Eliezer brought forward every imaginable argument, but they did not accept them. Said he to them: 'If the *halakhah* agrees with me, let this carob-tree prove it!' Thereupon the carob-tree was torn a hundred cubits out of its place—others affirm, four hundred cubits. 'No proof can be brought from a carob-tree,' they retorted. Again he said to them: 'If the *halakhah* agrees with me, let the walls of the schoolhouse prove it,' whereupon the walls inclined to fall. But R. Joshua rebuked them, saying: 'When scholars are engaged in a *halakhic* dispute, what have ye to interfere.' Hence they did not fall, in honour of R. Joshua, nor did they resume the upright, in honour of R. Eliezer; and they are still standing thus inclined. Again he said to them: 'If the *halakhah* agrees with me, let it be proved from Heaven!' Whereupon a Heavenly Voice cried out: 'Why do ye dispute with R. Eliezer, seeing that in all matters the *halakhah* agrees with him!' But R. Joshua arose and exclaimed: *"It is not in heaven"* (Deut 30:12). What did he mean by this? said R. Jeremiah: That the Torah had already been given at Mount Sinai; we pay no attention to a Heavenly Voice, because Thou hast long since written in the Torah at Mount Sinai, *After the majority must one incline* (Exod 23:2). *R. Nathan met Elijah and asked him: 'What did the Holy One, blessed be He, do in that hour?'* He laughed, he replied saying *'My sons have defeated Me, My sons have defeated Me.'* (B. Mes. 59b).

(C) It is related that a certain disciple came before R. Joshua at Yavneh and asked him, Is the evening *Tefilla* compulsory or optional? He replied: It is optional. He then presented himself before Rabban Gamaliel and asked him: Is the evening *Tefilla* compulsory or optional? He replied: It is compulsory. But, he said, did not R. Joshua tell me that it is optional? He said: Wait till the champions enter the Beth ha-Midrash. When the champions came in, someone arose and inquired, Is the evening *Tefilla* compulsory or optional? Said Rabban Gamaliel to the Sages: Is there anyone who disputes this? R. Joshua stood up and said: were I alive and he [the witness] dead, the living could contradict the dead. But now that he is alive and I am alive, how can the living contradict the living (i.e., how can I deny that I said this?) Rabban Gamaliel remained sitting and expounding and R. Joshua remained standing, until all the people there began to shout and to say to Huzpith the *turgeman* (a functionary who expounded the master's words aloud in the Academy). Stop! and he stopped. Then they said: How long is he [Rabban Gamaliel] to go on insulting him [R. Joshua]? On New Year last year he insulted him; he insulted him in the matter of the firstborn in the affair of R. Zadok; now he insults him again! Come, let us depose him! Whom shall we appoint instead? We can hardly appoint R. Joshua, because he is one of the parties involved. We can hardly appoint R. Akiba because perhaps Rabban Gamaliel will bring a curse on him because he has no ancestral merit. Let us then appoint R. Eleazar b. Azariah, who is wise and rich and tenth in descent from Ezra (a scribe and priest)....and wherever the expression 'on that day' is used, it refers to that day (of R. Gamaliel's ouster and R. Eleazar's appointment) — and there was no *halakhah* about which any doubt existed in the Beth ha-Midrash which was not fully elucidated (on that day) (*Ber.* 27b-28a).

Each of these texts appears in the Babylonian Talmud, a collection of oral discussions recorded late in the 5th century. Given the 400 year gap between the period referenced and the compilation of the Talmud, one can only speculate as to the historicity or precision of the accounts. They do, however, reflect rabbinic perceptions of the events described, conveying the "memories" which informed contemporary thought.

Text (A) projects a sense of the intrastrife which characterized the period of revolt against Rome (66-70 C.E.). Even as the Romans besieged Jerusalem, the Judaeans living within the walls of the city were utterly disunited. Rabban Yohanan ben Zakkai, a student of the famous teachers Hillel and Shammai, and, by the year 70, himself a respected, senior scholar, undertook to leave the city, arriving eventually at Yavneh (the story assumes the reader's knowledge that burial was always outside the walls of the city). While the Talmudic anecdote suggests that Yavneh was already inhabited by rabbinic sages, there is no other indication that Yavneh had such a population. This tradition thus reflects a later period, when the notion of "Yavneh and its sages" was well established. The passages, aims, in part, to answer the questions: "How did Yavneh come to be the center of rabbinic activity following the destruction of the Temple, and how did Yohanan ben Zakkai come to be the head of the Yavneh Academy?" Vespasian was, indeed, called to Rome as emperor during the siege of Jerusalem, and it was his son, Titus, who destroyed Jerusalem. Perhaps, as some historians have suggested, Yavneh was a detention center for Judaean prisoners during the war.[3]

Text (B) is "set" in Yavneh, not long after the period of Yohanan ben Zakkai's leadership. Students of Yohanan Ben Zakkai are embroiled in a disagreement over the status, with respect to the possibility of becoming liable to ritual impurity, of a particular type of earthen oven. While the virtually unanimous opinion of the rabbis is of one view, one disciple of Yohanan ben Zakkai is, adamantly, of a different opinion. Interestingly, it is that disciple, Eliezer ben Hyrcanus, who is, elsewhere, described by his teacher as "a cemented cistern which doesn't lose a drop,"[4] i.e., if he had heard a tradition relating to the matter at hand, one had it on the master's authority that he was, quite likely, correctly recalling the matter. Nonetheless, despite all manner of "natural" (or supernatural) proofs, the majority insists upon its position.

The text indicates that the rejection of a heavenly voice in support of R. Eliezer is grounded in the Torah itself, for the Torah establishes the requirement of following majority rulings. For centuries, however, dispute and alternative traditions had abounded in Judaea. Evident in this text is the sense of those putting it forward that normative standards of practice had to be established; anything less might lead to a renewal of sectarianism.

Text (C) describes the temporary ouster of R. Gamaliel, who had succeeded R. Yohanan ben Zakkai, as head of the Yavneh Academy. R. Gamaliel II, a descendant of Hillel, was acknowledged by the rabbinic scholars of the time as Nasi (Patriarch) of the Academy. Much has been written about the reasons for his ouster. As the text indicates, he had, on previous occasions, humiliated Rabbi Joshua, a popular scholar and a close disciple of R. Yohanan ben Zakkai. What has not always been emphasized in analyzing this passage, are the many issues which were voted upon during Rabban Gamaliel's removal from leadership. R. Elazar ben Azariah, a young rabbi of priestly lineage, was installed in place of R. Gamaliel, and, "on that day" a host of items was voted upon and concluded. Examination of those items reveals that many of them were matters dealing with the priests; issues which, prior to the destruction of the Temple, would have been dealt with by priestly courts. Perhaps, Rabban Gamaliel had not been prepared to extend rabbinic jurisdiction to the full range of priestly matters. By installing a "manageable" priest as head of the court for a brief period, and acting on matters hitherto reserved to priestly decision-making authorities, the sages at Yavneh extended rabbinic jurisdiction to include all matters of Jewish law. This accomplished, Rabban Gamaliel, the Talmud goes on to relate, was restored to his position.[5]

The period between the destruction of the Temple (70 C.E.) and the Bar Kochba War (132 C.E.) is richly significant. The generations of rabbinic leadership at Yavneh and the types of tensions described in such texts abound with issues for confrontation, analysis, interaction and internalization. Questions of authority, dissent, leadership and judicial process are central motifs which connect directly to the schools' aims of nurturing a deeper understanding of the Jewish past, developing a keener appreciation of and identification with the Jewish present and recognizing the interplay between Jewish history and western civilization.

Writing of biographical sketches of rabbinic personalities drawn from Talmudic sources, Judah Goldin observed:

> Such works are hardly biographies in the serious sense of the word, ... for not only do the primary sources disappoint us deeply in the amount of historical detail they provide, but even as regards the opinions and teachings of the Sages, one is left to guess what is early and what is late. In short, there is practically no way to get at development, surely and desperately necessary for the historian and the biographer.[6]

Understanding the limitations of *'aggadah,* in this case the Talmudic story, as a historical source is inherent in the critical study of such passages. The purpose of Talmudic stories is not to report things as they actually happened, but to present didactic lessons. These texts are replete with issues for expansive reflection and analysis.

The internal tensions at the time of the Revolt against Rome, laws of purities, the Flavian emperors and the Jews, the emergence of Yavneh as a judicial center late in the first century, the Sanhedrin, the priesthood, the lives of Yohanan ben Zakkai and Rabban Gamaliel (II), R. Akiva, R. Joshua, R. Eliezer ben Hyrkanus and R. Eleazar ben Azariah are but some of the topics which emerge from these passages. The secondary literature on this period is vast, and these materials invite students, after confrontation, analysis and interaction, to enter the realm of informed speculation and conjecture. Such texts, often glossed over in the course of "serious" Talmud study (because they are extra-legal passages) are significant "grist for the mill" in the high school Jewish history course.

Jewish Life in the Middle Ages

Medieval Europe was a corporate, hierarchical society, with defined group status for all tiers of inhabitants. Typically, high school students have studied European history and have a sense of feudal life. The Jewish history course introduces them to the place of Jews within this arrangement.

The Jewish corporate unit, *kehillah,* held a charter from the local king, recognizing the Jews' right to live under their ancestral laws and articulating the quid pro quo of communal taxes in exchange for royal protection. The external authority defined the *kehillah* as a unit to be regulated by its own power structure; internally, the *kehillah* wielded the threat of *herem* (excommunication) to ensure individual discipline. In the context of medieval society, *herem* could, in effect, strip a person of any identity or protected status. Throughout the middle ages, communities and, sometimes, clusters of communities, issued *takkanot* (ordinances) mandating expected community behaviors. Text (A) is an example of such *takkanot*, and relates to the issue of recourse to non-Jewish legal tribunals. Text (B) reflects the dramatic extent of jurisdiction and authority characteristic of some *kehillot*. Text (C) describes some of the most prevalent communal institutions of medieval Jewish life.

(A) At a synod at Troyes, about 1150, Rabbenu Tam and other authorities, with the assent of a large group of northern French and possibly western German rabbis, decreed:

"1. We have voted, decreed, ordained and declared under the *herem* that no man or woman may bring a fellow-Jew before Gentile courts or exert compulsion on him through Gentiles, whether by a prince or a common man, a ruler or an inferior official, except by mutual agreement made in the presence of proper witnesses.

2. If the matter accidentally reaches the government or other Gentiles, and in that manner pressure is exerted on a Jew, we have decreed that the man who is aided by the Gentiles shall have saved his fellow from their hands, and shall secure him against the Gentiles ... and he shall make satisfaction to him and secure him in such manner as the seven elders of the city will ordain....

3. He shall not intimidate the 'seven elders' (the "seven elders" were heads of the community) through the power of a Gentile. And because the masters of wicked tongue and informers do their deeds in darkness, we have decreed also excommunication for indirect action unless he satisfy him in accordance with the decision of the elders of the city."[7]

The power of rabbinic authorities to promulgate such legislative enactments as those of Troyes had long been recognized and practiced. The Talmud ascribes a series of enactments to Ezra the Scribe (5th century B.C.E.), and lists 9 *takkanot* (rabbinic ordinances) promulgated by Yohanan ben Zakkai at Yavneh.[8] The legal basis of this authority was attributed to the biblical verse, "According to the law which they shall teach thee and according to the judgment which they shall tell thee, thou shalt do, thou shall not turn aside from the sentence which they shall declare unto thee, to the right hand or to the left" (Deut 17:11). Such *takkanot* served to deal with situations not specifically addressed by existing law, to erect a "fence around the law" (*syag la Torah*), and at times, to modify the law and to meet the needs of the hour.

Charters issued to the Ashkenazic Jewish communities generally established the exclusive jurisdiction of rabbinic courts for Jewish litigants. Internally, the threat of *herem* served to secure respect for the primacy of rabbinic jurisdiction. The prohibition against recourse to non-Jewish law courts was not only rooted in the struggle to preserve judicial autonomy, but also in a belief that these tribunals were fundamentally unfair and corrupt. Such a text encourages discussion of medieval, corporate society, the internal workings of the *kehillah*, the power of Jewish law and its relationship to the law of the state and, of course, the personalities prominent in medieval Jewish life.

In Spain, rabbinic jurisdiction was in some respects more limited than in western Europe, and in other respects it was greater. Most Jewish courts in Spain were empowered to adjudicate criminal cases with the full support of the state's coercive force. Jewish courts used the prisons of the country to compel obedience to their orders. Floggings, fines, imprisonment, excommunications, and, in extreme cases, mutilation or death were among the penalties imposed by the Jewish courts. R. Asher ben Yehiel (1250-1327) who had moved to Toledo from Germany, observed: "When I first arrived here, I asked in amazement by what legal right Jews could, today, legally convict anyone to death without a Sanhedrin. In none of the countries that I know of, except here in Spain, do the Jewish courts try cases of capital punishment."[9]

Text (B) is from a Responsum of R. Asher ben Yehiel in a case involving a Jewish defamer of fellow Jews to Gentile authorities, whose acts were endangering Jewish life and property.

(B)   "While the four types of execution which the Sanhedrin (Jewish High Court) could impose null in Jewish law, since the Sanhedrin has gone into exile .... the sages have equated *the* person who would inform against his fellow Jew, in order to convey that fellow's property to gentiles, with the person who pursues another to kill him (and he can be killed)....

Therefore it has been customary throughout the Diaspora that in a case in which an informer has thrice informed (to the gentiles) about a fellow Jew, that we seek advice and counsel in order to remove an informer from the world as an extraordinary procedure for curbing lawless acts. This is *done as* a deterrent against the proliferation of informers, and to rescue all Israel the pursued from his land."[10]

This application of the concept of *rodef* (pursuer) has an all too familiar resonance at the end of the twentieth century. It was invoked in some quarters as a rationale for the assassination of Yitzhak Rabin, whose policies as elected head of a sovereign state were likened to the actions of a *rodef*. The same concept is applied by Jewish law to the unborn fetus which may be threatens the life of its mother (and which is aborted as a "pursuer"). A passage such as this opens up a tremendous range of issues for analysis and interaction, connecting the Jewish history curriculum to a broad range of issues important to the mission of the Jewish school and of interest to the student.

The Talmudic tractate Sanhedrin sets exacting standards of criminal procedure and requires that a court of twenty-three expert judges try capital cases. It was, as Rabbi Asher's observations reflect, a well-accepted principle that in the absence of a Sanhedrin, rabbinically ordered capital punishment was impossible. By the same token, with the lapse of ordination (*semikhah*), there was no body competent under Jewish law to decree flagellation or to levy any of the biblically prescribed fines.

The rabbis in Spain meted out "extralegal" punishments under the rationale that they were acting under exigency jurisdiction, *hora'at sha'ah*. Precedent for the rabbinic imposition of such punishment appears in both the Babylonian and Palestine Talmud, which establish that, for the preservation of the law, ordinary legal norms can be suspended. In addition to the precondition that it be invoked only for the purpose of protecting the Torah, such emergency authority must also be of a temporary nature, aimed at dealing with a specific, critical situation. The notion of *hora'at sha'ah* was associated with the verse in Psalms, "It is time to act for the L-rd: they have broken thy law" (Ps119:126).

Jewish law regulating communal life not only framed relations between Jews and the state, but governed the internal workings of the *kehillah*. Text (C) describes some of the social welfare mechanisms prevalent in medieval Jewish communities, as codified by Maimonides (1135-1204) in the *Mishnah Torah, Zeraim, 9*:

(C)

"1. Every Jewish community must appoint collectors of charity who are trustworthy men of repute, to go about among the people each Friday, taking from every one what he can afford to give, or what he is assessed. They are to distribute the money from Friday to Friday, giving every poor man sufficient food for seven days. This is what is called *kuppah* (fund).

2.   So too, collectors are appointed who fetch bread and foodstuffs from every courtyard, as well as fruit products or money, from anyone who donates for the needs of the moment. They distribute the collections among the poor in the evening, giving each pauper his daily provision. This is what is called *tamhuy*

3.   We have never seen or heard of a Jewish community without a charity fund. However, there are localities where the custom is to have one while in others it does not exist. Nowadays there is a widespread custom that fund collectors go around collecting every day and distribute on Fridays....

12. If one has stayed in a town for thirty days, he should be compelled to contribute to the community fund along with the population of the town. If he has stayed there for three months, he should be compelled to contribute to the *tamhuy;* if he stayed there for six months, he should be compelled to contribute toward the clothing of the local poor if he has stayed there for nine months, he should be compelled to contribute to all the burial needs of the poor."

The structure of Jewish communal life and the social welfare requirements of Jewish law are at the heart of this passage. How, why and whether such a system operated are complex issues which relate to the experiences of Jews and Judaism throughout the millennia. The communal institutions of contemporary Jewish life can, surely, be better understood against the backdrop of such traditions.

These sources, including *takkanot*, responsa and codes, invite examination and discussion of the corporate structure of society in the middle ages, the power of *herem*, the development and application of Jewish law, Ashkenazic and Sephardic Jewry, attitudes towards non-Jewish law courts and the law of the kingdom, informers, the law of the pursuer , capital punishment and the governance and social welfare system within the medieval Jewish *kehillah*. Study of these texts is enhanced by students' familiarity with European history of the middle ages and by their earlier exposure to the genres of texts examined, now, as historical sources. While the texts appear, here, in English translation, secondary Jewish day school students can, in many cases, examine such sources in their

Hebrew original, adding a dimension of identification with the primary language which has connected Jews across time and place.

Modernity

The changes in Jewish life over the last two centuries represent a transformation of which students in Jewish day high schools are legatees. Understanding the circumstances and ideas associated with this transformation is critical to the self-understanding of Jewish young adults in North America on the eve of the twenty-first century. The process of acculturation among Jews and the emerging patterns of religious adjustment in response to modernity can be seen through innumerable texts of this period. Three examples of oft cited historical sources are the declaration preceding the response to Napoleon of the French Assembly of Notables, the Constitution of the New Israelite Temple Association of Hamburg and the reactions to reform published by the traditional bet din of Hamburg in *Eleh Divrei ha-Brit*.

In May, 1806, Napoleon called for an assembly of the principal Jews in his empire to which, in July —when they were assembled — he communicated the text of twelve questions aimed at "reconciling the belief of the Jews with the duties of Frenchmen, and to make them useful citizens."[11] A clear symbol of the challenge of the state to the place of religion in the life of the Jews was the insistence that the assembly convene for its first session on Saturday, July 26. The deputies met for services that morning and proceeded to the meeting, which had been called for eleven o'clock. The desire of Napoleon, reported his senior representative, was "that you should be Frenchmen, it remains with you to accept of the preferred title, without forgetting that, to prove unworthy of it, would be renouncing it altogether."[12] The threat was clear: if the notables could not indicate that the Jews of the empire identified themselves above all else as Frenchmen, the Jews would be found unworthy of citizenship.

At its meeting of August 4, 1806, the assembly adopted a declaration, which was to precede its answers to the twelve questions. This declaration is Text (A):

> The assembly, impressed with a deep sense of gratitude, love, respect, and admiration for the sacred person of his Imperial Majesty, declares, in the name of all Frenchmen professing the religion of Moses, that they are fully determined to prove worthy of the favors His Majesty intends for them, by scrupulously conforming to his parental intentions; that their religion makes it their duty to consider the law of the prince as the su-

preme law in civil and political matters, that, consequently, should their religious code, or its various interpretations, contain civil or political commands, at variance with those of the French Code, those commands would, of course, cease to influence and govern them, since they must, above all, acknowledge and obey the laws of the prince.[13]

The self-definition of the deputies as "Frenchmen professing the religion of Moses" relates, immediately, to students who identify as nationals of a state in the modern era. The challenge of defining "state-religion" boundaries at a time in which the state was expanding its scope of jurisdiction encourages close examination of *dina de-malkhuta dina* ("the law of the kingdom is law") and its application to new situations by a variety of nineteenth century figures.[14] The emergence of Jewish religious responses to changing conditions is an exploration that leads very close to home for Jewish high school students on the eve of the 21st century.

Text (B), from the Constitution of the (Hamburg) New Israelite Temple Association, introduces discussion of religious responses to emancipation:

...Since public worship has for some time been neglected by so many, because of the ever decreasing knowledge of the language in which alone it has until now been conducted, and also because of many other shortcomings which have crept in at the same time—the undersigned, convinced of the necessity to restore public worship to its deserving dignity and importance, have joined together to follow the example of several Israelite congregations, especially the one in Berlin. They plan to arrange in this city also, for themselves as well as others who think as they do, a dignified and well-ordered ritual according to which the worship service shall be conducted on Sabbath and holy days and on other solemn occasions, and which shall be observed in their own temple, to be erected especially for this purpose. Specifically, there shall be introduced at such services a German sermon, and choral singing to the accompaniment of an organ.[15]

Issues which were of initial concern to reformers and the significance of the choice of "temple" as a reference to the synagogue center of Jewish religious reformers leap out of the text. Such a passage is also a springboard for discussion of contemporary Jewish religious movements. As "counterpoint" in the range of responses to emancipation, students can explore the reaction of the Hamburg Beth Din expressed in its publication, Text (C):

Worst of all, they have perpetrated a sore evil by removing all references to the belief in the Ingathering of the Exiles .... This belief is one of the major tenets of our holy Torah. All the prophets have been unanimous in affirming that the G-d of our fathers would gather our scattered ones, and this is our hope throughout our Exile. This belief in no way detracts from the honor of Their Majesties the Kings and ministers under whom we find protection, for it is common knowledge that we believe in the coming of the messiah and the Ingathering of the Exiles.[16]

The fundamental difference in world view between those who saw emancipation and integration into European society as the beginning of redemption and those who saw "emancipation" as but another phase within a fundamentally unchanged condition of exile is starkly in evidence. For Jewish day high school students, the identity issues emerging out of such texts are palpable. It is, perhaps, for this reason that initial efforts at developing textbooks for this population have been in the area of moden Jewish history.[17]

No less significant than the various religious responses to modernity, is the emergence of Jewish nationalism and Zionism as a response to modernity. For Jewish day high schools utilizing the prevailing methodology, Arthur Hertzberg's *The Zionist Idea*[18] is a ready reader. Each Zionist perspective invites confrontation, analysis, interaction and internalization, demanding, ultimately, consideration of the very nature of Jewish identity.

Conclusion

The development of educational curricula must, it has been aptly observed, take into account the learner, the teacher, the subject matter and the milieu. It is for this reason that the prevailing methodology in the study of Jewish history in Jewish day high schools has come to be built upon the study of primary sources. The prevalence of this methodology in the study of history, generally, contributes to the readiness of students and teachers to approach Jewish history in this way.

The study of Jewish history "speaks" to many learners in a way that other aspects of the Judaic studies program may not. There are those for whom a sense of historical context serves to enrich or enhance interest in other aspects of Jewish learning, Teachers of Jewish history tend to be drawn from the "ranks" of Judaic studies specialists, and they are equipped to explore primary sources as a central part of the curriculum. While at the present time, most teachers rely on self-generated curricula, it is to be anticipated that, as the system of Jewish high schools continues to grow, textbooks for an expanding market will be produced.

The types of sources referenced, above, are integral to an instructional methodology rooted in the four sequential steps of learning. Beyond giving expression to the educational mission of Jewish day schools, the study of Jewish history in secondary schools is creating a pool of highly knowledgeable students who will be proceeding to universities with prior, scholarly contact with primary Jewish sources. At a time of alarming polarization within Jewish life, the shared texts and experiences of Jewish history may provide a common language for communal conversation among elements of the emerging generation of American Jews. ✡

Endnotes

1. I am indebted to Rabbi Daniel Bouskila, Chairman of the Department of Jewish history at Shalhevet High School in Los Angeles for making his course syllabus available.
2. Zev Garber, ed., *Methodology in the Academic Teaching of Judaism* (New York, 1986), 2.
3. H. H. Ben-Sasson, ed., *A History of the Jewish People* (Cambridge, 1976), 320.
4. *'Avot* 2.11.
5. For a discussion of the demotion of Rabban Gamaliel and of various opinions relating to the account of it, see Gil Graff, "Priests, Sages and the Jurisdiction of the High Court, 50-100 C.E.," in *Shofar*, 8 .2 (Winter, 1990),1-7.
6. C. J. Adams, ed. *A Reader's Guide to the Great Religions* (New York, 1965), 223.
7. Louis Finkelstein, *Jewish Self-Government in the Middle Ages* (New York, 1964), 155-156.
8. *Rosh. Hash.* 31b.
9. *She'elot u-Teshuvot ha-Rosh*, 17, 8, quoted and translated in Abraham A. Neuman, *The Jews in Spain*, vol. 1 (Philadelphia, 1942), 138-139.
10. *She'elot u-Teshuvot ha-Rosh*, 17, 1 (the translation is mine).
11. Napoleon, *Correspondence*, 12:571-72, no. 10537, quoted and translated in Simon Schwarzfuchs, *Napoleon, the Jews and the Sanhedrin* (London, 1979), 55.
12. M. Diogene Tama, *Transactions of the Parisian Sanhedrin*, trans. F.D. Kirwan (London, 1807) , 132.
13. *Ibid.*, pp. 149-150.

14. See Gil Graff, *Dina de-Malkhuta Dina in Jewish Law, 1750-1848* (University of Alabama Press, 1985), especially 110-132.
15. Quoted and translated in Paul Mendes-Flohr and Jeduda Reinharz, eds., *The Jew in the Modern World* (New York, 1980), 145.
16. *Ibid.*, 151-152.
17. See, for example, David Bianco, *Modern Jewish History for Everyone* (Los Angeles, 1997) and Facing History and Ourselves Foundation, *The Jews of Poland* (Brookline, 1998).
18. Arthur Hertzberg, ed., *The Zionist Idea* (New York, 1975).
19. See selected essays by Joseph J. Schwab, in Ian Westbury and Neil J. Wilkoff, eds., *Science, Curriculum and Liberal Education* (Chicago, 1978).

Source Index

JUDITH R. BASKIN is chair of the Department of Judaic Studies at SUNY-Albany. She is the author of *Pharaoh's Counsellors: Job, Jethro and Balaam in Rabbinic and Patristic Tradition*, and the editor of *Jewish Women in Historical Perspective* and *Women of the Word: Jewish Women and Jewish Writing*. She is also co-editor of *Gender and Jewish Studies: A Curriculum Guide*, and is author of a number of articles on aspects of Jewish culture in late antiquity and the Middle Ages.

HERBERT W. BASSER is Professor of Religion, Queens University, Kingston, Ontario. He is co-editor of *Moses Kimhi: Commentary on the Book of Job* and *Approaches to Ancient Judaism*. He is also editor of *Pseudo-Rabad: Commentary to Sifre Deuteronomy* and *Pseudo-Rabad Commentary to Sifre Numbers*.

S. DANIEL BRESLAUER is Professor of Religious Studies at the University of Kansas, Lawrence KS. He has written over a dozen books, the most recent being *Toward a Jewish (M)orality: Speaking of a Postmodern Jewish Ethics*. He is currently working on a study of Jewish mythology.

ELLIOT N. DORFF is Rector and Professor of Philosophy at the University of Judaism in Los Angeles. He has written over one hundred articles about Jewish thought, law, and ethics and seven books, including two on issues of ethics: co-editor, *Contemporary Jewish Ethics and Morality: A Reader* and *Matters of Life and Death: A Jewish Approach to Modern Medical Ethics*. He is also the co-editor of *Contemporary Jewish Theology: A Reader.*

EUGENE J. FISHER has been Associate Director of the Secretariat for Ecumenical and Interreligious Affairs, National Conference of Catholic Bishops since 1977. He is consultor to the Vatican Commission for Religious Relations with the Jews and a member of the International Catholic-Jewish Liason Committee. He has published over twenty books and some 250 articles. His co-edited volume, *Spiritual Pilgrimage: Pope John Paul II on Jews and Judaism*, won the National Jewish Book Council Award in 1995.

ZEV GARBER, Editor of this volume, is Professor and Chair of Jewish Studies, Los Angeles Valley College and served as Visiting Professor in Religious Studies at the University of California at Riverside. A Past President of the National Association of the Professors of Hebrew, Associate Editor of *Shofar*, and Editor-in-Chief of Studies in the Shoah (UPA), among his many publications are *Methodology in the Academic Teach-*

ing of Judaism, Methodology in the Academic Teaching of the Holocaust, Teaching Hebrew Language and Literature at the College Level, Perspectives on Zionism, What Kind of God?, and *Peace, In Deed.* Recently, he taught for the Ziegler School of Rabbinics at the University of Judaism, Los Angeles.

GILL GRAFF is Executive Director of the Bureau of Jewish Education of Greater Los Angeles. A graduate of the UCLA School of Law, he earned a Ph.D. in Jewish history at UCLA and holds graduate degrees in Jewish Studies and educational administration. He has published numerous articles in the fields of Jewish history and Jewish education and is the author of *Separation of Church and State: Dina de Malkhuta in Jewish Law, 1750-1848.* He has taught Jewish Studies at the elementary, high school and university levels, most recently at the University of Judaism, Los Angeles.

HARRIS LENOWITZ is Professor of Hebrew in the Department of Languages and Literature and in the Middle East Center of the University of Utah. His latest book is *The Jewish Messiahs.*

JAMES F. MOORE is Professor of Theology at Valparaiso University. He is director of the CTNS-Templeton Foundation Chicago Area Summer Advanced Workshop on Science and Religion. He is the author of *Sexuality and Marriage* and *Christian Theology After the Shoah: A Reinterpretation of the Passion Narratives* as well as numerous articles on Jewish Studies, on Christian theology and the Holocaust, and on science and religion. He is on the editorial board of the Studies in Shoah series (UPA) and is an educational consultant to the Philadelphia Center for the Holocaust, Genocide and Human Rights.

GILEAD MORAHG is Professor of Hebrew literature at the University of Wisconsin-Madison. He is executive vice president of the National Association of Professors of Hebrew and immediate past president of the National Council of Organizations of Less Commonly Taught Languages. His publications include studies on Israel's new literature of the Holocaust, representations of Arabs in Israeli fiction, and the works of A.B. Yehoshua, David Shahar, Amoz Oz, David Grossman, and Yitzhak Ben-Ner. He also publishes regularly on the pedagogy and methodology of teaching Hebrew literature to English speaking learners.

DAVID PATTERSON holds the Bornblum Chair in Judaic Studies at The University of Memphis. He has published more than eighty articles in a variety of journals dealing with topics in philosophy, literature, Judaism, Holocaust, and education. His books include *Along the Edge* of *Annihilation, Sun Turned to Darkness, The Greatest Jewish Stories Ever Told, When Learned Men Murder, Pilgrimage of a Proselyte: From Auschwitz to Jerusalem, The Shriek of Silence, In Dialogue and Dilemma with Elie Wiesel,* and others.

MARVIN A. SWEENEY is Professor of Hebrew Bible at the Claremont School of Theology and Professor of Religion at the Claremont Graduate University. He is the author of *Isaiah 1-39, with an Introduction to Prophetic Literature*; *King Josiah of Judah: The Lost Messiah of Israel*; as well as many other books, studies, and reviews in Hebrew Bible and Jewish Studies. He is a past fellow of the Lilly Endowment, the W.F. Albright Institute, and the Hebrew University of Jerusalem. He has previously taught at HUC-JIR (Los Angeles) and the University of Miami.

CHARLES ELLIOTT VERNOFF is Professor of Religion at Cornell College of Iowa, having received graduate training at Harvard, the Hebrew University of Jerusalem, and the University of California at Santa Barbara. He was co-founder of Cornell's Institute for Holocaust Studies and has published in the areas of theory and method in the study of religion, comparative philosophy of religion, and Judaic thought. His articles have appeared in periodicals such as *JAAR, Journal of Ecumenical Studies*, and *Religious Studies Review* as well as in several edited volumes.

BRUCE ZUCKERMAN is currently an associate professor in the School of Religion at the University of Southern California, where he teaches courses in the Hebrew Bible, the Bible in Western Literature, the Ancient Near East, and Archaeology. He received his Ph.D. in Ancient Near Eastern Languages from Yale University and is a specialist in Northwest Semitic languages. Besides his teaching responsibilities, he directs the USC Archaeological Research Collection. Through West Semitic Research, a partnership with his brother Ken, he specializes in photographing ancient texts including numerous projects involving the Dead Sea Scrolls. He is the author of *Job the Silent: A Study in Biblical Counterpoint*. He is currently leading a project to disseminate electronic images of ancient texts through the West Semitic Research Project website www.usc.edu/dept/LAS/wsrp.